RETHINKING THE UNION
POST-CRISIS

In this important new book, Giandomenico Majone examines the crucial but often overlooked distinction between the general aim of European integration and the specific method of integration employed in designing a (ill-considered) monetary union. Written with the author's customary insight and precision, this highly topical and provocative book reviews the Union leaders' tradition of pushing through ambitious projects without considering the serious hurdles that lie in the way of their success. Regional and European integration topics are discussed, including credibility of commitments, delegation of powers, bargaining and influence activities, adverse selection and moral hazard. The author also offers a deeper examination of the specific crisis of monetary integration, arguing that integration might be achieved more effectively with inter-jurisdictional competition, and suggests how integration should be managed in the globalized world.

GIANDOMENICO MAJONE is Emeritus Professor of Public Policy at the European University Institute in Florence.

RETHINKING THE UNION OF EUROPE POST-CRISIS

Has Integration Gone Too Far?

GIANDOMENICO MAJONE

CAMBRIDGE
UNIVERSITY PRESS

University Printing House, Cambridge CB2 8BS, United Kingdom

Cambridge University Press is part of the University of Cambridge.

It furthers the University's mission by disseminating knowledge in the pursuit of education, learning and research at the highest international levels of excellence.

www.cambridge.org
Information on this title: www.cambridge.org/9781107694798

First published 2014

Printed in the United Kingdom by Clays, St Ives plc

A catalogue record for this publication is available from the British Library

Library of Congress Cataloguing in Publication data
Majone, Giandomenico.
Rethinking the union of Europe post-crisis : has integration gone too far? / Giandomenico Majone.
pages   cm
ISBN 978-1-107-06305-1 (hardback)
1. European Union countries – Economic integration.   2. European Union countries – Economic integration – Political aspects.   3. European Union countries – Economic policy.   4. European Union countries – Politics and government – 21st century.   I. Title.
HC241.M256   2014
337.1'42–dc23
2013046218

ISBN 978-1-107-06305-1 Hardback
ISBN 978-1-107-69479-8 Paperback

CONTENTS

ABBREVIATIONS

ACP	African, Caribbean, and Pacific (countries)
ANZCERTA	Australia–New Zealand Closer Economic Relations Trade Agreement
BRIC	Brazil, Russia, India, China
BVG	*Bundesverfassunsgericht*
CAP	Common Agricultural Policy
CFSP	Common Foreign and Security Policy
CJEU	Court of Justice of the European Union
Coreper	Committee of Permanent Representatives of the national governments
CUSTA	Canada–United States Free Trade Agreement
DSB	Dispute-settlement bodies
DSM	Dispute-settlement mechanisms
DSU	Dispute Settlement Understanding
EC	European Community
ECB	European Central Bank
ECHR	European Convention for the Protection of Human Rights and Fundamental Freedoms
ECJ	European Court of Justice
ECOFIN	Council of the finance ministers of the EU
ECSC	European Coal and Steel Community
ECU	European Currency Unit
EEC	European Economic Community
EFTA	European Free Trade Area
EMS	European Monetary System
EMU	Economic and Monetary Union
EP	European Parliament
EPU	European Political Union
ERM	Exchange Rate Mechanism
ESCB	European System of Central Banks
ESM	European Stability Mechanism
EU	European Union
EURATOM	European Atomic Energy Community
GATT	General Agreement on Tariffs and Trade

GDP	gross domestic product
GSP	Growth and Stability Pact
IMF	International Monetary Fund
ITF	International Transport Workers Federation
JHA	Justice and Home Affairs
MEP	Member of the European Parliament
MERCOSUR	*Mercado Común del Sur*
MTBO	Medium-term budgetary objective
NAFTA	North American Free Trade Agreement
NATO	North Atlantic Treaty Organization
OECD	Organization for Economic Cooperation and Development
OMC	Open Method of Coordination
PP	Precautionary Principle
SGP	Stability and Growth Pact
SPS	Sanitary and Phytosanitary (Agreement)
Stability Treaty	Treaty on Stability, Coordination and Governance in the Economic and Monetary Union 2012
TCE	Transaction-cost economics
TCP	Transaction-cost politics
TEU	Treaty on the European Union
TFEU	Treaty on the Functioning of the European Union
WTO	World Trade Organization

~

Introduction: varieties of regional integration

Regionalism, old and new

The revival of regional integration in the 1980s – which Jagdish Bhagwati (1993) labelled the 'Second Regionalism', in contrast to the 'First Regionalism' of the 1960s – raises a number of issues, starting with the question why the first regionalism failed (with the notable exception of the European Economic Community (EEC)), while this time regionalism is likely to endure. The conversion of the United States (US) to regionalism is of major significance in this respect. As the key advocate of multilateralism through the post-war years, its decision to travel the regional integration route seems to have tilted the balance at the margin from multilateralism to regionalism. A second important factor has been the widening and deepening of the European Community/Union (EC/EU). Thus, the fear that European investments would be diverted to Eastern Europe was cited by President Salinas of Mexico as a factor decisively pushing him toward the North American Free Trade Agreement (NAFTA). He felt that a free trade area embracing all of North America would enable Mexico to get the investments needed from the US and Canada, as well as from Japan (Bhagwati 1993; Vega Cànovas 2010). In his comment on Bhagwati's article, Robert Baldwin considered the likelihood of a gradual drift of the North American regional bloc to include a number of other Latin American countries. This enlargement would be driven by pressures from these countries to tap into the US market but another important factor that might drive the expansion of an American-centred bloc, according to Baldwin, 'would be the growing influence of the European Community in trade, macroeconomic and foreign policy matters. US political and economic leaders may adopt the view that it is necessary to expand such a bloc in order to match the increasing political and economic power of the Community' (Bhagwati 1993: 54).

A distinguishing characteristic of the new regionalism is the movement from shallow integration – integration based on the removal of barriers to trade at the border and limited coordination of national policies – to deeper integration, concerned with behind-the-border issues such as regulation of services and environmental and labour standards (see chapter 3). This feature of the new regionalism has tempted a number of analysts, including Robert Baldwin, to envisage a 'European' model of the future of regional integration. According to this model 'intensified economic integration implies stronger, more formal institutions that become wider and wider in scope. Institutions become more effective as they become more "state-like"' (Kahler 1995: 19). In reality, far from adopting or adapting the EC/EU model, the new or revived regional groups are seldom supported by significant supranational institutions or elaborate mechanisms for common decision-making. This is true also of regional organizations designed to be more than free trade areas or customs unions. Thus, MERCOSUR (Mercado Comùn del Sur) was established by Brazil, Argentina, Paraguay and Uruguay in 1995 with the objective of establishing a full common market in goods, capital, and people. However, executive power within MERCOSUR is with the national governments rather than with a European-style Commission. The highest decision-making body is the MERCOSUR Council, made up of the foreign and finance ministers of the four countries.

Even more striking (because more successful) is the Australia–New Zealand Closer Economic Relations Trade Agreement (ANZCERTA), which, despite its ambitious aims of deeper integration, including full liberalization of trade in services and harmonization of regulatory practices, 'is almost defiantly lacking in formal institutional development' (Kahler 1995: 108). ANZCERTA provides strong support for the thesis, espoused by a number of distinguished economists, that ambitious programmes of trade liberalization, including behind-the-border policies, do not require the support of significant supranational institutions or elaborate mechanisms for common decision-making. Thus the economic agreement between Australia and New Zealand is the clearest example of a model of regional integration that is explicitly alternative to the EU model. After the late 1980s, ANZCERTA entered a very ambitious phase in dealing with behind-the-border barriers to trade and issues of deep integration. By 1990 nearly all barriers to a single market were removed. Harmonization took place in regulatory practices, customs procedures, government purchasing, and technical barriers to trade.

In terms of economic integration, MERCOSUR has been much less successful than either NAFTA or ANZCERTA. According to some analysts this is due, at least in part, to the reluctance of Brazil to use its economic and political position as the regional leader to assume active regional leadership (Mattli 1999). As an increasingly influential member of the BRIC (Brazil, Russia, India, China) group of countries, however, Brazil may be willing to play a more active role in the near future. On the other hand, it seems unlikely that it will abandon its staunch opposition to any plan to accept for MERCOSUR anything like an EU-style Commission or supranational courts, not to mention a common currency.

In sum, despite repeated suggestions to the effect that 'the study of economic integration has been inspired if not dominated by the European example' (Pelkmans 1997: 2), the available empirical evidence points to the fact that the European example has elicited defensive reactions rather than emulative responses. In terms of comparative regionalism, the EU appears be the outlier rather than the model. The emphasis on process rather than concrete results as well as the deep ambiguity about ends discussed in the following chapters go a long way towards explaining the lack of attraction of European-style regional integration.

Process regionalism vs. outcome regionalism

In the article on regionalism and multilateralism mentioned above, Bhagwati considers the question whether regionalism – defined broadly as preferential trade agreements among a subset of countries – will get us closer to the goal of multilateral free trade for all countries than the process of trade negotiation. In this context he introduces a useful distinction between 'process multilateralism' – the process of trade negotiation – and 'outcome multilateralism' – the goal of multilateral free trade (Bhagwati 1993: 24). An analogous distinction can also be useful for comparing different models of regionalism. For example, when political leaders, policymakers, and analysts claim that the EU is the most successful model of regional integration, they may be right in terms of process – level of institutionalization, volume of legislation, territorial expansion, etc. – but not necessarily in terms of outcomes, such as 'closer union among the peoples of Europe', or even full market integration. In terms of performance criteria the superiority of the European model is far from being evident, and in fact it is increasingly disputed by the peoples of the EU themselves – see below. Indeed, there are several indications that even full economic integration – the only generally accepted goal of the process of European integration – may no longer be possible in a greatly enlarged and increasingly heterogeneous EU. Generally speaking, a mismatch between process and outcome provides *prima facie* evidence that the particular model of regional integration has been chosen for purposes other than the stated goal(s).

Even before the present crisis of the euro zone the evidence was clear that results produced by European integration remained well below what European leaders had repeatedly promised. Indeed, growth has stagnated, or even regressed, since the launching of the two most important economic projects: the Single Market Programme and Economic and Monetary Union (EMU). After the phase of very rapid catch-up with the US in the immediate post-war period, convergence in the levels of per capita income stopped at the beginning of the 1980s and has remained unchanged since, at around 70 per cent of the US level. A common trade policy, the customs union, a supranational competition policy, extensive harmonization of national laws and regulations, the Single Market project, and finally a centralized monetary policy, apparently made no difference as far as the economic performance of the EC/EU, relative to its major competitors, was concerned. While the American economy was generating employment as well as maintaining working hours, Europe's employment performance was weak and working hours fell consistently. During the 1990s growth of EU gross domestic product (GDP) was disappointing both in absolute terms and by comparison with the US.

The will to improve poor economic performance has driven EU policy over the last thirty years: from the Single Market Programme, meant to be a response to perceived 'Eurosclerosis' in the mid-1980s, to EMU in the 1990s, and the Lisbon Strategy for Growth and Jobs in the following decade. This 'Lisbon Strategy' provides a striking example of what at the national level would be considered a clumsy attempt to deceive the voters and, as such, likely to be punished at the polls, but which seems to involve no political costs at the European level. At the summit held in the Portuguese capital in March 2000 the heads of state and government of the EU (officially known as the European Council) announced extremely ambitious objectives, including the surpassing of the US economy by 2010. In order to achieve these objectives, it was assumed that the Union would grow at an annual average rate of 3 per cent, so as to create 20 million new jobs. Unfortunately, the data kept showing that far from closing the gap and then overtaking the US economy, the EU as a whole continued to lag behind in terms of growth rates, employment, and especially in terms of productivity. The experts knew all along that the goal announced in Lisbon was in fact unfeasible since it would have required an annual growth rate of productivity of about 4 per cent. Instead, in recent years productivity in Europe has been growing at about 0.5 to 1 per cent, while in the US productivity growth has been about 2 per cent per annum. The disappointing results finally convinced EU leaders that it was wiser to drop the target date of 2010, which they quietly did at the 2005 Spring European Council. By then businesses and economists were pronouncing the Lisbon economic reform process comatose, if not quite dead, while the three largest economies of the euro zone – France, Germany, and Italy – made little attempt to fulfil their Lisbon promises. No leader was punished by the voters because of the empty promises made in the Portuguese capital. On the contrary, press releases following the Spring 2007 meeting of the European Council reported that the Council 'acknowledged the success of the Lisbon Strategy for Growth and Jobs, reflected in higher growth and falling unemployment figures'. As it turned out, what the Council celebrated was only a cyclical upswing, not structural growth, as was shown by the data released by the European Statistical Office in August 2007: the Union was still dragging behind the US on practically all indicators.

The Lisbon Strategy – the complete failure of which was eventually admitted by Commission President Barroso, who used the failure as an excuse to announce a new 'Europe 2020' project – was an attempt to coordinate, in a flexible, non-binding way, the economic policies of the member states. But policy coordination is precisely what has *not* happened. Since the launching of the Lisbon Strategy in 2000, the governments of the major continental economies have each attempted to solve their structural problems in a different way, leading to large differences in key economic indicators. The reluctance of the member states to coordinate their policy actions has been demonstrated again in the first stages of the sovereign-debt crisis of the euro zone (see chapters 1 and 2).

Size, scope, and transaction costs

As noted above, a significantly lower level of institutionalization is a key feature distinguishing the regional organizations established in the 1980s and 1990s from the EU. Two other important differences from the European model are: the much smaller membership of the new organizations compared to the twenty-eight member states of the EU (now including Croatia), with many more to come in the near future; and also a more limited and more precisely defined scope of competences. The largest of the three regional groups already mentioned, MERCOSUR, has four members, possibly five in the near future; NAFTA, three members; and ANZCERTA includes only two countries. In the early 1990s it was expected that the free trade agreement between Canada, the US, and Mexico, would expand to include most countries of Latin America. However, plans for a Free Trade Area of the Americas did not materialize. Today, the US is apparently no longer interested in extending regional integration beyond North America, preferring instead to sign bilateral free trade agreements with other countries of Latin America. It is now generally acknowledged that the cost of integration on NAFTA terms is probably too high for many Latin American countries – an expression of economic and political realism largely absent in the EU. At the same time, the regional leader in South America, Brazil, does not seem to be interested in giving up its position of dominance within MERCOSUR for membership in a regional organization dominated by the US.

The size of regional organizations matters for at least two reasons. First, a small organization economizes on bargaining, influence, and other transaction costs: see chapter 4. Second, the small size facilitates the development of a system of reputations based on mutual trust, and such a system, in turn, facilitates the enforcement of agreements among the members of the organization. Because the contract – in the general meaning of voluntary agreement – is the basic unit of analysis in transaction-cost economics, economists of this school have given a good deal of attention to problems of contract enforcement. They point out that in situations in which detailed contracts cannot be written, making legal enforcement difficult, enforcement may still be possible if the parties themselves have enough information to evaluate each other's past behaviour, which information is a basic requirement of any system of reputations. Even if it is possible to write detailed contracts, a good reputation can often allow the decision-maker to avoid that expense as well as the use of costly and error-prone legal contract enforcement mechanisms. One of the ways that people enhance the effectiveness of a system of reputations is by narrowing the range of people with whom they do business. Also, frequent transactions allow trust to flourish. If these conditions are not satisfied, however, then recourse to legal contract enforcement mechanisms may be unavoidable. The legal system, however, has many disadvantages for contract enforcement. Because it is a general system, it relies on general rules that may be poorly tailored for the particular context where the dispute arises. Also, legal procedures tend to be cumbersome, time-consuming, and expensive, while legal rules based on historical precedents may be unresponsive to changing technologies and other changing realities. The relevance of these observations to the case of the EU will be demonstrated in chapters 3 and 4 in the present book.

Regional economic integration need not lead to centralized, law-based institutions that tend to expand the scope of their own competences. As already noted, most of the new regional organizations have deliberately minimized recourse to legal and bureaucratic institutions. According to the 1988 Canada–United States Free Trade Agreement (CUSTA), for example, prospective trade conflicts were to be treated by consultations and a variety of dispute-settlement mechanisms. The other institutional provisions similarly minimize the use of legal means, favouring instead recourse to mediation and arbitration, supported by the appropriate kind of expertise and, if necessary, by the threat of retaliation. Many of the novel features of the Canada–US Agreement were retained in the design of NAFTA, which was ratified in 1993. In particular, NAFTA's dispute-settlement mechanisms closely resemble those of CUSTA in most respects, while moving beyond them in others. While in the EU disputes over trade and investment must be resolved by the European courts applying European law – a system that mimics the legal central- ism prevailing at the national level – the dispute-resolution mechanisms established by NAFTA represent a new experiment in international governance, see chapter 9. Legal centralism maintains that disputes require access to a forum external to the original social setting of the dispute, and that remedies will be provided according to rules designed by experts who operate under the auspices of the state. In reality, most disputes between market actors, including many disputes that could be brought to a court, are resolved by more flexible means, as will be seen in chapter 3. In many instances the participants can devise more satisfac- tory solutions to their disputes than can professionals constrained to apply general rules on the basis of limited knowledge of the dispute. Because of the serious limitations with which court ordering is beset, the costs of contract implementation can be quite significant. The NAFTA arrangements for dispute resolution depend much less on legal central- ism and court ordering than the corresponding arrangements in the EU, and for this reason they are likely to be more cost-effective, as well as more transparent, than the more traditional, state-like mechanisms adopted by the Union.

A widely used label to characterize the European model of regional integration is 'integration through law'. The label is appropriate because it suggests that European law has been used not only as a substitute for democratic politics, but also to compensate by legal means the lack of mutual trust among a growing number of member states. A good example is the Stability Pact, which was meant to force members of the euro zone to respect the Maastricht parameters, see chapter 1. By now even pro-integration experts agree that there were no valid economic reasons to impose a common currency on a group of structurally very different national economies. Consequently, the old Stability Pact was not so much geared towards coordinating as towards disciplining the fiscal policies of the members of the euro zone. According to some analysts, this is precisely the reason why it failed. This emphasis on punitive mechanisms of contract enforcement shows the absence of mutual trust in a group of countries that is supposed to move toward 'ever closer union'. The architects of regional organizations such as the CUSTA, NAFTA, and ANZCERTA were apparently more aware than European leaders of the risks of forcing integration beyond the limits voters are prepared to accept. One of the standard arguments used in the 1990s to justify the introduction of a common European currency was that exchange-rate instability would disrupt trade in the common market. However, a monetary union between Canada and the US has never been seriously considered even though the trading relationship between these two countries is the largest bilateral trading relationship in the world – with about two-thirds of Canada's imports coming from the US, and three-quarters of its exports going to the US; about one-fifth of US imports coming from Canada and one-quarter of US exports going to Canada. The fact that Canadian and US traders, like traders in Australia and New Zealand, continue to operate, apparently with success, using their own currencies shows that the empirical evidence that currency swings dampen trade is far from being convincing. The two Pacific countries, like the countries of North America, provide ample evidence that a single market does not require a single currency.

Integration for its own sake?

The arguments and evidence presented in the preceding sections strongly suggest that the EU, far from being a source of inspiration for the designers of new regional organizations, was actually rejected by them as a useful model. On the other hand, scholars who insist on the *sui generis* nature of the Union implicitly deny the possibility of any meaningful comparison with other regional blocs. They do not tell us, however, what makes the EU essentially different from other schemes of regional integration. One such distinctive feature would be a commitment to full economic *and* political integration. However, nowadays there are very few advocates of fully-fledged political union – the old vision of the United States of Europe. Even political and intellectual leaders who claim that the present general crisis of European integration can only be solved by the magic formula 'more Europe' acknowledge the impossibility of a federal solution, see chapter 7. The political content of the magic formula remains, however, wholly indeterminate. The only clear objective is the continuing expansion of EU powers: process regionalism.

The competences of the EU have grown so much since establishment of the EEC by the 1957 Treaty of Rome that according to some specialists of European law the Union's 'policy-making powers now [touch] almost every imaginable public policy objective' (Curtin *et al.* 2013: 1). More than twenty years ago a distinguished legal scholar and member of the EU's Court of First Instance (renamed General Court by the Lisbon Treaty) could claim that 'there is no nucleus of sovereignty that the Member States can invoke, as such, against the Community' (Lenaerts 1990). Indeed, in the euphoria created by the Single European Act and the very successful marketing of the 'Europe 1992' programme it became tempting to imagine that there were no effective barriers to the continuous, if incremental, expansion of European competences.

According to EU leaders, this continuous expansion of supranational powers has produced a steady flow of benefits for the citizens: 'European integration has delivered 50 years of economic prosperity, stability and peace. It has helped to raise standards of living, built an internal market and strengthened the Union's voice in the world.' These opening lines of the Commission's White Paper on *European Governance*, published in 2001 (Commission 2001), were repeated almost verbatim by Chancellor Angela Merkel, as rotating president of the European Council, on the occasion of the fiftieth anniversary celebrations of the signing of the Treaty of Rome. The flow of benefits generated by the steady expansion of the legislative and policymaking powers of the EU should have produced a steadily growing popular support for European integration. Unfortunately, this is not at all the case. Over the years popular attitudes towards integration have changed from a 'permissive consensus' – when a large majority of citizens in all the member states were either not interested in European integration or took the supranational institutions for granted as an accepted part of the political landscape – to outright hostility. Recent opinion surveys have measured the extent of the hostility.

According to the extensive survey conducted by the Washington, DC-based Pew Research Center in 2012, Germany is the only member of the EU in which most people (59 per cent) think their country has been helped by European integration. The most negative were the Greeks, with 70 per cent saying that European integration has hurt them, followed by the French with 63 per cent. The survey, entitled *European Unity on the Rocks, Greeks and Germans at Polar Opposites*, was conducted in eight EU countries – Britain, France, Germany, Italy, Spain, Greece, Poland, and the Czech Republic – and the US, and queried 9,108 people between 17 March and 16 April 2012. According to the report, what started out in 2009 as a sovereign-debt crisis has now triggered a full-blown crisis of public confidence: in the economy, in the benefits of European economic integration, in membership in the EU, in the euro, and in the free-market system. In particular, Europeans largely oppose further fiscal austerity to deal with the crisis; are divided on bailing out indebted nations; and oppose Brussels' impending over-sight of national budgets. Across the eight EU member states surveyed, a median of only 34 per cent think that European economic integration has strengthened their country's economy. Indeed, majorities or near majorities in most nations now believe that the economic integration of Europe has actually weakened their economies. This is the opinion in Greece (70 per cent), France (63 per cent), Britain (61 per cent), Italy (61 per cent), the Czech Republic (59 per cent) and Spain (50 per cent). Only in Germany do most people (59 per cent) say that their country has been well served by European integration. Among the five members of the euro zone surveyed, a median of only 37 per cent believes having the euro as their common currency has been a good thing. This includes just 30 per cent of the Italians and 31 per cent of the French. A median of about four-in-ten Europeans (39 per cent) surveyed think favourably of the European Central Bank (ECB), the institution at the centre of the debate over how to deal with the euro crisis. That includes just 15 per cent of the Greeks, 25 per cent of the Spanish, and only 40 per cent of the Germans. At the same time, the three non-euro zone countries surveyed are quite happy they have kept their own currencies, including nearly three-quarters of the British (73 per cent). The conclusion of the Pew Report is that the European project is a major casualty of the on-going European sovereign-debt crisis (Pew Global Attitudes Project 2012).

Later surveys confirm the negative data of the American research centre concerning the benefits of European integration. Thus the survey conducted by Ipsos-Publicis (2013) in France and in the other five larger members of the EU revealed that membership in the EU was considered a disadvantage rather than a benefit by 64 per cent of United Kingdom (UK) citizens but also by 58 per cent of Germans and 53 per cent of Italians. Only in Poland a large majority of the people interviewed (70 per cent) still see membership in the Union as a benefit. Again, no more than 29 per cent of interviewees in the six countries had a positive opinion of the European institutions, while the discipline imposed by the Fiscal Compact was assumed to have negative consequences for the economy by 76 per cent of the Spaniards, 71 per cent of the French, 66 per cent of the Italians and, rather surprisingly, also by a majority (54 per cent) of the German sample.

A few years ago even confirmed Euro-sceptics would have found it hard to believe that such negative views of the EU and of the integration process were so widely shared. Certainly, the crisis of the euro zone has a lot to do with this change of attitudes. The seeds of discontent were sown long before, however, as it became increasingly difficult to conceal the unsatisfactory results, or outright failures, of significant European projects. Thus, the earliest attempt to transfer to the European level the domestic interventionism of the governments of the member states, namely the Common Agricultural Policy (CAP), resulted in what *The Economist* of 29 September 1990 called 'the single most idiotic system of economic mismanagement that the rich western countries have ever devised'. In spite of widespread dissatisfaction with its results, almost 40 per cent of the EU budget still goes to the CAP. The complete failure of the promise solemnly made by the heads of state and government at the Lisbon summit of March 2000 to make the EU 'the most competitive, knowledge-based economy in the world' by 2010 has already been mentioned. Also the much advertised promise of a single European market by 1992 is still far from having been fulfilled, as will be seen in chapter 1. It is at any rate true that neither these nor the many other policy failures of the past generated anything like the present crisis of public confidence in the benefits of membership in the EU. The reason is fairly obvious. The permissive consensus of the past was only possible as long as Euro-elites managed to keep European issues out of the political debate. This de-politicization of supranational issues was facilitated by the fact that most European policies were implemented by the national administrations, so that it was difficult for ordinary citizens, and sometimes even for experts, to allocate responsibility for unsatisfactory outcomes as between 'Brussels' and the national governments. At any rate most European policies of the past, including CAP, interested only limited segments of the population.

In this respect monetary union represents a clear break with the traditional approach of 'integration by stealth' (Majone 2005). What makes the crisis of the euro zone so politically significant is the fact that the actual consequences of decisions taken at the European level are now so much more visible than they were in earlier stages of the integration process. Buyers are typically interested in the quality and price of a finished product, not in the way it is produced, or in the internal organization of the firm that produces it. Similarly, the 'buyers' of public policy, voters and the citizens at large, are interested in the quality and tax-prices of specific policy outcomes, not in administrative procedures and decision-making processes. Thus an important consequence of monetary union, and of its crisis, is the possibility, now open to anybody, of seeing an important European policy in operation – and of assessing its effectiveness. Unlike most policy decisions taken in Brussels, the decisions taken by the ECB in Frankfurt are widely advertised, and their consequences – whether on home mortgages, on consumer credit, or on the availability of publicly financed services – have a direct impact on the welfare of all inhabitants of the euro zone, indeed of the entire EU. Also the Bank's non-decisions, for example, concerning variations in the discount rate, are often discussed in the media. Since the beginning of the crisis of the euro zone, moreover, everybody realizes that integration entails costs as well as benefits, and that a positive net balance of benefits over costs can no longer be taken for granted. This new realism is likely to generate a much stronger demand for accountability by results – precisely what is foreign to the political culture of total optimism of EU leaders, see chapter 2. Once results become visible, however, the political consequences of failure to deliver the goods can be significant.

European integration in a new key

In the early stages of the integration process it was not unreasonable to assume that a community of six fairly homogeneous states would evolve, sooner or later, into a politically integrated bloc – perhaps even into something like a federation. That assumption is no longer tenable in a Union of almost thirty member states at vastly different stages of socioeconomic development, with different geopolitical concerns, and correspondingly diverse policy priorities. Hence the growing resistance to the view of the European integration process as a sort of straight-line evolution from the nation state to a supranational union doing pretty much the same things, only on a bigger scale: from a common agricultural policy to common foreign, security, trade, and monetary policies. Under present conditions, not orthogenesis (as biologists call straight-line evolution) but evolution with several side-branches seems to be the appropriate metaphor. As a matter of fact, the general pattern of European integration since the end of World War II reveals several distinct branches – a number of, often overlapping, state groupings established for purposes of cooperation in a variety of fields: political, economic, protection of human rights, security, science and technology. An important example is the Council of Europe founded in 1949, which at present has more than forty member countries. The Council may concern itself with all political, economic, and social matters of general European interest and thus has an even broader mandate than the EU. True, it does not have the power to make binding laws. The two instruments at the Council's disposal are non-binding resolutions and conventions effective only between the states that ratify them. The most important convention enacted under its auspices is the European Convention for the Protection of Human Rights and Fundamental Freedoms (ECHR) of 4 November 1950. With the creation of the European Court of Human Rights, located in Strasbourg, the ECHR provides an enforcement structure which subjects the states to a 'European' supervision of their compliance with the provisions of the Convention. For this reason, it has been argued that the ECHR constitutes a first expression of supranationalism in the European integration process. It is interesting to note that despite the non-binding character of the norms, levels of compliance with the ECHR and with the decisions of the Strasbourg Court do not appear to be at all lower than levels of compliance with EC law (Majone 2009).

The variety of modes of integration and of inter-state cooperation was always the distinguishing feature of the European polity – a variety which has made Europe different from, and more dynamic than, the centralized empires of the past. As Eric Jones has stressed, for most of its history Europe formed a cultural, economic, even a political unity. Of course, it was a special type of unity that did not exclude frequent, if limited, wars. Not the unity of the Chinese, Mogul or Ottoman empires; rather, unity in diversity, embodied in a system of states competing and cooperating with each other. Such a system realized the benefits of competitive decision-making and the economies of scale of the centralized empire, giving Europe some of the best of both worlds. In the words of the British historian:

> This picture of a Europe which shared in salient respects a common culture...and formed something of a single market demonstrates that political decentralisation did not mean a fatal loss of economies of scale in production and distribution. The states system did not thwart the flow of capital and labour to the constituent states offering the highest marginal return.
>
> (Jones 1987: 117)

The European states system always opposed any attempt to unify the continent under the leadership of a great power that would pre-empt the sovereignty of the other members of the system. Even at the peak of their power neither Spain nor France nor Germany succeeded in establishing a European empire. Each time the freedom of the European system of states hung precariously in the balance. Yet each time, the forces seeking to preserve the balance in the system were victorious over those that would upset it (Dehio 1962).

As will be seen in some detail in chapter 8, the member states of the EU are also extremely reluctant to accept the leadership of one member of their group; indeed, even the largest and economically most powerful member of the Union is extremely reluctant to assume such a role. This reluctance is rooted in history, but also in the contemporary ideology of European integration. A key element of this ideology is the basic equality and equal dignity of all the member states, from the smallest to the largest: no leader but a 'collective leadership' as the principle of equality of all member states has sometimes been characterized. This principle of formal and (to the extent possible) substantive equality has inspired all the European treaties and also the day-to-day practice. It is reflected in the design and *modus operandi* of the European institutions. A direct consequence of this principle is the fact that nobody can claim to govern the Union and, as a corollary, the total absence of the traditional government–opposition dialectic. The European Commission, which many Euro-enthusiasts used to see as the would-be kernel of the future government of a federal Europe, in fact looks more and more like an international bureaucracy and less and less like a proto-government. Knowledgeable observers of the European scene have recently noted that even the European Council – the most likely candidate to provide leadership at the supranational level – is only able to achieve what the member states want it to achieve, with agreements hammered out, often bilaterally, beyond its walls. What most students of European integration have failed to analyse, however, are the limits of what a polity based on collective leadership can be expected to achieve.

The alleged comparative advantage of the EU model with respect to other regional organizations has usually been attributed to the extent of the powers delegated to the supranational institutions. But as pointed out above and in more detail in chapter 4, a high level of supranational institutionalization entails high transaction costs, so that in terms of the *net* benefits of integration the superiority of the European model is far from being obvious. The results achieved by regional organizations such as NAFTA and ANZCERTA show that extensive economic integration is possible without elaborate institutional and legal superstructures. Harry Johnson and other distinguished economists had argued the same point in the early days of the EEC, without however influencing the public discourse. Unless we are willing to assume that the founding fathers of communitarian Europe were either naive or uninformed we must conclude that the rationale behind the unique institutional development of the European supranational institutions was political rather than economic.

The problem is that a politically integrated Europe, in the sense in which 'political integration' is commonly understood today, was and continues to be an elitist project. In the course of more than half a century of integration efforts, a certain Europeanization of intellectual, economic, and political elites has taken place, yet this process has hardly touched the vast majority of European citizens. All attempts to induce a transfer of loyalties from the national to the supranational level – not only by propaganda and cultural actions but, more concretely, by such measures as the direct election of the European Parliament (EP), various social-policy measures, including the 'welfare state for farmers' represented by the CAP, or policies of regional aid – failed completely in this respect, when they did not increase the degree of conflict among the member states of the EU. In the early stages of integration the reaction of the Euro-elites to this unsatisfactory situation was to claim that popular support was not, after all, necessary. Thus Ernst Haas and his neo-functionalist school argued that the bureaucratized nature of European states implies that all crucial decisions are made by elites: public policymakers, as well as economic elites, trade unions, professional associations, business lobbies, etc. Public opinion at large, on the other hand, was deemed to be unimportant. The basic problem for the neo-functionalists, but also for some political leaders, was not how to 'Europeanize the masses', but how 'to make Europe without Europeans' (Schmitter 2005). Thus Paul-Henri Spaak, Belgian political leader and ardent federalist, maintained that supranational institutions had become indispensable for peace and prosperity in Western Europe, regardless of what those institutions might be or do. 'For me', he once told a group of journalists, 'everything which tends towards European organizations is good' (citation in Milward 1992: 324).

Unfortunately neo-functionalist scholars and integrationist leaders alike overestimated the effectiveness of supranational institutions. The superior problem-solving capacity of these institutions – a superiority assumed a priori rather than supported by concrete evidence – was supposed to produce a sufficient normative basis for the integration project by inducing the progressive transfer of the loyalties and political demands of social groups from the national to the European level. Since the 1970s, however, the effectiveness of the supranational institutions has been increasingly questioned. As was indicated above, today most opinion surveys show that the supranational institutions in Brussels and Frankfurt are increasingly perceived less as potential sources of solutions than as causes of some of the problems that most concern the citizens of the EU. In addition, the micro- and macroeconomic evidence mentioned in the following chapters supports the growing conviction that an ever-widening and deepening integration process has proved impotent to arrest the decline of Europe's economy relative to its major competitors. What is increasingly questioned is less the general idea of integration than the particular integration method followed so far. It is time, therefore, to consider more carefully alternative approaches suggested in the past by a few critics of the prevailing orthodoxy.

An alternative approach to regional integration, advocated by David Mitrany in the 1940s (see Eilstrup-Sangiovanni 2006) and by Ralph Dahrendorf in the 1970s (Dahrendorf 1973), is based on a functional, rather than territorial, view of integration. A territorial union, according to Mitrany, binds together some interests which are not of common concern to the group, while it inevitably 'cuts asunder some interests of common concern to the group and those outside it'. To avoid such 'twice-arbitrary surgery' it is necessary to proceed by 'binding together those interests which are common, where they are common, and to the extent to which they are common'. Thus the essential principle of a functional organization of international activities 'is that activities would be selected specifically and organized separately, each according to its nature, to the conditions under which it has to operate, and to the needs of the moment' (see chapter 10). At the same time, Mitrany was sceptical about the advantages of political union. His main objection to schemes for continental unions was that the closer the union the more inevitably would it be dominated by the more powerful member. Also Dahrendorf's notion of integration à la carte led to the conclusion that there should be common European policies only in areas where the member states have a common interest. While not excluding a priori the possibility of a European political union, eventually, the future Lord Dahrendorf maintained that no country should be forced to participate in everything. Integration à la carte was not ideal, but it was much better than 'avoiding anything that cannot be cooked in a single pot'.

Neither these nor other ideas of differentiated integration were based on, or inspired by, any formal social-scientific theory. Today James Buchanan's economic theory of clubs may be used to provide a robust conceptual basis for the analysis of integration à la carte and of other forms of functional integration, see chapter 3. The economic theory of clubs emphasizes the advantages of institutional pluralism, and implies that an efficient assignment of tasks between different levels of governance need not coincide with existing national boundaries: there may be significant externalities and a need for coordination between some, but not all, regions within a country or group of countries. This theory also explains why a number of tasks which used to be assigned to central governments are today performed by private, increasingly transnational, organizations. Thus, despite the strong historical correlation between standardization and the emergence of the sovereign territorial state, current views on standardization have changed radically as a result of the advance of globalization, the development of technology, and the growing variety and sophistication of technical standards. As far as a given community of users is concerned, standards are collective goods – in that they fulfil specific functions deemed desirable by the community that shares them – but this does not mean that they must be established by government fiat. A good standard must reflect the needs, preferences, and resources of the community of users, rather than some centrally defined vision of the 'common interest'. According to economist Alessandra Casella (1996), the fact that in today's integrating world economy the relevant community of standards users need not be territorially defined, distinguishes the traditional approach from the contemporary understanding of standards as a special class of 'club goods' – public goods made available only to those who contribute to their production. Moreover, as the complexity of a society increases, perhaps as the result of integration of previously separate markets, the number of clubs tends to increase as well. This is because greater diversity of needs and preferences makes it efficient to produce a broader range of club goods, such as product standards. The general implication of this argument is that top-down harmonization may be desirable when the market is relatively small and homogeneous. In a large market, on the other hand, harmonization tends to be brought about by the recognition of similar demands, rather than by a policy imposed from the top. Hence a multiplicity of club goods replaces policy harmonization.

As will be seen in chapters 9 and 10, the view of Europe as a 'club of clubs', rather than as a would-be federation, has deep roots in the history of the Old Continent. As several distinguished historians have argued, the European global dominance of the past was made possible not by centralization, but by fragmentation and by the competition stimulated by fragmentation. The mistake of today's integrationist leaders has been to assume a unilinear development from the nation state to something fulfilling much the same functions, on a grander scale and allegedly more effectively. History suggests that there is something unnatural in this approach, as far as our continent is concerned. European unity has never been the unity of empire or even of a large transnational federation, but a much subtler unity in diversity achieved through a unique mixture of competition, cooperation, and imitation.

An ever closer and larger Union?

In December 2003, on the eve of the EU's 'big bang' enlargement that was to add ten new member states from Central and Eastern Europe, two perceptive German journalists raised a question which political leaders and European institutions had carefully avoided for too many years: 'Europe: couldn't we have it one size smaller?' (Pinzer and Fritz-Vannahme 2003). Their article, which appeared in the influential weekly *Die Zeit*, expressed well the feelings of many Europeans about the apparently unstoppable growth of EU competences, and the steady expansion of its borders. It is becoming increasingly clear, they wrote, that the Union is overstepping itself. In the past it managed to appear so successful by making incompatible commitments: ever deeper supranational integration that would not, however, touch the rights and privileges of the national governments; a monetary union that would not interfere with the economic policies of the member states; a common security policy which in no way should compromise either the sovereignty of the member states or their commitments to North Atlantic Treaty Organization (NATO). Already ten years ago perceptive observers of the European scene, like these two German journalists, knew that such empty promises were no longer credible. Poland and the other member states from Eastern Europe made it clear that they were in favour of economic integration but were not willing to give up the national sovereignty they had just recovered. And EMU could be implemented only by 'dropping the E', as Jacques Delors is supposed to have sadly admitted. Today we are experiencing the consequences of that 'total optimism' which made monetary union possible, see chapter 2. The depth of the current crisis justifies the widespread opinion that integration has gone too far. But it is also important to keep in mind that this critique applies to the particular method of integration followed by the national governments and by the supranational institutions since the Treaty of Rome. As indicated above, other methods exist and need to be developed further, both conceptually and practically. In this sense European integration has not gone far enough: we must go beyond a simple linear extrapolation of the traditional nation state model. The search for alternative integration methods, however, must start from the realization that despite globalization and regional integration the nation state is still vitally important, as argued in the final chapter of this book. Hence current attempts to solve the present crisis of monetary union by reducing the autonomy of democratically elected national governments are likely to be self-defeating.

1

Monetary union as a metaphor

The rhetoric of European monetary union

The agreement on EMU included in the 1992 Treaty on European Union (Maastricht Treaty) represents the most daring move towards fully-fledged integration undertaken by European leaders so far. However, the crisis of the euro zone, its origins and political and economic consequences, cannot be discussed only in terms of that fateful decision, but must be viewed as part of a more general crisis of the particular approach to European integration that has been followed since the 1950s. Piris (2011) distinguished three dimensions of this crisis: the risk of a collapse of monetary union; popular distrust in the European institutions and widespread disenchantment with the very idea of European integration; and dysfunctional institutions and ineffective decision processes in a Union of twenty-eight highly heterogeneous member states. The best way to understand the nature of the general crisis, I submit, is to start from EMU because monetary union, with all its gaps and fragilities, is a metaphor for the entire process of European integration as it has developed so far.

The essence of metaphor is 'understanding and experiencing one kind of thing in terms of another' (Lakoff and Johnson 1980: 5). In particular, structural metaphors 'allow us. . .to use one highly structured and clearly delineated concept to structure another' (ibid.: 61). In the following pages and chapters I shall use EMU primarily as a structural metaphor.

Precisely because monetary union is a highly structured and clearly delineated concept it allows us to better understand important features of the traditional methods of integration which tend to be overlooked – often deliberately. As we shall see in more detail in chapters 2 and 3, for example, a characteristic feature of the traditional approach to integration is the much greater importance attached to process, in particular to institution building, rather than to concrete results, of the type which citizens can understand and evaluate. This primacy of process over outcome is evident in the criteria generally used to assess the success of strategic decisions taken at European level. An agreement to proceed in a certain direction may be advertised as an achievement of historic significance, though many important issues still remain unresolved, and ultimate success is far from being certain: what really counts is having reached a collective agreement. Thus, agreement on EMU was celebrated as a turning point in European integration, even though the Maastricht Treaty left a number of fundamental policy questions unanswered. In order to make political agreement possible, questions concerning measures to coordinate economic policies, or to provide compensatory budgetary transfers, were simply sidestepped. Also, issues of external monetary policy, unitary external representation of the monetary union, exchange-rate policy, and political accountability were left unsettled. Even the basic question: whether it made economic sense to adopt a one-size-fits-all monetary policy for such structurally different national economies, was never properly discussed. As a result, EMU turned out to be a high-risk project with no easy exit option if things went wrong. The chosen strategy simply assumed an irrevocable commitment to the single currency and accorded no place to failure (Tsoukalis 1993).

The absence of contingency plans – which, as we shall see in the next chapter, is a typical feature of policymaking at EU level – is another consequence of the primacy of process over results. Also the fact that 'it took only a few weeks for the euro to become the single European currency used in daily transactions from Finland to Portugal and from Ireland to Greece' has been seen as definite proof of the success of the single currency: 'The success of the launch of the euro is not only technical and economic, it is also and foremost political. The euro is the most visible and practical symbol of the progress towards a political union in Europe' (De Grauwe 2004: 363). In this as in many other cases, the process was celebrated without waiting for the actual results. What makes this premature celebration notable is less the tone than the fact that the enthusiastic writer is not a pro-integration political leader or a self-interested Brussels bureaucrat but a distinguished monetary economist. One is more prepared to discount the rhetoric of official documents, such as the Commission's White Paper on *European Governance*, or to understand the optimism of EU leaders celebrating the fiftieth anniversary of the signing of the Treaty of Rome (Majone 2009: 81–7).

In sum, to understand why the great expectations that accompanied the introduction of the euro were bitterly disappointed so soon is to grasp the basic problems of policymaking in the EU – and to perceive them more clearly than would be possible by analysing other, less obvious, cases of policy failure. It is indeed hard to find a better example of the willingness of EU leaders to compromise their collective credibility by committing themselves to over-optimistic goals. Nor can one find, in the entire history of European integration, a better illustration of the complete disregard, not only of expert opinion, but also of such basic principles of crisis management as the timely preparation of contingency plans and careful attention to signs that may foretell a crisis. As will be seen in the following chapter, these are not isolated and more or less random accidents, but structural flaws of policymaking in the EU.

No royal road to political union

The process of monetary union was supposed to take the member states to the point of no return on the road to economic and political integration. In fact, since its inception this process was marked by deep differences of opinion among the main participants – disagreements about the purpose, design, and management of monetary union that have never been fully resolved. Plans for monetary union were almost contemporary with the establishment of the EEC in 1957. One could assume, therefore, that the problems and consequences – both intended and unintended – of such a far-reaching integrationist move would have been reasonably well understood by the time the European Council, meeting in Brussels in May 1998, decided to begin EMU on 1 January 1999. We shall see that this was not at all the case.

As soon as the Treaty of Rome was signed, Jean Monnet asked one of his closest associates, Pierre Uri, and the Belgian monetary economist Robert Triffin to draft a plan for a European monetary system (Uri 1989). The main focus of the Rome Treaty was of course on creating a customs union and a common market, but in its text one also finds some recognition of the importance of macroeconomic policies, and of monetary policy in particular. The CAP itself, being based on common prices for agricultural products, by implication made it necessary to pay attention to exchange rates, and indeed the treaty referred to the exchange rates between the currencies of the member states as a matter of Community interest. A monetary committee consisting of senior officials from the finance ministries was set up as early as 1958; it was followed in 1964 by a committee of governors of the national banks, established to minimize the risk of conflicting monetary policies by the member states, but also to co-opt the central bankers. Actually, the usefulness of a regional monetary union was not obvious in the 1960s since the Bretton Woods regime governed the world economy for the first three decades following the end of World War II, while the US dollar was the undisputed monetary standard. Only when the US proved unable, or unwilling, to ensure monetary stability, did plans for EMU revive.

By the late 1960s, the currency crises which threatened the preservation of the international monetary system were pushing toward the creation of a currency bloc in Europe. In fact, one of the inadequacies of Bretton Woods acknowledged at the time was that the American emphasis on universal organization (multilateralism) led to the neglect of regional arrangements and how such arrangements could be accommodated to the universal design (Meier 1982). Moreover, while monetary stability was still considered important for the smooth functioning of the European common market, everybody understood that beyond (or behind) the technical objectives there was a much more important political aim: monetary union was to be *'la voie royale vers l'union politique'* – the royal road to political union, as the French liked to put it (Tsoukalis 1993: 178). For all these reasons, in the 1970s EMU was to replace the customs union as the main goal of the EEC.

At the Hague summit in December 1969, the heads of state and government of the EEC decided to reduce exchange-rate flexibility and to move towards economic and monetary union. EMU was to replace the customs union as the main goal of the new decade. A high-level group – chaired by the prime minister of Luxembourg, Pierre Werner – was entrusted with the preparation of a report on the establishment of monetary union. In October 1970 Werner presented an ambitious seven-stage plan to achieve this goal within ten years(!) by means of institutional reforms and closer political cooperation (see Tsoukalis 1993: 225–7; Marsh 2010: 53–67). The plan glossed over serious differences of opinion concerning the strategy to be adopted during the transitional period in order to achieve a sufficient harmonization of national economic policies. The crucial difference was whether the Community would move towards monetary alignment – irrevocably fixed parities and the elimination of margins of fluctuation – before the effectiveness of the system of policy coordination had been demonstrated. The countries of the so-called 'monetarist' bloc (led by France and also including Belgium and Luxembourg, with widespread support in the European Commission) held the view that the EEC should move towards monetary alignment even before the system of economic policy coordination had proved its effectiveness. Hence, they were in favour of early steps to fix the exchange rates, as a prelude to full monetary union. While agreeing that imbalances in balance of payments were a sign of financial disequilibrium, the 'monetarists' believed that responsibility for correcting such imbalances lay equally with surplus and with deficit countries.

In practice this meant that strong-currency countries with balance of payments surpluses (like Germany) should support economically weaker countries (such as France and Italy) through currency intervention and the pooling of foreign exchange reserves. But this was exactly what Germany and the Netherlands, the members of the 'economist' bloc, wished to avoid. German and Dutch leaders insisted that convergence in the real sector and in the setting of policy goals was a necessary, even if not sufficient, condition for stable exchange rates. Hence, monetary union required a tight coordination of the economic, fiscal, and even social policies of the prospective members of the union. Expounding the policy that Germany would advocate for a quarter of a century, Karl Schiller, the economics and finance minister of the Federal Republic, announced that monetary union would happen only after European economies had converged (Marsh 2010: 53).

The Werner Plan attempted to minimize the differences between 'monetarist' and 'economist' positions by proposing parallel progress in both monetary integration and economic policy coordination. The final report of the Werner Group was based on a consensus among its members concerning the ultimate objective of monetary union, and a rather vague compromise between 'economists' and 'monetarists' about the intermediate stages. Paradoxically – but characteristically for planning at the European level – the main conflict within the Werner Group concerned, not the feasibility of EMU within the short time-scale envisaged, but the strategy to be adopted during the transitional period. The apparent consensus on the feasibility of the goal and the unresolved disagreements about the means turned the realization of EMU into a question of political will, but this entailed another paradox. As Tsoukalis pointed out (1993: 227), this political view of monetary union implied the risk of neglecting the economic costs associated with the loss of monetary sovereignty, and in particular with the abandonment of such an important policy instrument as the exchange rate. In fact, the plan soon became a victim of the sclerosis that afflicted the EEC in the 1970s, while high inflation and growing economic divergence made nonsense of the 1980 target date. In fairness to the prime minister of Luxembourg and his group, it should be pointed out that the Werner Report, unlike later documents on monetary union such as the Delors Report (1989), was quite explicit about the connection between monetary and political union:

> The transfer of competences [from the member states to the EEC] is a process of fundamental political significance, which presupposes a progressive development of political cooperation. Hence, Economic and Monetary Union is a stimulus for the development of a political union without which [EMU] could not survive in the long run.
>
> (citation in Sarrazin 2012: 66; my translation)

Anyhow, faced with the demise of the Bretton Woods system as a result of President Nixon's measures of August 1971, the six members of the EEC forgot the objective of EMU and produced instead a variety of national exchange-rate regimes. Thus EMU became 'the biggest non-event of the 1970s...With the benefit of hindsight it can be argued that the ambitious initiative, originally intended to transform radically the economic and political map of Western Europe, had been taken at the highest level without much thought of its wider implications' (Tsoukalis 1993: 182). As we shall see in the following pages, the same thoughtless attitude concerning the risks and long-term implications of the project characterizes all the following stages of the process that eventually led to the adoption of the common currency.

Fighting the 'tyranny of the Mark': from the Werner Plan to the beginning of the euro crisis

The demise of the Bretton Woods system and the subsequent 'float' of major currencies against each other were seen as a serious threat to economic cohesion in the EEC. Accordingly, in April 1972 the member states launched the 'Snake', a regime to keep fluctuations between each pair of Community currencies within a narrow margin. By the mid-1970s, however, widely divergent inflation rates and economic performance in the member states completely undermined the Snake arrangement. In the debate preceding the formation of the European Monetary System (EMS) in March 1979, 'greater symmetry' became the French slogan for reduced German influence on European monetary policy. Germany's influence over European money – the 'tyranny of the Mark' – was, according to the Banque de France, a major factor complicating France's aim to return to the Snake. In the Snake arrangement – as later in the EMS – the German currency eventually became the real centre of the system, the anchor to which all other currencies were pegged. With the D-Mark at its centre, the arrangement was asymmetrical, just as the Bretton Woods arrangement with the dollar as its anchor, had been asymmetric. The attempt made to design rules which would guarantee a certain degree of symmetry between strong and weak currencies proved almost totally ineffective. The asymmetry in the EMS reached its highest point during the second, and most successful, phase between 1983 and 1987. The calm after the 1987 realignment ended abruptly in the autumn of 1992, when exchange rate distortions became unsustainable and the UK and Italy decided to withdraw from the Exchange Rate Mechanism (ERM) of the EMS rather than devalue their overvalued currencies. During the period 1987–1992 many observers and market participants had assumed that something closely resembling fixed exchange rates had arrived, so that investments in high-interest countries, but without commensurate exchange risk, had become possible. Accordingly, capital flowed to the countries with the highest interest rates. In August 1993, however, the margins of permissible exchange-rate fluctuations of ERM currencies were expanded to plus or minus 15 per cent, so that the system came to resemble one of flexible exchange rates. Three other important events marked the later part of the third phase in the history of EMS. First, the liberalization of capital movements; second, the decision to proceed to economic and monetary union, starting in July 1990; and, third, the unification of Germany, with profound effects, not only on the German economy but also on the other members of the system and more generally on European politics.

Concerning the decision to proceed to EMU the crucial problem facing France and the other 'monetarist' countries was how to keep moving towards monetary union without allowing the German central bank's low-inflation monetary policy to become the pace-setter for the entire Community. What in retrospect seems an inevitable development was not accepted without a good deal of reluctance, when not open resistance, by French and other European leaders. Initially, the ERM was meant to operate symmetrically for all members, and symmetry was to be achieved by making the European Currency Unit (ECU), rather than the D-Mark, the centre of the ERM. The ECU was a basket of currencies, consisting of fixed amounts (to be revised every five years) of each EEC currency, including those not participating in the ERM. It was to be the ECU against which the currencies of the member states would establish their central rates. France's hope was that the currency-basket mechanism would force the Bundesbank to intervene to lower the D-Mark before other central banks were obliged to defend their own currencies. Germany, however, made few concessions to the French desire to end the hegemony of the D-Mark. Currency interventions and debt settlement rules within the EMS still required weaker countries to support their currencies rather than the stronger members to weaken theirs. Thus, the EMS contained only minor concessions to the positions of France and the other members, or supporters, of the 'monetarist' group, including the European Commission. Interviewed by David Marsh in May 2007, former Bundesbank President Hans Tietmeyer was quite explicit:

> The Bundesbank desire to have the system based on the anchor of the D-Mark, and to prevent a move towards 'symmetry' of intervention and settlement obligations, won the day. The EMS turned out to be not much more than a legal enshrinement of the basis of the 'Snake'.
>
> (Marsh 2010: 87)

For France and its allies this was precisely the problem with the EMS. Hence, by the second half of the 1980s European leaders, led by France, begun to consider reviving the monetary union project. At the June 1988 European Council in Hannover, EU heads of state or government charged Jacques Delors – president of the European Commission and a key protagonist in the revival of the single currency project – with developing a plan for EMU. The committee formed for this purpose delivered its report the following year (Delors Report 1989). The report's conclusions formed the basis for the part of the 1991 Maastricht Treaty dealing with monetary union, while the decision to begin EMU on 1 January 1999 was made by a special European Council meeting in May 1998.

It has already been suggested that monetary union, as a structural metaphor, can help us to perceive more clearly features of the traditional methods of integration which may be otherwise overlooked. France's position with respect to Germany provides another example of the heuristic value of our metaphor: the self-centred position of the Paris government is by no means unique to monetary union. As Tony Judt pointed out in his brilliant history of post-war Europe, the key problem for France since the end of World War II was: how were the resources of (West) Germany to be both contained and yet mobilized to French advantage? The Schuman Plan envisaging the creation of the Coal and

Steel Community represented a first solution to the problem that had vexed France since 1945. According to the Schuman scheme, the High Authority of the European Coal and Steel Community:

> would have the power to encourage competition, set pricing policy, direct investment and buy and sell on behalf of participating countries. But above all it would take control of the Ruhr and other vital German resources out of purely German hands. It represented a European solution to a – *the* – French problem.
>
> (Judt 2010:156; italics in the original)

Monetary union, too, was supposed to be a European solution to the French problem of how to contain the power of a reunited Germany. But despite French hopes and the activism of French President Sarkozy, the crisis of the euro zone has proved beyond doubt that the future of monetary union depends largely on Germany. The problem, though, is that the largest and economically most powerful member of the EU is very reluctant to play the role of the benevolent hegemon, as we shall see in chapter 8.

The 1992 Maastricht Treaty provided a legal framework for monetary union, but left many basic institutional and political questions unresolved. Thus, nothing was said about what to do to contain and resolve systemic crises – except for a very explicit, if later violated, 'no-bail-out' clause prohibiting the members of the euro zone, the ECB, and the other European institutions from rescuing member states which found themselves in serious financial difficulties. Another unsettled issue was the design of the external monetary policymaking machinery. The issue of the exchange rate of the euro was dealt with in Article 109 of the Treaty, but most experts agree that the Article is so ambiguous that in practice nobody is responsible for the exchange rate of the euro. This ambiguity, like the other ambiguities and omissions of the Treaty, was not the result of bad drafting, but rather of unresolved disagreements among the member states about key aspects of monetary union. Because of such disagreements, the only way to move ahead was to produce a treaty article open to all interpretations. The fact that nobody is clearly in charge of the external value of the common currency has been referred to by economist Charles Wyplosz (2000) as the 'dark secret' of monetary union. At Maastricht, governance issues and all remaining open questions were left to be settled in the future. The priority of the Delors Committee – which in 1989 had outlined the three stages by which the member states could achieve EMU – and of other integrationist leaders was to make the integration process irreversible, while different national governments accepted monetary union for different, largely incompatible, reasons. For France, in particular, a key benefit of monetary union was the possibility of replacing the existing exchange-rate arrangement, centred on the D-Mark, with a formal European institution where each national central bank governor would have a seat at the table of monetary decision-making.

Officially, monetary union was presented as the necessary complement of the Single Market project, as suggested by the title of a study published in 1990 by the European Commission: *One Market, One Money* (Commission 1990). In spite of clear evidence that very close trade relations, such as those between the US and Canada, are definitely possible even without monetary union (see the Introduction and chapter 2) the Commission report stated emphatically that only a single currency allows the full potential of a single market to be achieved. A single currency, the Commission argued, would enhance the credibility of the internal market programme and the gains associated with its completion: 'one market', 'one legal system', and now 'one money'. A common monetary policy vis-à-vis the rest of the world would also produce a 'European monetary personality', as it was called, and hence gains in prestige and political power. The Maastricht Treaty provided a legal framework for monetary union but, to repeat, left many basic institutional and policy questions to be settled in the future. The incompleteness of the Treaty in crucial matters of monetary policymaking did not particularly worry EU leaders since the basic motivations for monetary union were not economic but political: for integrationist leaders, to make the integration process irreversible; for France, to eliminate, once and for all, the dominating position of the Bundesbank in Europe; for Germany, to facilitate acceptance of German reunification.

Even a 'good European' like Mario Monti, for eight years Single Market, then Competition Commissioner in Brussels and eventually Italy's prime minister, in an interview published by the Italian financial newspaper *Sole-24 Ore* of 24 November 2005 (Monti 2005), admitted that monetary union had so far failed to accomplish all the positive results that had been promised. The euro, according to Professor Monti, is a currency in search of a single market – a single market which does not yet exist because of the protectionism still practised by the national governments, and the reluctance of the same governments to undertake the necessary structural reforms. Note the circularity of the arguments in favour of deeper integration: during the debate on EMU people were told that monetary union was needed to complete the single market, and also to force the national governments to undertake structural reforms; after the common currency was introduced, the message was that the single currency could not produce the hoped-for benefits unless a fully-fledged single market was established, and the requisite structural reforms were carried out. A similar circularity, concerning the causal relation between monetary and political union, will be noted in chapter 7. More recently (Monti 2011) Professor Monti has argued that the real problem with the EU is excessive deference to the larger member states. He supports this argument with two examples: the failure to enforce the old Stability and Growth Pact (SGP) against France and Germany in 2003; and Germany's opposition to a Commission proposal to strengthen the Lisbon Strategy for Growth and Jobs by publishing a score board so as to put more pressure on member states by 'naming and shaming'. We have here another instance of the paradox noted in the preceding section in connection with the debate on the Werner Plan: the tendency to discuss the best means to a given end, without examining whether the end itself is feasible. Also the goal of the Lisbon Strategy, as officially stated in March 2000, was to make the EU 'the most competitive, knowledge-based economy in the world', capable of surpassing the American economy by the year 2010, just as the Werner Plan had assumed that monetary union could be achieved by 1980. Once more, no questions about the feasibility of the goal were raised.

On 1 January 2002, the euro was introduced among enthusiastic predictions of faster economic growth, far-reaching structural reforms by the governments of the euro zone, greater productivity, further intensification of intra-EU trade, and price stability. Those forecasts, like so many previous ones, soon proved to be too optimistic. Early in December 2009 the heads of government of all members of the EU met in Brussels to discuss the alarming financial situation of Greece. The budget deficit of this country had reached almost 13 per cent of GDP, and its public debt, 113 per cent. The possibility of a state bankruptcy seemed quite real, and the media were already referring to the Greek situation as a 'time bomb for the euro'. The concerns of EU leaders were increased by the fact that the international rating agency Fitch had already downgraded Greece's rating, and also Standard & Poor was considering the possibility of a lower rating. For the first time since the beginning of monetary union a member of the euro zone was no longer in the AAA class. For Greece the downgrading meant that it would have to pay higher interest rates in order to borrow, further aggravating its budget deficit. In spite of this precarious situation, the member states agreed that Greece must solve its own problems without financial help from the EU. They also pointed out that Greece had conducted unsound macroeconomic policies for years. Responding to these criticisms the Greek finance minister assured his colleagues that Greece would take care of its own problems without external financial help.

In spite of the rigid position against financial aid taken at the Brussels summit – a position reasserted in the first months of 2010, especially by the German government – many observers continued to believe that in an extreme situation the other countries would come to the rescue of the Athens government. Even though Greece produces only about 2.6 per cent of the GDP of the euro zone, most EU governments feared a domino effect, with Portugal, Spain, and possibly Italy following Greece, and a serious loss of credibility for the entire euro zone in case of default by a member state. Thus by the Spring of 2010, European institutions and national governments had accepted the idea that financial help for Greece, and possibly for other members of the euro zone, was unavoidable, even if that meant breaking the rules. Commissioner Almunia had been one of the first to announce that Greece would not be allowed to default, adding that the EU had enough instruments to prevent a collapse. This was a diplomatic way of saying that help from the International Monetary Fund (IMF) was not welcome. Also the president of the ECB had clearly indicated his opposition to an IMF role beyond some technical assistance. But M Trichet suffered an embarrassing defeat when on 25 March 2010 the government leaders of the euro zone agreed that 'substantial IMF financing' would be part of a Greece bail-out. A more serious defeat, with potentially far-reaching consequences for the future status of the ECB and the credibility of the common currency, was inflicted two months later, when the leaders of the euro zone bullied the Bank into monetizing the sovereign debt of Southern European members.

In May 2010, under pressure from its euro-partners who feared a repetition of the Greek crisis, Spain adopted a series of deficit-cutting measures of unprecedented severity. The plan presented by Prime Minister Zapatero – which should reduce the country's deficit from the level of 11.2 per cent of GDP (the third largest in the euro zone) to 3 per cent by 2013 – was approved by the narrowest majority (just one vote) in the history of Spanish democracy, and only thanks to the abstention of the conservative Catalan party, CiU. The immediate result, however, was another downrating of the Spanish public debt. The rating agencies were afraid that such drastic debt-cutting measures might not be politically sustainable, or else they might bring about a severe depression, and a long period of no, or very little, growth. As for Ireland, in November 2010 the government of Prime Minister Brian Cowen was forced to follow the example of Greece and accept the financial help of the EU and the IMF, together with the harsh conditions imposed by the rescuers. At the same time, the unpopularity of this decision forced the prime minister to announce new national elections as soon as Parliament had passed the new budget law. By this time, even the most optimistic observers of the European scene could not fail to notice the consequences of adopting the same monetary policy for such a heterogeneous group of countries. Actually, doubts about the limit of centralized policy harmonization had already been raised in the 1970s. Before discussing monetary union from the perspective of (total) policy harmonization, however, it is instructive to see how in the 1990s EU leaders tried, rather reluctantly, to strengthen the governance structure of the euro zone in order to avoid possible crises in the future.

The ECB, the Euro-Group, and the Stability and Growth Pact

As noted above, many issues were left undecided in the design of the institutions of monetary governance in the EU. To close at least some of these gaps, two potentially significant policy innovations were introduced in the post-Maastricht period: the Growth and Stability Pact – a set of rules and procedures for mutual surveillance of the fiscal policies of the members of the euro zone, and the imposition of penalties when countries have excessive deficits; and what later has been called the Euro-Group: a subset of the Council of the finance ministers of the EU (ECOFIN), made up of the finance ministers of the countries of the euro zone. The idea of some sort of 'stability pact', or treaty, was in the air in 1995, when German public opinion was becoming very negative towards EMU. Already in 1992, the Council of Economic Advisers of the German government had demanded in its annual report that the sanctions foreseen by the Maastricht Treaty be made more precise, and be applied in a strict manner. Also the Social-Democratic Party, then in opposition, was campaigning about the dangers to monetary stability stemming from the EMU project, and demanding stricter rules, in line with the position of the Bundesbank (Heipertz and Verdun 2010). Responding to such political pressures, in November 1995 Theo Weigel, the German finance minister, announced his version of a stability plan. Weigel's plan built on the language of the Maastricht Treaty regarding excessive government deficits. It included a procedure for increased policy surveillance, specific penalties to be imposed on countries with excessive deficits, and the automatic imposition of those penalties. Germany's partners agreed on the principles of mutual surveillance and reinforced dissuasion of excessive deficits but did not accept automatic sanctions. The compromise reached at the European Council meeting in Dublin in mid-December 1996 instead of automatic sanctions included a political pledge to aim for low deficits. French President Chirac was particularly vocal in his opposition to large automatic fines on countries breaking the rules. On French insistence, the European Council declared that growth as well as price stability would be an explicit goal of future EMU monetary policy. Hence the arrangement for policing budgetary policy was renamed 'Stability and Growth Pact' (Marsh 2010).

In theory, the SGP should have replaced at least some of the discipline previously imposed by the financial markets, by the rating agencies, and by the IMF, when they express their opinion on the pricing of sovereign debt of individual countries. A surrogate discipline and coordination device of the members' fiscal policies was seen to be particularly needed in the absence of a common stability culture, of strong public support of monetary union, and of common institutions to back up the independence of the ECB. Experts doubted that the compromise that emerged from the 1996 Dublin summit could succeed in imposing sufficiently strict constraints on the fiscal policy of the national governments. The fear was that the finance ministers of the members of the euro zone would shy away from harsh implementation of the Pact once member states got into difficulties. The concerns of the experts were justified: the SGP proved to be ineffective as a tool of fiscal discipline and policy coordination – not to mention as a stimulus to growth. This ineffectiveness was due in good part to the traditional Franco–German disagreement about the character and organization of economic policymaking in Economic and Monetary Union, with French leaders always insisting that monetary power should be balanced by political power. Thus, President Chirac and his prime minister Alain Juppé used a French–German summit at Nuremberg in December 1996 to plead for a political EMU Advisory Council with the ability to influence ECB decisions, but the proposal was forcefully rejected by the German delegation. On the other hand, at the EU summit in Dublin in mid-December Chirac did succeed in toning down German proposals for inclusion in the SGP of large automatic fines on countries violating the rules of the Pact.

Similar disagreements emerged on the occasion of the establishment of the Euro-Group to act as a forum for policy coordination within the euro zone. In October 1997 France and Germany agreed that the finance ministers of the euro zone should meet regularly with the president of the ECB and with the Commission, in order to discuss issues of economic policy. As already mentioned, a crucial issue left unresolved by the Maastricht Treaty was exchange-rate policy. The French intended the Euro-Group to assume responsibility not just for overall exchange-rate strategy but also for short-run currency movements. The French finance minister and future managing director of the IMF, Dominique Strauss-Kahn, insisted on the political necessity of strengthening political supervision of the ECB: 'In the absence of a visible and legitimate political body, the ECB might soon be regarded by the public as the only institution responsible for macroeconomic policy' (cited in Marsh 2010: 199). Germany, however, viewed a strong role for the Euro-Group as a threat to the independence of the ECB. The German position was that the group of finance ministers should serve merely as an informal body to promote information exchange, and that the SGP would provide direction on the appropriate fiscal policies. In the end the idea of a political counterweight to the ECB was rejected; the Euro-Group could not even fine member states violating the Pact, since the decision to fine presupposes a vote to that effect, and all formal voting takes place within the entire ECOFIN.

The ECB had an obvious interest in making sure that the rules of the SGP were obeyed. Reacting to calls to reform the Pact after the first violations of the Pact's rules by several members of the euro zone (see below) it asserted that the principles of budgetary discipline embodied in the Pact are 'indispensable for economic and monetary union', and a 'necessary complement to reinforce the bank's own monetary policy' (citations in Howarth and Loedel 2004: 835). The ECB has consistently defended the SGP, going as far as claiming to be ready to raise interest rates in order to encourage member state compliance with the Pact. In fact, the empirical evidence for the first years of operation of the SGP suggested that 'the ECB's bark is definitely worse than its bite and that when breaking the [SGP] rules does not significantly contribute to inflation the member states will not be punished by ECB interest rate rises (at least in the short term)' (ibid.: 838). On the other hand, it must be kept in mind that the ECB's mandate is quite narrow: to ensure price stability, not the fiscal discipline of euro zone member states, much less macroeconomic conditions for growth. With the central bank unable, and the Council of finance ministers unwilling, to impose fiscal discipline on the members of the euro zone, it was perhaps inevitable that the rules of the Pact would be violated, sooner or later.

Portugal was the first member state to break the rules in 2001, with a deficit of 4.1 per cent of GDP; but the situation became paradoxical the following year, when Germany declared it would be unable to meet the very rules it had devised in order to restrain other, supposedly less virtuous, member states. With national elections approaching, German chancellor Schroeder lobbied vigorously to prevent a vote within ECOFIN to accept the Commission's recommendation of a politically embarrassing formal warning, as required by the SGP. After some debate, ECOFIN agreed unanimously not to issue the warning, in exchange for a German promise to respect its commitment to a balanced budget by 2004. Similar promises on controlling government spending were made by Portugal. Then in late November 2003 a majority of the finance ministers decided to suspend the procedures for excessive deficit initiated by the Commission against France and Germany. Instead, the finance ministers of the EU recommended reductions of the structural deficits of the two countries sufficient to bring the deficits below 3 per cent of GDP by the end of 2005. France and Germany promised to do their best to achieve this goal, but this was a political, not a legally binding, commitment. One consequence of the events of November 2003 was clear: the SGP would not be altogether discarded, but it would eventually be reformulated along lines set by ECOFIN rather than by the Commission. This assessment is not contradicted by the fact that on 13 July 2004 the European Court of Justice (now called the Court of Justice of the European Union (CJEU), but hereafter referred to as the ECJ or just the Court) overturned the decision of the finance ministers to suspend the sanctions procedure against France and Germany.

In January 2004 a badly divided Commission had finally agreed to bring the decision of ECOFIN before the ECJ. While the ruling of the Court partially vindicated the Commission's challenge of the Council's decision, the Brussels executive lost in the second, and more important, part of its case, where it claimed that ECOFIN had a duty to adopt the Commission's recommendations. The reform of the Pact in June 2005 in the end eliminated the elements of automatism in the original agreement and introduced considerable room for intergovernmental margins of manoeuvre. As a result, the increased uncertainty surrounding the determination of acceptable intermediate budget balances made it even more difficult for the finance ministers to trigger sanctions against errant member states. A few years after the ECJ decision of 13 July 2004, Europe was hit with full force by the global financial crisis ignited by the bankruptcy of Lehman Brothers. Large banks and important financial groups in France, Germany, Belgium, and the Netherlands had to be saved from collapse with spectacular financial rescue packages. In October 2008 French President Sarkozy hosted two crisis meetings of European leaders. One of the results of the meetings was an effective suspension of the SGP as a means of offsetting recessionary risks, thus opening the way to an unprecedented expansion of the debt and deficit levels of the members of the euro zone. What the narrative of the preceding pages shows is that policymaking in the EU is a process of baroque complexity, even in the supposedly technocratic field of monetary policy.

EMU and the paradox of policy harmonization

Another illustration of the heuristic advantage of using monetary union as a metaphor can be provided by considering EMU from the perspective of policy harmonization. Harmonization of the laws and policies of the member states is one of the three legal techniques which the Treaty of Rome (Article 100) made available to the European Commission for establishing and maintaining a common European market – the other two techniques being liberalization and the control of anti-competitive behaviour. The legal literature distinguishes three main modes of harmonization: total, optional, and minimum harmonization. From the early 1960s to the early 1970s the Commission's approach was characterized by a distinct preference for total harmonization – detailed measures designed to regulate exhaustively the problems in question, to the exclusion of previously existing national policies. Under total harmonization once European rules have been put in place, a member state's capacity to apply stricter rules by appealing to the values referred to in Article 36 of the Treaty – such as the protection of the health and life of humans, animals, and plants – is excluded. The ECJ initially supported this exclusive Community competence, judging it to be necessary to the construction of the common market and, more generally, to the autonomy of the Community system, and against the tendency of the member states to reduce European law to a branch of international law. Already by the mid-1970s, however, the limits of total harmonization had become visible. The idea of a common market structured by one body of uniform European rules had to be given up once it was realized that total harmonization confers on the Community an exclusive competence which it is ill-equipped to discharge (Weatherill 1995). The emphasis shifted from total to optional and minimum harmonization, and to mutual recognition. Optional harmonization aims to guarantee the free movement of goods, while permitting the member states to retain their traditional forms of regulation for goods produced for the domestic market. Under minimum harmonization, the national governments must secure the level of regulation set out in a directive but are permitted to set higher standards, provided that the stricter national rules do not violate Community law.

The principle of mutual recognition – first enunciated by the ECJ in the *Cassis de Dijon* judgment of 1979 (*Rewe-Zentrale v. Bundesmonopol Verwaltung fuer Branntwein* (Case 120/78) (*Cassis de Dijon*) [1979] ECR 649) – was supposed to reduce the need for ex ante, top-down harmonization, and to facilitate regulatory competition among the member states. This principle requires member states to recognize regulations drawn up by other EU members as being essentially equivalent to their own, allowing activities that are lawful in one member state to be freely pursued throughout the Union. In this way, a virtuous circle of regulatory competition would be stimulated, which should raise the quality of all regulation and drive out rules offering protection that consumers do not, in fact, require. The end result would be ex post harmonization, achieved through market processes rather than by administrative measures. However, the high hopes raised by the *Cassis de Dijon* judgment and by what appeared to be the Commission's enthusiastic endorsement of the Court's doctrine were largely disappointed. For political, ideological, and bureaucratic reasons, ex post, market-driven harmonization was never allowed seriously to challenge the dominant position of the centralized, top-down version (Majone 2009: 117–24).

As already mentioned in the Introduction, the idea that economic integration requires extensive ex ante harmonization of national laws and regulations has been criticized by distinguished economists since the early years of the European Community. Thus, Harry Johnson wrote: 'The need for harmonization additional to what is already required of countries extensively engaged in world trade is relatively slight...The problems of harmonization are such as can be handled by negotiation and consultation according to well-established procedures among the governments concerned, rather than such as to require elaborate international agreements' (Johnson 1972, cited in Kahler 1995: 12). In opposing the harmonization bias of the early literature on economic integration, Johnson pointed out that the eventual gains from harmonization should be weighed against the welfare losses produced by harmonized rules that are not tailored to national preferences except in a rough, average sense. The welfare losses entailed by centralized harmonization have become a major theme in the more recent literature on free trade and harmonization (Bhagwati and Hudec 1996). EMU proves that in spite of all warnings the system of policymaking in the EU is still based on the principle that 'one-size-fits-all', inherited from the time when the goal was to establish a common market among six, rather homogeneous, countries.

Concerns about what already in the 1970s some member states considered excessive centralization became more intense after the Single European Act, by way of derogation from Article 100 of the Rome Treaty, introduced qualified majority voting for harmonization measures having the internal market as their object. In an attempt to allay such fears, the Treaty of Maastricht defined, for the first time, new European competences in a way that actually limits the exercise of Community powers, and explicitly excluded any harmonization of national laws in a number of policy areas. In its *Tobacco Advertising* judgment of October 2000 (*Germany v. Parliament and Council* (Case C-376/98) [2000] (ECR 1-8419)), the ECJ showed how strictly the limits of the Community's conferred powers are taken today. Long before the *Tobacco Advertising* judgment, Alan Dashwood had observed that in the EEC:

> [H]armonization tended to be pursued not so much to resolve concrete problems encountered in the course of constructing the common market as to drive forward the general process of integration. This. . .was bound to affect the judgment of the Commission, inclining it towards maximum exercise of the powers available under Article 100 and towards solutions involving a high degree of uniformity between national laws.
>
> (Dashwood 1983: 194)

The problem of centralized harmonization is much more serious today than when Professor Dashwood wrote these lines. The reason is the high level of socioeconomic heterogeneity produced by the latest enlargement of the EU. Relative to previous enlargements, income disparities between the new member states from Central, Eastern, and South-Eastern Europe and the old EU-15 are considerably larger. Thus, the income levels of three Mediterranean countries (Greece, Spain, and Portugal), when they joined the Union in the 1980s, were around 65 per cent of the EU-10 average income. The average income of the new Eastern members was only about 40 per cent of the EU-15 average. This is about the same difference as that between the GDP of a Western Europe reduced to ruins by the war, and that of the US in 1945. Actually, income inequality is today much greater in the socially minded EU than in the supposedly arch-capitalist US: while the average household income in New Jersey is about twice as large as the corresponding measure in Mississippi, average per capita income in Luxembourg or Denmark is at least ten times as large as in Romania. When socioeconomic conditions differ so much, it is not only politically difficult but also inefficient to harmonize national laws and policies: if countries have significantly different needs and hence different national priorities, the policies that maximize aggregate welfare ought to be different rather than harmonized. This is true even in the case of minimum harmonization – unless the minimum standard is so low as to be exceeded by all national standards, in which case it is simply irrelevant.

The shifts from total harmonization to less stringent forms, such as optional or minimum harmonization, were 'the inevitable adjustments to the notion of uniformity demanded by a Community structure that is supporting an ever-increasing number of Member States and an ever-increasing range of functions' (Weatherill 1995: 148). Since these lines were written the number of member states has almost doubled, the range of EU competences has greatly expanded, and socioeconomic diversity has increased exponentially. In spite of all these changes, the boldest experiment in total harmonization was launched on 1 January 1999, when the final stage of monetary union entered into force with the irrevocable fixing of the exchange rates of the currencies of eleven (soon to become twelve, and eventually eighteen and more) member states, and the pre-emption of national action in the monetary area. What is most striking about this rather paradoxical return to total harmonization is the contradiction between the centralization of monetary policy and the mutation of the fairly homogeneous EU-15 into a highly heterogeneous bloc of twenty-eight states – a contradiction which, as noted above, tends to reduce the benefits of a common monetary policy. What two American experts, Eichengreen and Frieden, argued in 1995 is even truer today:

> Given the risks and uncertainties that pervade the process [of monetary integration] there would have to be a clear margin of benefits over costs for economic considerations, narrowly defined, to provide a justification

for such a radical departure in policy. The absence of such a margin
implies that the momentum for monetary union must therefore derive
from other, primarily political, factors.

(Eichengreen and Frieden 1995: 274)

Unfortunately, the political benefits of monetary union are even more
doubtful than the economic ones. This is particularly true in the case of
Germany. German leaders worked hard to convince their voters that the
sacrifice of their beloved D-Mark was justified by the prospect of a
decisive advance towards political union. In reality, the introduction of
the common currency has hardly increased the credibility of the commitment of Germany's partners to political union. In Germany itself
popular support for the political integration of Europe has significantly
decreased in recent years. After the reunification of the country, the
disappearance of the Soviet menace, and a fading memory of the horrors
of World War II, Germany is no longer so dependent on the political
support of its European partners. It has even been argued – in particular
by the well-known columnist Wolfgang Muenchau writing in *Spiegel On
Line* of 26 September 2012 (Muenchau 2012b) – that a united and
economically powerful Germany sees itself less as a member of the EU
than as an autonomous, medium-size power that can deal directly with
Americans, Chinese, and Russians, without worrying too much about its
EU partners.

Also the new members from Central and Eastern Europe do not seem
to be interested in the political integration of the continent. The loss of
national sovereignty during the period of Soviet domination explains the
importance these countries attach to national values. Hence, it is hardly
to be expected that the new member states will support wholeheartedly
the cause of political union, even after joining the euro zone. In this
connection it should be kept in mind that since monetary union is
considered part of the *acquis communautaire*, the new member states
must join EMU once they satisfy the so-called convergence criteria: they
are not allowed to opt out of monetary union as some older member
states did. However, it seems likely that after the current debt crisis the
new member states will reassess more carefully the benefits and costs of
monetary union, as was suggested by Slawomir Skrzypek, the late president of the National Bank of Poland. Shortly before dying in the
Smolensk air crash in which the president of Poland and numerous
other personalities lost their life, Mr Skrzypek published an article in
the *Financial Times* of 13 April 2010, titled: 'Poland should not rush to

sign up to the euro'. In this article, the central banker pointed out that in 2010, when Europe was plagued by concerns over excessive public debt in Greece and elsewhere, the Polish economy was projected to grow by 2.7 per cent, accelerating to 3 per cent in 2011. One important reason for this, he wrote:

> is that as a non-member of the euro, Poland has been able to profit from the flexibility of the zloty exchange rate in a way that has helped growth and lowered the current account deficit without importing inflation. . .Because Poland's currency is not bound by the Exchange Rate Mechanism II, we have been able to adjust the value of the zloty in line with domestic requirements.
>
> (Skrzypek 2010)

The decade-long story of peripheral euro members drastically losing competitiveness, Mr Skrzypek added, has been a salutary lesson. The 'Greek imbroglio' (as he called it) shows that there is no substitute for countries' own efforts to improve competitiveness, boost fiscal discipline, and increase labour and product market flexibility – whether or not they are in the euro zone. This banker's advice to his fellow citizens:

> [W]e must temper the wish to adopt the euro with necessary prudence. We should not tie ourselves to timetables that may be counterproductive. Solid economic growth and sensible policies are possible both within and outside the euro zone. Nations in a hurry to join the euro may end up missing their overriding objectives.
>
> (Ibid.)

A cautious approach similar to the one suggested by Mr Skrzypek has been followed by Sweden since it joined the EU in 1995. This country, not a member of the EU when the Maastricht Treaty was ratified, could not obtain a *de jure* opt-out from EMU, as the UK and Denmark did. It did however ask, and was granted, a derogation – in practice, a *de facto* opt-out – when it became a member of the Union. Swedish leaders have decided that future membership of their country in the euro zone shall depend, not on EU prescriptions but on the approval of the voters in a popular referendum. Since the beginning of the sovereign-debt crisis opinion polls show growing popular opposition to joining monetary union, so that the prospect of Swedish membership in EMU keeps receding into the future. According to a survey conducted in July 2010, 61 per cent of the Swedes were against joining monetary union; one year earlier the negative votes were 44 per cent. One important reason for the growing opposition to the euro is the fact that Sweden, like Poland, has weathered the financial crisis rather well, also thanks to its independent monetary policy. The Swedish economy, which is heavily dependent on exports, has profited significantly from the weakness of the national currency, the krona. Recently, Sweden had the lowest budget deficit of all EU member states and one of the highest rates of economic growth, providing additional evidence in support of Mr Skrzypek's assessment of the advantages of an independent monetary policy.

It is quite possible that a number of Central and Eastern European countries may decide to follow Mr Skrzypek's advice and join Sweden in the camp of the *de facto* opt-outs, regardless of the duty of membership in the euro zone imposed on them by the *acquis communautaire*. The Czech Republic and Hungary have already linked their acceptance of the common currency to approval by popular referendum or by a super-majority in the national parliament. Moreover, in a greatly enlarged and increasingly heterogeneous monetary union even the original members of the euro zone may conclude that the policies of the ECB no longer correspond to their national conditions as well as they did before the enlargement. This is because the original members will more often than today be outliers, in terms of inflation and output, compared to the average that the ECB will have to focus on. As a consequence, some older members may realize that the calculus of the benefits and costs of monetary union has become less favourable (De Grauwe 2007: 97–101). In sum, while the philosophy of the advocates of EMU was based on the notion that all member states should accept the total harmonization of national monetary policies as a precondition of political union, the paradoxical result seems to be the final breakdown of the notion of one set of policies that apply to all member states. But here another paradox arises: while the Lisbon Treaty, ratified in 2009, admitted, for the first time in EU history, the possibility that a member state may wish to drop out of the EU, even if only on a temporary basis, membership in the euro zone continues to be considered irreversible. Monetary union being still considered part of the *acquis communautaire*, the official slogan continues to be: 'The euro is forever.'

The *acquis communautaire*: means of commitment or outworn straightjacket?

Since the beginnings of European integration in the 1950s the key problem facing national leaders and supranational institutions was how to induce sovereign states to credibly commit themselves to a project which, if successful, would necessarily entail the acceptance of limits on national sovereignty. How to achieve such credible commitments is another example of a general problem which is most clearly perceived in the case of monetary union. First, however, we need to understand better how the issue of credible commitments arises, and to this end some concepts discussed at greater length in chapters 3 and 4 will be anticipated here. To begin with, European treaties, like all international treaties and national constitutions, are 'incomplete contracts', to use the language of transaction-cost economics. This means that the parties are unable to foresee accurately all the relevant contingencies that might arise in the implementation of the treaties, and are also unable or unwilling to determine and agree upon a course of action for each possible contingency. Contractual incompleteness can lead to problems of imperfect commitment, such as various forms of pre- and post-contractual opportunism. The founding fathers of the EEC attempted to meet the problems of contractual incompleteness by delegating to the Commission and the ECJ the task of filling the gaps in the Rome Treaty. As we shall see in later chapters, this solution created its own problems.

Making the so-called *acquis communautaire* binding for all present and future member states was meant to be another device for eliciting credible commitments to the unfolding integration process. The European Commission has defined the *acquis communautaire* as 'the rights and obligations, actual and potential, of the Community system and its institutional framework'. This means that in principle a member state has to accept en masse the provisions of the treaties, the decisions taken by the institutions pursuant to the treaties, and the case law of the ECJ developed in more than half a century. At first sight the requirement may seem reasonable: after all, anybody wishing to join a club must accept to follow its rules. As a commitment device, however, the *acquis* is problematic, not least because the rules developed by the EC/EU over more than half a century are many, complex, and often ambiguous. They have to be interpreted, and considerable discretion is thus involved in their application. For example, we saw that the UK and Denmark were officially exempted from the duty of joining the monetary union, while Sweden obtained a *de facto* opt-out when it joined the EU in 1995. On the other hand there is no *de jure* or *de facto* opt-out for countries that joined the Union in 2004–2007 or later; the new members, as well as future members, must (in theory) introduce the common currency as part of the *acquis communautaire*. They must first satisfy the convergence criteria, of course, but the collective judgement concerning the satisfaction of the admission criteria is a political decision, as was the case with Greece and other older members of the EU at the beginning of monetary union.

Moreover, the criteria for admission to the monetary union are purely financial, hence they do not reflect the socioeconomic conditions of a country. This can produce rather paradoxical results. For instance, according to some projections of the European Commission only one member of the EU-27 was expected to satisfy all the criteria of the Stability Pact in 2010: Bulgaria. This country, one of the poorest members of the EU, had the lowest budget deficit of all the member states in 2009, and expected its budget to be balanced in 2010. For Bulgaria, as for many other new member states, the only problematic parameter had been inflation, but because of the global economic crisis inflation had also sharply declined. Thus, the Bulgarian government hoped that the national currency, the lev, would enter the Exchange Rate Mechanism II (a sort of waiting room for countries planning to introduce the euro) in the Spring of 2010, and adopt the common currency by 2013 or 2014, ahead of economically more advanced countries (Martens 2009).

The imposition of the *acquis communautaire* on new member states has already produced some unexpected consequences. The accession negotiations for each Central and Eastern European country were structured through bilateral Accession Partnerships setting timetables for harmonization ('alignment') in various areas, closely monitored by the Commission. This approach left little scope for the candidates to set their own pace and priorities, and caused considerable criticism about the language of 'partnership' being a euphemism for the imposition of EU priorities. In some cases the minimum social standards set by the European directives turned out to be lower than the national standards of the new members, giving their governments an excuse for lowering the level of social protection. Thus, it has been pointed out that the transposition of the Information and Consultation Directive was used by the Polish, Slovak, and Estonian governments to weaken the national standards in this area. Also the 1993 Working Time Directive was used by some governments to reduce the cost of overtime, and to support management demands for more flexible working times (Meardi 2007). In these and other cases, social standards in the new member states have been reduced, rather than raised, by the transposition of EU directives. Thus, acceptance of the *acquis communautaire* has undermined the *acquis national* of the new members, just as policy harmonization in the older member states has often undermined the priorities set by the democratic process at national level (Majone 2009).

At the same time, formal acceptance of the *acquis* by older member states has not eliminated such consequences of incomplete commitment as adverse selection and moral hazard. Adverse selection refers to the kind of pre-contractual opportunism that arises when one party to a bargain has private information that can be used to reduce the net benefits of the other contracting partner(s); while moral hazard is a form of post-contractual opportunism that arises when actions required under the contract are not easily observable by the other contracting partners. It is by now more or less openly acknowledged that these two types of opportunism have played a major role in the sovereign-debt crisis of the euro zone, see chapter 4. The crisis of monetary union has made the traditional opportunism of the member states too visible to be denied or ignored, as so often in the past. Thus it was always suspected that Greece, as well as other countries with large public debts, engaged in various forms of pre-contractual opportunism in order to be admitted to monetary union as soon as possible. Early admission was considered important for reasons of national prestige, but even more in the hope that transferring power over monetary policy to a European central bank supposedly modelled on the Bundesbank, would allow the national governments to import, or free-ride on, Germany's reputation for fiscal discipline. Thus, perverse incentives to conceal information on the true condition of public finances (adverse selection) were present from the very beginning of monetary union. What made the temptation irresistible for some countries was the fact, mentioned above, that most national governments supported a 'political' decision concerning the flexible application of the Maastricht parameters. They did this in order to start the monetary union with as large a group of participants as possible. As a consequence, countries like Belgium and Italy, with public debts well over 100 per cent of GDP, were allowed to join EMU from the beginning, while the financial data presented by Greece and other countries were accepted without any serious scrutiny.

The political decision to adopt a common currency for a group of countries with different economic structures and different approaches to public finance was bound to generate perverse incentives for at least some of the contractual partners. Before the final decision on EMU was taken, the then president of the Bundesbank tried in vain to convince European leaders that '[m]ore than a single currency, the emerging single European market needs converging policies, which are still not in place in all participating countries. The repeated references to alleged huge savings in transaction costs for the countries of a single currency area are not in the least convincing' (Poehl 1990: 36). The truth is that for most political leaders the warnings of the experts about a premature monetary union counted very little when compared with the immediate advantages of monetary union. As soon as a country adopted the euro, its public debt received the highest grade by the international rating agencies, and consequently its government could borrow at about the same interest rate as the most virtuous members of the bloc. This meant that countries like Greece, Portugal, or Spain could borrow at rates well below the double-digit rates they had to pay before adopting the euro.

In turn, the possibility of borrowing at low cost in the international financial market is what made possible the Spanish real-estate boom. As a result of the euro-induced boom, wages and inflation grew much faster in Spain than in Germany or France. At the same time, the ECB, being mainly concerned with the level of inflation in the largest economies of the euro zone – Germany, France, and Italy – allowed the interest rate to remain low: too low for the conditions prevailing in Spain. This is also what happened in the case of Ireland. For a number of years, inflation in this country had been considerably higher than the average inflation in the euro zone. The ECB, however, was mainly concerned with the average level of inflation in the euro zone, which average depended heavily on the price level in the larger economies. As a consequence, it kept the interest level much too low with respect to what would have been appropriate for the booming Irish economy. Naturally enough, Irish families took advantage of what were, in real terms, *negative* interest rates to engage in their favourite activity, buying property, until the real-estate bubble exploded.

Today the political willingness in favour of significant enlargement of the euro zone, eventually to include all the new member states, has significantly declined. As a result, it is likely that the Maastricht convergence criteria will be used as an instrument to postpone new entries. But also the new member states have started having second thoughts about the net benefits of membership in an exclusive but increasingly demanding club. One of the earliest and clearest expressions of these doubts has been given by a late president of the National Bank of Poland (see the preceding section). Today, even further enlargement of the EU – let alone enlargement of the euro zone – is viewed with growing scepticism. In an interview published by the influential German newspaper *Die Welt am Sonntag* (Lammer 2012), the president of the Bundestag, Norbert Lammer, warned against expanding the EU further, at least in the near future. We have so many urgent tasks to finish in order to consolidate the present Union, he argued, that we should avoid the past mistake of letting enlargement move ahead of the necessary stabilization of the EU. Referring to the problems caused by the premature admission of Romania and Bulgaria, Lammer suggested that even Croatia was not ripe for admission in 2013 – in spite of all the assurances to that effect given in Brussels and by many national leaders. Given such an atmosphere of consolidation, if not retrenchment, the view of monetary union as an obligation imposed by the dogma of the *acquis communautaire* seems increasingly outdated. Even assuming that in the early days of European integration the *acquis* was a useful commitment device, one should not forget the old adage about yesterday's good sense being today's or tomorrow's mistake. All these doubts concerning the future development of the euro zone, and of the EU itself, contribute to the fragility of the present monetary union.

The fragility of an incomplete monetary union

Even before the Maastricht Treaty was ratified, Nigel Lawson, the former British chancellor of the Exchequer expressed strong reservations about the Treaty's most significant innovation. In an article titled 'The folly of a single currency', published in *The Evening Standard* of 4 November 1991, he argued that if a political union could be successful then a monetary union might work. However, since a European nation does not yet exist, Lawson did not believe that a political union could work. He concluded that 'monetary union may bring the nemesis of the European Community' (citation in Wincott 1995: 603).

More than twenty years later Lord Lawson found his worst fears confirmed by the crisis of the euro zone:

> A successful eurozone is an impossibility. European Monetary Union...was doomed from the start. The disaster which we see unfolding today, most acutely in Greece but increasingly elsewhere in the eurozone, too, was not only predictable but predicted...A monetary union, for its very existence, requires there to be automatic, not occasional and discretionary, transfers from the more successful to the less successful parts of the union, which in turn requires there to be, at the very least, a single system of taxation and benefits. There also needs to be a high degree of central control of budget deficits. In other words, a single finance ministry within a single government. Even then, it would not be economically beneficial within an area as large and diverse as the European Union...But of course [monetary union] was never an economic venture in the first place. It was always entirely political. The architects of

European monetary union knew full well that it could not work without full-blooded political union, and that was their objective from the start. It is hard to imagine anything more arrogant and irresponsible. It was arrogant, since, in a democracy, political union requires the consent of the people, which plainly does not exist...And it was grossly irresponsible, since it was always clear that, should their gamble fail and political union prove unachievable, the consequences of monetary union alone would be as disastrous as we see unfolding today.

(Lawson 2012: 7)

The sceptical stance of the British politician since the early 1990s was shared by a number of experts and policymakers, including the leaders of Germany's central bank. The leaders of the Bundesbank reasoned that other member states, after formally surrendering their monetary autonomy, could not also effectively surrender control of fiscal policy without the possibility of counting on compensatory financial transfers. The practical consequence would be the entrenchment of Germany as the paymaster of the EU. In a lecture given at the London School of Economics shortly before becoming president of the Bundesbank, Hans Tietmeyer made clear that the monetary policymakers wanted to avoid at all costs a situation where the German government could face strong pressures to bail out fiscally irresponsible member states: 'If such transfers are demanded and are then forthcoming in larger volumes...this could not only weaken the willingness to adjust but also and in particular place too great a burden on the countries that pay' (citation in Wincott 1995: 607).

What Tietmeyer feared in 1992 is exactly what has happened from 2009 to the present, and most likely will continue to happen at least for a few more years. The insistence of the Bundesbank on what it called the 'parallelism' between political and monetary union could be interpreted as a stratagem to slow down the process of monetary integration, but its leaders also used other arguments. In particular they kept stressing the point made by Karl Schiller and other German policymakers since the 1970s, namely that a considerable degree of economic integration should be regarded as a precondition for monetary union. As mentioned above, for example, even before the final decision on EMU was taken, the president of the Bundesbank told European leaders that a single European market required convergence of national policies even more than a single currency. Recent developments in the euro zone confirm the soundness of this and other early warnings that monetary union was premature for a group of countries still characterized by a high degree of economic diversity and limited political cohesion.

Risky as the strategy of monetary union appears today, not only to experts but also to the general public, it is not very different from the general approach to European integration followed since the 1950s – an approach based on the twin principles of fait accompli and of the primacy of process over outcome (see also chapter 3). The strategy of fait accompli – which consists in pushing ahead with ambitious projects, without worrying about either feasibility or popular support – is the foundation of the so-called Monnet method. The most pungent characterization of this method has been provided by Pascal Lamy, former European Commissioner and erstwhile lieutenant of Commission President Jacques Delors: 'Europe was built in a St Simonian [i.e., technocratic] way from the beginning, this was Monnet's approach: The people weren't ready to agree to integration, so you had to get on without telling them too much about what was happening'. However, Lamy was honest enough to add: 'Now St Simonianism is finished. It can't work when you have to face democratic opinion' (cited in Ross 1995: 194). As was already mentioned in the Introduction, the primacy of process was proclaimed most explicitly by Paul-Henry Spaak, who assumed that 'everything which tends toward European organizations' was good. For him, any kind of European authority was a guarantee for post-war security, regardless of what that authority might be or do. The two principles of fait accompli and primacy of process support and complement each other: if only process and institution building count, then one can push ahead without worrying too much about concrete results and public opinion.

The risks inherent in the Monnet–Spaak approach to European integration can no longer be overlooked: the euro crisis is making the economic costs of a premature monetary union too obvious to be ignored. The political costs may in the end be even more significant. All the possible solutions of the crisis discussed in Brussels and in the national capitals so far prescribe greater centralization of fiscal, social, and countercyclical policies, and the establishment of supranational authorities with the requisite powers – all of this without prior political integration, and at a time when popular hostility towards 'Europe' is reaching unprecedented levels of intensity. European leaders had many occasions to examine both the economic and the political aspects of monetary union. The relation between monetary union and political integration was a much debated issue during the process of negotiation and ratification of the 1993 Treaty on European Union. Few people remember, or even know, that the move to EMU was supposed to be accompanied by a parallel move to European Political Union (EPU). One of the arguments used by Chancellor Kohl to persuade the German voters to give up their beloved D-Mark in favour of a common European currency was that EMU would be the final step before political union. Although no agreement could be reached on EPU or even on effective coordination of national fiscal policies, it was decided to proceed with monetary union. Thus EMU became the prime example of fait accompli, while the relation of monetary to political union continued to remain an unsettled question.

The reluctance to consider anything that could raise doubts about the wisdom of the strategy of fait accompli led EU leaders to ignore another basic fact, namely that the benefits of monetary union can exceed the costs of giving up a national currency only under rather stringent conditions. These include high mobility of labour and the possibility of compensating fiscal transfers across the monetary union to make up for uneven economic developments – conditions which were not even approximately satisfied in the EU when the Maastricht Treaty was ratified, and are still unfulfilled today. The possibility of compensating fiscal transfers across the monetary union presupposes, if not political union, at least a tight coordination of fiscal policies. The member states were not prepared to give up their autonomy in such a politically sensitive area, but in December 1996 they did come to an agreement on procedures for increased policy surveillance, specific penalties for countries having excessive deficits, and for the automatic imposition of those penalties. As we saw, this arrangement for policing budgetary policy was named (or rather renamed) the SGP in an attempt to convince public opinion that growth as well as price stability would be an explicit goal of future European monetary policy. In practice, the SGP did not prove to be an effective tool for fiscal coordination; instead, it disintegrated into squabbles over its application. The Pact started to play an active role only in 2009, with the explosion of the Greek debt crisis. By then all the risks which the Pact and the Maastricht criteria concerning public debts and deficits were supposed to prevent, had already materialized.

The disruptive consequences of the decision to proceed with monetary union regardless of economic and political risks became evident some fifteen years later with the near bankruptcy of Greece, Portugal, and Ireland, and a general crisis of the euro zone which not only speculators but also a growing number of experts and policymakers see as threatening the collapse of monetary union, perhaps of the EU itself. Recent experience has confirmed what economists and economic historians have known for a long time; namely, that monetary union without political union is, if not impossible, at least fragile as shown, for example, by the short life of the Latin Monetary Union. Founded in 1865 by France, Italy, Belgium, and Switzerland; joined by Greece and Romania two years later, this monetary union ended with the Franco-German war of 1870–1871, by which time the system had already been undermined by the monetary manipulations of some member states. What we understand more clearly today is the extent to which membership in a monetary union without political union makes a country economically fragile. This fragility, as Martin Wolf wrote:

> is inherent in the construction: members are neither sovereign states nor components of a federation. The big challenge for the eurozone is to resolve this contradiction. Given the state of public opinion today, as revealed by electoral results and surveys, from Finland to Hungary, and from Sweden to Portugal, a federal solution is impossible. Does this mean that the members of the eurozone can resolve the contradiction only by recovering their sovereignty in the monetary field?

> (Wolf 2011)

The problems connected with leaving EMU will be discussed later on in this book (see in particular chapter 8). To conclude this section let me recall what was said at the beginning of the present chapter: structural metaphors allow us to use something that is clearly understood in order to expose something which is less clearly perceived – or perhaps deliberately concealed. The fragility of an incomplete monetary union reminds us that the entire EU is, in many important respects, seriously incomplete and hence fragile. For example, responsibilities are distributed across European and national levels in a process which is by no means complete, and hence is open to different interpretations and frequent contestations. According to Otmar Issing, the case of monetary policy is different since 'there is only a *single* monetary policy for the euro area, which is set in a centralized decision-making process' (Issing 2008: 55; emphasis in the original). However, recent experience has shown that in a crisis situation monetary policy for the euro area is not under the control of a single decision centre. The situation is further complicated by the problem of Germany as the 'reluctant hegemon', see again chapter 8.

Also the Single European Market, which should have been achieved by 1992, is still an incomplete project. On the one hand, the services sector – which represents more than two-thirds of the GDP of all advanced economies – is still largely regulated at the national level. On the other hand, the steady enlargement of the EU has increased, and will continue to increase, the socioeconomic heterogeneity of the member states, making it impossible to devise common rules without sacrificing the needs and priorities of at least some members. One of the attempts made in the past to mask the incomplete, tentative nature of the integration process was to create a feeling of familiarity by giving key European institutions the same name as national institutions, even though the latter operate according to quite different principles and perform rather different functions. As will be seen in the following chapters, as well as in last section of the present chapter, such homonymy is particularly misleading in the case of the ECB and the EP.

Misleading analogies

The received view of EMU has it that the ECB is a clone of the Bundesbank, the continuation of German monetary policy by other means. 'Why has the German model prevailed?' asks the author of a standard textbook on the economics of monetary union, whose seventh edition appeared shortly before the beginning of the euro crisis (De Grauwe 2007: 163). As we saw in a previous section, a key benefit of EMU, for France and other members of the 'monetarist' group of countries, was precisely the opportunity monetary union seemed to offer of replacing the existing exchange-rate arrangement, centred on the D-Mark, with a European-level institution where each national central bank governor would have a seat at the table of monetary decision-making. Ironically, the ECB turned out to be even more exclusively committed to price stability than the old Bundesbank, and as jealous of its own political independence – at least until the beginning of the euro crisis. In fact, the ECB is not a politically independent institution operating in the context of a democratic government, like the Federal Reserve in the US or the pre-EMU Bundesbank in Germany. Rather, it is a 'disembedded' non-majoritarian institution, free (indeed, obliged) to operate in a political vacuum, without a European government, or at least a European finance minister, to balance its powers, see chapter 5. The irony of this outcome was compounded by the fact that the exceptional independence of the ECB found its strongest defender in Jean-Claude Trichet – a former director of the French Treasury and governor of the Banque de France – who in the past had opposed both

EMU and central bank independence (Marsh 2010: 185–6). As president of the ECB, however, Trichet became Germany's main ally in matters related to the political independence of the Bank, and to the limited role of the so-called Euro-Group – the finance ministers of the members of the euro zone. With reference to Trichet's change of mind concerning central bank independence David Marsh (ibid.: 226, 317) speaks of a 'Becket effect', drawing a parallel to Thomas à Becket, chancellor of Henry II of England, who opposed the king after he was made archbishop of Canterbury – and was murdered for his change of allegiance. As Marsh reports, one German central banker spoke approvingly of Trichet as 'our convert', while another banker commented that it was incomparably better for Germany to have a French ECB president carrying out a Bundesbank-style policy in Frankfurt than to have a German president carrying out a Banque de France-style in Paris.

It is also true that the Bundesbank-style policy of the ECB is matched, in part, by a formal structure and rules that in many ways mimic the Bundesbank. For example, the ECB's disclosure rules tend to follow the Bundesbank thirty-year pattern, in significant contrast with the practices of the US Federal Reserve Board and of the Bank of England, which publish minutes of their interest rate-settings sessions a few weeks after the meetings take place. Despite continuing pressure from the EP and from expert opinion to give more information on its decision-making, it is unlikely that the ECB will start to release minutes of its proceedings: to do so would, in David Marsh's words, 'fly in the face of the Bundesbank long-term practice'. Also its location in Frankfurt was supposed to make it easier to skew the ECB's corporate culture towards the Bundesbank model. Many observers expected that the superior performance of the German economy in recent years would stamp the imprint of the German model on ECB policymaking even more strongly. Even the most favourably disposed observers, however, could not reasonably expect that monetary policymaking in the EU could match the performance of the German or other successful national models. The very fact that European monetary policy must be of the one-size-fits-all type means that many decisions of the monetary authority are bound to be suboptimal for some, if not all, members of the euro zone, as discussed in a previous section. It is also the case that the voting system in the ECB seems to privilege nationality over the needs of the euro zone as an economic area. In addition to these more or less inevitable difficulties, however, the efficiency of the mechanisms of monetary governance has been reduced by the political compromises that were necessary in order to make monetary union at all possible. In a number of important cases these political compromises took the form of non-decisions: controversial issues were left unresolved, leaving big holes in the policymaking machinery.

At any rate, the euro crisis has altered dramatically both the ECB's behaviour and the political and economic context in which the ECB operates. In particular, the main concern of the Bank is now less the stability of prices than the very survival of monetary union. In repeating the slogan that 'the euro is forever', the leaders of the central bank reveal their intention of doing anything necessary to save the common currency, pretty much regardless of what the rules say. In a perceptive article published in *Spiegel On Line* of 15 February 2012 (Muenchau 2012a), Wolfgang Muenchau discusses the changed behaviour of the ECB in the crisis – the flooding of the markets with cheap money, and the buying of state bonds of doubtful quality – but especially he rejects what may be called the Clausewitzian view of the ECB as a continuation of the old Bundesbank by other means. This Associate Editor and columnist of the *Financial Times* argues that the crisis of the euro zone has definitely shown that the ECB is not a clone of the German central bank. In fact, it should have been clear all along that the Bundesbank model could not have been replicated at the European level, for at least three reasons.

First, the broad domestic consensus concerning the importance of price stability, budgetary discipline, and international competitiveness does not exist in other countries of the euro zone having greatly different histories and political cultures. The second reason is the economic, social, and political homogeneity of Germany, which contrasts with the great heterogeneity of the euro zone. The third, and according to Muenchau most important, difference between the ECB and the Bundesbank is that the German economy, for all its robustness, is fairly small relative to the world economy. This means that the old Bundesbank did not have to worry too much about the impact of its decisions outside Germany or, at most, outside Europe. By contrast, the ECB cannot overlook the impact of its policies on the world economy because of the size of the euro zone. A clear indication of the international significance of the EU, we may add, is the concern of the president of the US, as well as of the leaders of the BRIC countries (Brazil, Russia, India, and especially China), about the risk of sovereign defaults in the euro zone. Thus, none of the three conditions which made it possible for the Bundesbank to operate successfully at the national level are satisfied at the European level.

But the ECB is also different from the Federal Reserve, which, according to its statute, must pursue not one but two objectives: price stability *and* full employment. Thus in early 2011, the ECB raised the interest rate because of the risk of higher inflation, while the Federal Reserve was easing monetary policy because of a rise in unemployment. The main difference between the two institutions, however, is that the governor of the Federal Reserve has a political counterpart in the Secretary of the Treasury, while the political counterparts of the president of the ECB are almost twenty heads of state or government, as many finance ministers, the president of the European Commission, and the Commissioner responsible for economic and monetary affairs. It follows that the president of the ECB will never be able to play a role with respect to the multi-headed governance of the euro zone comparable to that of the governor of the Federal Reserve vis-à-vis the federal government of the US. Muenchau concludes that as an institutional 'hermaphrodite' the ECB cannot play the decisive role in the current crisis (Muenchau 2012a).

In other words, the ECB is essentially different from any national bank, but also the other European institutions differ in crucial respects from national institutions bearing the same, or similar, names. This difference is particularly evident in case of the EP. As I pointed out in a previous work (Majone 2009: 155–7), the EP differs from the legislatures of parliamentary democracies not only because it lacks their power to tax and spend, to initiate legislation, and to validate a government's actions, but most fundamentally because of the absence of the traditional government–opposition dialectic in the EU. One of the significant consequences of this absence is the fact that EU voters, being denied an appropriate political arena in which to hold European governance accountable, are almost pushed into supporting any organized opposition to Europe. Hence the transformation of popular referendums on new treaties into contests for or against the EU. The *sui generis* nature of the EP is also revealed by the attitude of its members: many Members of the European Parliament (MEPs) see themselves as policy specialists rather than as partisan politicians, and insist that the Commission should be a neutral institution, and that individual Commissioners should forget their party affiliation, if any. This attitude may also account, at least in part, for the fact that the EP has never seriously contested the Commission's monopoly of legislative initiative.

Finally, the EP does not represent a (non-existent) European people in the same sense in which a national parliament represents an historically defined *demos*, and thus cannot represent, even in theory, a generally recognized European interest which is something more than the sum of the various national interests. Individual interests, on the other hand, are still largely rooted at the national level, and hence find their natural expression in national parliaments and political parties. In fact, where important national interests are at stake, the EP tends to vote along national, rather than party, lines. One example among many that could be cited: when the EP turned down a Commission proposal for a Takeover Directive, in July 2001, the MEPs voted overwhelmingly to protect national economic interests, rather than the 'common interest' in the integration of Europe's capital markets, or even according to party-political (left–right) positions (Knudsen 2005). In the enlarged EU structural differences among the national economies have increased significantly, so one may expect that this process of 're-nationalization' of the EP will acquire momentum in the future.

All this explains why the real arena of democratic politics continues to be the nation state, and why European elections are 'second-order elections': useful perhaps to gauge the popularity of the incumbent *national* government, but meaningless as an arena where European issues would be debated and settled. It also explains why voter partic-ipation in European elections has been constantly decreasing since 1979, the year of the first direct European elections, and why the EP does not enjoy sufficient democratic legitimacy to be able, in turn, to legitimate European policies, or other European institutions such as the Commission (see chapter 6). Treaty after treaty the member states have increased the powers of the EP, but the results have been quite disappointing, to the point that some knowledgeable observers, such as Jean-Claude Piris (2011), now doubt even the democratic legitimacy of the supranational parliament. The fact is that while in national elections the voters choose their governments, this is not the case in European elections. Again, some of the most important issues for the voters – including monetary policy, foreign and security policy, social security, public health and education – are not within the competence of the EP.

The other main example of striking differences between a national institution and the apparently corresponding European institution, the ECJ, will be discussed in chapter 3. In all these cases, the ambiguous behaviour of supranational institutions that are supposed to solve tech-nical (legal or economic) problems but that also pursue the political goal of 'more Europe' mirrors the institutional and political ambiguity of the EU itself: a creation of international law aiming at 'ever closer union'; an association of democratic states suffering from a serious, and growing, democratic deficit; member states that are no longer sovereign states but neither members of a federation. This ambiguity is compounded by the fact that in an EU continuously moving the boundary posts of its own powers, it is increasingly difficult to separate the responsibilities of national and supranational policymakers. As long as the member states hold very different views about the nature and purpose of European integration, and are differently committed to the integration project, it is highly unlikely that all these ambiguities will be resolved.

2

A political culture of total optimism: its rise and fall

Fait accompli and total optimism

According to the Treaty on European Union (TEU), Article 107 (1), 'The ESCB [European System of Central Banks] shall be composed of the ECB and of the national central banks.' This wording makes clear that the authors of the treaty had assumed that *all* member states of the EU would join the monetary union – an overly optimistic assumption, as it turned out. As we shall see in the present chapter such a priori optimism is (or was until recently) a characteristic feature of the political culture of European integration – and one reason why crises always find EU leaders unprepared. When the euro was introduced, an American political economist wrote: 'Prudence might have counselled that the European Union take certain steps well before the creation of the euro area' (Henning 2000: 41). He was referring to what economist Charles Wyplosz has called the 'dark secret' of monetary union: the fact that the relevant article of the Maastricht Treaty is so ambiguous that it is not clear who is actually responsible for the exchange rate of the euro, see chapter 1. Even Wim Duisenberg – who as (first) president of the ECB should have been better informed about the financial conditions of would-be members of the monetary union – was absolutely delighted when, in January 2001, Greece adopted the euro. Like many other Euro-enthusiasts the Dutch central banker was convinced that for the sake of European integration it was important to have as many countries as possible in the monetary union. Thus, possible risks were totally ignored (Lévy 2012). These are only few examples of the unconcerned, not to say reckless, attitude which until recently prevailed among EU leaders – not just in monetary policy but in all areas of European competence. Henning, like the majority of American experts, counselled prudence, but the truth is that prudential reasoning is foreign to the Monnet strategy of fait accompli which, as mentioned in chapter 1, goes back to the beginnings of European integration.

This approach to European integration implies that the success of a collective decision is determined by the decision-makers themselves – by the very fact that they agreed on the decision – rather than by those who will be affected by the eventual outcomes. This emphasis on the process of decision-making rather than on actual results excludes a priori the possibility of failure. 'Technocratic' – the adjective often used with reference to decision-making in the EU – is the wrong label for such an attitude, since the first task of the expert consists in analysing the conditions under which a given task is at all feasible, and then determining whether the eventual obstacles – economic, political, or technological – may be removed, at acceptable costs, before the decision is implemented (Majone 1989: 70–81). As already noted in chapter 1, the question of feasibility has been systematically ignored by integrationist leaders. Thus, there is no indication that the feasibility of the goal of the Werner Plan – monetary union by 1980 – was ever seriously considered. The so-called 'bicycle theory' of European integration – according to which integration must keep moving forward, especially in a crisis, for the bicycle (that the EU is seen to be) not to fall – provides the conceptual justification of the strategy of fait accompli. Over the years systematic application of this strategy has generated what may be called a political culture of total optimism. The basic features of this peculiar political culture emerged in the 1960s and early 1970s – the age of 'permissive consensus', when the integration project, being taken for granted by European publics, did not seem to require any justification in terms of results. Such a benign attitude was facilitated by the fact that most European policies were too remote from the daily problems of the people to seriously concern public opinion. True, policies such as the CAP or particular regulatory measures have been questioned and criticized often enough; but controversies and contestations always remain confined within fairly narrow political and academic circles, or within particular interest groups.

I have borrowed the expression 'political culture of total optimism' from the historian Geoffrey Parker, who used it in his discussion of the grand strategy of Philip II of Spain. According to this historian, 'Spain's strategic culture absolutely demanded such total optimism: since it had to be assumed that God fought on Spain's side and would therefore send success, any attempt to plan for possible failure could be construed as either "tempting Providence" or denoting a lack of faith'. Of course, many other rulers of the past, as well as modern statesmen and strategists, also made the mistake of not taking the possibility of failure into account. 'Philip II, however, left more to chance – or to "Providence" – than most statesmen, thanks to his complete confidence that God would make good any deficiencies and errors'. The consequences of the king's total optimism were 'a willingness to cast all caution to the winds and, equally dangerous, a failure to make contingency plans' (Parker 1998: 107–8).

A political culture of total optimism could hardly survive in the conflictive politics of modern mass democracies, but it did take root at the supranational level, where it could facilitate collective decision-making by small elites. The total optimism of EU leaders – revealed most clearly by their systematic failure to make contingency plans – does not spring from confidence in 'Providence', but from two more worldly sources. On the one hand, federalists derive confidence in the final success of their cause from the conviction that the nation state is no longer viable, at least in Europe. Like some intellectual leaders of the 1930s, such as Ortega y Gassett and Julien Benda, latter-day federalists believe that only the political union of the continent – a nation state 'writ large' – can save Europe from becoming irrelevant in a world dominated by a few superpowers of continental dimension. Sooner or later European citizens will acknowledge the necessity of political union, and will also understand why in certain situations it is necessary to accept risks that would be considered unacceptable in different contexts. On the other hand, EU leaders who are not in favour of full political union also find it convenient to display total optimism concerning the outcomes of the collective decisions taken at the supranational level. This is because they have a vested interest in the preservation of a system that, among other things, allows them to take unpopular measures *in camera* rather than in a direct confrontation with the opposition parties at home.

This display of optimism, regardless of actual results, is facilitated by the fact that most decisions taken at the EU level must satisfy different, even conflicting, interests. As we saw in chapter 1, for example, the decision to proceed with monetary union was supported by leaders who saw EMU as a necessary step towards political union; by governments that wished to terminate the 'tyranny of the German Mark'; and by leaders who correctly assumed that membership in the euro zone would immediately improve the credit rating of their countries, allowing them to borrow at significantly lower rates of interest. A decision that has to satisfy many different interests must necessarily be ambiguous or incomplete or, most likely, both. In December 2011 the Brussels correspondent of the *Frankfurter Allgemeine Zeitung*, Werner Mussler, summarized in the following terms his experience of sixteen summits in two years to discuss the euro crisis: 'It is one of the peculiar features of decision making in the EU that the compromises reached at the summits leave much room for different interpretations, so that afterwards everybody can claim victory. But this only means that many questions remain unresolved' (citation in Sarrazin 2012: 213).

A consequence of the prevailing political culture is the fact that long-term consequences are heavily discounted or altogether ignored. This explains not only the absence of contingency plans and of any other instrument of crisis management, but also the willingness of European leaders to increase the risk of future failure for the sake of immediate advantages. Such considerations provide additional evidence in support of the heuristic usefulness of viewing monetary union as a metaphor of the entire integration project. It is indeed hard to find a better example of the willingness of EU leaders to compromise their collective credibility for the sake of short-term benefits than their decision to proceed with monetary union before there was any agreement on political union, and leaving a number of technical and institutional problems unresolved. Nor can one find, in the entire history of European integration, a better illustration of the complete disregard, not only of expert opinion, but also of such basic principles of crisis management as timely preparation of contingency plans and careful attention to signs that may foretell a crisis. The lax application of the convergence criteria of the Maastricht Treaty, and of the subsequent rules of the SGP (see chapter 1) are other examples of the same tendency to increase the risks of an already risky project. Similar, if less striking or less well-known, examples can easily be found in most other areas of EU policymaking.

Management consultants have introduced the notion of 'culture audit', meaning a systematic recording of all the factors that go into making a company's culture. Such an audit is a useful way to recognize that corporate culture is not just defined by hard factors like mission statements and administrative structures; it is also determined by softer factors such as beliefs, attitudes, and symbols. For political scientists, values, beliefs, and attitudes constitute the political culture of a given community. The notion of political culture has rarely been used to study how plans and decisions are made at the European level, but I submit that the refusal of EU leaders to contemplate the possibility of failure is best explained in terms of the kind of political culture discussed above. In fact, an attitude of total optimism is evident, not only in the plans and decisions of EU leaders, but also in the analyses of many students of

European integration. Thus a legal scholar writes of 'the inherent ability of the EU integration process to constantly reinvent itself as part of an evolutionary process of political and economic survival' (Szyszczak 2006: 487). Another specialist of European law claims that the approach to integration followed for half a century is still basically valid, and capable of evolving in response to changing pressures and new priorities (Dougan 2006). Equally favourable prognoses have been issued by political scientists and commentators who over the years have absorbed the EU culture of total optimism. Thus, shortly before the French and Dutch voters rejected the Constitutional Treaty, a well-known American student of European integration wrote that the 'constitutional compromise' embodied in the multi-level system of governance of the EU 'is unlikely to be upset by major functional challenges, autonomous institutional evolution, or demands for democratic accountability....When a constitutional system no longer needs to expand and deepen in order to assure its own continued existence, it is truly stable' (Moravcsik 2005: 376).

Ignoring feasibility

Total optimism implies a total disregard of the many constraints – technical, economic, political, institutional, cultural – that even under the best conditions severely limit the range of possible choices in political and social life. As Michael Polanyi once observed:

> The existence of social tasks which appear both desirable and feasible and yet are in fact impracticable has set the stage throughout history for a wide range of human conflicts. All the battles of social reform were fought on these grounds, with conservatives often harshly overstating and progressives recklessly underestimating the limits of manageability.
>
> (Polanyi 1951: 169)

Feasibility analysis – a core element of the theory and practice of policy analysis – was developed precisely to help policymakers avoid both harsh overstatements and reckless underestimation of the limits of manageability of political and social tasks. The aim of this branch of policy analysis is to identify the most important constraints, separate them from fictitious obstacles, evaluate their significance for different implementation strategies, and estimate the costs and benefits of relaxing those constraints that are not absolutely binding. Good policy analysts know that it is a mistake to define feasibility only in terms of a few, easily quantifiable limitations, such as technical or budgetary constraints. The second-best theorem of welfare economics explains why sub-optimal solutions of public policy problems are usually the only feasible ones. Essentially, the theorem states that the first-order conditions for an optimum are not, in general, valid policy criteria in a situation where, because of some constraints added to the usual budgetary and technical limitations, the conditions cannot all be simultaneously satisfied. But if sub-optimal or second-best solutions are the only feasible ones, then it follows that feasibility, rather than optimality, should be the main concern of policy analysts and, a fortiori, of policymakers (Majone 1989: 75–8).

The insouciance about the feasibility of even the most ambitious goals, which is so characteristic of decision-making in the EU, is evident in the examples mentioned in the preceding section. If additional evidence is desired, it can easily be provided. Thus at the summit held in the Portuguese capital in March 2000 – less than two years before the introduction of the euro – the European Council launched the so-called Lisbon Strategy for Growth and Jobs. As mentioned in the Introduction, the European leaders promised that by the year 2010 the Union would become 'the most competitive, knowledge-based economy in the world', leaving the US economy lagging behind. In order to justify such an ambitious goal it was assumed that the EU would grow at an annual average rate of 3 per cent, so as to create 20 million new jobs; while maintaining a commitment to solidarity and equality and, of course, respecting the environment. The experts knew all along that the goal was in fact unfeasible, and the Lisbon Strategy was declared dead in 2011 by Commission President Barroso who, instead of explaining the reasons for the failure, used the occasion to announce the launching of a new 'Europe 2020' project.

The large-scale enlargement of the years 2004–2007, with the consequent dramatic increase in socioeconomic heterogeneity within the EU, may be mentioned as another manifestation of the same unconcern about potential problems. The original plans of opening accession negotiations with no more than five countries from Central and Eastern Europe – five being the number favoured by the Commission, while the government of Chancellor Kohl would have preferred to start with only Poland, the Czech Republic, and Hungary – were soon superseded by the decision to open formal accession negotiations with all ten Central and Eastern Europe candidates, plus Malta and Cyprus. The basic reason for the large-scale enlargement decided at the Luxembourg European Council of December 1997, was national or institutional self-interest, with each incumbent member state pushing for its own favoured candidates, and the Commission attempting to present enlargement as feasible without an increase in the budget, and without demanding too many sacrifices from the older member states. As Sedelmeier and Wallace (2000: 453) write, these assurances of the Commission 'implied some very optimistic assumptions, notably real growth of the budget through annual growth in EU GDP of 2.5 per cent, but politically the important message was that the reforms needed for enlargement were "yesable".' The point was that Eastern enlargement gave the Brussels bureaucracy an extraordinary opportunity to play, for the first time, a role of political leadership, and also, through the direct grants, the role of the patron vis-à-vis the Central and Eastern Europe countries. Thus the politically important message the Commission intended to convey was that the reforms needed for enlargement were feasible at no cost to the older member states. If the position of the Commission can be reasonably explained only in terms of institutional self-interest, the acceptance by the member states of the 'big bang' solution indicates a less rational attitude of general unconcern about possible future problems. Indeed it is difficult to see how, having already admitted ten countries from Central and Eastern Europe, the Union could refuse to admit, sooner or later, other South-Eastern countries, in addition to Croatia: Montenegro, Bosnia-Herzegovina, Serbia, Kosovo, Macedonia, and Albania, as well as Moldova, Ukraine and, possibly, Turkey and Georgia. Another 'big bang' enlargement as in 2004–2007 is highly unlikely, but in the not too distant future the EU could comprise more than thirty countries at vastly different levels of development, and with correspondingly different policy preferences and national priorities.

Lack of concern about future problems entails not only a lack of preparations to meet the new situation, but also a sense of shocked surprise when problems arise. Consider the surprise caused in 2005 by the rejection of the draft Constitutional Treaty by impressive majorities of French and Dutch voters – 55 and 65.1 per cent, respectively. In an extraordinary meeting in Brussels in early June 2005 the presidents of the Commission, of the EP, and of the European Council at first tried to minimize what had happened. They insisted that the ratification process continue, so that at the end of 2006, when it was scheduled to be completed, a general reassessment of the situation could be made. Their hopes were dashed by the British decision to postpone indefinitely the referendum originally planned for the first half of 2006. Denmark, the Czech Republic, and Poland soon followed the British example, reinforcing the general impression that the Constitutional Treaty was effectively dead. According to informed observers, moreover, the draft Constitution would not have passed popular consultations, not only in Euro-sceptic countries like the UK, Denmark, or the Czech Republic, but even in Germany. Yet, the possibility of a rejection of the draft Constitution had never been seriously considered in Brussels: by explicit admission of the president of the European Commission, no 'Plan B' existed.

After the bad experience with the Constitutional Treaty, the Lisbon Treaty has been carefully drafted to avoid any reference, however remote, to terms like constitution, federalism, or political integration – the new Treaty even fails to mention rather innocuous symbols of statehood such as the European flag and anthem. The Treaty framers have also been generous in granting opt-outs, in the hope of convincing the national governments that ratification by popular referendum was unnecessary. However, all these stratagems failed to impress the Irish voters, who used the chance offered to them to vent their dissatisfaction with the European project by voting against the Treaty. Unsurprisingly, given these precedents and the present state of public opinion, popular referendums are now viewed as potential hazards for the integration process, not just in traditionally Euro-sceptic countries but in most member states, as well as in Brussels. Some authors go as far as speaking of a 'referendum roulette', but it seems highly unlikely that in the future it will be possible to force the referendum genie back into the bottle.

After the first Irish vote against the Lisbon Treaty, demands for popular ratification of future European treaties have been advanced by leaders of different countries and political hues. In July 2008 Werner Faymann, then the Social-Democratic candidate for the Austrian federal election to take place the following September, came out in favour of popular referendums for all future treaty amendments and on other important EU issues. The Austrian Parliament had already ratified the Lisbon Treaty in April, but the Social-Democratic leader was obviously trying to improve his electoral chances by taking advantage of wide-spread Euro-fatigue: at the time Eurobarometer data indicated that only 28 per cent of Austrian citizens still supported the EU, while in 1994 66.6 per cent had voted in favour of joining the Union. It remains to be seen how many national leaders will dare to submit to popular ratification the new Treaty on Stability, Coordination and Governance in the Economic and Monetary Union (Stability Treaty), signed in 2012 as an international (rather than European) treaty between all member states other than the UK and the Czech Republic.

From the federal vision to co-management of the national economies

An important expression of a political culture is the symbols and the terminology it uses. In the preceding chapter we noted the tendency to give European supranational institutions the same, or similar, names as national institutions which in reality perform rather different functions. This is due less to a lack of imagination than to the desire to take advantage of the symbolic status enjoyed by such national institutions as parliaments, central banks, and constitutional courts. What in chapter 1 I called misleading analogies, were seen by supporters of political union as pre-figurations of the future role of European institutions as organs of a supranational federal state. Thus in the 1960s some German legal scholars claimed that the institutions of the European Communities had been designed with the idea of replicating the model of the German Federal Republic. The Council of Ministers, the organ for the participation of the member states in the decisions of the Communities, was said to correspond to the German Bundesrat; the European Commission, the body responsible for implementing the Council's decisions, and would-be kernel of the future government of a united Europe, was the analogue of the federal executive; finally, the ECJ was, obviously, the constitutional court of the future federation. Hans Peter Ipsen, the author of one of the earliest treatises on European law, warned about the risk of taking these analogies too seriously. In a purely structural or organizational perspective, Ipsen wrote, one may compare the institutions of the European Communities with certain institutions of the German federal state, but it is methodologically wrong to derive from such analogies conclusions about the federal, or pre-federal, nature of the EEC; to argue that the founding treaties contain an inherent, automatic tendency toward a federal outcome of the integration process (Ipsen 1972: 190–1).

Despite these and other warnings, the use of symbols of statehood has continued unabated up to the present. A European logo and flag, an EU anthem, a standardized European passport and driver licence, EU citizenship, Brussels-sponsored games and sport events, an official 'Europe Day' public holiday: these and other 'cultural actions' were meant to create a new kind of European consciousness, but the results were much below expectations. Ironically, all those culture-building initiatives seemed to echo many of the techniques and methods used in the past by nationalist elites to forge Europe's existing nation states – precisely the model EU supporters seek to transcend (Shore 2006). More recently, integrationist elites saw monetary union as the decisive move towards a European federal government. Speaking on French television before the 1991 EU InterGovernmental Conference leading to the Maastricht Treaty and monetary union, Jacques Delors declared: 'My objective is that before the end of the Millennium [Europe] should have a true federation. The Commission should become a political executive which can define essential common interests. . .' In 1999 Romano Prodi, newly appointed president of the Commission, was still pursuing a similar vision. In an interview with the Spanish newspaper *El Pais* he announced: 'Here in Brussels, a true European government has been born' (citations in Shore 2011: 290).

Then the atmosphere seemed to change. The opening lines of one of the best-known documents of the Prodi Commission – the White Paper on *European Governance* (2001) – were still suffused with the culture of total optimism:

> European integration has delivered 50 years of stability, peace, and economic prosperity. It has helped to raise standards of living, built an internal market and strengthened the Union's voice in the world. It has achieved results which would not have been possible by individual Member States acting on their own. It has attracted a succession of applications for membership and in a few years' time it will expand on a continental scale. It has also served as a model for regional integration across the world.
>
> (Commission 2001: 9)

Yet, this optimism seems to be contradicted, or at least seriously qualified, by a series of admissions appearing immediately after the celebration of the past and future successes of the EU. Despite these achievements, the White Paper continues, many Europeans feel alienated from the Union's work, and the decreasing turnout in the EP elections reveals the widening gulf between the EU and the people it serves. It is true, the Commission admits, that the Union seems to be unable to act effectively in a number of important policy areas, and also on the world scene; but even where the Union does act effectively, it rarely gets proper credit for its actions. Finally, people do not understand how the system operates, and do not feel that European institutions act as an effective channel for their views and concerns. In sum, people no longer trust such a complex system to deliver what they want. The conclusion of the White Paper was that the Union must start a serious process of reform, not of the European 'government' – the word suddenly disappeared from the Commission's vocabulary – but of its system of 'governance'.

Much has been written in recent years about the EU's 'Governance Turn'. Governance, the Commission explained, 'means rules, processes and behaviour that affect the way in which powers are exercised at European level, particularly as regards openness, participation, effectiveness and coherence' (ibid.: 11). In its enthusiastic reception of the old/new concept of governance, however, the Commission ignored all the negative or problematic aspects of this fashionable paradigm. At the heart of the concept of governance is the realization that public policy is not the exclusive competence of a centralized, hierarchical system, but is made and implemented by a variety of actors – public and private, national and sub-national, international or supranational – generally operating under different systems of rules and unclear definitions of competences and responsibilities This multiplicity of actors and operational codes creates problems which the European Commission chose to overlook. Diffuse accountability is one of the most serious of these problems. Conventional notions of accountability, Rod Rhodes (2006: 439) points out, do not fit when authority for service delivery is divided among several agencies. This 'problem of many hands' arises where responsibility for policy in complex organizations is shared, and it is correspondingly difficult to find out who is responsible. It is also the case that even if the constituent organizations in a polycentric network hold the relevant decision-makers to account, multiple accountabilities necessarily weaken central control. For these and other reasons one may conclude that in the EU the accountability deficit is even more serious than the much deplored democratic deficit, see chapter 6.

The Open Method of Coordination (OMC) is generally considered one of the most significant expressions of the new governance paradigm. In an effort to bring about change in such areas as employment, health, migration, and pension reform, where the Community has limited or no competence, the new method employs non-binding objectives and guidelines, commonly agreed indicators, benchmarking, and persuasion. The philosophy underlying the OMC and related 'soft law' methods is that each state should be encouraged to experiment on its own, and to craft solutions fit to its national context. While the classic Community method creates binding uniform rules, provides sanctions if they fail to do so, and allows challenges for non-compliance to be brought before the ECJ, the OMC provides no formal sanctions for member states that do not follow the guidelines. Advocates of the new approach argue that the method can be effective despite – or even because of – its open-ended, non-binding, non-justiciable qualities (Trubek and Trubek 2005). Unfortunately, the OMC seems to have fallen far short of such optimistic expectations even in areas – such as employment and health – where one might have presumed it to have yielded the most significant results. In fact, expectations about the effectiveness of the method were quite high: OMC was seen as a key instrument for achieving the ambitious goal of the Lisbon Strategy: the EU as the most competitive, knowledge-based economy in the world by 2010!

As a matter of fact, the Commission White Paper did not share the general enthusiasm for the OMC, in which it saw a potential competitor of the Community method. It warned that 'the [OMC] must not upset the institutional balance nor dilute the achievement of common objectives in the Treaty...The open method of coordination should be a complement, rather than a replacement, for Community action' (Commission 2001: 39). The model for the future, the Commission suggested, should be a 'reinvigorated' Community method: 'The Community method has served the Union well for almost half a century. It can continue to do so, but it must be brought up to date' (ibid.: 64–5). This new, 'reinvigorated' version is simply a variant of the traditional separation-of-powers model: the Commission as the sole executive power, but keeping the monopoly of legislative initiative; the Council and the EP (without the power of initiative) as the legislative bodies; and national and sub-national actors involved, somehow, in the EU policy process. The general message was still highly optimistic: overall, things are going well and if improvements seem desirable, these can only be made under the motto 'more Europe'.

Even the most severe crisis in more than sixty years of European integration has not shaken the belief of some European leaders in 'the inherent ability of the EU integration process to constantly reinvent itself as part of an evolutionary process of political and economic survival' (to cite again from Szyszczak 2006). At present, the shibboleth of 'more Europe' has found application in a system of co-management by member states and EU institutions – what the new Stability Treaty calls a 'budget and economic partnership' – to control and correct the economic, fiscal, and ultimately the social policies of euro zone members in serious financial difficulties, see chapter 6. This process of co-management of the national economies represents an unprecedented interference with national sovereignty, at a moment when popular hostility towards the EU and its institutions has reached an intensity never experienced before. Once more, EU leaders do not seem to be particularly concerned about the political and normative implications of their attempts to rescue a premature and poorly designed monetary union. Their immediate concern is to convince the peoples of Europe that 'there is no alternative' to what they are doing. Part of their new rhetorical strategy consists in replacing the traditional optimism of official statements by catastrophic visions of what it would mean for monetary union to fail.

From total optimism to catastrophism

In January 2009 EU leaders celebrated the tenth anniversary of the successful launching of EMU. This success, the Euro-enthusiasts claimed, was not only technical and economic, but also, and foremost, political: the common currency was going to be the solid foundation of a politically united Europe. One year later, the same leaders were facing the possible bankruptcy of some members of the euro zone. Chancellor Angela Merkel, on the occasion of the Bundestag debate on financial help to Greece of 7 May 2010, went as far as asserting that the crisis of the common currency was nothing less than an existential threat for Germany and for Europe. The monetary union, she concluded, is a 'community of destiny' (*Schicksalsgemeinschaft*): 'if the euro fails then Europe fails'. And Wolfgang Schaeuble, her finance minister, added: 'We must defend this common European currency as a whole. . .By defending it we defend at the same time the European project' (citations in Jung *et al.* 2010: 80). Few other European leaders went as far as linking the future of European integration to the future of the euro, but then the Berlin government had to convince its highly sceptical voters of the necessity of a fund of 750 billion euros to avert the risk of default by Greece and other members of the euro zone. Only a few years before, a sovereign-debt crisis of such proportions would have been simply inconceivable. At that time all euro zone governments could borrow at about the same cost as Germany. Even after the first signs of the debt crisis appeared – with Ireland and Greece having to offer interest rates that by March 2009 were already significantly higher than Germany's – no euro zone government was willing to discuss the possibility of aid measures for countries in serious financial straits. One year later, even the spokes-person of the Greek Ministry of Finance denied the need for any European aid package, saying that reports to that effect were 'talk, only talk'. In fact, by then Germany and other EU countries were considering the possibility of an aid package of the order of 25–30 billion euros, but only as an extreme measure. The official position remained that the Maastricht Treaty prohibits the member states of the EU, as well as the European institutions, from providing financial aid to individual mem-bers of the euro zone. Each government, it was said again and again, must keep its own finances in order so that no country becomes depend-ent on another. But when state bankruptcy – not in South America or South-East Asia but right in Europe – became a real possibility, the official position changed and the 'no-bail-out clause' (Article 125(1) of the Lisbon Treaty) was conveniently forgotten, without a word of apology or explanation.

How can we explain the switch from the traditional mood of total optimism to the catastrophism of the leaders of the largest European economy? As already suggested, the most obvious explanation is that by insisting that the survival of the EU depends on the survival of monetary union, the German leaders were attempting, first of all, to impress their own voters with the exceptional gravity of the situation. At the same time they wanted to convince present and future euro zone members of the need to accept tighter coordination and closer control of national eco-nomic and fiscal policies, as well as greater harmonization of important aspects of social policy. These ambitious objectives were clearly spelled out by the German chancellor when, at the end of January 2011, she advanced the idea of a 'Pact for Competitiveness' as a first step towards a future economic government of the euro zone. The pact would have obligated all euro zone members to adhere to sound fiscal *and* social policies, including an age limit for pensions to reflect demographic developments, and modest wage increases that would no longer be adapted automatically to rising prices. Also finance minister Schaeuble expressed the hope that the sovereign-debt crisis of the euro zone could convince the other member states that a centralized monetary policy must be supported by the delegation of responsibility for macroeco-nomic policymaking to the supranational level, as well as far-reaching harmonization of domestic, and in particular social, policies. In this way the sovereign-debt crisis would actually help to achieve those quasi-federalist aims which, after the rejection of the Constitutional Treaty and the difficult ratification of the Lisbon Treaty, had seemed to recede into an ever more distant future. However, even leaders of countries that traditionally supported Germany's position, such as the Netherlands, Luxembourg, and Austria, were severely critical of Merkel's Pact for Competitiveness. It is true that because of the debt crisis countries like Greece, Portugal, and Ireland, and to some extent also Spain and Italy, adopted tough and legally binding measures of fiscal discipline, but such measures were forced on them, not freely agreed to, and as such were deeply resented. Indeed, one has to go back to the years immediately following the end of World War II to find such levels of mutual resentment between the publics of the Southern and the Northern members of the would-be core Europe – surely one of the most unintended and undesirable consequences of monetary union.

Brinkmanship

This widespread reluctance to accept the German viewpoint does not prove that the more obvious explanation of the catastrophism of the German leaders – an attempt to impress voters with the exceptional gravity of the situation – is wrong, rather that it is incomplete: it captures only one dimension of a complex strategy of crisis control. The bleak scenario painted by Angela Merkel and her finance minister in May 2010 should be understood not only as an exercise in persuasion, but also as a strategic move of brinkmanship. As mentioned above, the position of the German government during the first year of the debt crisis was that the Maastricht Treaty simply prohibits the members of the EU from providing financial aid to individual euro zone members. However, Germany's refusal to help lacked credibility. Every European government is well aware of the importance the largest and economically most powerful member of the EU has historically attached to the collective good of 'European integration'. It is true that a reunited Germany has shown increasing unwillingness to continue to play the role of paymaster and problem-solver for the rest of Europe, but as long as this country – for historical, political, and economic reasons – attaches greater importance to European integration than other member states, it is unlikely to provide a counterexample to Mancur Olson's theorem about the exploitation of the great by the small in the financing of collective goods, see chapter 8.

At any rate, as long as Germany's European partners remained convinced that this country is still strongly committed to European integration, its refusal to help heavily indebted members of the euro zone – a decision wholly under the control of the German government – lacked credibility. On the other hand, the warning that the collapse of the euro could entail the end of the EU designs a new scenario, where events do not depend only on German decisions. Thus, Berlin's later position is best understood as a move in a strategy of brinkmanship. The essence of brinkmanship is the deliberate creation of risk. 'This risk should be sufficiently intolerable to your opponent to induce him to eliminate the risk by following your wishes...In fact brinkmanship is a threat, but of a special kind' (Dixit and Nalebuff 1991: 207). With brinkmanship one is willing to create a risk, but one remains unwilling to carry out the threatened act if the occasion arises. To convince other players that the threatened consequences will occur, however, one also needs a device of commitment, such as the toss of a coin, which takes the actual action out of one's control. But as Dixit and Nalebuff point out, in many circumstances a generalized fear that 'things may get out of hand' can serve the same purpose. Thus, with reference to President Kennedy's announcement of a naval quarantine of Cuba during the Cuban missile crisis of October 1962, they write:

> The fact that Kennedy's decisions had to be carried out by parties with their own procedures (and sometimes their own agenda) provided a method for Kennedy to credibly commit to taking some of the control out of his hands. The ways in which a bureaucracy takes a life of its own, the difficulty of stopping momentum, and the conflicting goals within an organization were some of the underlying ways in which Kennedy could threaten to start a process that he could not guarantee to stop.
>
> (Ibid.: 213)

Since the threat of strictly limiting Germany's role in the sovereign-debt crisis did not prove to be credible, in spite of being supported by explicit treaty rules, a new strategy had to be developed. The warning of a possible collapse of the entire European project as a result of the actions or inactions of *all* the member states (Angela Merkel's 'community of destiny') is more credible. The uncertainty scales down the threat, making it more tolerable to the threatening party, and therefore more credible to the other parties. The replacement of certainty by the perspective of a deliberately created risk is, to repeat, the essence of brinkmanship. It does not seem, however, that brinkmanship worked for the German chancellor as well as it did for President Kennedy. In fact, the assertion that the collapse of the euro would imply the break-up of the EU – a catastrophe which, it was said, could only be avoided by linking punitive interest rates with any EU aid payment in order to force indebted states to save – was not taken too seriously either by Germany's European partners or by most experts. The decision by the Euro-Group, in March 2011, to establish the European Stability Mechanism (ESM, effectively a European monetary fund with a capital of 700 billion euros), to start operations in 2012 rather than in September 2013 as originally planned, shows that the scepticism of the majority of member states and the doubts of the experts were justified.

Caught unawares?

EU leaders were surprised and shocked by the first serious crisis of the common currency. This is the impression one gathers from the evident absence of contingency plans, the overreaction of some leaders, the abrupt and unexplained changes of attitude – for example, concerning the proper roles of the ECB and of the IMF in the crisis, or about the stringency of the no-bail-out clause. The finance minister of Germany's Christian-Democratic and Social-Democratic coalition government was one of the first European leaders to speak about the unspeakable. At an event organized by his Social-Democratic Party in Dusseldorf on 16 February, 2009, Peer Steinbrueck acknowledged that some states of the euro zone were in a 'very difficult situation', thus confirming what until then only currency market speculators or independent researchers had dared to say. Then the finance minister went a good deal further: 'If one euro zone [member] gets into trouble, then collectively we will have to be helpful.' The admission was tantamount to a complete reversal of previous positions concerning the euro crisis. Until then, as we saw, no political leader had been willing to discuss the possibility of aid measures for countries in a financial emergency. Now Steinbrueck was conceding that '[t]he euro-region treaties don't foresee any help for insolvent countries, but in reality the other states would have to rescue those running into difficulty'. Just one week before the Dusseldorf meeting, the same German politician had struck a very different tone, telling the other finance ministers of the euro zone that they should not take too seriously the 'horror scenarios' painted by the media. Also the then president of the ECB, Jean-Claude Trichet, had commented on reports of the problems some governments were starting to have in obtaining fresh capital with the words: 'I think these rumours are unfounded' (all citations in Reiermann 2009).

It would take another year before European institutions and national governments would admit that the procedures then in place to coordinate policies and re-establish economic equilibrium were insufficient for weathering a serious crisis. A report made available by the European Commission in January 2010 noted what should have been clear all along, namely that the members of the euro zone differ greatly in terms of competitiveness, and also that some countries had taken advantage of the low interest rates, following membership in the monetary union, to accumulate enormous deficits. EU aid for Greece was still excluded with the argument that it would set a dangerous precedent for other countries such as Portugal, Spain, or Ireland. Already the following month, however, the heads of government of the EU agreed to help Greece, but only in case of absolute necessity, i.e., in case of a serious risk of state bankruptcy. In March 2010, the German chancellor went so far as to suggest that the member states should seriously consider the possibility of expelling from the euro zone a repeated rule-breaker. The EU kept insisting that it had a plan to help Greece, should the need arise, but lacking details as to what the plan might look like commentators were inclined to doubt that assertion. The dearth of details offered by Brussels was especially disturbing to Greece. The Greek prime minister tried to put some pressure on his European partners by hinting that he was thinking of approaching the IMF for assistance. Up to that time, Germany, France, and most other member states, as well as the European Commission and the ECB, had categorically excluded that the IMF could play within the euro zone a role similar to the one it had traditionally played in the less developed countries of Asia and Latin America. Eventually, however, it had to be admitted that the IMF's financial assistance and technical expertise were both needed in the case of serious problems of members of the euro zone.

The confusion of EU leaders confronted by the first crisis of the new monetary union was obvious and to some extent understandable in light of the prevailing political culture of total optimism. Still, the total absence of contingency plans is particularly striking in this case because of the many early warnings concerning the risks of a monetary union without political union, and even in the absence of fiscal coordination. Thus, Tsoukalis' widely used textbook on the economics of European integration, published shortly after ratification of the Maastricht Treaty, explained clearly why monetary union was a high-risk project with no easy exit options if things went wrong. As mentioned in the preceding chapter, the Greek economist concluded his discussion by pointing out that the chosen strategy accorded no place to failure. Ten years later the same economist noted that the combination of a complete centralization of monetary policy, a highly decentralized fiscal policy, and a disconnected European political system, had no precedent in history: 'The architects of Maastricht have produced a complex design of arguably postmodern inspiration, which seems to defy the law of gravity' (Tsoukalis 2003: 169).

Early warnings about the risks of monetary union had been issued by a number of European and American experts, but they had all been ignored by the leaders of the EU. A very articulate argument about the political and economic risks of the project was advanced by Martin Feldstein – professor of economics at Harvard, former chairman of the Council of Economic Advisers of the US President, and head of the prestigious National Bureau of Economic Research – in an article published in *The Economist* of 13 June 1992 (Feldstein 1992), even before the Maastricht Treaty came into force. Feldstein begins by rejecting the claim, made by a number of EU leaders and especially by the European Commission, that the adoption of a single currency was necessary to perfect the single market's free trade in goods and services. He points out that it is possible to have all the benefits of free trade without a common currency: nobody seriously suggests that Canada, the US, and Mexico, as members of NAFTA, should form a currency union. Even before the formation of NAFTA, trade relations between Canada and the US were extremely close, much closer than between any two members of the EU, but no monetary union between the two countries had ever been seriously considered. The case for linking monetary union to the creation of the single market was based on the notion that eliminating currency fluctuations within Europe would increase trade among the members of the EU. However, statistical studies that measured the effect of exchange-rate volatility on trade in Europe failed to find any significant impact. Further evidence that currency volatility does not inhibit trade, Feldstein adds, is the sharp increase in the volume of American imports during the 1980s when the dollar gyrated widely. Also, the fluctuations of the yen relative to the dollar and to European currencies have never been a serious barrier to the ability of Japanese firms to increase exports.

Having disposed of this specious argument in support of monetary union, the American economist goes on to remind his readers of two conditions that have to be met to make it worthwhile for a group of independent countries to adopt a single currency: first, the economic shocks that hit the individual countries should be similar, so that the appropriate monetary policy is generally the same everywhere; and, second, labour should be highly mobile among countries adopting the common currency. It is easy to see that Europe was not, and is not, an optimal currency area. Individual countries tend to suffer substantially different shocks because of differences in the mix of the products they produce, in the foreign markets to which they sell, and in a host of other relevant socioeconomic factors. Labour mobility across Europe, on the other hand, is and will remain limited by differences in language and culture and, one could add, by differences in such important factors as the types of welfare state regimes.

If Europe is not an optimal currency area, as all experts agree, then it becomes crucially important to understand the disadvantages of losing an independent national monetary policy. Textbooks on international trade tell us that if the demand for the products of a country falls, the country will suffer lower employment and output unless wages and prices fall as well. In practice, wages and prices adjust only slowly, so output and employment suffer. These negative effects can be mitigated with devaluation of the national currency or lower domestic interest rates – both remedies being impossible, however, if the country is a member of a monetary union. Why then have most EU member states opted in favour of a monetary union that was not necessary to facilitate trade, but likely to add to cyclic instability of incomes and employment? One common answer to this question is that a single currency and an independent, supranational central bank are an effective way to restrict the ability of national governments to pursue inflationary monetary policies. According to Feldstein this anti-inflationary argument was very much weakened by the success of the EMS.

The system worked, at least for a number of years, enabling countries with a weak track record in terms of monetary stability to borrow credibility by pegging their currency to the D-Mark and pursuing a German-style anti-inflationary policy. Inflation in countries like France and Italy came down sharply, converging towards the low inflation rate of Germany. Why, then, accept a monetary union that would force every country to give up the possibility of countercyclical domestic monetary adjustments and flexible nominal exchange rates to prevent hypothetical inflationary policies by their own central banks? Feldstein clearly understood that the very success of the German model within the EMS was an important motivation for monetary union. As we saw in chapter 1, France and other member states were very much against letting the Bundesbank make monetary policy for all of Europe. The creation of a

European central bank to manage a European currency was a matter of national pride, especially for France. The American economist did not ignore other political reasons behind the decision to proceed with monetary union. Thus he found it quite understandable that those who favoured a politically united Europe were prepared to accept the adverse economic effects of monetary union in order to achieve a federal union that they favoured for non-economic reasons. But Feldstein could not understand 'those who advocate monetary union but reject any movement towards a federalist political structure for Europe. That is a formula for economic costs without any of the supposed political benefits' (Feldstein 1992: 22).

Thus more than twenty years ago the risks of monetary union had been pointed out in detail by one of America's best-known economists, but his warnings were totally ignored by EU leaders. Similar, if less detailed, warnings have been issued by a number of other well-known experts, including Nobel Prize-winning economist, Milton Friedman, who went as far as predicting that EMU would not last more than fifteen years. Hence the obvious question: how could democratic policymakers launch the most ambitious integration project in complete disregard of expert opinion and without a contingency plan spelling out what to do in case of a serious crisis? Again, how could the same political leaders take on such risks without informing their voters, or even against the opposition of a large majority of their voters, as in the case of Germany? The most direct answer to both questions is that this is the way all important decisions have been taken in the EEC/EU for more than half a century. What was possible in the past, however, is no longer acceptable today. Even aside from the current crisis, monetary union has changed the character of European integration in one crucial respect: the integration process has become politicized. However, this late politicization has not produced the kind of popular support EU leaders had hoped for. On the contrary, the euro crisis is causing a popular backlash in both debtor and creditor countries. People are no longer content with process: they want to see results.

Process vs. outcomes

One of the lessons to be learned from the crisis of monetary union is the importance of distinguishing between two basic criteria used to evaluate any activity, including institutional design and policymaking: by process or by results. Despite its significance, this distinction is seldom clearly made, either in teaching or in research about European integration; and it seems to be totally ignored by EU political leaders and European institutions alike. As already pointed out in the Introduction, decisions and policies made at the European level are generally evaluated in terms of process – decision-making procedures, institution building, volume of legislation, expansion of competences, whether or not consensus was achieved on a particular Commission proposal – rather than in terms of results which the citizens can assess. In the Commission's 2001 White Paper on *European Governance* (Commission 2001), for example, the good governance principles are largely concerned, not with the ultimate decision/policy to be adopted, but with the way in which decisions are reached (Smith 2012: 276; Shore 2006: 719). The primacy assigned to process has enabled political leaders, Eurocrats, and most scholars, to depict European integration as a positive-sum game for everybody concerned. A good example is the opening lines of the 2001 White Paper claiming that European integration has delivered fifty years of stability, peace, and economic prosperity. As already mentioned, the same optimistic message has been sent by EU leaders on every possible occasion, at least before the beginning of the euro crisis. Now we know that the truth is less rosy. In terms of such concrete results as faster growth, higher productivity, rising employment levels, or greater technological innovation the empirical evidence presents a rather different picture.

It is certainly true that Europe experienced unprecedented prosperity in the decades immediately following the end of World War II. The doubts raised by economists and statisticians concern the causal influence of the integration process on the economic development of the continent. If that causation cannot be clearly established – and most accurate quantitative studies indicate that the gains from the Common Market were very small in relation to the increases in income that the member states enjoyed in the 1950s and 1960s – then it must be admitted that the myth of fifty years of prosperity made possible by European integration rests on the *post hoc, ergo propter hoc* fallacy: inferring a causal connection from a mere sequence in time (Majone 2009: 81–3). After the phase of very rapid catch-up with the US in the immediate post-war period – that is to say, even before the EEC was established – convergence in the levels of per capita income stopped at the beginning of the 1980s and have remained unchanged since, at around 70 per cent of the US level. During the 1990s growth of EU GDP was disappointing both in absolute terms and with regard to the US; overall growth slowed from the 1980s, which itself had slowed from the 1970s. A common trade policy, the customs union, a supranational competition policy, extensive harmonization of national laws and regulations, the Single Market, and finally a centralized monetary policy, apparently made no difference as far as the economic performance of the EEC/EU, relative to its major competitors, was concerned. While the American economy was generating employment as well as maintaining working hours, Europe's employment performance was weak and working hours fell consistently (Sapir *et al.* 2004). As a matter of fact, not only are we still far from having a single European market, but the EU market is today even more segmented along national lines than it was a couple of decades ago. The main reason for this paradoxical state of affairs is that in all advanced economies the services sector has been continuously growing in terms of share of GDP. Today it represents about 72 per cent of the GDP of the old EU-15, and services are still largely regulated at the national level.

Also monetary union has been assessed in terms of process, at least in its early stages. The launch of the common currency in 1999, and the smooth introduction of euro notes and coins and phasing out of the national currencies in 2002 were taken, even by some experts, as more or less conclusive evidence of success of the most risky project in the history of European integration. As we saw in chapter 1, shortly after the introduction of the common currency a well-known monetary economist, Paul De Grauwe, claimed that the launch of the euro had been a technical, economic, but especially a political success. Some years later, Otmar Issing – a member of the executive board of the ECB from 1998 to 2006, who later became a severe critic of the Trichet presidency – would still write that 'the common currency has become an irreversible reality...Over the nine years that have passed since its birthday on 1 January 1999, the euro has been a striking success' (Issing 2008: 1–2). In fact, recent data show that per capita GDP in the euro zone, outside Germany, has actually declined since the beginning of monetary union, see chapter 4. Empirical evidence only confirms what policy analysts have known for a long time, namely that evaluation by process is quite different from evaluation by results; and that these two modes of policy evaluation serve different purposes and appeal to different publics (Majone 1989: 170–5).

The main reason why people did not notice for so long the gap between poor or mediocre results and official enthusiastic evaluations in terms of process criteria is that most EU policies were too remote from daily problems to seriously concern public opinion. Moreover, it was difficult for ordinary citizens, and sometimes even for the experts, to allocate responsibility for unsatisfactory outcomes as between 'Brussels' and the national governments. Occasional complaints about the disappointing economic performance of the EU could be answered by reminding the critics that Community competences did not include macroeconomic policymaking. What makes the crisis of the euro zone so important also from the point of view of policy evaluation is the fact that the actual consequences of decisions taken at the European level are now so much more visible than they were in earlier stages of the integration process. As the buyers of finished products are typically interested in the quality of the product, not in the production process so, we already noted, the 'buyers' of public policy, voters and the citizens at large, are interested in the quality and tax-prices of specific policy outcomes, not in administrative procedures and decision-making processes. Thus, an important consequence of monetary union has been to make it possible for everybody to question the effectiveness of European policies. Unlike most policy decisions taken in Brussels, the decisions taken by the ECB are widely advertised, and their consequences – whether on home mortgages, on consumer credit, or on the availability of publicly financed services – have a direct impact on the welfare of all inhabitants of the euro zone, indeed of the entire EU. Also the Bank's non-decisions, for example, concerning variations in the discount rate, are often discussed in the media. Since the beginning of the crisis of the euro zone, moreover, everybody realizes that integration entails costs as well as benefits, and that a positive net balance of benefits over costs can no longer be taken for granted. This new realism is likely to generate a much stronger demand for accountability by results – precisely what is foreign to the political culture of total optimism of EU leaders. And once results become visible, the normative consequences of failures to deliver the goods can be significant.

Legitimacy, writes Martin Lipset, involves the capacity of a political system to engender and maintain the belief that its institutions are capable of resolving the major problems facing society. He goes on to explain that while effectiveness is primarily instrumental, legitimacy is evaluative. Nevertheless, the two concepts are linked:

> After a new social structure is established, if the new system is unable to sustain the expectations of major groups (on the ground of 'effectiveness') for a long enough period to develop legitimacy upon the new basis, a new crisis may develop...On the other hand, a breakdown of effectiveness, repeatedly or for a long period, will endanger even a legitimate systems stability.
>
> (Lipset 1963: 65, 67–8)

It is this connection between effectiveness, legitimacy, and systemic stability which makes so worrisome the unsatisfactory economic performance of the last decades, and especially the present crisis of the euro zone. Indeed, the basic reason why today public debate and hostile public reactions have replaced the permissive consensus of the past – when the integration project was seemingly taken for granted by European voters as part of the political landscape – is precisely the fact that monetary union has put an end to the primacy of process as *the* criterion of policy evaluation in the EU. As long as the permissive consensus lasted, the issue of the democratic deficit did not arise. The consensus began to erode as the EC/EU enlarged and acquired more powers, first with the Single European Act and later with the Maastricht Treaty. Indeed, the ratification crisis of the latter treaty – which led to the opt-outs of Great Britain and Denmark from monetary union – showed that by the early 1990s a permissive consensus no longer existed. This was the time when the democratic deficit became a serious issue.

Some EU leaders now argue that even if European integration has not delivered all the hoped-for economic benefits, at least it has delivered fifty years of peace and stability in Europe. It is certainly true that since the end of the World War II Western Europe has enjoyed over half a century of uninterrupted peace. What is doubtful, however, is the causal role of European integration in preserving peace in the old continent. A moment's reflection suggests that it is hardly believable that, after the disastrous results of two world wars, in fifty years Europeans had either the resources or the will to use again military means to resolve their conflicts – a conclusion which the distinguished Princeton political economist, Albert Hirschman, had already reached three decades ago: '[T]he European Community arrived a bit late in history for its widely proclaimed mission, which was to avert further wars *between* the major Western European nations; even without the Community the time for such wars was past after the two exhausting world wars of the first half of the twentieth century' (Hirschman 1981: 281; emphasis in the original). Aspirations to enduring peace and the 'repudiation of war' expressed in the post-1945 constitutions of countries like Germany and Italy reveal the reluctance of the member states of the EU to engage in military actions – not only in distant theatres, but even in Europe's backyard. When the Yugoslav crisis broke out in June 1991, Jacques Poos, then foreign minister of Luxembourg and president of the European Council for the first six months of that year, declared: 'This is the hour of Europe, not the hour of the Americans' (cited in Gordon and Shapiro 2004: 33).

Unfortunately, the EU proved unable to enforce stability and peaceful coexistence among the peoples of the former federation, and had to appeal to the US for help. The civil war in Bosnia was ended by the intervention of the American superpower, which then mediated and guaranteed the Dayton Agreement of November 1995 between Serbs, Croatians, and Moslems. Four years later, this time in Kosovo, the EU again displayed its inability to ensure peace and respect for basic human rights even in areas of clear European interest (Majone 2009: 87–90).

To conclude, a most important, if unintended, consequence of monetary union has been the injection of a good dose of realism in the discourse about European integration. The implications of this change are vast. On the one hand, a culture of total optimism cannot survive once the benefits and costs of European integration are assessed more realistically; on the other hand, this new realism means that it is no longer possible to de-politicize the integration process. The times are past when integrationist leaders managed to keep European issues out of the political debate. The immediate consequence of this process of politicization is that political entrepreneurs now have the opportunity of differentiating themselves from more traditional parties in terms of European issues, so that bargains struck in Brussels may now be contested at the national level. From Stockholm to Prague, from Berlin to Rome, the trend is becoming too visible to be ignored or dismissed as irrelevant for the future of European integration.

Exit scenarios

Until recently, European leaders refused to admit the possibility that a member state could wish to withdraw from the Community or the Union. The Treaty of Rome was silent on the issue of secession, but most commentators agreed that unilateral withdrawal would have been illegal under European law. The silence of the Rome Treaty, and of all subsequent treaties up to the latest amendments, is understandable from a federalist perspective. Indeed, the inadmissibility of secession is generally considered a distinguishing feature of the federal model – the American Civil War was fought to prevent the withdrawal of the Southern states from the federation. On the other hand, secession is a fully acknowledged right of every member of a confederation, since the confederate Pact is a formal contract among sovereign states. Hence the significance of the new Article 50 TEU, according to which 'Any Member State may decide to withdraw from the European Union in accordance with its own constitutional requirements.' The procedure to be followed is spelled out in the second paragraph, while the last paragraph foresees the possibility that a state which has withdrawn from the Union may later ask to rejoin. Surprisingly, Article 50 TEU and the related Article 218 (3) of the Treaty on the Functioning of the European Union (TFEU), which effectively sanction the transition from a federal to a confederal model for the EU, have attracted few political or even scholarly comments. Nevertheless this important precedent suggests that it is time to also consider the problem of withdrawal from monetary union.

The euro was supposed to be the visible symbol of the irresistible advance towards a politically united Europe. Actually, EMU has split the EU into several different camps – perhaps permanently. Instead of the Commission's slogan 'One Market, One Money' we now have a Union divided into two main groups: the present and future members of the euro zone, and the *de jure* (UK, Denmark) or *de facto* (Sweden) opt-outs. But a third group may emerge in the not too distant future. In 2006 Kenneth Rogoff, professor at Harvard and former chief economist at the IMF, predicted that in the future the EU may be split into three camps with the addition of the future drop-outs of the euro zone – countries with a large public debt, which in the next five to ten years may have to give up the euro. Interviewed by the German magazine *Der* Spiegel, Rogoff argued that Portugal and Italy, and possibly other countries as well, may be forced to abandon the common currency because rigorous implementation of the Maastricht parameters could entail social and economic costs too high for their voters to accept (Mueller 2006). Other experts advanced the hypothesis that countries with sound public finances could also find out that in a greatly enlarged euro zone the economic benefits of a common currency no longer compensate the costs of a one-size-fits-all monetary policy, and thus decide to leave the euro zone.

Since the Greek debt crisis economists have started to examine the costs and benefits of withdrawal. The argument of supporters of the exit option goes something like this: Greece and other countries of the Southern periphery of the EU have lost competitiveness since the introduction of the euro, hence it will be very difficult for them to repay their debts. If they remain in the euro zone they will weaken the common currency, eventually leading to the formation of two groups: a bloc of Northern countries favouring a strong currency, and a Southern rim of countries preferring a weak currency. The net result would be a weaker common currency and a severe loss of credibility for the entire monetary union. If instead the weak-currency countries decide to go back to the national currency, or to form a new bloc of structurally fairly similar economies, they can devaluate their currency in order to again become competitive, and reduce the weight of their public debt by restructuring it. Even a German expert who pleads that '[t]he euro-zone should be given another chance', acknowledges that if Greece and other Southern European countries decide to remain in the euro zone they will have to improve their competitiveness. But this is only possible if the wages in these countries grow less than German wages. However, wages in Germany have hardly grown in real terms for quite some time. Hence the attempt to recover competitiveness by doing better than Germany would lead to sinking nominal wages in the Southern countries, and to deflationary developments in the entire euro zone. The only way to avoid deflation would be for German wages to grow much more than in the recent past. Professor Bofinger concludes that '[t]he euro-zone has a future only if nominal wages in Germany grow for several years at the rate of about 3 per cent' (Bofinger 2010: 40, my translation). Given the dependence of the German economy on exports, however, this scenario seems unrealistic.

Recently, the Hungarian-born American financier George Soros has also entered the debate on the future of monetary union and of the EU itself. In an essay published in September 2012, he argued that in order to avoid a definitive split of the euro zone into creditor and debt countries, and thus a possible collapse of the EU itself, Germany must resolve a basic dilemma: either assume the role of the 'benevolent hegemon' or else leave the euro zone. If Germany were to choose the second alternative the euro would depreciate, and since all debts are denominated in the common currency, their weight, for the countries remaining in the euro zone, would be reduced in real terms. The debtor countries would export more because of the reduced (real) price of their products, while importing less; hence their competitiveness would be restored. Creditor countries, on the other hand, would suffer losses on their investments in the euro zone and also on the credits accumulated within the euro-clearing system. The end result, according to Soros, would be the fulfilment of Keynes' dream of an international monetary system in which both creditors and debtors share responsibility for the stability of the system. At the same time Europe would escape a threatening economic depression. However, Germany could achieve the same result at lower cost if it was willing to play the role of the benevolent hegemon. Such a role would entail two conditions: first, debtor and creditor countries should be able to refinance their debts on near equal terms; and, second, a nominal growth rate of up to five per cent should be aimed at. Through growth, Europe could reduce the burden of its debts, but the level of inflation would probably exceed what the Bundesbank is prepared to accept. At any rate, both conditions could be satisfied only with significant progress on the road to a politically integrated EU in which Germany accepts the responsibilities implied by its role as the leader – a role which Germany continues to reject, see chapter 8.

Soros concludes that if the members of the euro zone cannot live together except by pushing the Union into a long-lasting depression, then a consensual separation of debtor and creditor countries seems preferable. Were a debtor country to leave the euro zone, this could improve somewhat its competitiveness but the country could no longer service its euro-denominated debt, with incalculable consequences for the financial markets, especially in the case of large countries like Spain or Italy. If instead Germany were to give up the common currency, leaving the euro zone in the hands of the debtor countries, all problems that now appear to be insoluble, could be resolved through depreciation, improved competitiveness, and a new status of the ECB as lender of last resort. The common market would survive, but the relative position of Germany and of other creditor countries that might wish to leave the euro zone would change from the winning to the losing side. They would be exposed to strong competition from the euro zone, and would suffer significant losses from their euro-denominated assets and their credits under the so-called Target payment system, which connects the existing payment systems of the members of the euro zone. After the initial shock, however, Europe would manage to get out of the present debt trap (Soros 2012).

Thus according to most experts, but contrary to the brinkmanship tactics of the German chancellor with her repeated warnings that the future of the EU depends on the future of EMU, a return to the D-Mark would not necessarily mean a complete collapse of monetary union. German economists favouring the formation of two, internally more homogeneous, monetary clubs point out that under the present arrangements bad debt threatens both weak and strong economies, and also call attention to the decreasing share of German exports going to other countries of the euro zone: from 46.5 per cent in 1995 to 42.6 in 2008, with a continuing downwards trend. Together with other recent evidence – such as the June 2009 ruling of the German Constitutional Court on the Lisbon Treaty (which informed observers have interpreted as threatening future steps towards closer European integration) these data tend to support the impression of a growing disengagement of Germany from the European project, see again chapter 8.

Most opinion polls indicate that today the large majority of German voters, and a rapidly growing percentage of public opinion in other countries, agree with the idea that monetary union was not such a good idea, after all. Instead of counteracting such spreading scepticism with concrete evidence about the *net* benefits of monetary union, EU leaders prefer to follow the defensive tactic of all fait accompli strategists: emphasize the cost of change. They also try to convince the markets and the public at large that the structural flaws revealed by the crisis can be corrected by a rigid application of the new Stability Treaty. The markets do not seem to believe that the illness can be cured by increasing the dose of a medicine which proved to be ineffective in the past; while voters everywhere fear that a strict disciplinary approach to monetary union will aggravate an already serious economic recession.

If a lesson can already be drawn from the crisis of the euro zone it is that EU leaders must abjure, once and for all, fait accompli as a strategy for speeding up the integration process. What these leaders face today are fundamental questions about the nature and limits of European integration. Open-ended commitments such as striving for 'ever closer union among the peoples of Europe' will no longer do. This and other similarly hazy goals have provided for some time an ideological justification for the continuous expansion of European competences. But as Edward Carr noted long ago: 'The conception of politics as an infinite process seems in the long run uncongenial or incomprehensible to the human mind' (Carr 1964: 89). Just as the development of a true European political identity has been made practically impossible by the absence of well-defined and stable geographical boundaries (Majone 2009), so the absence of a finite political goal has impeded the development of a long-term strategy capable of bringing commitments and available resources into balance.

3

Integration and its modes

From shallow to deep integration

The significance of the distinction between 'shallow' and 'deep' modes of economic integration has been increasingly recognized since the 1990s (see in particular Kahler 1995). As we saw in the Introduction to the present volume, shallow integration, at the global or regional level, is economic integration based on the removal of barriers to exchange at the border, with limited coordination of national policies. Under a regime of shallow integration domestic policies are regarded as matters to be determined by the preferences of the nation's citizens and its political institutions. Such a mode of economic integration imposes minimal constraints on domestic policymaking. Thus, the Bretton Woods regime of the post-war era permitted national policymakers to focus on domestic problems while enabling global trade to recover from the war, and indeed to flourish during the 1950s and 1960s. Governments were left free to run their own independent economic policies and to erect their preferred versions of the welfare state. The General Agreement on Tariffs and Trade (GATT) and the IMF were core global institutions in the management of shallow integration. While the GATT negotiations were responsible for sharp reductions in at-the-border restrictions on trade in goods and services, the problems of using the GATT to govern the increasingly complex world trading system were becoming more and more obvious by the 1980s.

As economic integration advanced it became clear that domestic, 'behind-the-border' policies that had not been previously subjected to international scrutiny, could pose serious impediments to trade. Thus issues of deep integration emerged on the international agenda. Instead of the older agenda of removing barriers that block exchange at national borders, these new agenda items included conflict over domestic regulatory regimes and perceived policy spillovers, as well as concerns over environmental externalities and risk management. In short, the transition to deep integration seemed to require analysis of the economic, political, and scientific aspects of virtually all domestic policies, regulations, and practices. As a consequence the distinction between domestic policy and international trade policy tends to disappear under deep integration since any discretionary use of domestic regulations can be construed as posing an impediment to – and transaction costs on – international trade: 'Global rules, in effect, become the domestic rules' (Rodrik 2011: 83).

Reflecting these changes in the global agenda, the World Trade Organization (WTO), which came into being on 1 January 1995, has a much wider remit than the GATT. This includes the old GATT (now called the GATT 1994, to take account of the changes agreed to in the Uruguay Round); the new General Agreement on Trade in Services; the Trade-Related Aspects of Intellectual Property Rights and Trade-Related Investment Measures; several plurilateral agreements on such matters as government procurement and civil aviation; and, most important, the Dispute Settlement Understanding (DSU). The DSU combines a quasi-judicial procedure for settling disputes with an innovative safety valve: the new Appellate Body to which a losing party can appeal. A decision of the Appellate Body can be overturned, but only by unanimity in the General Affairs Council. The desire to gain access to the effective enforcement mechanism provided by the DSU is the main reason why the WTO mandate was expanded to include the protection of intellectual property despite the existence of the World Intellectual Property Organization. The same attraction of the new enforcement mechanism was also the main motivation behind proposals to expand the mandate to include the protection of core labour standards, despite the existence of the International Labour Organization.

A good example of the effectiveness of the new system is the *Beef Hormones* case, which has involved the EU and WTO in a long dispute concerning the appropriate use of the Precautionary Principle (PP) in risk regulation (Majone 2005: 125–31). The EU's commitment to, and application of, the PP has been repeatedly criticized by the WTO, the US, and by many other developed and developing countries. What international organizations and third countries fear is that something as poorly defined as the PP may be too easily misused for protectionist purposes. Such fears are fed by episodes like the controversy over the use of growth hormones in cattle raising. The EU hormones regime stems from the European Directive 81/602, as amended by Directive 85/358. The 1985 Directive prohibited the use of hormones in livestock farming. Even then the prohibition was controversial. The UK brought suit against the Directive, arguing *inter alia* that in enacting the Directive the Council should have taken into consideration a report by the Commission's scientific experts, according to which growth hormones used following good veterinary practice would result in no significant harm.

In 1997 the US and Canada filed complaints with the WTO against the European ban of meat products containing growth hormones, submitting that this measure violated the Sanitary and Phytosanitary (SPS) Agreement. This agreement allows WTO members to adopt health standards that are stricter than international standards, provided the stricter standards are supported by a formal risk assessment. Unfortunately, the risk assessment conducted by the Community's scientific experts had not established any significant health risk. Hence the Commission was forced to meet the WTO challenge with arguments similar to those used in rejecting the UK's complaint against Directive 85/358. In particular, the Commission pointed to various incidents since the early 1980s, when hormones that entered the European food market had allegedly made European consumers wary of beef. It concluded that a ban of beef containing growth hormones was necessary to restore consumer confidence.

The WTO's Dispute Resolution Panel decided against the EC. The Panel raised three objections: first, more permissive international standards existed for five of the hormones; second, the EC measure was not based on a risk assessment, as required by Article 5(1) of the SPS Agreement; finally, the EC policy was not consistent, hence in violation of the no-discrimination requirement of Article 5(5). The Appellate Body agreed with the panel that the EC had failed to base its measure on a risk assessment and decided against the EC essentially for two reasons: because the scientific evidence of harm produced by the Commission was not 'sufficiently specific to the case at hand'; and, second, because 'theoretical uncertainty' arising because 'science can never provide absolute certainty that a given substance will never have adverse health effects' is not the kind of risk to be assessed under Article 5(1) of the SPS Agreement. The objections raised by these WTO bodies were a severe blow to the reputation of the EU system of risk regulation. The Commission tried to explain the European position with its *Communication on the Precautionary Principle* of 2 February 2000, but the experts were hardly convinced by the arguments, and the attempt to promote the PP as 'a general principle of international economic and environmental law' (Commission 2000: 3) largely failed.

Deepening integration

Formally, economic integration in Europe has always been of the 'deep' variety. In reality the Rome Treaty envisaged something closer to shallow integration, even as far as the free movement of goods was concerned, see the Introduction. What is significant in the European case, therefore, is less the formal commitment to deep integration than the steady process of deepening, and especially the interaction with two other processes: widening and enlargement. Today's EU is largely the result of these three processes: *deepening*, in the sense of institution building and of increasing penetration of supranational policies and regulations into the domestic arena; *widening*, in the sense of increasing the scope of the EU's competences; and the *enlargement* of membership. For a long time it was tacitly assumed that these processes were mutually compatible; according to some over-optimistic European leaders, the processes were even mutually reinforcing. Unfortunately, deepening, widening, and enlargement, far from being compatible, let alone mutually reinforcing processes, provide a good example of what in chapter 10 will be called an 'impossible trinity', or trilemma: meaning that we cannot have deepening integration, continuing enlargement, and expanding competences at the same time. Enlargement entails increasing socioeconomic heterogeneity of the member states and consequent welfare losses caused by common, one-size-fits-all European policies, making deepening increasingly difficult. In particular, the greater heterogeneity induced by enlargement increases the difficulty of harmonizing the services sector; a sector still largely regulated at the national level despite its steadily growing economic importance. Other, more political factors limit the extent to which deep integration may be pushed. In the absence of radical institutional reforms, moreover, an expanding membership further complicates already cumbersome policymaking processes, making the expansion of European competences increasingly problematic (Piris 2011).

The significance of the transition from shallow to deep integration is best seen, not at the European or regional level, but at the global level – by comparing the GATT and the WTO rules and enforcement mechanisms. As the process of deepening advances, however, similar concerns arise both at the regional and at the global level. 'What happens when different nations desire or need different rules? Can *any* model of deep integration prove sustainable when democratic politics remains organized along national lines?' (Rodrik 2011: 83). Today such questions are as significant in the case of the EU as at the global level – the level with which Rodrik is primarily concerned. In fact, it could be argued that they are even more urgent at the European level since deep integration has advanced so much more in the EU than in the rest of the world. It follows that European monetary union is a good metaphor, not only for the integration of the Old Continent, as suggested in chapter 1, but to some extent even for the larger globalization process. In the following chapters we shall come back again and again to the two questions raised by Dani Rodrik. Before considering these and related issues in more detail in the next and in later chapters, however, we must complete our discussion of various modes of integration. In the European context, 'deepening' is closely linked to a preference for 'positive' over 'negative' integration, as discussed in the following section.

Positive and negative integration

In one of the first contributions to the theory of regional economic integration, Béla Balassa (1961) distinguished five stages of the integration process: *Free Trade Area*, when tariffs and quotas are abolished for imports from members of the area; *Customs Union*, entailing the suppression of discrimination for member states in product markets; *Common Market*, meaning a customs union plus free movement of the factors of production; *Economic Union*: a common market with some degree of harmonization of national economic policies; *Total Economic Integration*, characterized by the unification of monetary, fiscal, social, and countercyclical policies, and the establishment of a supranational authority enabled to take decisions that are binding for the member states. Concerning this scheme, it has been pointed out that although the five stages are presented sequentially, there is no compelling reason to assume that the order of the sequence would be rigidly followed in practice. The sequence also exhibits a sharp discontinuity in that while *negative* integration – prohibiting tariffs, quotas and other forms of economic discrimination – characterizes the first three stages, *positive* integration, in the form of harmonization or even unification of national policies, suddenly appears at the stage of economic union. However, some policy harmonization usually takes place already at the stage of a free trade area as, for example, in the case of NAFTA. Again, the experience of the EEC suggests that a common market may require fairly extensive reliance on policy harmonization and other measures of positive integration, such as re-regulation at the supranational level. In fact, the temptation to impose uniformity has always been so strong that national rules and policies have been harmonized even when a satisfactory level of economic integration could be achieved by other means, such as better cooperation among national regulators, or ex post harmonization induced by regulatory competition among the member states (Majone 2009).

Balassa's hierarchical arrangement of the stages of integration has contributed to the diffusion of the mistaken idea that positive integration is intrinsically superior to negative integration. In fact, the Treaty of Rome did not attach any normative connotation to this distinction. The common market was to be achieved by both methods, but in fact by greater reliance on negative law – witness the significance of such requirements as Articles 12–17 (elimination of customs duties); 30–37 (elimination of quantitative restrictions to intra-Community trade); 48–73 (free movement of persons, services, and capital); and 85–94 (rules against distortion of competition). More recently, however, positive integration has often been identified with positive values like social protection and the correction of market failures; negative integration, with deregulation and the narrow interests of traders. In reality, economic and other special interests often find it convenient to support measures of positive integration, while fundamental rights and the diffuse interests of consumers are generally better protected by measures of negative integration: the most dramatic results in the fight against discrimination on grounds of gender have been achieved by Article 119 of the Rome Treaty in its original, 'negative', formulation, see the following section.

To see how positive integration can be used to favour special interests, consider the perverse redistributive effects of what, in terms of funding, is still the largest programme of positive integration: the quasi-federal CAP. Already in 1992 the European Commission reported that the richest 20 per cent of European landowners and agribusiness companies received 80 per cent of EU farm aid, and it seems that the situation has not changed significantly since then. Until recently, moreover, the recipients of EU agricultural subsidies remained mostly undisclosed. In 2005, for example, the Dutch minister of agriculture was called before the country's Parliament to answer questions about payouts to his own farms. Knowing that his subsidies would soon be made public, the minister disclosed that his farms in the Netherlands and in France received at least 185,000 euros in 2004. What is even more shocking, among the largest receivers of CAP subsidies are some of the most prestigious aristocratic families of Britain, as well as the present owners of the large collective farms privatized after the fall of East Germany's communist regime. According to a study by professor Richard Baldwin of the Graduate Institute of International Studies in Geneva (reported by the *International Herald Tribune* (Castle 2007) in the 2003–2004 farming year, the Queen of England and Prince Charles received 360,000 euros in EU farm subsidies, the Duke of Westminster 260,000 euros, and the Duke of Marlborough 300,000 euros. Incidentally, the capture by powerful national interests of what was supposed to be the core of a 'welfare state for farmers' exemplifies the kind of problems that a European welfare state – advocated by some to correct the alleged neo-liberal bias of the EU – would have to face.

In this connection it is worthwhile to recall that the Treaty of Rome rejected the view, fairly common even in the 1950s, that differences in social conditions between the member states can represent a form of 'unfair' competition, so that positive integration (harmonization) is needed in order to prevent 'social dumping' or a 'race to the bottom'. The Treaty nowhere prescribed that social policies be harmonized prior to, or even concurrently with, trade liberalization within the common market. Rather, it maintained, in line with the conclusions of the 1956 Spaak Report, that harmonization should in general be regarded as a corollary of, rather than a requirement for, market integration. This sequence – free trade first, followed by a more or less spontaneous harmonization of social standards – was generally accepted by European policymakers until the mid-1970s. After a decade of hesitation, a clear shift in the direction of ex ante harmonization occurred in the mid-1980s. Several factors contributed to this shift: the enlargement of the Community, creating large differences in labour costs between member states; high unemployment and stagnating real wages; and, not least, the social activism of the Delors Commission (Sapir 1996: 550–7).

Many, perhaps most, measures of positive integration in the areas of health, safety, and environmental regulation, have been justified by the argument that without EU-level harmonization member states would engage in a socially undesirable 'race to the bottom' in order to attract foreign investments. It has been shown, however, that race-to-the-bottom arguments are seriously flawed. At the end of such a race, two states starting with equally high environmental standards, say, would have adopted sub-optimally lax standards, but have about the same level of industrial activity as before engaging in the race; in equilibrium the two states will not experience any inflow or outflow of industry. Such arguments are also incomplete because they fail to consider that there are more direct means of attracting foreign direct investments. The advocates of harmonization implicitly assume that states compete over only one variable, such as environmental quality. Given the assumption of a 'race', however, it is more reasonable to suppose that if harmonization prevents competition over environmental standards, states would try to compete over other variables, such as worker safety, minimum wages, or taxation of corporate profits. To avoid these alternative races, the central regulators would have to harmonize all national rules, so as to eliminate the possibility of any form of inter-state competition altogether. This would amount to eliminating any trace of national autonomy, so that race-to-the-bottom arguments are, in the end, arguments against subsidiarity (Revesz 1992).

The positive side of negative integration

While the actual impact of positive integration has been generally over-rated, the role of negative integration in advancing and legitimating the process of European integration may not have been sufficiently appreciated (Majone 2005: 155–9). Negative integration ('negative law') is not only about removing national restrictions to the free movement of the factors of production. It is also about limiting monopoly power and market dominance, protecting the diffuse interests of consumers, and about fighting discrimination on grounds of gender, nationality, age, and other factors. The best-known example of negative law in the area of individual rights is the already mentioned Article 119 of the Treaty of Rome, which requires application of the principle of equal pay, for male and female workers, for equal work or work of equal value. The Article itself conferred no positive regulatory power until it was amended by the Treaty of Amsterdam. The new paragraph (3) inserted by that Treaty extends the scope of the Article to positive measures ensuring equality of opportunity and is thus not restricted to measures simply outlawing discrimination. So far, however, the most dramatic results have been achieved by Article 119 in its original, 'negative', formulation.

In the *Second Defrenne* case (*Defrenne v. Sabena*, Case 43/75) the ECJ held that the Article is directly enforceable and grants rights to an individual if remedies do not exist under national law. It decided that the policy of the Belgian airline Sabena – forcing stewardesses to change job within the company (at a loss in wages) at the age of forty, but imposing no such requirement on cabin stewards doing the same work – was discriminatory, and required Sabena to compensate Ms Defrenne's loss of income. In the *Bilka* case of 1986 (*Bilka-Kaufhaus v. Karin Weber von Hartz* (Case 170/84) [1986] ECR 1607), the Court indicated its willingness, absent a clear justification, to strike down national measures excluding women from any employer-provided benefits, such as pensions. In a later case, the ECJ held that all elements of pay are due to all employees in a particular activity, without regard to the hours worked. At that time, in Germany employees who worked less than ten hours a week for a commercial cleaning company did not receive statutory sick pay. Mostly women were affected by this regulation. The Court saw the regulation as an indirect discrimination against women, hence as a violation of Article 119. Since the discriminatory impact on women of the hours requirement lacked an objective justification – or at least, one was not provided by the German government – the claimant won her case.

The *Barber* case (*Barber v. GRE* (Case C-262/88) [1990] ECR I-1889), in which the Court extended the meaning of Article 119 to cover age thresholds for pension eligibility, demonstrates the symmetric effect of this norm. Mr Barber, having been made redundant at age 52, was denied a pension that would have been available immediately to female employees. Instead, he received a lump-sum payment. The Court held that this treatment was illegal since pensions are pay and hence within the scope of Article 119. The decision, which required massive restructuring of pension schemes, caused a 'Barber Protocol' to be included in the Maastricht Treaty, to the effect that *Barber* was not to be applied retroactively. Nonetheless, the implications for future pension plans were considerable (Ostner and Lewis 1995). These and other rulings of the ECJ show the impact negative law can have on national legislation and legal practice by outlawing direct and indirect discrimination both in individual and in collective agreements. It is instructive to compare this direct impact, with the uncertain, and often sub-optimal, outcomes of many measures of positive integration.

While the actual results of positive integration are often uncertain, in part because of their dependence on implementation by national bureaucracies with their idiosyncratic methods and different levels of efficiency, the results of negative integration are clear-cut, and generally implemented – albeit reluctantly – by the affected member states. The strength of negative integration was demonstrated once more by the ECJ's decision of October 2007 against the German law protecting

Volkswagen (VW) from hostile takeovers (*EC v. Germany* (Case C-318/ 05) [2007] ECR I-6957), and making possible higher wages and shorter working hours for workers lucky enough to be employed by VW rather than by other car companies. The Court's decision was an impressive demonstration of the power of negative law, and a significant victory for the Commission which, in an effort to get rid of the law, had taken the German government to court in October 2004. This victory followed the decision by Microsoft to surrender in its nine-year battle with the Commission over its dominance of the software market. Microsoft agreed to apply the decision globally, thus acknowledging that the Commission's reach as a competition regulator extends beyond Europe. Comparing these successes with the failures, or limited success, of so many measures of positive integration (for instance, in the area of environmental policy, see Majone 2005: 117–24), we can see that negative integration still works – not always but at least in a number of important cases.

Integration through the judiciary

The key role played by the ECJ (now CJEU) in the integration process is generally acknowledged by both Euro-sceptics and Euro-philes. The judicial doctrine of the supremacy of European law; the inviolability of the existing body of rules and legislation mandated by the EU (the so-called *acquis communautaire*); the disciplinary-legalistic approach to monetary union exemplified by the SGP – are eloquent testimony of the crucial importance of supranational law and legal institutions in the European model of regional integration. In this model, law tends to be used as an ersatz for both political economy and democratic politics. Since the very beginnings of the integration process, European institutions, and particularly the ECJ, have done all they can to differentiate the EEC from other international or regional organizations, emphasizing instead its proto-federal features. This emphasis corresponded to the aspirations of at least some of the founding fathers, who intended the EEC to be only a first step towards a full political union – the United States of Europe. Distinguished legal scholars have claimed that the judicial doctrines of supremacy and direct effect of EU law (see below) have established a pattern that would usually be recognized as a federal system of law. It is, however, important to appreciate that the federal analogy applies, if at all, only to the legal system of the EU, in particular to the judiciary; it definitely does not apply to the area of politics and policy, including such vital matters as legislative and executive powers, taxation, and foreign and defence policy. The economic and monetary union introduced by the Treaty on European Union (Maastricht Treaty) was supposed to be the decisive step towards political union, thus closing the chasm between the legal and the political spheres. In fact, the EU has never been so divided as since the introduction of the common currency. On the other hand, the sovereign-debt crisis of the euro zone – in particular the failure of the SGP, which was supposed to obviate the lack of a centralized budget – has revealed the risks of attempting to pursue monetary union before having reached any agreement on political union. Even in the field of regulatory policy, the early hopes of a 'federal pre-emption' of national rules and standards through total harmonization had to be scaled down to what could be achieved in an expanding and increasingly heterogeneous association of states, see chapter 4.

Instead of using the politically controversial term 'federalism', when applied to the EC/EU, many authors prefer to speak of 'supranationalism' as the feature distinguishing the European model from other regional organizations. The notion of supranationalism includes such features as the independence of an organization and its institutions from the member states; its ability to bind the member states by a majority or weighted-majority vote; and the direct binding effect of laws emanating from the organization on natural and legal persons. However, the deep cleavage between the legal and the political-economic evaluation of the progress of European integration persists also in terms of supranationalism, as a number of knowledgeable commentators have noted. More than thirty years ago Joseph Weiler affirmed the clear superiority of legal ('normative') supranationalism over political-economic ('decisional') supranationalism in the case of the EC (Weiler 1981). The superiority of legal supranationalism in the EC/EU largely rests on two principles not even mentioned in the founding treaties, having been announced by the ECJ in the 1960s: the direct effect (self-execution) and supremacy of European law. According to the doctrine of direct effect – introduced by the ECJ in 1963 and developed subsequently – Community legal norms that are clear, precise, and that do not require further legislative measures by the authorities of the Community or the member states, must be regarded as the law of the land in the sphere of application of European law. Direct effect applies to all actions producing legal effects in the EU, but its full impact is realized in combination with the doctrine of supremacy. In a series of cases starting in 1964 the ECJ has formulated the doctrine that in the sphere of application of Community law, *any* Community law trumps conflicting national law whether enacted before or after the Community norm. Supremacy is absolute: 'even the most minor piece of technical Community legislation ranks above the most cherished [national] constitutional norm' (Weatherill 1995: 106). Additionally, although this has never been stated explicitly or generally accepted by the member states, the ECJ claims to be the body that determines which norms come within the sphere of application of Community law.

The practical implications of this claim are even more far reaching than may be suggested by the terminology used. As Weiler (1999: 21) pointed out, the principle of supremacy could be expressed in a less uncompromising version than the one chosen by the ECJ: namely, that each law (Community or national) is supreme within its own sphere of competence. The Court's inflexible understanding of the principle renders crucial the question of defining the sphere of competence, and in particular the institutional question of which court will have the final decision as to the definition of spheres – i.e., what German jurists call the *Kompetenz-Kompetenz* question. In other words, who ultimately gets to police the jurisdictional boundaries between the national and European polities? The German, Danish, and other highest courts have asserted that they have the residual authority to determine whether EU legislative acts are enacted *ultra vires*. These courts do not contest the authority of the ECJ to review the legality of EU legislative acts, which includes the review of whether the acts are within the competences of the Union. But, the national courts point out that the ECJ is itself an EU institution that can act *ultra vires* when it attempts to amend a European treaty under the guise of interpreting it. If the European Court then endorses EU legislative acts based on such interpretation, the national courts have a constitutional duty to step in and render such laws inapplicable in their respective jurisdictions (Kumm 2005: 264).

Even in 'monist' countries – where international treaties upon ratification are transposed automatically into the national legal order, and may even be recognized as having direct effect – the national legislature, if it dislikes an internalized treaty norm, can simply enact a conflicting national measure, thus eliminating all the practical effects of the treaty norm. Because of the principle of supremacy this remedy is not available to the legislatures of the member states of the EU. Hence this principle brings the key difference between international law and EU law into sharp relief, explaining why direct effect and supremacy have been hailed as core elements of the 'constitutionalization' of European law. The paradoxical aspect of this perspective is the implication that constitutional rules may be imposed, by judicial fiat, on persons who did not participate, through their representatives, in the making of those rules. The paradox arises because '*all* binding acts of Community law are endowed with supremacy, whether or not the European Parliament played a role in their adoption. Supremacy even extends to acts adopted by the Commission, which certainly is executive law-making *par excellence*' (De Witte 1999: 208; emphases in the original).

The paradox is made even more pungent by the genesis of the doctrines of direct effect and supremacy, on which the status of the ECJ as the real 'motor of integration' – rather than the Commission – largely rests. As recent research has shown (Vauchez 2010), these doctrines were not the inescapable logical consequence of two 'landmark' decisions (the 1963 *Van Gend en Loos* case (*Van Gend en Loos v. Nederlandse Administratie der Belastingen* (Case 26/62) [1963] ECR 1) and *Costa v. ENEL* (*Flaminio Costa v. ENEL* (Case 6/64) [1964] ECR 585) of the following year); nor did they burst full-grown from the collective mind of the Court. It is also the case that none of the three Community treaties – the 1951 Paris Treaty establishing the Coal and Steel Community and the two Rome Treaties establishing Euratom and the EEC – mentioned the principles of direct effect and supremacy; while legal commentators by and large ignored the issue. In fact, the two principles are the result of the efforts of a fairly small group of legal experts: some ECJ judges and Advocates General; the head of the Legal Service of the European Commission – an institution notoriously devoted to the cause of widening and deepening the integration process; academic specialists in EC law who wished to differentiate their emerging sub-discipline from the more traditional areas of comparative and international law; and, not least, a small but influential group of 'gentlemen-politicians of law' – notables from legal professions playing on both sides of the political/legal fence. While alerting a variety of audiences – lawyers, academic circles, the press – these activists turned the ambiguous *Van Gend en Loos* decision, which did not express any opinion on the question of supremacy of EC law, into a clear-cut and far-reaching judicial fiat, with the supremacy of European law as its 'logical consequence'. As Vauchez (2010: 14) writes:

> On the whole, it all occurred as if a kind of second judicial deliberation had been initiated, one that would fabricate the overall reach of *Van Gend*

en Loos by extending in manifold ways the sense and the validity of its 'message', well above and beyond the relative prudent and balanced considerations of the (original) decision itself...The multifaceted activism of some of the jurists who had taken part in the case (hereafter referred to as ECJ paladins or ECJ promoters) was essential in securing an extensive interpretation of the Court's decision.

Through this interpretive activism, Vauchez continues, the case ceased to be the mere resolution of a dispute between a Dutch transportation company, Van Gend en Loos, and the Dutch tax authorities, nor just an interpretation of Article 12 of the Rome Treaty on customs duties. Rather, for the small band of legal activists the judgment came to represent a trail-blazing judgment founding EC law's relationship with European integration, and entailing the ECJ's future agenda (ibid.:15). Thus *Van Gend en Loos* and *Costa v. ENEL* were solidly linked together, to become the cornerstone of a far-reaching doctrine, with the ECJ leading the integration process, and the development of European law protected from direct political oversight. But why did the member states of the European Community accept these developments, which in no way corresponded to their idea of what market integration implied? The principle of the supremacy of European law can be legally effective only to the extent that national courts are willing to accept it, and the evidence shows that this acceptance is selective and generally based on the national courts' own constitutional terms. How did the ECJ overcome this potential obstacle? These are the questions to be discussed in the following section.

The member states and the ECJ: common agency and the loss of control

Direct effect and supremacy are two legs of the tripod on which the judicial redefinition of European integration rests. The third leg is provided by the preliminary ruling procedure spelled out in Article 177 of the Rome Treaty. This procedure enables, and in some cases requires, national courts to suspend their proceedings when a question of interpretation of Community law arises. The issues at stake are then referred to the ECJ, which considers them in the light of observations submitted by the parties to the national proceedings, by member states, and by Community institutions, especially the Commission. The judgment of the European Court is then referred back to the national court that submitted the question(s). Finally, the national court applies the ECJ ruling to the case which it must decide. Already in the early stages of the integration process the ECJ developed the key legal principles of EC law – including direct effect and supremacy – through its preliminary ruling judgments. Then, in a kind of boot-strap operation, direct effect and supremacy have been used to transform the preliminary ruling system from a mechanism primarily designed to allow individuals to challenge EC laws into a mechanism to challenge the compatibility of national law with European law. In this way a means was created for individuals to pull the ECJ into national policy debates, and for national courts to set aside laws and policies that violate European law. Because of references by national courts to the supranational court, national governments found their ability to keep national policy issues out of the EC legal arena considerably reduced (Alter 2001). As already mentioned, higher national courts tend to be reluctant to accept the doctrine of the supremacy of European law (see Gerards 2011 for additional evidence). In contrast, the relationship between the ECJ and lower national courts remains more cooperative than competitive. Most legal scholars agree that many lower national courts have used the relationship to enhance their own authority and independence, not just vis-à-vis higher courts in their country but also in relation to their national executives and legislatures.

In the late 1990s an extensive empirical study of the relations between the member states of the EU and the supranational institutions came to the conclusion that the jurisprudence of the ECJ did not reflect the position of even the most powerful member states. More generally, the authors interpreted the evidence as showing that national governments do not control the integration process in any real sense. The governments behave reactively rather than proactively: they act to ratify transfers of governing authority from the national to the supranational level, or to slow down the pace at which these transfers are made (Stone Sweet and Caporaso 1998). Such a generalized loss of control was somewhat overstated even then, but without doubt the ECJ did succeed, not only in establishing and defending its own independence, but also in subverting the original intentions of the member states as 'Masters of the Treaty'. Several factors have been mentioned as possible explanation of the success of the Court in expanding the EU legal system so far from the desire of the member states, and beyond their control. First, the transformation of the preliminary ruling procedure allowed the supranational court to enlist the national courts as powerful allies, thus raising the financial and political costs to the national governments of ignoring its decisions. A second factor is the different time horizons of courts and politicians: while the desire to be re-elected makes democratic politicians discount the long-term effects of their actions or inaction, the ECJ, as a non-majoritarian institution independent of the electoral cycle, was able to expand its authority by establishing legal principles but not applying the principles to the cases at hand. In this way, the Court was able to build doctrinal precedents without arousing political concerns about the broad, long-term implications of the precedents. (Alter 2001). A third explanatory factor is the phenomenon of 'common agency' (i.e., an agent with multiple principals) and the special significance of this phenomenon in the EU context. In spite of its importance, the problem of common agency – a particular aspect of the general principal–agent problem – has attracted little analytic attention among students of European integration. Because of this, more attention will be devoted to this particular explanation of the ability of the highest European court to escape member states' control.

The problem of common agency is also well known at the national level since it appears whenever the lines of authority are blurred. Even in separation-of-powers systems, such as the US, each branch of government wields some power over the other's agents, and other influences – such as courts, interest groups, or the media – can be quite significant. The fact that each government agency or bureaucracy is simultaneously answerable to multiple principals who are trying to influence its actions in different directions, has been emphasized in the more recent literature on bureaucracy (Wilson, 1989), and also in some of the more rigorous transaction-cost analyses of the principal–agent problem. From the point of view of transaction-cost economics, this problem boils down to the general question of how to motivate a person, or an organization, to act on behalf of another. The solution depends on the availability of suitable incentives, but also on the design of institutions to gather information, protect investments, allocate decision and property rights, and so on. Now in the case of common agency there are multiple principals, whose interests in the output of the agency are at least partly in conflict. The conflict may result from the fact that different principals value the agent's actions differently. Suppose that two principals, A and B, are trying to influence the agent, who controls two tasks, a and b. Principal A is primarily interested in the outcome of a, and principal B in that of b. Because of time and other constraints, more effort devoted to a by the agent necessarily means less spent on b, and vice versa. Therefore, principal A will be tempted to offer an incentive scheme that responds positively to a-output and negatively to b-output. Similarly, B offers a scheme that rewards the agent for producing more of b and penalizes him for producing more of a. How do incentive schemes work in such a situation? Dixit (1996: 98) has shown that in general the power of incentives in the equilibrium among several such principals is weakened, sometimes dramatically. The situation could be improved if all principals were to get together and offer the agent a combined incentive scheme, however such collusion is excluded by the assumption that the interests of the principals are in conflict. Hence the conclusion that '[t]he agent's actions may often be influenced better by prohibiting certain activities than by rewarding others with conventional marginal incentives' (ibid.: 100).

In case of the relationship between the member states and the ECJ, the principals – the member states as masters of the treaties – lack credible means to penalize the Court when it interprets existing EC laws in ways that they had not intended. One reason for the absence of credible threats is the general lack of consensus to attack the authority of the Court. Small member states have an interest in a strong EU legal system that can protect them from an excessive influence of the larger members. It is also the case that within the ECJ small member states have disproportionate voice since each judge has one vote and decisions are taken by simple majority. Again, the decisions of the supranational court usually affect different states differently, hence it is difficult to form a coalition large enough to make it possible to change the disputed legislation. Finally, reversing an ECJ decision based on the treaty would require a treaty amendment – a threshold that is even harder to reach since it requires unanimous agreement of the member states plus ratification of the changes by all the national parliaments and, increasingly, by popular referendums. Karen Alter (2001) rightly concluded that the difficulty of changing the Court's mandate given the requirement of unanimity and given the lack of political consensus implies that the ECJ's room for manoeuvre may be even greater than that of the US Supreme Court or other constitutional courts, at least in some respects.

As mentioned above, there are good theoretical reasons to suggest that the actions of a multi-principal agent can be influenced more effectively by prohibiting certain activities than by designing sophisticated schemes of positive and negative incentives. This is precisely the strategy followed by the member states since the 1990s. Recognizing that in established areas of EU competence political threats to alter the ECJ's role lack credibility, the national leaders came to the conclusion that what they could do was to exclude the Court from new areas. Thus the Maastricht Treaty excluded the ECJ from the Common Foreign and Security Policy (CFSP) and also from Justice and Home Affairs (JHA). The small member states were particularly unhappy about the exclusion of the Court from JHA, and in 1997 the Treaty of Amsterdam acknowledged the competence of the Court in some aspects of JHA, but only in a limited way. A similar strategy was adopted with respect to one of the key legal instruments available to the European Commission: the harmonization of national laws and regulations. Controlling the discretion of the Commission is in many respects even harder than in the case of the ECJ. This is because the Commission is not only a multi-principal but also a multi-task agent: it alone can make legislative and policy proposals; it also implements EU decisions, and acts as the guardian of the treaties. The multiplicity of tasks and principals make it extremely difficult not only to control the Commission, but also to enforce a good system of accountability, see chapter 6. Thus, when the member states began to realize that the Commission was pursuing harmonization not so much to resolve concrete economic or legal problems as to drive forward the general process of integration, they could do little more than try to prevent similar abuses in new areas.

The Treaty of Maastricht defined for the first time new European competences in a way that actually limits the exercise of EU powers. For example, Article 126 added a new legal basis for action in the field of education, but policy instruments were restricted to 'incentive measures' and to recommendations; harmonization of national laws was explicitly ruled out. Likewise, Article 129 created specific powers for the EU in the field of public health protection, but this competence was highly circumscribed as subsidiary to that of the member states. Harmonization was again ruled out, though the Article states that health-protection requirements shall form a constituent part of the other European policies. The other provisions of the Treaty – defining new competences in areas such as culture, consumer protection, and industrial policy – were similarly drafted. Unwilling to continue to rely on implicit powers, which seemed out of control, the framers of the Treaty opted for an explicit grant that delimits the mode and the reach of action (Weiler 1999). Such has been the approach followed thereafter by the Amsterdam, Nice, and Lisbon Treaties.

As will be discussed in more detail in the next chapter, European treaties, like all international treaties, are incomplete contracts. This means that the parties are unable to foresee accurately all the relevant contingencies that might be important to them in the course of the contract, and are also unable or unwilling to determine and agree upon a course of action for each possible contingency. Hence contingencies will arise that have not been accounted for because they were not foreseen, or were considered highly unlikely, at the time of contracting. The founding fathers of the EEC attempted to meet the problems of incomplete contracting by delegating to the Commission and the ECJ the task of filling the gaps in the Rome Treaty. However, subsequent experience showed that it had been unwise to assume the self-restraint of the supranational institutions. Unable to reform the existing body of legislation, rules, and general principles such as the direct effect and primacy of Community law, the national governments took the initiative in amending the treaties every few years, using the amendment process to define new competences in the way described above, namely by limiting the exercise of EU powers in new policy areas. Other approaches to regional economic integration, as embodied for example in NAFTA and in MERCOSUR, have avoided such problems, and their costly consequences, by deliberately minimizing the role of supranational institutions.

It may be argued that the flexible, decentralized systems of rule enforcement and dispute resolution are made possible by the small membership of NAFTA and of other regional organizations. A large supranational organization like the EU, with twenty-eight members at present and more to come in the not too distant future, on the other hand, needs a much more centralized system. But aside from the fact that the foundations of the present system were laid when the EC included only six countries, three of which were quite small, the evidence shows that a decentralized system can be reasonably effective even in the case of an international organization with a membership of well over one hundred countries, like the WTO. Trade disputes under the WTO are subject to a system of binding adjudication significantly influenced by the NAFTA model. As already mentioned, the present arrangement provides a unified dispute-settlement system for all parts of the GATT/WTO system; no longer do different subjects have different dispute-settlement procedures, as in the old GATT. A complaining government has a right to have a panel process initiated, while earlier practice was vulnerable to such blocking. Under the new appellate procedure (which requires a consensus to block a dispute rather than to approve one) it is practically impossible to block a panel report. The quid pro quo is an appellate process, with the possibility of an appeal to a panel of three experts drawn from a permanent roster of seven such experts (Jackson 1999: 124–7). These and other innovations are such that the new dispute-settlement process is a striking contrast to the early days of the GATT, when the 'working parties' set up to report on disputes between member states were really a forum for encouraging negotiation, not a third-party investigation for the purpose of coming to objective conclusions on the merits of the case. As Dani Rodrik (2011: 78) writes: 'Evading the trade regime's judicial verdict had been child's play under the GATT; now it became virtually impossible.'

The ECJ, the WTO, and the EU constitutional narrative

It seems reasonable to assume that as the EU institution with the largest stake in legal centralism, the ECJ would not be in favour of more flexible, decentralized systems for the settlement of disputes. The Court's attitude towards the WTO system confirms this assumption. Some distinguished international lawyers have seen parallels between the integration process in Europe and the development of the world trading system, and thus concluded that the ECJ should give direct effect to WTO law as it requires the EU member states to give direct effect to legal norms of the EU order. Over the years, however, the European Court has expressed strong reservations concerning the legitimacy of the WTO system. The main reason adduced by the Court is that, unlike the EU, the WTO has not yet developed into a constitutional order as shown by the important role that the principle of reciprocity plays in it. The WTO focuses on one single issue, the enhancement of global trade, while other policy concerns are only considered incoherently, as exception clauses in particular trade agreements. Moreover, since members of the dispute-settlement bodies (DSB) are, in general, experts in trade issues, the WTO jurisprudence is said to suffer from a bias as a consequence of which international trade issues are given priority vis-à-vis other policy concerns. From these alleged shortcomings of the WTO system the highest European Court concludes that DSB decisions lack the legitimacy to deserve an unconditional reception by the EU legal order. This denial of direct effect was explicitly asserted in the 2005 *Van Parys* judgment (Case C-377/02, [2005] ECR I-1465). The case refers to the banana import system established by the EC, which differentiates between bananas imported from the African, Caribbean, and Pacific (ACP) countries – mostly former European colonies associated through the

Yaounde, Lomé, and Cotonou Conventions – and those imported from non-ACP states.

The ACP conventions have been predicated on the concept of fostering development and thus have been based on granting EU market access rather than on reciprocity. In 1997 the WTO Appellate Body found that the provision concerning the importation of bananas from ACP countries was incompatible with the most-favoured-nation principle, according to which any concession made by one country to another must be immediately and unconditionally extended to like products originating from other members of WTO. In 1998 and 1999 Van Parys, the plaintiff, applied for import licences for bananas from Ecuador, but because of EC regulations was only granted a certain quota by the Belgian authorities. Van Parys took legal action against these decisions, claiming that they should not be based on the EC regulations since the latter were incompatible with WTO law. In its decision the ECJ referred to its established jurisprudence that WTO law has no direct effect in the EU legal order. The arguments used by the Court are infused with the philosophy of legal centralism. Thus the European judges pointed out that the WTO dispute-settlement system is not a fully developed judicial system since it accords considerable importance to negotiation between the parties, even after a DSB decision has been issued. If such decisions had direct effect, they argued, this would deprive the European institutions of considerable room for manoeuvre, preventing them from playing a significant role in the negotiation process. Moreover, some members of the WTO, notably the US, deny the direct effect of World Trade law within their domestic legal order. Since the WTO system is built on the principle of reciprocity this would again deprive the political organs of the EU – the Commission and the Council of Ministers – of room for manoeuvre. In other cases the Court had ruled that the terms of the WTO agreements themselves do not specify precisely what their own methods of enforcement are to be, given that compensation is permitted in certain circumstances as an alternative to direct enforcement, and that there is scope for negotiation over the recommendations of the DSB. In sum, the ECJ insisted that the WTO system, based as it is on the principle of mutually advantageous negotiations rather than on clearly and precisely binding legal commitments, is still legally underdeveloped, and certainly very far from being a constitutional order. The majority of academic commentators, however, find that the legal reasoning of the Court is less than convincing, while the political motivation is pretty clear: not to deprive the EU institutions of the room for negotiation afforded by the procedural provisions of the WTO system (Craig and De Búrca 2003: 193–201).

The argument that the WTO is not a fully-fledged constitutional order appears especially implausible when it is used for denying the direct effect of WTO law in the EU legal order. As the reader will recall from the previous section on integration by the judiciary, the doctrine of the direct effect of European law in the legal orders of the member states emerged in the early 1960s when the EC was actually little more than a customs union, certainly nothing like a fully developed constitutional system. Moreover, we now know that the principles of direct effect and supremacy are not the inescapable logical consequence of some 'landmark' decisions, but are the result of the efforts of a small band of legal experts and practitioners of law (Vauchez 2010). Thanks to their efforts, both direct effect and supremacy eventually came to be viewed as core elements of the 'constitutionalization' of European law, with the implication noted by Bruno De Witte (1999) that constitutional rules may be imposed by judicial fiat on persons who did not participate through their representatives in the making of those rules. In this way the ECJ and its allies pretended to erase a distinction that was already well understood in ancient Greece by the end of the sixth century BC, when *thesmos*, the law as set down by the law-giver, was replaced by *nomos*, the law as approved and enacted by the people itself, see chapter 6.

Ironically, the *Van Parys* decision happened to be announced in the same year in which the French and Dutch voters rejected the Treaty establishing a Constitution for Europe that included for the first time a clause explicitly confirming the primacy of EU law. The negative outcomes of the two referenda, it has been said, 'have cast a dim shadow over the very possibility of the EU achieving full constitutional status by political means' (Dani 2009: 325). In fact, the Presidency Conclusions of the European Council of June 2007 acknowledged that the constitutional concept had to be abandoned, and assured that the Reform (Lisbon) Treaty would not have a constitutional character. On this occasion, the Council proved to be realistic enough to realize the failure of the attempt to use constitutional language as a catalyst for the reforms necessary to the EU; and to appreciate that constitutional language had probably performed more in attracting criticism than mobilizing positive engagement by EU citizens (ibid.: 326). As the institution that has invested most in the possibility of the EU achieving full constitutional status – as understood by legal centralism, i.e., in the traditional terms of statehood – the ECJ is bound to be seriously affected by the present constitutional disenchantment. It is true that the time horizons of courts and politicians are significantly different – which fact, as has been pointed out, made it possible for the ECJ to expand its authority by establishing legal principles but not applying the principles to the case at hand. However, time may no longer work in favour of the Court because disenchantment is no longer limited to the claims of supranational constitutionalism or even to the role of the ECJ as the motor of European integration, but extends to other key aspects of the method of integration followed so far. The euphoria that accompanied the launching of the Constitutional Treaty signed in Rome in October 2004, but rejected by the voters the following year, is comparable to the euphoria of the integrationist elites when, on 1 January 2002, the euro was introduced among enthusiastic predictions of faster economic growth, and gains in prestige and political power produced by a currency able to rival the US dollar on world markets. Today we have good reasons to doubt that future historians will view legal and monetary centralism as milestones on the road to a united Europe.

Beyond legal centralism

'Integration through law' is a well-known characterization of the European approach to regional integration. However, 'legal centralism' seems to be a better description of what distinguishes the European from other models of regional integration such as NAFTA or MERCOSUR. The legal centralism which characterizes the traditional European approach and, in particular, the role of the ECJ as 'engine of integration', rather than as a true constitutional court, suggest a deficit of mutual trust among the member states of the EU. Among the causes of this deficit is the different level of commitment by countries that are traditionally considered to be 'Euro-sceptic', like Great Britain and Denmark, and those of more integrationist member states such as Germany, Italy, Spain, or Belgium. Even within the latter group, however, there is no agreement about how far integration should go, with the majority of countries favouring economic, rather than political, integration. Also the new member states from Central and Eastern Europe, while favouring economic integration, are determined not to surrender their recently recovered national sovereignty.

In its traditional version, legal centralism maintains that disputes require access to a forum external to the original social setting of the dispute, and that 'remedies will be provided as prescribed in some body of authoritative learning and dispensed by experts who operate under the auspices of the state' (Galanter 1981, cited in Williamson 1985: 20). The underlying assumption is that effective rules of law regarding disputes are in place and are applied by courts in an informed and low-cost way. More generally, legal centralism has a marked statist character: it takes the state as the central element of the legal and political world. In the context of European integration, legal centralism not only emphasizes the supremacy of European law, but also envisages the EU as a federal state in the making. At the policymaking level this perspective entails a strong bias in favour of total harmonization of national rules and regulations, see chapter 1.

A central tenet in Oliver Williamson's version of transaction-cost economics (to be discussed in chapter 4) is the greater efficiency of 'private ordering', that is, of bilateral and trilateral (arbitration) mechanisms for settling disputes between contractual partners. We know that all contracts, except for the simplest ones, are incomplete, and that incomplete contracting leads to problems of imperfect commitment – a strong temptation to renege on the original terms of the agreement because what should be done in case of an unforeseen contingency is left unstated or ambiguous, and hence open to different interpretations. The root difficulty is that the incentives of contractual partners in the implementation stage may no longer be the same as the incentives in the contract-writing stage. Legal centralism simply ignores the problems raised by contractual incompleteness, as well as the transaction costs that are incurred in tackling such problems. The greater efficiency of private ordering (compared to court ordering) in situations of incomplete contracting is the reason why most disputes between market actors, including many disputes that could be brought to a court, are resolved by more flexible means. In many instances contractual partners can devise more satisfactory solutions to their disputes, such as arbitration, than can judges constrained to apply general rules on the basis of limited knowledge of the dispute.

Moreover, given the very real limitations with which court ordering is beset, the costs of contract implementation cannot be disregarded. Taking issue with the tradition of central legalism, transaction-cost economics insists that the ex ante and ex post costs of contracting are interdependent, hence they must be addressed simultaneously rather than sequentially. Costs of both types are often difficult to quantify, but the difficulty is mitigated by the fact that transaction costs are always assessed in a comparative institutional way, in which one mode of contracting is compared with another: it is the difference between transaction costs, rather than their absolute magnitude, that matters. Such considerations lead institutional economists to reject the claim that the courts are well suited for administering justice whenever contract disputes arise, and to prefer bilateral and trilateral efforts to settle disputes. Rather than employing a legalistic approach to contract enforcement, the concept of contract as a general framework is emphasized instead. Hence, disputes are not routinely litigated, and the courts are used for ultimate appeal, as protection against egregious abuses (Williamson 1985: 20–2; 164–6).

In his 1995 book on the political economy of regional integration Miles Kahler argued that economic integration need not lead to centralized, law-based institutions that tend to expand the scope of their competences (Kahler 1995). In fact, most, if not all, regional organizations outside Europe have deliberately minimized recourse to legal and bureaucratic institutions. Thus the arrangements for dispute resolution of the NAFTA depend much less on legal centralism and court ordering than the corresponding arrangements in the EU, and for this reason they are likely to be more cost-effective, as well as more transparent, than the more traditional, state-like mechanisms adopted by the Union. It is true that the level of integration achieved by the EU is very much deeper than anything achieved, or even aimed at, by other regional groupings. There is, however, fairly general agreement among both scholars and informed observers that further expansion, or even preservation of the present level of integration, will require greater institutional flexibility and also more differentiated modes of integration in Europe. A more radical solution of many of today's problems would consist in shifting the present mode of integration from an emphasis on territory, i.e. the member states, to one based more on functional links.

Functional vs. territorial integration

The severity of the monetary crisis should not make us forget that the integration project is facing another, potentially even more explosive, problem: the growing economic, social and political diversity of an EU whose already large membership is still supposed to grow. This is precisely the mistake committed by those who propose a two-speed Europe, with the members of the euro zone forming the avant-garde. Not only is the present Euro-Group already highly heterogeneous, as noted above; in the future it is bound to become even more diverse, unless the principle of the *acquis*, which obliges every new member state to join the euro zone, is given up. Thus, if we want to think constructively about the future of European integration after the crisis of monetary union, we must consider alternatives that are reasonably robust against the two main problems the EU is facing today: excessive centralization in some key domains, and a level of internal diversity that is changing the very nature of the enterprise. Jean-Claude Piris saw the problem clearly when he wrote: 'Although the EU includes 27 Member States at very different levels of socioeconomic development, the current decision-making system is still largely based on the principle of "one-decision-fits-all"' (Piris 2011: 6). His proposal of a two-speed Europe, however, does not adequately reflect this insight. Given the level of socioeconomic heterogeneity, the model of integration à la carte certainly looks more flexible, hence more robust, than the two- or multi-speed alternative. As already mentioned, for Dahrendorf (1973), integration à la carte meant that there would be common European policies in areas where the member states have a common interest, but not otherwise. This, he said, must become the general rule rather than the exception if we wish to prevent continuous demands for special treatment, destroying in the long run the coherence of the entire system – a prescient anticipation of the present practice of moving ahead by granting opt-outs from treaty obligations. Unfortunately, none of the forms of differentiated integration discussed by Dahrendorf and by other writers in the 1970s were based on, or inspired by, any formal social-scientific theory. This is also true of more recent proposals, such as the ideas advanced by the then German foreign minister Joschka Fischer in his Humboldt University speech of May 2000 (Fischer 2000), which was considered by many to have been the catalyst that led to the calling for the Convention on the Future of Europe in 2002.

As far as functional integration is concerned, a sound conceptual basis is provided by the economic theory of clubs, originally developed by James Buchanan (1965), and later applied by Alessandra Casella (1996), to study the interaction between expanding markets and the provision of product standards. Casella argues, *inter alia*, that if we think of standards as being developed by communities of users, then 'opening trade will modify not only the standards but also the coalitions that express them. As markets. . .expand and become more heterogeneous, different coalitions will form across national borders, and their number will rise' (ibid.: 149). The relevance of these arguments extends well beyond the narrow area of standard-setting. In fact, Casella's emphasis on heterogeneity among traders as the main force against harmonization and for the multiplication of 'clubs' suggests an attractive theoretical basis for the mode of integration advocated by Dahrendorf (and, before him, by David Mitrany, see below). To see this more clearly we need to recall a few definitions and key concepts of the theory.

Public (or collective) goods, such as national defence or environmental quality, are characterized by two properties: first, it does not cost anything for an additional individual to enjoy the benefits of the public goods, once they are produced (joint-supply property); and, second, it is difficult or impossible to exclude individuals from the enjoyment of such goods (non-excludability). A 'club good' is a public good from whose benefits individuals may be excluded; an association established to provide an excludable public good is a *club*. Two elements determine the optimal size of a club. One is the cost of producing the club good – in a large club this cost is shared over more members. The second element is the cost to each club member of the good not meeting precisely his or her individual needs or preferences. The latter cost is likely to increase with the size of the club. The optimal size is determined by the point where the marginal benefit from the addition of one new member, i.e. the reduction in the per capita cost of producing the good, equals the marginal cost caused by a mismatch between the characteristics of the good and the preferences of the individual club members. If the preferences and the technologies for the provision of club goods are such that the number of clubs that can be formed in a society of given size is large, then an efficient allocation of such excludable public goods through the voluntary association of individuals into clubs is possible. With many alternative clubs available, each individual can guarantee herself a satisfactory balance of benefits and costs, since any attempt to discriminate against her would induce her to exit into a competing club. The important question is: what happens as the complexity of the society increases, perhaps as the result of the integration of previously separate markets? It has been shown that under plausible hypotheses the number of clubs tends to increase as well, since the greater diversity of needs and preferences makes it efficient to produce a broader range of club goods such as product standards. The two main forces driving the results of Casella's model are heterogeneity among the economic agents, and transaction costs – the costs of trading under different standards. Harmonization is the optimal strategy when transaction costs are high enough, relative to gross returns, to prevent a partition of the community of users into two clubs that reflect their needs more precisely. Hence harmonization occurs in response to market integration, but possibly only for an intermediate range of productivity in the production of standards, and when heterogeneity is not too great.

Think now of a society composed not of individuals, but of independent states. Associations of independent states (alliances, leagues, confederations) are typically voluntary, and their members are exclusively entitled to enjoy certain benefits produced by the association, so that the economic theory of clubs is applicable to this situation. In fact, since excludability is more easily enforced in the context envisaged here, many goods that are purely public at the national level become club goods at the international level. The club goods in question could be collective security, policy coordination, common technical standards – or a common currency: several proposals on how to resolve the euro crisis (see chapter 2) boil down to changing the nature of monetary union, from a public good to a club good. In these and many other cases, countries unwilling to share the costs are usually excluded from the benefits of inter-state cooperation on a particular project. Now, as an association of states expands, becoming more diverse in its preferences, the cost of uniformity in the provision of such goods – for example, the total harmonization of monetary policies – can escalate dramatically. The theory predicts an increase in the number of voluntary associations to meet the increased demand for club goods more precisely tailored to the different requirements of various subsets of more homogeneous states. In sum, the key idea of the theory of clubs is that aggregate welfare is maximized when the variety in preferences is matched by a corresponding variety of institutional arrangements.

But of course clubs, in the sense of the theory sketched here, need not be formed by governments. In fact, the theory explains why a number of important tasks which used to be assigned to central governments are today performed by private, increasingly transnational, organizations. Although there is a strong historical link between standardization and the emergence of the sovereign territorial state (Spruyt 1994), current views of standardization have changed radically as a result of the advance of globalization, the development of technology, and the growing variety and sophistication of technical standards. Standards are indeed public goods – in the sense that they fulfil specific functions deemed desirable by the community that shares them – but this does not mean that they must be established by government fiat. A good standard must reflect the needs, preferences, and resources of the community of users, rather than some centrally defined vision of the 'common interest'.

The economic theory of clubs provides a good conceptual foundation for the functional (rather than territorial) approach to international governance advocated by David Mitrany in the 1940s. A territorial union, Mitrany argued, 'would bind together some interests which are not of common concern to the group, while it inevitably cut asunder some interests of common concern to the group and those outside it'. To avoid such 'twice-arbitrary surgery' it is necessary to proceed by 'binding together those interests which are common, where they are common, and to the extent to which they are common'. Thus the essential principle of a functional organization of international activities 'is that activities would be selected specifically and organized separately, each according to its nature, to the conditions under which it has to operate, and to the needs of the moment' (citations in Eilstrup-Sangiovanni 2006: 57–8). On the other hand, Mitrany was sceptical about the advantages of political union. His main objection to schemes for continental unions was that 'the closer the union the more inevitably would it be dominated by the more powerful member' (ibid.: 47). This point, which has been largely overlooked by later writers on European integration, is directly linked to the discussion of Germany as a potential (but reluctant) hegemon, see chapter 8.

A Europe of clubs organized around functional tasks would not exclude the possibility of large projects supported by all the member states – as long as there is clear evidence (by referendum, supermajorities in national parliaments, etc.) of sufficient popular support. This is precisely what Dahrendorf had emphasized. The Single Market project, for example, seems to enjoy broad support even in so-called Euro-sceptic countries. Hence, this would be a natural starting point from which to assess the extent of democratic acceptance of further movement towards closer integration. But once decisions about the extent of integration are no longer taken *in camera* but are submitted to the decision of the voters, the provision of correct information about expected benefits and costs, about successes and failures, becomes truly indispensable. Even in case of a project like the Single Market, the general public should know that the promise of reaching that goal by 1992 is still far from being fulfilled. The aim of the internal market project was to open the internal borders of the EU to the free movement of goods, services, capital, and workers, as within a nation state. This aim, writes Piris (2011: 15):

> is presented as having been more or less achieved, but the truth is that it is not complete., especially in the services sector. In many areas the Single

Market exists in the books but, in practice, multiple barriers and regulatory obstacles fragment the intra-EU trade and hamper economic initiative and innovation.

In fact, Piris points out, 'the development of a single market in services' was still one of the proposals made by Mario Monti in 2010 in a report commissioned by the president of the European Commission (Report 2010). But what the member states of the EU need today is not more top-down, one-size-fits-all harmonization, but more flexibility and inter-state competition. Probably, a single market in services is not achievable because of deep-rooted differences of historical and cultural traditions, as well as in levels of economic development. Not top-down harmonization but a multiplicity of clubs seems to be the appropriate response to this problem.

4

Deepening integration: transaction costs and socio-political limits

From transaction-cost economics to transaction-cost politics

In spite of its growing importance in the new institutional economics and in political science, the transaction-cost approach to the analysis of institutions has not yet found significant applications in studies of regional, and in particular European, integration. Since this and related approaches – such as the economic theory of clubs discussed in the preceding and in later chapters – play an important role in the general argument developed in the present book, it seems advisable to introduce at this point the key ideas of the transaction-cost approach. Generally speaking, transaction costs are the costs of operating an economic, a political, or a social system. In case of the market system, Ronald Coase's characterization is still the clearest:

> In order to carry out a market transaction it is necessary to discover who it is that one wishes to deal with, to inform people that one wishes to deal with and on what terms, to conduct negotiations leading up to a bargain, to draw up the contract, to undertake the inspection needed to make sure that the terms of the contract are being observed, and so on.
>
> (Coase 1988: 15)

Thus the costs of using the market system may be classified as: (1) costs of preparing contracts, i.e., *search and information costs*, narrowly defined; (2) costs of concluding contracts: *bargaining and decision-making costs*; and (3) *costs of monitoring and enforcing the contractual obligations*. Such costs are clearly different from the costs of producing goods and services – the only costs considered by neo-classical economics – but they are as real and significant as production costs. Following Williamson (1985) we can think of transaction costs, whether they arise in economic or in political systems, as the social equivalent of friction in physical systems. The same author also emphasizes the comparative nature of transaction-cost analysis, which consists in calculating 'the comparative costs of planning, adapting, and monitoring task com-pletion under alternative governance structures' (cited in Dixit 1996: 31). The writings of scholars such as Ronald Coase, Oliver Williamson, and Douglass North have led to the recognition that various transaction costs are the primary reason why competitive markets do not function as effectively as suggested by neo-classical theory.

The idea of studying the political process in the transaction-cost mode seems to have originated with Douglass North (1990) who, however, focused on a particular type of transaction cost, namely a failure of 'instrumental rationality' for participants in the political process. He argued that the informational feedback is inadequate to convey to the participants in this process the correct theory of how their world oper-ates; this affects the individuals' decisions and in turn the outcome of the process and the information it generates. Since North's 1990 paper other types of political transaction costs have been identified in the literature. Thus Furubotn and Richter define political transaction costs as the costs of supplying public goods by collective action. Specifically, these are: (1) *the costs of setting up, maintaining, and changing a system's formal and informal political organization;* and (2) *the costs of running a polity* (Furubotn and Richter 2000: 47). Actually, all forms of economic transaction costs also appear in political processes; but political pro-cesses are likely to be even more beset by transaction costs than are economic processes and relationships. This observation suggests that a transaction-cost politics (TCP) perspective, developed along the lines of transaction-cost economics (TCE), may provide new insights.

This is precisely the research programme sketched by the distin-guished Princeton economist Avinash Dixit in his *The Making Of Economic Policy* (Dixit 1996). Dixit begins by noting that in TCP, as in TCE, the contract is the basic unit of analysis. In TCE, a contract is a voluntary agreement among people who recognize their mutual interests and agree to modify their behaviour in ways that are mutually beneficial. The agreement may specify the sort of actions each contractual partner is to take, the rules and procedures that will be used to decide matters in the future, and the behaviour that each might expect from the others. Such agreements are contracts, regardless of whether they have the legal status of contracts. In fact, voluntary agreements may be completely unarticu-lated and implicit, and yet perform the same functions that formal contracts do, and even more (Milgrom and Roberts 1992).

In TCP, the parties to a political contract are voters or interest groups, on the one hand, and politicians and/or bureaucrats, on the other. The contract is the promise of a policy in return for votes (or contributions). Beyond this basic parallel, however, political contracts differ from economic contracts in several ways, all of which make them more complex and harder to enforce. Thus, political contracts are rarely between two clearly identifiable partners, and their terms are generally much vaguer than those of economic contracts. Hence they leave much room for interpretation, and many opportunities to blame third parties or force majeure for failure to deliver. Also, many political promises are not subject to any external enforcement mechanism. If a politician fails to deliver on such a 'contractual obligation', the only recourse may be to remove him or her from office. Again, political contracts tend to be seriously incomplete. Most contracts considered by TCE are incomplete, in the sense that they do not attempt to foresee and unambiguously describe every contingency that might possibly be relevant to the contractual partners, see the next section. The bounded rationality of real people – their limited foresight, imprecise language, the costs of writing down a detailed plan of action – means that not all contingencies are fully accounted for. In practice all but the simplest types of contract – such as spot contracts governing goods or services that are traded 'on the spot' – are incomplete. Political contracts are even more incomplete than economic ones, and bounded rationality has more serious bite. In countries governed by a close-knit group of politicians and civil servants working in collaboration with business and labour groups, such as Japan from the 1950s to the 1980s, some of the uncertainties may be reduced because of the mutual trust of these actors. But such close governance systems are becoming less prevalent and less successful, while 'the European Union is likely to be too heterogeneous and too much influenced by its sovereign members' to foster mutual trust (Dixit 1996: 154).

Next, Dixit presents a taxonomy of transaction costs using the categories introduced by Williamson in the context of TCE, but interpreting them in light of the TCP framework. The first category is 'information impactedness', meaning all aspects of limited and asymmetric information. This category includes such problems as (1) adverse selection – a term coined in the insurance industry to denote a situation of pre-contractual informational advantage for one of the parties; (2) non-observability of the agent's action; and (3) non-verifiability of information by outsiders. Adverse selection leads to screening costs; non-observability, to costs of monitoring; and non-verifiability, to auditing costs. Such information asymmetries are often more prevalent and more serious in TCP than in

TCE. An example of TCP-relevant information asymmetry is the fact that political parties' true intentions are often hidden behind their publicly announced platforms, forcing voters to infer the truth from observation of policy outcomes.

It must be observed, however, that in a democracy voters can use evidence provided at little or no cost by opposition parties or by political entrepreneurs. Anthony Downs, who was the first scholar to give serious attention to the question of political information in modern mass democracies, argued that voters have strong incentives to develop methods for significantly reducing the costs of information acquisition. Thus they use a variety of rules to determine what to make use of and what not to make use of. These rules serve to focus attention upon only the most relevant data, allowing voters to form political preferences and make political decisions without becoming fully informed about the content and details of political issues. Moreover, political entrepreneurs can expend the resources needed to acquire information and then transmit it to the voters. By such means the voters can 'avoid the staggering difficulty of knowing everything the government has done during the election period and everything its opponents would have done were they in office' (Downs 1957: 217). As we shall see in a later section, the costs of information asymmetries, and other political transaction costs, are much higher in a polity like the EU, where the role of the voters is seriously limited.

The second group of transaction costs arises from (pre- and post-contractual) opportunism, i.e., 'self-interest seeking with guile' (Williamson 1985). As mentioned above, moral hazard is a particularly serious problem caused by post-contractual opportunism; it arises when actions required or desired under the contract are not freely observable. Today it is generally recognized that both moral hazard and adverse selection (i.e., pre-contractual informational advantage for one of the parties) are at the root of the sovereign-debt crisis of the euro zone, most clearly in the case of Greece. Opportunistic behaviour is a particularly serious problem in case of contractual incompleteness. When contingencies arise that could not have been foreseen at contracting time, some contractual partners may be tempted to use the unforeseen circumstances to renege on the original agreement. When the reneging takes the form of not carrying through on the agreed actions, it may affect efficiency both directly and indirectly. The costs of opportunism may be quite high when the actions of agents are not observable. Governance structures are characterized by various agency relationships in economics as well as in politics, but such relationships are often much more complicated and significant in TCP than in TCE. First, in politics it is not always clear who are the principals and who are the agents. Second, the output of an agency may be not only unobservable, but also unknowable. If the agency goal is so vague as to be meaningless, the principal (for example, the administrator) often will not know what to do and thus cannot be expected to tell the subordinates what to do, much less evaluate the work after the fact. Third, the lines of authority are often blurred, since a public agency may be answerable to multiple principals, a situation known in the literature as common agency, see chapter 3. An agency may also be assigned multiple tasks, in which case it has ample room for opportunistic behaviour in the choice of the goals to be pursued. The European Commission is a particularly striking example in this as in other respects: it has been assigned a variety of executive, legislative, and quasi-judicial functions, and this multiplicity of roles expands the scope of the institution's discretionary choices while at the same time complicating the task of evaluating the overall quality of its performance (Majone 2005: 38–40).

The third group of transaction costs arises in connection with 'asset specificity'. In economics this condition exists when, in a contract between two parties to exploit a mutually beneficial opportunity, at least one party must make an irreversible investment. Once it has done so it will become vulnerable to demands of the other party to renegotiate the contract and get for itself a greater share of profit, using the threat of dissolving the whole relationship. Economic investments in specific assets may be deterred by fear of a 'political hold-up' such as a shift in government policy. The early history of American regulation of public utilities, an industry characterized by irreversible investments, provides a good illustration of this. In the nineteenth century Chicago gas companies were reluctant to invest for fear that consumers might capture the city's regulatory apparatus and secure passage of an ordinance requiring gas companies to charge very low rates. Because gas mains locked producers into the Chicago market, they could not have avoided the regulation by physically relocating their plant and capital. Before investing in Chicago, therefore, gas companies needed assurances that once they installed their mains city authorities would not impose onerous regulations. As Werner Troesken (1996) has shown in an instructive case study, the problem was resolved by various political and institutional means, which included moving the regulation of public utilities from the city to the state level.

Until recently, membership in the EC/EU could be considered a kind of irreversible investment which potentially made a new member vulnerable to demands of the more integrationist member states and to future decisions by the ECJ and the other supranational institutions. The Treaty of Rome was silent on the possibility of voluntary withdrawal from the Community, but most legal authorities agreed that secession would have been illegal under European law. In addition, all member states were supposed to apply in full the body of legislation, rules, and policies mandated by the EU. Since ratification of the Maastricht Treaty, this *acquis communautaire* includes also membership in the monetary union. Hence, as already mentioned, the new member states from Central and Eastern Europe are expected to adopt the common currency as soon as they satisfy the Maastricht 'convergence criteria' concerning the budget deficit, public debt levels, low and convergent inflation rates, and a stable exchange rate. Membership in the monetary union is considered an irreversible investment: 'the euro is forever' is the slogan often repeated in Brussels, in Frankfurt, where the ECB is located, as well as in Berlin. Paradoxically, since ratification of the Lisbon Treaty in 2009, membership in the EU is no longer 'forever'. According to Article 50 of the Treaty: 'Any Member State may decide to withdraw from the Union in accordance with its own constitutional requirements'. Moreover, a state which has withdrawn from the Union may ask to rejoin. A number of proposals recently made by independent experts to solve the crisis of the euro zone assume a similar regulation of membership in the euro zone.

One final point I would like to emphasize before concluding this introductory section is that the reduction of political transaction costs through better design of governance structures has both normative and efficiency implications. The public-choice school in economics has popularized the notion that while economic markets tend to be efficient, political markets are affected by various forms of failure associated with information problems, such as voters' ignorance, opportunism. logrolling, etc. This view has been challenged by Anthony Downs, as we saw above, and more recently and in more general terms, by Wittman (1995) and Breton (1996), who argue that democratic political markets are highly competitive, and that democratic institutions are designed to reduce transaction costs. One does not have to subscribe in full the claim that 'democratic markets are organized to promote wealth-maximizing outcomes. . .and political and bureaucratic entrepreneurs are rewarded for efficient behaviour' (Wittman 1995: 2), to accept the conclusion that democracies are more efficient than non-democratic regimes, where competition is thwarted and transaction costs are high. Even the more modest claim is sufficient to support the proposition that the EU's much discussed democratic deficit has not only normative but also important efficiency implications. Lacking many of the instruments democracies use to reduce transaction costs, the Union is bound to be comparatively inefficient. In the following pages I support this general proposition by comparing how fully-fledged democracies, on the one hand, and the EU, on the other, deal with some important instances of political transaction costs: information problems; the trade-off between credible commitment and flexibility; and problems of institutional design. Let us begin by seeing how transaction-cost analysis tackles the problem of how to achieve credible commitments.

Technologies of commitment

As we know, the basic unit of analysis in both TCE and TCP is the contract; hence, the credibility of contractual commitments is a central question for the entire transaction-cost approach. The issue of credible commitments is also crucially important for understanding the evolution of the integration process in Europe. As already mentioned, the key problem facing national leaders and supranational institutions since the 1950s was how to induce sovereign states to credibly commit themselves to a project which, if successful, would necessarily entail the acceptance of limits on national sovereignty. Formal ratification by the national parliaments of the treaties transferring powers from the national to the European level could not by itself ensure a credible commitment to the integration project. This is because European treaties, like all international treaties and national constitutions, are incomplete contracts, so that contingencies will arise that have not been accounted for because they were not foreseen, or were considered highly unlikely, at contracting time. For this reason, contractual incompleteness can lead to problems of imperfect commitment, such as reneging on the deal or asking for ex post renegotiation.

A partial remedy to contractual incompleteness is an arrangement known as 'relational contracting', where the parties agree on general principles rather than detailed plans of action. A relational contract settles for a general agreement framing the entire relationship, recognizing that it is impossible to concentrate all bargaining at the ex ante contracting stage. The 1957 Treaty of Rome establishing the EEC is a good example: with a few exceptions, the Treaty only provides general principles and policy guidelines, and delegates to the European institutions – in particular, to the Commission – the tasks of specifying the concrete measures to be taken in order to achieve the broad Treaty objectives in a constantly evolving situation. In this perspective, Article 235 of the Rome Treaty (which enables the Council of Ministers, acting on a proposal of the European Commission, to take appropriate measures in cases where action by the Community is found to be necessary and there is no specific power under the Treaty available for that purpose) was part of the general response of the member states to the incompleteness of the founding Treaty – no such provision would have been necessary if the founding fathers had been infinitely wise and prescient. For more than two decades the powers of the Community and the reach of European law were expanded, sometimes dramatically, without any formal treaty amendment. Starting with the Maastricht Treaty, however, the national governments have taken the initiative in amending the treaties every few years; and have used the amendment process to define new competences in a way that actually limits the exercise of Community powers, and in particular limits the jurisdiction of the ECJ in new policy areas. This activism of the member states, their repeated reminders that they, not the Commission or the Court, are the masters of the treaties, clearly indicates a loss of confidence in the self-restraint of the supranational institutions, and marks the beginning of a search for methods of integration alternative to legal centralism and to the so-called Community method, see chapter 7. Delegation of powers to supranational institutions is no longer seen as the best, let alone the only, strategy for achieving credible commitments.

In fact, the so-called technology of commitment (Dixit and Nalebuff 1991: 144–63) includes a number of different strategies for achieving credibility. Here I shall mention only two strategies that have played a significant role in the course of European integration: breaking down large commitments into smaller ones; and building and using a reputation. The first one – moving in small, frequent steps – should be followed whenever a large commitment is unfeasible and hence not credible. The strategy consists in breaking down the total commitment into a number of small steps such that the scale of commitment of each is sufficiently reduced to be credible. As a striking violation of this sensible strategy in the EU context one can mention the commitment made at the Lisbon summit of March 2000 to make the EU the world's most competitive economy by 2010. The commitment was not credible because, given the rigidity of most national economies, a decade is not long enough to permit breaking down such an ambitious goal into a number of smaller, more credible commitments. In general, however, the strategy of moving in small steps ('piecemeal integration') has been applied frequently in the EU, not without some notable successes. In the area of JHA, for example, one can trace the various steps from the creation of the Trevi Group (as part of European Political Cooperation) by the Rome European Council of December 1975; the first Schengen Agreement in 1985 and its sub-sequent incorporation in the Amsterdam Treaty; the transformation of JHA into a fundamental treaty objective, also at Amsterdam; the Tampere European Council of October 1999, a landmark for both the policy and institutional development of JHA; down to the 2009 Lisbon Treaty, which provided for full application of Community decision rules to almost all internal security matters and made binding the Charter of Fundamental Rights for the application of internal security measures.

The case of EMU is particularly instructive from the point of view of this particular commitment strategy. Before the final decision to proceed with full monetary integration in 1999 – a quantum jump whose long-term results are still uncertain – this major area of European policy-making also generally exhibited a similar strategy of small steps, with one significant exception. The Treaty of Rome contained very little in terms of binding commitments in the field of macroeconomic policy. At the Hague summit of December 1969, however, the political leaders of the then six member states adopted, for the first time, the target of full economic and monetary union within a decade. In the situation of monetary instability following the collapse of the Bretton Woods system in 1971, this ambitious target turned out to be impossible to reach. As Tsoukalis writes: 'EMU became the biggest non-event of the decade...Very senior west European politicians had made political commitments but had not by and large translated them into the appro-priate economic policies. Finally they gave way under market pressure' (Tsoukalis 2003: 152).

After this serious setback, the strategy of small steps was followed pretty consistently for almost two decades. After 1972 what was left of the over-ambitious Werner Plan for EMU was the 'Snake', a fixed exchange-rate regime including, in addition to Germany, the Benelux countries, as well as Denmark, Austria, and Switzerland – in practice, a D-Mark block. Although the 'Snake' was short-lived, it was a decisive step in the process of ever closer cooperation among European central bankers. The EMS – a system of fixed, but periodically adjustable, exchange rates between EC currencies – was established in March

1979. The early years of the EMS were still characterized by high inflation rates and persisting divergences between the national economies, but from the early 1980s and especially during the 1990s the convergence downwards of inflation rates became pronounced. In turn, price convergence, coupled with the growing credibility of stability-oriented policies, brought about the gradual convergence of nominal long-term interest rates. The decision to liberalize capital movements, taken in 1988 as part of the Single Market programme was another important step on the road leading gradually from an extensive coordination of national policies to the centralization of monetary policy at EU level.

The strategy of small, credible steps came to a sudden halt with the reunification of Germany in 1989 and the collapse of the Soviet Union. For many people in Paris, Rome, Brussels, and in other capitals, the transformation of the geopolitical context called for a deepening of the integration process and a strengthening of the ties binding the new, larger Germany to its European partners, see chapter 1. In Germany itself, the official position had always been that political union should precede monetary union. After the fall of the Berlin wall, however, Chancellor Helmut Kohl and other key decision-makers came to regard European monetary union as the price to be paid for German unification. The fact that monetary union between East and West Germany had preceded the political reunification of the two states was even taken by some as a good omen for the European case. At any rate, it seems very likely that without the fall of the Berlin wall and the reunification of Germany, opposition to European monetary union would have prevailed in the Federal Republic. Here the drafting of the Maastricht Treaty coincided with a period of emotional exhaustion and concentration on domestic problems. In Autumn 1991, Chancellor Kohl took the momentous decision to accept European monetary union even without political union (Sarrazin 2012: 65–70). After that, the economic and political desirability of EMU was not seriously questioned during the negotiations leading to the Treaty of Maastricht. The matter was supposed to have already been settled. The doubters, of which there were many, kept a low profile, preferring to concentrate on specific problems instead of challenging the main principles and objectives. Nevertheless, the decision to move to a single currency and a European central bank by 1 January 1999 left a number of crucial issues still unresolved, as already mentioned.

After Maastricht, but before the onset of the euro crisis, the only attempt to meet widespread concerns about the insufficient coordination of the fiscal and economic policies of the members of the euro zone was the SGP, adopted at the Amsterdam summit in October 1997. Shortly after its introduction, Wim Duisenberg, the first president of the ECB, claimed that the existence of the Pact had made a centralized budget unnecessary. In reality, the Pact never worked the way it was intended to. Its reform in June 2005 in the end eliminated the elements of automatism in the original agreement and introduced considerable room for inter-governmental margins of manoeuvre. Thus the credibility of EMU had been undermined even before the sovereign-debt crisis, especially in view of the decision to start monetary union with a much larger number of members than originally contemplated, see chapter 1.

'Building a reputation' is another important strategy for achieving credibility. Reputation can arise only in a context of repeated interactions, which create a link between current and expected future decisions. In such a context two different methods of building and using a reputation may be distinguished (Milgrom and Roberts 1992). The first method applies when, although it is not possible to specify in advance what to do in any specific situation, the parties themselves have enough information to evaluate each other's past behaviour. When the latter condition does not hold – for example, because the situation is ambiguous and thus open to different and conflicting interpretations – a system of reputa-tions can work, if at all, only with the help of independent third parties, such as courts or rating agencies. Both methods have been used exten-sively in the context of European integration. Deferring the discussion of reputations aided by institutions to the following section on delegation of powers, here I consider the case where the parties have enough information to evaluate each other's behaviour. For example, the fre-quent meetings of the Council of Ministers – at least once a month for major Councils like General Affairs, Agriculture, and Economic and Financial Affairs, and much more frequently in crisis situations – create a situation of repeated interactions where reputation can become a very valuable asset. Concerning the presidency of the Council, for example, Fiona Hayes-Renshaw wrote: 'With so much attention focused on the President-in-office, it has become a point of pride for the outgoing office-holders to be viewed by their colleagues as having conducted a "good presidency"' (Hayes-Renshaw 2002: 60).

Among the criteria used in forming such judgements this author mentions: whether Council business was dealt with efficiently and impartially; whether the main objectives outlined in the presidency programme were achieved; and 'whether unpredictable events were dealt with calmly, efficiently, and effectively'. Reputation seems to be quite important also below the ministerial level. Indeed, because of the more frequent interactions at the lower levels, reputation may be an even more valuable asset there. To quote Hayes-Renshaw again:

> A certain *esprit de corps*, similar to that perceptible in Coreper [the Committee of Permanent Representatives of the national governments]... is noticeable among the members of the working groups that meet on a regular basis. The personal relations forged through continuous interaction between individuals in the group (many of whom may be long-serving members) eventually fosters an appreciation of differing points of view and a desire to reach agreement by consensus, in an attempt to keep everyone on board.
>
> (Ibid.: 55)

According to Jeffrey Lewis, the members of Coreper 'exemplify a brand of diplomacy based on thick bonds of mutual trust, understanding, responsiveness, and a willingness to compromise' (Lewis 2002: 280). The norm of thick trust is 'reconfirmed weekly through the normal cycle of meetings, trips, and lunches'. There is also a norm of mutual responsiveness that is best described as a shared purpose to understand each other's problems. Finally a 'culture of compromise' favours a self-restraint in the calculation and defence of interests (ibid.: 291). However, the punitive approach of the new Stability Treaty is a clear indication that the era of mutual trust and good feelings may be over, not only for the euro zone but for the entire EU, see chapter 6.

Delegation of powers

As was mentioned in the preceding section, in relational contracting the task of interpreting the original agreement in light of unforeseen circumstances may be delegated to one of the parties or, more likely, to a third party. A relevant consideration is that the delegate should have much to lose from a damaged reputation. It follows that the delegate is likely to be a person (or an institution) with a longer time horizon, more visibility, and greater frequency of transactions than the other contractual partners. One of the most striking features of the institutional architecture of the EC/EU is the extensive delegation of powers to supranational institutions. The member states, Miles Kahler writes, 'have delegated more important and extensive functions to European institutions than has been the case with the members of other international or regional institutions. The Commission, for example, surpasses even the strongest secretariat of an international organization.' (Kahler 1995: 85) There are two main reasons for political principals to delegate some of their powers to agents rather than exercising those powers themselves: first, to reduce decision-making costs, for example by taking advantage of administrative or technical expertise; the second reason is the one mentioned above, namely to enhance the credibility of long-term policy commitments. Both reasons are relevant in the context of European integration, although the second reason is in many respects the more important one. When the purpose is to reduce decision-making costs, the key problem facing the principals is bureaucratic drift, that is, the ability of the agent to enact outcomes different from the policies preferred by those who originally delegated powers. This is the only problem considered by most works on the principal–agent model, with which delegation theory is often identified (see, for example, Epstein and O'Halloran 1999). According to this body of literature, the first-best solution of the delegation problem would be for principals to appoint agents who share their preferences. If this is impossible or too costly, then bureaucratic drift should be reduced with the help of various mechanisms of ex ante and ex post control. It is recognized that controls are imperfect, so that there will always remain a difference between the policy enacted and what is implemented, and this residual non-compliance is an important component of 'agency costs'. To calculate the net benefits of delegation, agency costs are to be subtracted from the gains in decision-making efficiency.

The situation is rather different when credibility is the main reason for delegating powers. In this case the best strategy to enhance the credibility of a long-term policy commitment may be to choose a delegate whose policy preferences actually differ from the preferences of the delegating principal(s). For example, if a government wants to credibly commit itself to price stability, it can delegate responsibility for monetary policy to a central banker who values ex post inflation less than the government itself. If distortions in the labour market cause the rate of inflation to be too high, for example, then society can be made better off by having the central bank place a higher weight on price stability. One of the best-known formalizations of this idea is Rogoff's model of the 'conservative' central banker, meaning that the banker is more inflation-averse than the government. The government's commitment to a lower average rate of inflation becomes credible precisely because the delegate values ex post inflation less than his or her political principals. It should be noted that this and similar models do not assume that the central bank is fully independent (Rogoff 1985). In fact, we shall see below that in a crisis situation the cost of a rigid commitment to price stability may be too high in political and welfare terms. In such a situation the best solution is for the government to assume control of both monetary and fiscal policy.

Alesina and Grilli (1994) applied Rogoff's model to the case of the ECB. In their model, each member state evaluates the consequences of monetary integration according to its own preferences. The authors show that participation in the monetary union can increase national welfare if the preferences of the ECB are more 'conservative' than national preferences. In such a case, monetary union allows countries to credibly commit themselves to anti-inflationary policies. This explains why elite support for monetary union was strongest in countries with a historically high inflation bias, such as Italy, Spain, and Greece. Apparently, the political leaders of these countries felt that the enhanced credibility for price stability, and the resulting reduction in the cost of servicing the public debt, more than compensated for the potential costs in terms of unemployment. Economists who, like Alesina and Grilli, supported European monetary union, assumed, rather naively, that all the members of monetary union would abide by the rules of fiscal discipline imposed by the Maastricht Treaty and by the SGP. Today we know that things went quite differently because of the pre- and post-contractual opportunism of some member states, leading to problems of adverse selection and moral hazard – problems well known to economists, but surprisingly overlooked, not only by political leaders and policymakers, but also by academic supporters of European monetary union, see the following section.

Arguments based on the different preferences of political principals and their agents, can also be used to explain why members of the EU Commission tend to be more in favour of European integration than the national governments that choose them. Governments may believe that integration of the national economies is the optimal long-run policy, but they also know that they could be tempted by short-run incentives to renege on their commitment to respect European rules, such as those disciplining state aid to industry. Choosing as Commissioners people who are more pro-integration than the government is a way for the member states to enhance the credibility of their commitment to integration. Despite these obvious advantages, doubts concerning the net benefits of delegation to supranational institutions had already emerged at the time of the drafting of the Maastricht Treaty, as mentioned in the preceding section. Such doubts seem to be justified when one considers the transaction and legitimacy costs of delegation on the scale practised in the EU.

One of the most striking features of the EU institutional arrangements is the monopoly of agenda setting enjoyed by the non-elected Commission: in all matters related to market integration, only the Commission can make legislative and policy proposals. It is important to understand clearly what is implied by such an extensive delegation of powers. First, other European institutions, including the Parliament, cannot legislate in the absence of a prior proposal from the Commission. It is up to the latter institution to decide whether the EU should act and, if so, in what legal form, and what content and implementing procedures should be followed. Second, the Commission can amend its proposal at any time while it is under discussion in the Committee of Permanent Representatives of the member states, or in the Council of Ministers, while the Council can amend a Commission proposal only by unanimity. Moreover, if the Council unanimously wishes to adopt a measure which differs from the proposal, the Commission can deprive the Council of its power of decision by withdrawing its own proposal. Finally, neither the Council nor the EP nor a member state can compel the Commission to submit a proposal, except in those few cases where the Treaty imposes an obligation to legislate.

As I had occasion to point out some time ago, this monopoly of legislative and policy initiative granted to a non-elected body represents a violation of fundamental democratic principles that is unique in modern constitutional history, and fairly rare even in ancient history (Majone 2009: 30–5). It is, of course, true that in contemporary parliamentary systems most legislative proposals are introduced to parliament by the executive as draft legislation. Once legislators receive such proposals, however, they are free to change or reject them; this is not the case in the EU where amendments are possible only under the strict requirement of unanimity, as just mentioned. In parliamentary systems, moreover, the executive cannot pre-empt the right of initiative of parliamentary parties and of individual members of the legislature. Such heavy legitimacy costs do not seem to be compensated by significant gains in efficiency terms. The Commission's monopolistic power of initiative is the pillar of the so-called Community method, which defines the roles of the various European institutions and the modes of their interactions. Hence, the effectiveness of the Commission as a policy initiator may be estimated on the basis of the actual results achieved in sixty years of application of this method. As we saw in chapter 2, even the semi-official Sapir Report in 2004 (Sapir *et al.* 2004) came to the conclusion that these results were far from being satisfactory.

The method adopted for monetary union may be considered a variant of the Community method (Dehousse 2011), but having a common currency did not in fact improve the performance of the European economy. According to the data of the EU statistical office (Eurostat) pro capita GDP (measured in purchasing power parity, with EU 27=100) in 1999 was 113 for the euro zone, 121 in Germany, 162 in the US; in 2008 it was 109, 116 and 147, respectively; in 2009: 109, 116, 145; in 2010 the pro capita GDP was 148 in the US, 108 in the euro zone and 118 in Germany (Sarrazin 2012: 109, table 3.3). Thus pro capita GDP in the euro zone outside Germany has actually declined since the beginning of monetary union. One may well wonder whether the disappointing results achieved by the EU so far justify the transaction costs of operating such cumbersome institutional machinery. I come back to this question in a later section where some of the most significant transaction costs caused by extensive delegation of powers to the supranational institutions, in particular bargaining and influence costs, will be discussed. Before discussing this general issue, I conclude the present section by considering some problematic aspects of the delegation of exclusive responsibility for monetary policy to the ECB.

We have seen that the delegation of powers to a more or less independent central bank is meant to restrain the temptation of democratic politicians to assign greater weight to short-run considerations and thus to default on long-term commitments. In the area of monetary policy, where credibility is essential to success, delegation to an autonomous central bank can be an effective way of achieving a credible long-term commitment to monetary stability. However, it is now recognized that from the point of view of policy effectiveness the government should have the option of overriding the central bank's decisions – under particular conditions and following well-defined procedures. This means that the optimal mode of delegation to the central bank should strike a balance between credibility and flexibility, for example, by applying a non-linear decision rule according to which in case of large disturbances the bank would follow the government's preferences. In the words of a well-known economist: 'if the government is not free to respond to adverse future conditions flexibly, that can create its own cost in terms of future economic performance' (Dixit 1996: 66). Hence the solution suggested by Dixit and by other experts combines some of the advantages of both commitment and flexibility. It consists in using an unconditional rule at some times, keeping flexibility at others, and defining threshold levels of contingencies at which policy would switch from one regime to the other:

> A switch from the commitment regime to the flexible regime should be made when the disequilibrium becomes so large, and the net advantage of flexibility over commitment grows so large, that it provides a sufficient rate of return on the sunk lump-sum cost of switching. The reverse switch should be made when the disequilibrium is small enough to justify that move using a similar calculation.
>
> (Ibid.: 67–8)

Of course, the solution suggested by the experts presupposes a close cooperation between the central bank and a fully-fledged, democratically accountable government. But this is precisely what is missing at the European level. Unlike the situation in the US, say, where the Federal Reserve is placed within a political structure in which Congress, the President, and the Treasury Department supply all the necessary political counterweights, the ECB operates without a European government to balance its powers. As we shall see in chapter 5, the political and social 'disembeddedness' of supranational institutions enjoying such extensive powers is one of the most serious problems of European governance.

Information, bargaining, and influence costs

Discussing the transaction costs connected with limited and asymmetric information in the first section of the present chapter, it was pointed out that in a democracy voters can use evidence provided by opposition parties or by political entrepreneurs, to find out what the government has done, and perhaps also what its opponents would have done had they been in office. On the other hand, the cost of obtaining political information can be quite significant for the citizens of a polity like the EU, where democratic institutions – including an electorally accountable government and opposition – are either absent or poorly developed. In the EU there is no central power to be conquered in a competition among political parties, and while European competences extend from competition policy, economic and monetary union, and trade policy to agriculture, regional policy, and the environment, such policies are not decided upon by an elected government but by political exchange among the three law-making institutions: Council of Ministers, EP, and

Commission. In such a context, only interest groups have sufficient incentives to incur the cost of acquiring reliable information concerning the nature and possible consequences of European policies. The other two categories of cost discussed in the present section are even more outside the purview of the average voter.

'Bargaining costs' are the transaction costs involved in negotiations among different parties. They include not only the opportunity costs of bargainers' time, but also resources expended trying to improve one's bargaining position, the costs of monitoring and enforcing the agreement, and the losses from failure to reach an agreement. A most important source of bargaining costs is the opportunistic behaviour of bargainers mainly interested in private (rather than collective) benefits and costs. Such behaviour makes it impossible to resolve satisfactorily the inescapable tension between cooperative moves to create value jointly (expanding the pie) and competitive moves to gain individual advantage (dividing the pie). In the EU context, opportunistic behaviour becomes particularly evident in crisis situations. The most striking example is provided by the difficulty of reaching agreement on what to do in order to save monetary union, as shown by the sixteen crisis summits held between 2010 and 2012. At each summit a breakthrough seemed to be within reach only to discover, perhaps a few days later, that some government was not willing to accept the proposed solution. Similar patterns of behaviour may also be observed in the case of other, less serious, crises of the past. Consider, for example, how the member states reacted to the rejection of the draft Constitutional Treaty by the French and Dutch voters in May–June 2005. One of the most obvious, and most disturbing, consequences was the return to brutal methods of defence of the national interest. Of course, national interests always become highly visible in critical situations. Still, an implicit rule had developed over the years according to which the defence of the national interest should not exclude concessions to the other member states, and at least a formal acknowledgment of the existence of a higher common interest. At the Brussels summit of 16–17 June 2005 – where the financial framework for the period 2007–2013 was to be defined – the mode of interaction among the national leaders reached a degree of brutality seldom experienced before (Majone 2009: 41–2).

Spain's attitude at that summit was particularly revealing of the resurgence of naked national-interest thinking in the wake of the constitutional debacle. After his unexpected electoral victory in April 2004, Prime Minister Zapatero repeatedly proclaimed his intention of placing

Spain 'at the centre of Europe', together with France and Germany. At the Brussels summit of June 2005, however, Zapatero presented himself as the most strenuous defender of a narrowly conceived national interest. The Spanish prime minister was well aware of the economic advantages his country derived from EU membership, and in his first official visit to Berlin he had announced Spain's willingness to share with poorer member states the help so generously provided by the Union. But at the Brussels summit he presented a list of rigid conditions for Spain's acceptance of the 2007–2013 financial framework – including an absolute refusal that Spain become a net contributor to the EU budget before 2014. In the end, the Spanish prime minister sealed the failure of the summit by rejecting the last compromise proposed by European Council President Juncker. The agreement on the 2007–2013 financial framework finally reached in December 2005 was made possible only by postponing any serious discussion about the CAP, and by the decision of Chancellor Angela Merkel to increase her country's contribution to the EU budget – a return to the 'checkbook diplomacy' of Helmut Kohl, that had been abandoned because of the parlous state of Germany's public finances in those years.

While naked self-interest may be the most important source of bargaining costs, not only in the EU, another significant source is private information about preferences. As Milgrom and Roberts (1992: 77) put it: 'Unless the parties' valuations of a good being traded are common knowledge, the parties may be delayed in reaching an agreement or may even fail to agree at all, because they may misrepresent the good's value.' One implication of research by Bailer and Schneider (2006) on the importance of constraints in legislative bargaining in the EU is that negotiations risk breaking down if governments are not well informed about the domestic constraints of their bargaining partners. These authors present evidence that meetings of both the European Council and the Council of Ministers are strongly affected by the strategic moves of some national governments. The approval of important directives has often been held up for years in the Council of Ministers precisely for this reason. Such problems are even more serious in the case of the European Council – the institution bringing together the heads of state or government, and around which the whole EU system revolves. According to one of the most knowledgeable students of this institution, 'European Councils frequently fail to reach decisions, creating "leftovers" which means postponing decisions to a future date' (De Schoutheete 2006: 55).

A system of inter-state bargaining that manages to give, or at least to promise, something to everybody should be quite stable. As a matter of fact, scholars who praise the stability of the EU base their arguments on the capacity of the system to satisfy a variety of demands through a series of package deals both within and across issue areas. Since not all demands can be satisfied simultaneously, an agreement on x today may be exchanged for the promise to discuss y tomorrow. The participants who receive such promises acquire an interest in the maintenance of the bargaining forum itself; they become 'locked in, and socialized by, the intensity and rewards of their interactions' (Hayes-Renshaw and Wallace 1997: 254–5). Hence, it is hardly surprising that bargaining costs are so high in the EU. This writer is not aware of any systematic quantitative estimates, or even of attempts to identify the major categories of such costs; but given the number of the bargainers and the pervasiveness of bargaining at all levels of European governance, the total investment of resources to gain bargaining advantages must be staggering. Such investment is typically unproductive for the group of member states as a whole, yet it is incurred in the hope of shifting the distribution of gains.

One of the functions of identifying major sources of bargaining costs in business organizations is to explain practices that arise in order to minimize such costs. In the EU the rule that the Council of Ministers can only modify a Commission proposal by unanimity (see chapter 2) may be understood as an attempt to reduce bargaining costs. In politics as well as in business 'take it or leave it' is a frequently used device for this purpose. The rule about the Council and Commission proposals suggests that the founding fathers of the EEC understood that the elaborate institutions they were establishing entailed the risk of high bargaining costs. In this they were more astute than their followers, who proved unable to control the explosion of these, as of other transaction costs caused by a continuous increase in membership and a parallel growth of European competences.

'Influence costs' are the costs incurred in attempts to bias the decisions of the central institutions in a self-interested fashion, in attempts to counter such influence activities by others, and by the resulting degradation of the quality of decisions. Judging from the extensive literature on interest groups in the EU, influence costs are at least as pervasive, and potentially even more serious, than bargaining costs in their distorting consequences. Students of economic organizations have suggested that influence costs are one important reason why a merged organization cannot do everything the separate components did, and more. Two conditions are necessary to make influence costs likely to occur: first, decisions must be made that can influence how the benefits and costs in the organization are distributed; and, second, the affected parties must have open channels of communication to the central decision-makers, as well as the means to influence them. Hence the general proposition that any centralization of authority, whether in the public or private sector, creates the potential for intervention and so gives rise to costly influence activities. It follows that influence costs are one of the largest costs of big government:

> Direct governmental expenditures are just the tip of the iceberg. The resources expended by others to influence judges and juries, legislators and regulators, inspectors...and other government employees may far exceed those expended by the government itself on making and even on implementing the decisions that are influenced. The reason the size of government enters into the analysis is that larger governments have larger agendas, more decision makers, and more issues to resolve. The opportunities for influencing governmental decisions grow along with the size and scope of government.
>
> (Milgrom and Roberts 1992: 270–1)

Compared to other regional organizations, the EU is 'big government' in both its size and its scope of activities. Hence it is a safe inference that influence costs are much higher in case of the EU than in smaller, more focused, and less institutionally developed regional organizations, such as NAFTA or MERCOSUR, see chapter 9. The CAP, the Fisheries Policy, and the way the Cohesion and Structural Funds operate, provide ample evidence of the extent of influence activities in the EU. The 'complete independence' of the European Commission – the Treaty injunction that in the performance of their duties members of the Commission 'shall neither seek nor take instructions from any government or from any other body' – is of course meant to prevent, as much as possible, influence activities within the EC/EU. In spite of this injunction, doubts about the independence of the Commission, or at least of some of its members, have been expressed for a long time. Recently a very knowledgeable observer like Jean-Claude Piris (2011) has argued that the principle of the independence of the Commissioners from their country of origin has become theoretical. For this reason, the most important measure of the Lisbon Treaty to increase the effectiveness of the Commission was the reduction of the number of Commissioners from one per member state to two-thirds of the number of member states, with a system of equal rotation. However, after the failure of the first Irish referendum to ratify the Treaty, in June 2008, the European Council promised to abandon the planned reduction of the number of Commissioners, in order to facilitate the success of the second referendum. The problem, Piris argues, is that a Commission with one Commissioner per member state runs the risk of falling into intergovernmentalism since the member states tend to identify 'their' Commissioner as their representative in the Commission. The consequence is that decisions are made by consensus, so that, with twenty-seven (now twenty-eight) member states, the Commission can hardly take decisions. In such a case, future analysts will have to consider another kind of transaction costs: the cost of non-decisions.

Adverse selection, moral hazard and the debt crisis of the euro zone

In discussing the transaction costs of reaching mutually acceptable agreements, i.e., bargaining costs, we noted the existence of incentives for bargaining partners to misrepresent the value attached to the proposal. A second kind of incentive problem arising from pre-contractual information asymmetries is known as adverse selection. When discussing various kinds of transaction costs at the beginning of the present chapter, we noted that 'adverse selection', a term originally coined in the insurance industry, now refers also to the kind of pre-contractual opportunism that arises when one party to a bargain has private information about something that affects the other's net benefit from the contract. Also moral hazard was originally an insurance term referring to the tendency of people with insurance to reduce the care they take to avoid or reduce insurance losses. In TCE the term refers more generally to the form of post-contractual opportunism that arises when actions required under the contract are not freely observable. The difficulty or cost of monitoring and enforcing appropriate behaviour creates the moral hazard problem. As a consequence, contracting is incomplete since there is no point to writing a contract specifying in detail particular behaviour when the desired actions cannot be observed and consequently the contract cannot be effectively enforced.

It was already noted that in the context of the EU's sovereign-debt crisis several member states, but especially Greece, have provided textbook examples of both pre-contractual and post-contractual opportunism. Greece entered the third stage of EMU and adopted the euro in

January 2001. Despite persistent doubts about the reliability of the data provided by the Greek government, the European Council resolved that Athens had satisfied the convergence criteria and could therefore join a bloc of countries that included such champions of fiscal discipline as Germany, the Netherlands, and Austria. The major international rating agencies assigned the top AAA grade, the same grade given to German bonds, to the Greek public debt and to the bonds of less fiscally virtuous members of the euro zone that were suspected, like Greece, of having indulged in creative accounting. As a result, in the euro zone, the debt of each member of the euro zone faced similar prices, even though the risks were in fact quite dissimilar. Even after adoption of the euro in January 2001, successive Greek governments continued to play Russian roulette with the national economy, and to conceal what they were doing by manipulating the official statistics. In addition to concealing the extent of their financial problems, these governments also engaged in various practices of 'creative public finance' such as contract swaps, with the help of international banks Goldman Sachs and JP Morgan – a clear case of post-contractual opportunism. The loose governance of the euro zone provided again the wrong incentives. Already in 2004 and 2005 there had been problems with the economic data provided by Athens. The EU's statistical office, Eurostat, then asked for more powers to verify how the data had been produced, but it was refused the additional authority which might have averted the present crisis, see chapter 6. In reality, national governments, European institutions, and international bodies all cooperated in creating such problems of pre- and post-contractual opportunism.

Although responsibility for the Greek disaster is widely shared, official reports and public commentary prefer to focus only on the misbehaviour of the Athens government. Ten years after its admission to the supposedly exclusive Euro club, Greece was being treated as an EU protectorate, if not as a colony. During negotiations between Athens and the so-called troika – the ECB, IMF, and European Commission in June and July 2011 – troika's officials revealed what they wanted: to make Greece's 50 billion euro privatization programme happen, outsiders were to be brought in to run it. And because Greece seemed incapable of collecting taxes, international experts would come in to do that too. Such rigour should have been applied much earlier, and not only in the case of Greece. The same countries and European institutions that supported, or at least accepted, a large and economically highly heterogeneous monetary union, regardless of the risks involved, invoke the strictest disciplinary measures now, when it may be too late to rescue the common currency.

Already several years ago, long-time official participants in the EMU project stated privately that some form of fiscal federalism – i.e., a more federal European structure with centralized redistributive policies of taxing, borrowing, and spending – was a certainty in the long run (McNamara 2006). At the time this was a taboo idea, but since the beginning of the debt crisis such voices have become more insistent and openly articulated. Thus, Jacques Attali, who was the founding president of the European Bank for Reconstruction and Development as well as a former adviser to French President Mitterand, believes that Greece will never be able to repay its debts because the numerous aid plans, even if they have so far succeeded in avoiding default, failed to clear the long-term liabilities. On the other hand, the current crisis cannot be resolved by Greece exiting from the euro zone: 'If we let Greece go bankrupt, the euro will disappear. The very principle of the European Union will be challenged.' According to the French expert, the only possible solution requires the political courage of implementing a plan that includes the establishment of a European Ministry of Finance; the issuing of European Treasury bonds that would stretch out the debts payments of Greece, Portugal, Ireland, and other countries; and assessing a broad-based European Value Added Tax that would raise the necessary funds to repay the debt (Attali 2011).

Like most other experts, Attali fails to consider the limits of what Greek and other European voters may be willing to support. In fact, the defenders of EMU claim that the present debt crisis can be solved only by imposing the tightest fiscal discipline on debtor countries, even if this means enlarging the democratic deficit of the EU to a point where, given the state of public opinion today, it may well become politically unsustainable, see chapter 6. These 'good Europeans' refuse to admit that the root problem is their principle of fait accompli – pushing ahead with integration regardless of political, social, and economic consequences. The culture of total optimism, which prevailed until recently, prevented them from seeing those limits on supranational integration which Friedrich Hayek had perceived so clearly almost eighty years ago.

Hayek on redistributive limits to deep integration

The general approach to political and social questions by this Nobel Prize winning economist consisted in calling attention to the constraints facing would-be problem solvers, rather than in elaborating on the desirability of an optimal solution. In this, Hayek's approach was similar to that of another great Anglo-Austrian thinker, Karl Popper. The federalist movement of the inter-war period was largely driven by the ambition of restoring Europe to its former position at the centre of the world. This was to be accomplished by means of the economic and political integration of the continent. Hayek was open to federalist ideas but, characteristically, he focused attention on the constraints that would have to be overcome in order to deepen political and economic integration. His ideas on socio-political limits to integration have been expressed most cogently in one of his least cited papers – a short essay published in September 1939 in a rather obscure journal, the *New Commonwealth Quarterly*, and titled 'The Economic Conditions of Inter-state Federalism' (reprinted in Hayek 1948). In this paper, Hayek was actually addressing proposals concerning the transformation of the British Commonwealth into a federation, but his ideas are equally, if not more, relevant in the European context. Integration, Hayek argued, cannot proceed beyond a certain point without running into serious constraints at both the national and the supranational levels. In the first part of the paper he raises an important, if today fairly obvious, point, namely that political union could hardly be possible without economic union, which means that the economic powers of the member states of the future federation would have to be severely limited in the monetary and fiscal field, as well as in the area of industrial policy. But, he adds, it is not only the powers of the member states that would have to be limited: if there is great heterogeneity of socioeconomic conditions among the member states, which is likely to be the case in a large federation, the powers of the union would also have to be severely constrained. Whereas federalists saw in a European federation the optimal solution to all the problems of the continent, Hayek pointed out that in case of a high level of socioeconomic heterogeneity a federal government would be unable to undertake policies with identifiable winners and losers in different members of the federation:

> [T]he existing sovereign national states are mostly of such dimensions and composition to render possible agreement on an amount of state interference which they would not suffer if they were either much smaller or much larger...Planning, or central direction of economic activity, presupposes the existence of common ideals and common values; and the degree to which planning can be carried is limited by the extent to which agreement on such a common scale can be obtained or enforced. It is clear that such agreement will be limited in inverse proportion to the homogeneity and the similarity in outlook and tradition possessed by the

inhabitants of an area. Although, in the national state, the submission to the will of a majority will be facilitated by the myth of nationality, it must be clear that people will be reluctant to submit to any interference in their daily affairs when the majority which directs the government is composed of people of different nationalities and different traditions. It is, after all, only common sense that the central government in a federation composed of many different people will have to be restricted in scope if it is to avoid meeting an increasing resistance on the part of the various groups which it includes…There seems to be little possible doubt that the scope for the regulation of economic life will be much narrower for the central government of a federation than for national states.

(Hayek 1948: 264–5, footnote omitted)

The implications of such apparently common-sense observations are far reaching:

The conclusion that, in a federation, certain economic powers, which are now generally wielded by the national states, could be exercised neither by the federation nor by the individual states, implies that there would have to be less government all round if federation is to be practicable. Certain forms of economic policy will have to be conducted by the federation or by nobody at all. Whether the federation will exercise these powers will depend on the possibility of reaching true agreement, not only on *whether* these powers are to be used, but on *how* they are to be used…In many cases in which it will prove impossible to reach such agreement, we shall have to resign ourselves rather to have no legislation in a particular field than the state legislation which would break up the economic unity of the federation. Indeed, this readiness to have no legislation at all on some subjects rather than state legislation will be the acid test of whether we are intellectually mature for the achievement of suprastate organization.

(Ibid.: 266)

Hayek was writing these words before the rise of the expansive welfare states of the post-war years. His argument is even more relevant today since it implies that a European federation would be unable to pursue precisely those policies which characterize and legitimate the contemporary nation state: health, social policy, industrial policy, income redistribution, and, more generally, all policies favouring particular socioeconomic groups at the expense of other identifiable groups. But a European super-state unable to provide such public goods would lose whatever popular support it may have enjoyed initially. To emphasize this important point, let us assume that in a moment of federalist enthusiasm a majority of EU citizens expressed themselves in favour of full political integration. Given sufficiently broad popular support, the new federal entity would certainly be established on democratic principles, so that the democratic-deficit problem of the present EU would be solved – at least initially. As explained by Hayek, however, the federation would be unable to provide the variety of public goods that Europeans are accustomed to expect of their own national welfare state, and hence it could not retain for long the loyalty of its citizens. In turn, this loss of legitimacy would prevent the federal government from acting energetically even in areas, such as foreign policy and defence, where the European national states do need to pool their sovereignty in order to play a more incisive international role.

By calling attention to the distributive, cultural, and ultimately political constraints that limit the powers of a federation of very heterogeneous states, Hayek also helps us perceive more clearly the fundamental flaw of both federalist and 'neo-functionalist' theories of European integration: the inability to imagine a united Europe other than as a national state 'writ large'. But as historian Eric Jones has convincingly argued – and as will be discussed in more detail in later chapters – for most of its history Europe formed a cultural, economic, even a political unity. But it was not the unity of an empire or of a large super-state; rather, it was unity in diversity, embodied in a system of states competing and cooperating with each other. Such a system realized the benefits of competitive decision-making and the economies of scale of a centralized empire, giving Europe some of the best of both worlds. In the words of the British historian: 'This picture of a Europe which shared in salient respects a common culture...and formed something of a single market demonstrates that political decentralisation did not mean a fatal loss of economies of scale in production and distribution. The states system did not thwart the flow of capital and labour to the constituent states offering the highest marginal return' (Jones 1987: 117).

Constitutional and political limits to deeper integration

High transaction costs and the growing socioeconomic heterogeneity of the member states of the EU are not, of course, the only constraints facing the advocates of deeper integration. At least as important are the limits to the transfer of national sovereignty set by the national constitutions of the member states. It is impossible to discuss here the limits to the depth of European integration set by the different constitutional provisions of each member state of the EU. The case of Germany, however, deserves at least a brief mention, not only because of the political and economic weight of this country, but also because the decisions of Germany's Federal Constitutional Court (*Bundesverfassunsgericht*, here BVG) influence other constitutional courts, especially those of the countries of Central and Eastern Europe. As soon as the German Parliament approved the Fiscal Compact and the permanent rescue mechanism for members of the euro zone facing serious financial problems – the ESM – on 29 June 2012, five different complaints were submitted to the BVG by politicians representing the entire spectrum of opinion represented in the federal Parliament (Bundestag). Nobody expected an outright declaration of unconstitutionality of the two treaties, but what the complainants hoped to get from the Court were stricter limits on the discretion of the German government in its attempts to solve the crisis of the euro zone by deepening European integration – the 'more Europe' recipe often invoked by the German chancellor and by her finance minister, see chapter 7.

Already in the judgment on the constitutionality of the Lisbon Treaty, the Court had affirmed that core elements of the state identity could not be changed, even by means of constitutional amendments. Then, in September 2011, the BVG had been asked to rule on the constitutionality of the aid packages for Greece, Portugal, and Ireland agreed to by the German and the other governments of the euro zone. Germany had committed sums equivalent to more than half of the national budget without consulting the parliament and without providing sufficient public information about the various anti-crisis measures taken with the other governments of the euro zone. The BVG decided that the financial aids granted so far did not violate the rights of the Bundestag under the German Constitution. However, the judges set strict limits to the discretion of the executive. Thus they argued that German taxpayers could not be made responsible for the debts of other countries without explicit agreement of their parliament. Other strict limits to deeper integration concerned the impossibility that a future 'European economic government' – an idea often discussed at the time by the German chancellor and by French President Sarkozy – could affect the powers of the Bundestag concerning the national budget. The position of the BVG concerning constitutional limits on further integration was clearly expressed by the president of the Court, Andreas Vosskuhle, in an interview published by the *Franfurter Allgemeine Zeitung* (Amann and Kloepfer 2011). Asked whether the German Constitution ('Basic Law') allows more European integration, he answered: 'I think the possibilities have been largely exhausted.' And if politicians wished to go further? the interviewers wished to know. Vosskuhle's answer: 'The sovereign statehood of Germany is guaranteed by the Basic Law. It could not be renounced even through a constitutional revision by the legislature because of the "eternal guarantee" embedded in the Basic Law.' Could the budgetary sovereignty of the Bundestag be transferred in part to European institutions? was the next question. The answer: 'There does not seem to be much room left for transferring core competences to the European Union. To move beyond these limits it would be necessary to give Germany a new constitution. This would require a popular referendum. Without the people [such a move] is impossible.'

In a judgment published on 19 June 2012, the BVG insisted particularly on the duty of the executive to respect the right of the German Parliament to be involved in matters concerning the EU, and to be fully and timely informed about the decisions to be taken at the European level, as required by Article 23(2) and (3) of the Basic Law. According to the constitutional judges, the government led by Angela Merkel has systematically violated the rights of the German Parliament by not informing it 'comprehensively and as quickly as possible' about important developments in the EU. Instead, the decisions taken by the chancellor to solve the debt crisis of the euro zone have systematically presented the Bundestag with a fait accompli. As reported by Christian Geyer (2012: 29), the judges produced abundant empirical evidence concerning the asymmetry between the information available to the government and that communicated to the Bundestag. Some members of the German Parliament had to get information from Austrian sources, and in case of a draft of the EMS treaty dated 6 April 2011, the parliamentarians were informed by unofficial sources, even though the text of the draft was available to the executive. The judges of the BVG kept insisting on the temporal dimension of the government's duty to report to Parliament. The federal government has a duty to communicate to the Parliament more than the final text of a treaty; it must also make available, as soon as possible, early drafts and partial conclusions. The right to know of the representatives of the German people cannot be limited with the excuse of secrecy or urgency: the pressure of time does not justify a limitation of democracy. The president of the BVG rejected the accusation that in this way the judges slow down the process of European integration. He pointed out that the rules which the Basic Law prescribes for decisions concerning important political questions must also be upheld in crisis situations. 'This means, above all, that Parliament must be informed, that it must be allowed to take part in important decisions. This is the red line that runs through all our own decisions.' It is also the line that increasingly limits the policy discretion of the German government, and which explains the rigid, or sometimes contradictory, positions which the German chancellor takes at the European level.

In fact, the oscillating behaviour of the German government during the euro crisis shows with particular clarity that the attitude of the national electorates increasingly conditions the relations among the member states, as well as the general attitude towards European integration – a potentially disruptive development for a project launched and carried out by political and economic elites. As I have argued elsewhere, it is impossible to understand the course of the European integration process since the early 1950s without taking into consideration the failed Europeanization of the masses – the failure to achieve something comparable to the 'nationalization of the masses' which occurred in Germany and in most other countries of Western Europe during the nineteenth century (Majone 2009: 22–5). Since the end of World War II a certain Europeanization of the national elites has taken place, yet this process has hardly touched the vast majority of citizens. Students of European integration have always minimized, when they have not completely ignored, the implications of insufficient popular support for the integration project. The authors of the first social-scientific analyses of regional integration in the Old Continent – Ernst Haas and his neo-functionalist school – argued that the bureaucratized nature of European states entailed that all crucial decisions are made by political and economic elites, see chapter 5. In the age of the 'permissive consensus' it was tempting to assume that popular support was indeed unnecessary. However this permissive consensus began to erode with the first enlargement of the European Community in 1973 – which included two countries, Britain and Denmark, that from the outset rejected any idea of political integration – and especially with the first significant expansion of European competences under the Single European Act of 1986. After the controversial decision to proceed with monetary union despite the repeated warnings of the experts and the opposition of the vast majority of German voters, and after the rejection of the draft Constitutional Treaty by the French and Dutch voters in 2005, what remained of the mood of permissive consensus turned into Euro-fatigue, even into outright Euro-scepticism. These changes of European public opinion probably explain the unwillingness of the national governments to cooperate with each other and with the European institutions in the solution of problems concerning the entire EU – for example, on the occasion of massive illegal immigration following the recent changes of regime in North Africa. Despite the official rhetoric about the determination of the member states 'to lay the foundations of an ever closer union among the peoples of Europe', the process of deepening integration seems to have reached its limits. It is even conceivable that a regressive movement may set in. Thus in chapter 1 I quoted the opinion of economist De Grauwe – a strong advocate of European integration – that in an increasingly heterogeneous monetary union even the original members of the euro zone may conclude that the policies of the ECB no longer correspond to their national conditions as well as they did before the enlargement, and so decide to give up the common currency.

5

European integration and the decoupling
of politics and economics

Rise and decline of a liberal principle

The possibility of separating economics and politics was a key, if implicit, assumption of the founders of the EEC. It was not a new idea, but rather a return to a classic liberal tenet which in the nineteenth century and up to World War I had made it possible for the world economy to develop in such a fashion that 'between national and international economic integration there was only a difference in degree but not in kind' (Roepke 1954: 219). During the mercantilist era of the seventeenth and eighteenth centuries, the relationship between state power and international trade was seen as a problem of exceptional importance, one which was formulated as a debate about the interventionist obligations of rulers rather than as a matter of free trade (Brewer 1989). Against the mercantilist promotion of the power of the state, state regulation of trade, and the subordination of economic goals to political power, liberalism advocated the widest possible separation of the two spheres of politics (government) and economics. By aid of this principle of separation it was possible to reduce to a minimum the economic implications of the coexistence of sovereign states with their different legal orders and systems of administration, their frontiers, and separate citizenship. Applying this same principle of separation between politics and economics to the monetary field, it was possible to create an effective international monetary order: the gold standard. Absent a world government, there could not exist a genuine *de jure* world money system guaranteeing the possibility of payments at stable exchange rates, but the gold standard made it possible to achieve, in practice, the same result: if not a *de jure* at least a *de facto* world monetary system. As Roepke (1954: 225) has argued, in no area can the significance of the principle of the de-politicization of the economic sphere be seen as clearly as in the case of money. In the heyday of the international gold standard, the

1870s to 1914, surrender of national monetary sovereignty was considered not only acceptable but positively beneficial. On the one hand, no serious problems seemed to arise from the application of the essential conditions, or 'rules of the game', for operation of a gold standard – including the condition that within each country of the system there must be a high degree of wage flexibility. On the other hand, surrender of monetary sovereignty fit perfectly classical liberal theory, according to which the role of government and government itself were to be reduced to a minimum.

The gold standard was a monetary order which, by linking money to gold and not to arbitrary decisions of governments, was a perfect example of the principle of the de-politicization of the economic sphere. As Roepke puts it, it was an 'economic' but not a 'political' currency system. But the gold standard was bound to break down when the predominantly liberal system of states was gradually replaced by an interventionist, 'welfare-state' system. The increasing politicization of economic life was bound to destroy a monetary order based on the principle of de-politicization. In fact, a monetary policy independent of financial policy is possible only so long as government expenditure constitutes a comparatively small part of all payments, and as long as the government debt constitutes only a small part of all credit instruments. Today such conditions no longer exist: '[A]s long as government expenditure constitutes as large a part of the national income as it now does everywhere, we must accept the fact that government will necessarily dominate monetary policy and that the only way in which we could alter this would be to reduce government expenditure greatly.' (Hayek 1960: 327; footnote omitted).

In all the nation states of Western Europe the increasing politicization of economic life and the rise of the welfare state were already clearly visible in the 1950s. The possibility of separating politics and economics was not, however, an unreasonable assumption at the European level, given the limited competences of the EEC (largely confined to measures of negative integration, see chapter 2) and the small size of the Community budget. In fact, the Treaty of Rome never mandated that social policies should be harmonized prior to, or concurrently with, trade liberalization inside the common market. Rather, it suggested that social harmonization should be regarded as a possible corollary rather than a requirement for the common market. The only significant exception to this stance was Article 119 of the Treaty, stating the principle that men and women should receive equal pay for equal work. As already mentioned, this Article was inserted at the demand of France which, having introduced similar legislation before 1957, feared the competition of other countries in sectors (such as textiles) employing a high proportion of female workers. At any rate, the application of Article 119 was blocked for a long time by lack of political agreement between the member states on its compulsory nature.

The assumption of the founding fathers concerning the possibility of separating economics and politics was basically shared by many members of the German 'ordo-liberal' school, who viewed the 1957 Treaty of Rome as an 'economic constitution' guaranteeing the basic economic freedoms, the opening up of the national economies and a system of undistorted competition. This same view also imposed limits on the Community itself: discretionary economic policies as well as a continuous expansion of supranational competences were considered illegitimate and unlawful. Thus:

> The ordo-liberal European polity consists of a two-fold structure: at supranational level, it is committed to economic rationality and a system of undistorted competition, while, at the national level, re-distributive (social) policies may be pursued and developed further...social policy at European level could, at best, be said to have been handled through intergovernmental bargaining processes.

> (Joerges and Roedl 2009: 4)

The subsequent expansion of the powers and increased activism of the EC/EU went well beyond such limits. Unsurprisingly, the strongest critique of the Maastricht Treaty, with its unprecedented expansion of European competences and commitment to monetary union, came from Germany's ordo-liberals, who interpreted the treaty as a break with the economic constitution embedded in the Rome Treaty.

The 'Coase Theorem' and the Treaty of Rome

The difficulty of separating economic and political criteria at the macro level may be better appreciated by considering how strict are the conditions that allow separation of efficiency and distributive criteria even at the microeconomic level. As economists tell us, economic decisions are much simpler when efficiency considerations – the size of the pie – can be separated from distributive considerations – how the pie gets divided; in other words, when the issue of how value is created is separable from that of the distribution of value. When such separation is possible, a group decision is said to be efficient if it maximizes the total value (or the aggregate welfare) of the members of the group. Moreover, for any inefficient decision, there exists another (total-value maximizing) decision that *all* the group members strictly prefer. The celebrated proposition known as 'Coase Theorem' states that if the parties bargain to an efficient agreement and there are no significant transaction costs and no 'wealth effects' – i.e., if the choices of the bargainers do not depend on the amount of resources at their disposal – then the value-creating activities that they will agree upon do not depend on the bargaining power of the parties or on what assets each owned when the bargaining began. Rather, efficiency alone determines the choice of the activity; the other factors can affect only decisions about how the costs and benefits are to be shared (Milgrom and Roberts 1992). The Coase Theorem is the foundation of TCE, but its validity depends on the absence of significant transaction costs. This apparent paradox has been cleared up by Ronald Coase himself:

> The world of zero transaction costs has often been described as a Coasian world. Nothing could be further from the truth. It is the world of modern economic theory, one which I was hoping to persuade economists to leave. What I did. . .was simply to bring to light some of its properties. I argued that in such a world the allocation of resources would be independent of the legal position, a result which Stigler dubbed the 'Coase Theorem'.
>
> (Coase 1988: 174)

The formal analysis of economic problems is greatly simplified when wealth effects can be ignored. This assumption allows the analyst to focus on questions of efficiency, setting aside, at least for the time being, questions concerning the distribution of the gains. However, the assumption of no wealth effects is a good deal more restrictive than may appear at first sight, hence its range of meaningful application is pretty narrow. As Milgrom and Roberts (1992: 35–8) explain, for the assumption of no wealth effects to hold, three conditions must be satisfied. First, given any two alternative decisions there is a definite amount of money, or other valuable resources, that would be sufficient to compensate the decision-maker to switch from one alternative to the other. Second, if the decision-maker were first given an additional amount of wealth, then the amount needed to compensate the decision-maker for the switch from one alternative to the other would be unaffected. Finally, the decision-maker must have enough resources to absorb any wealth reduction necessary to pay for a switch from the less preferred to the more preferred option. A moment's reflection will suggest a number of situations in real life, both at the individual and at the collective level, where one or more of these conditions would not be satisfied. Thus for some people there may be no amount of money that they would accept as compensation for a serious risk of loss of life, or for being forced to live far from family and friends. Again, a poor country will often lack the resources to pursue a policy that a richer one would.

It seems reasonable to assume that the drafters of the Treaty of Rome assumed something like a no-wealth-effects condition, and that this assumption allowed them to separate efficiency from distributive considerations in the process of European integration. Thus the Treaty never mandated that social policies should be harmonized prior to or concurrently with trade liberalization inside the common market. Another piece of evidence concerning the assumptions of the founding fathers is the much greater importance which the Rome Treaty attaches to negative than to positive integration, see chapter 2. Other significant factors suggesting the applicability of the Coase Theorem to our case are the small number, socioeconomic homogeneity, and cultural similarity of the countries that established the EEC – essentially the same countries which formed the core of Charlemagne's empire! True, the treaty foresaw a higher level of institutionalization than seemed to be justified by a simple customs union, thus possibly raising transaction costs to a level where the assumptions of the theorem may no longer hold. This emphasis on institutionalization was due to a number of factors: the influence of a relatively small group of federalist political leaders; the lack at the time of alternative models of regional integration that might have suggested the possibility of achieving the goals of the treaty by institutionally simpler means; and, perhaps, also the statist tradition of continental Europe. An important point to keep in mind about the level of institutionalization, however, is that the founding members of the EEC had quite different ideas about the roles of the supranational institutions than what eventually came to be accepted. Thus in creating the ECJ they intended to create a court that could not significantly compromise national sovereignty or national interests (Alter 2001). In fact, the ECJ did change the EU legal system – in particular by turning the preliminary ruling system from a mechanism to allow individuals to challenge EC law in national courts into a mechanism to challenge national law in national courts.

At any rate, the possibility of separating politics and economics was a reasonable, even a useful, assumption as long as the competences of the

EEC remained limited. In the formative years of the Community, law and economics – the discourse of legal and economic integration – provided a sufficient buffer to achieve results that could not be directly obtained in the political realm. Not only were national governments required to abstain from measures that would create unjustified obstacles to free movement in the common market; the European institutions themselves, rather than mimicking the interventionism of the national policymakers in their efforts to bring about the economic integration of Europe, were to rely primarily on measures of negative integration. The moderation of the initial objectives explains why the issue of the 'democratic deficit' was never raised before new treaties, starting with the Single European Act, greatly expanded the powers of the Community.

A neo-liberal bias?

The emphasis of the Rome Treaty on negative integration and the view, embedded in the Maastricht Treaty, of monetary policy as a non-political field to be delegated to independent experts have been used by some commentators as evidence of the liberal, or rather 'neo-liberal', character of the EC/EU. According to this interpretation, the neo-liberal bias of the original project, rather than an excessive expansion of supranational competences, is at the origin of the democratic deficit: only a strong social dimension could legitimate the integration project. This is the position, for example, of the Belgian political leader and convinced federalist, Guy Verhofstadt, but also of renowned members of the intelligentsia like Juergen Habermas. The German philosopher chose to interpret the rejection of the draft Constitutional Treaty by the French and Dutch voters in May and June 2005 as a rejection of the neo-liberal stance of the EU, and as the expression of popular demand for a more welfare-oriented Union. In an article published in the *Suddeutsche Zeitung*, Habermas (2005) argued that with the achievement of the basic economic freedoms, the common market, monetary union, and the SGP for the euro zone, the neo-liberals had achieved all their objectives. Now, he warned, it is time to deepen the social dimension, and in particular to soften the impact of monetary union by means of the progressive harmonization of fiscal, social, and economic policies. According to the German philosopher, the entire integration process is distorted by the neo-liberal philosophy which pervades the European treaties. This is the original sin which 'Social Europe' is supposed to redeem.

Even a casual acquaintance with the history of post-war Europe is sufficient to cast serious doubts on the plausibility of this interpretation. In the 1950s liberalism, as a political and economic ideology, was at its nadir in Western Europe, with the partial exception of Germany. Central planning, industrial policy, public ownership as the main mode of economic regulation, were advocated by practically all political parties, including most liberal groupings. The nationalization of key industries, in particular, was seen as the most effective solution to all sorts of problems: not only to eliminate the political power and economic inefficiency of private monopolies, but also to stimulate regional development, redistribute resources in favour of particular social groups, protect consumers, foster industrial democracy, and, not least, ensure national security. These, or very similar, views were held by political leaders of the right and of the left; they were important ingredients of the contemporary zeitgeist. Those same years also witnessed the rise of the European welfare state, hence the puzzle: how could the authors of the Treaty of Rome – who at home accepted, indeed practised, interventionism in all sectors of the economy and of social relations – espouse economic liberalism at the European level? A sudden ideological conversion has to be excluded since the same political leaders, and those who followed them, continued to support interventionist policies domestically, at least until the 1980s – and some still do.

Liberal ideas concerning the working of the economic system were revived in the 1980s, but it is certainly wrong to consider monetary union a neo-liberal project, as Habermas does in the article mentioned above and keeps repeating in later publications. Indeed, no other European project has been as politically motivated, and as persistently pursued by integrationist leaders over many years, as the monetary union of national economies characterized by deep structural differences, and in the absence of a serious coordination of the economic and fiscal policies of the member states. The political motivation of EMU has been clear to competent observers from the very beginning, see chapter 1. It is also noteworthy that the UK, the most 'neo-liberal' member of the EU, has not joined the euro zone, and gives no indication of wanting to do so in the foreseeable future. Hence, European monetary union is exactly the reverse of the gold standard: if the latter was, in Roepke's terms, a strictly 'economic' currency system, the former is a unique example of a 'political' currency system. Once the political nature of EMU is clearly understood, it is difficult to believe in the constitutional (i.e., treaty-based) principles allegedly guiding the monetary policy of the EU: the non-political character of this policy and its separation from fiscal policy; the complete independence of the ECB and of the ESCB; price stability as absolute priority, etc. If the debt crisis of the euro zone proves anything, it is the impossibility of conceiving monetary union as a technical solution to well-defined economic problems; rather, its history since the Werner Plan of the 1970s shows EMU to be the result of a long-drawn political bargaining between France and Germany, with the connivance of a few other European actors, as discussed in chapter 1.

But what about the more general point made by Habermas and by a number of other writers, namely the alleged neo-liberal bias of the European treaties themselves? The truth is that different economic and social philosophies coexist in the founding treaties and in all subsequent texts (Majone 2009: 90–8). What the critics fail to see, or prefer to ignore, is that those elements of a liberal economic constitution that can be found in the treaties have only instrumental value – they do not express an ideological commitment; rather, they serve integrationist and other political objectives. This was already evident in the 1951 Treaty of Paris establishing the European Coal and Steel Community (ECSC). Although the declared objective of the Treaty was the elimination of trade barriers and the encouragement of 'normal' competition (rather than competition per se) in the sectors of coal and steel, many specific provisions were hardly compatible with economic liberalism. Thus the High Authority, the supranational executive of the ECSC, was given extensive powers of intervention, including the right to levy taxes, to influence investment decisions, and even in some cases to impose minimum prices and production quotas. Given the limited scope of the ECSC, and also of the generally forgotten but still surviving European Atomic Energy Community ('Euratom'), the corresponding treaties could largely avoid questions of general economic philosophy. Such questions played a much larger role in the preparatory work for the establishment of the EEC, when it was realized that the integration of highly regulated national markets would have been impossible without a serious effort to deregulate and liberalize the economies of the member states.

In other words, the well-known fact that monopolies and cartels have an inherent tendency to carve up markets was the main motivation for introducing strict competition rules. It would indeed be useless to bring down trade barriers between the member states if the national governments or private industry remained free to use subsidies or cartel-like arrangements to divide markets, or to reserve them for home producers.

Even a customs union, let alone a common market, must worry about the effects of cartels and concentrations: as tariff barriers go down, firms and governments might resort to various non-competitive practices, or non-tariff barriers, in order to offset the effects of the removal of protection. On the other hand, a customs union – which is what the EEC initially was – represents a preferential trade agreement among a subset of countries, and as such it was always considered with suspicion by economic liberals, who much preferred multilateralism (free trade for all countries) and the most-favoured-nation principle of the GATT and WTO charters. For this reason Wilhelm Roepke was opposed to the establishment of the EEC. According to the first Commissioner responsible for the competition policy of the European Community, 'Roepke was not prepared to acknowledge that the EEC (Rome) Treaty was based upon the market economy philosophy and that the rules of competition in particular were in accordance with neo-liberal ideas and were now being extended to international trade within the Community' (von der Groeben 1987: 48). Also the father of the German 'economic miracle', the Minister of Economic Affairs, Ludwig Erhard was quite sceptical about preferential trade agreements, favouring instead a multilateral approach to free trade. A significant number of German academics of the 'Ordo-liberal' school, took the same position, and also opposed early projects of monetary union, supporting instead the idea, popularized by Hayek, of competing national currencies.

The instrumental character of the alleged liberal bias of the EU is best seen in the field of international trade, and this explains the opposition of liberal economists like Roepke and of a liberal statesman like Ludwig Erhard to the EEC's regional approach to free trade. Customs unions cut tariffs for their members but not for other members of the GATT (or of the WTO after 1995), which are thus denied the benefit of the most-favoured-nation rights. In fact, the compatibility of the Treaty of Rome with GATT rules was hotly contested by a number of countries. In particular, strong objections were raised regarding the association between the Community and the 'Overseas Territories' – mainly former colonies and territories of France and the Benelux countries. This association was seen by third countries as effectively dismantling the ceiling placed on preferences in force at the time the GATT was established (1947), thereby creating a new and wider preferential system. Because of this and other complaints, no agreement was ever reached on the compatibility of the Rome Treaty with Article XXIV of the GATT, which deals with the formation of customs unions and free trade areas. The issue was resolved pragmatically, i.e., by shelving it, but only because the US threw its weight behind a relaxed interpretation of Article XXIV in favour of the EEC. Not surprisingly, relations between the EC/EU and its trading partners have been problematic from the very beginning. It would suffice to recall the international problems created by the protectionism of the CAP but these are not, in fact, the only problems.

The EU has also been accused of using food safety regulations, in particular those based on the so-called Precautionary Principle, as protectionist devices. From the perspective of many trading partners of the EU it must appear rather odd that the Union is accused by some European intellectuals and integrationist leaders of being 'neo-liberal'. In fact, the Commission's Communication on the PP reveals, in addition to a poor understanding of the logic of decision-making under uncertainty (Majone 2005: 138–42), also a serious disregard of the distributive implications of the principle, in particular the impact of precautionary standards on the welfare of developing countries. The European Commission maintains that in considering the positive and negative consequences of alternative risk strategies, one should take into consideration '*the overall cost to the Community*, both in the long- and short-term' (Commission 2000: 19; emphasis added). Such Euro-centrism could perhaps be justified if the cost of precautionary measures was borne only by exporters in rich countries, but what if it also is borne by very poor countries? The EU claims to be deeply committed to assisting, financially and otherwise, developing countries, especially African ones. However, estimates by World Bank economists of the economic impact of certain precautionary standards proposed by the Commission in the late 1990s, tell a different story. Using trade and regulatory survey data for the member states of the EU and nine African countries between 1989 and 1998, the World Bank economists estimated that the new standards would decrease African exports of cereals, dried fruits, and nuts to the EU by 64 per cent, relative to regulation following international standards (Otsuki, Wilson, and Sewadeh 2000). The total loss of export revenue for the nine African countries amounted to 400 million US dollars under EU standards, compared to a gain of 670 million US dollars if international standards were used. Moreover, studies conducted by the World Health Organization lead to the conclusion that the costs imposed on some of the poorest countries in the world would hardly be justified by the miniscule health benefits provided to Europeans by the precautionary standards.

We may conclude that the influence of 'neo-liberalism' on the European treaties and on European policies is much more limited than the critics claim. To the extent that such an influence may be detected, as in the case of the competition rules, the reason is not ideological, but strictly utilitarian: the impossibility of integrating a group of heavily regulated economies without some limits on the interventionist tendencies of national governments and the cartelization tendencies of private and public enterprises. The instrumental role of the rules on competition and state aid is also indicated by the fact that EU competition rules take the place of WTO-authorized countervailing duties to offset the damage caused by export subsidies to the industries of importing nations. It is the combination of rigid market access rules with flexible safeguards that has permitted multilateral trade integration to proceed so far without any domestic policy harmonization. Members of the WTO not only enjoy domestic policy autonomy but must also respect the exercise of that autonomy by other WTO members (Roessler 1996: 50–1). The member states of the Union, on the other hand, have surrendered their policy autonomy in matters relating to intra-EU trade, relying instead on the existence of a European competition policy.

At any rate, even the Treaty of Rome, although more 'neo-liberal' than the ECSC and Euratom Treaties, contains a number of interventionist features, most strikingly in the articles dealing with the CAP. The objectives of the CAP, as defined by the Treaty, are complex and partly contradictory, but the ECJ realistically interpreted them so as to give priority to maintaining farmers' incomes over increasing agricultural productivity or ensuring reasonable prices for consumers. Thus the Court recognized the essentially redistributive character of a policy which still absorbs almost 40 per cent of all budget expenditures of the EU (down from about 75 per cent in 1980). These redistributive objectives – aiming at establishing what has been called a 'welfare state for farmers' – are pursued by a variety of interventionist and protectionist means. The operational core of the CAP is the common organization of the markets for specific products, based on the instruments of common, politically determined prices, Community preferences, and financial transfers. To appreciate the importance attached to the CAP by the Treaty of Rome one should keep in mind that in post-war Europe 'agriculture became the equivalent of a large nationalized industry, managed by interventionist policies which sought to impose macroeconomic objectives in return for exemptions from the forces of open economic competition' (Milward 1992: 229). Short of leaving agriculture outside the scope of the European common market – an option favoured by some countries but categorically rejected by France – the only solution was to move state intervention to the European level. The CAP is the most obvious, but certainly not the only, sign of the influence of interventionist philosophies in the Rome Treaty. As Walter Hallstein, the first president of the European Commission, is supposed to have said: 'the Communities are in politics, not in business' (cited in von der Groeben 1987: 31).

The fundamental fallacy of neo-functionalism

The possibility of separating economics and politics was not only a basic principle of classic liberalism and a reasonable assumption of the founding fathers of the EEC. It was also Jean Monnet's working hypothesis, as well as an assumed premise of Ernest Haas and his neo-functionalist school. As stated above, the assumption of the founding fathers was not unreasonable because they envisaged a Community limited to a customs union, eventually developing into something like a common market. Also at the national level certain important public functions are delegated to unelected ('non-majoritarian') institutions such as regulatory authorities, central banks, and courts of law. Neo-functionalism, on the other hand, was meant to be a theory of regional *political* integration, to be achieved primarily by economic means – a strategy which badly underestimated the importance of popular support for the viability of the integration project. As already mentioned, Haas assumed that the bureaucratized nature of European states entailed that all crucial decisions are made by elites: public policymakers, as well as economic elites, trade unions, professional associations, business lobbies, etc. Public opinion at large, on the other hand, was deemed to be unimportant. Andrew Moravcsik has aptly summarized this elitist stance: 'Elite groups most intensely concerned with an issue, Haas asserts, have the greatest impact on national decision-making, which is why a majority, in the strict sense, is not required to make policy' (Moravcsik 2005: 352). Like Jean Monnet, but unlike the post-war generation of federalists, Haas and his school thought that the basic problem was not how to 'Europeanize the masses'; rather, the problem was how to make 'Europe without Europeans' (Schmitter 2005).

The success of the neo-functionalist strategy depended on the assumption that the superior problem-solving capacity of the supranational institutions would induce the progressive transfer of the loyalties and political demands of social groups from the national to the European level. The effectiveness of the supranational institutions was supposed to legitimate, ex post, the technocratic methods of integration. Unfortunately, this effectiveness has been increasingly questioned in recent years: rightly or wrongly 'Brussels,' and now also 'Frankfurt,' are perceived less as potential sources of solutions for problems that cannot be solved at the national level, than as causes of other, even more serious, problems. Thus, the mounting awareness that an ever-widening and deepening integration process has proved impotent to arrest the decline of Europe's economy relative to its major international competitors contributed to the dissatisfaction that found dramatic expression in the French and Dutch rejections of the draft Constitutional Treaty, and in the Irish 'No' to the Lisbon Treaty. The uncertainties and delays in tackling the sovereign-debt crisis have further increased an already high level of dissatisfaction with the problem-solving capacity of the European institutions, see chapter 8.

The British prime minister Clement Attlee used to warn against the 'fundamental fallacy' of believing that 'it is possible by the elaboration of machinery to escape the necessity of trusting one's fellow human beings' (citation in Judt 2010: 730). Attlee was reflecting on his Labour Party colleagues' obsession with the techniques of party-political management. The fundamental fallacy of both Monnet and the neo-functionalist school was the belief that the political integration of Europe could be achieved by political and economic elites with the help of legal and managerial instruments, but without the active participation of Europeans. This mistaken belief was further aggravated by later attempts to force the pace of integration, EMU being the most significant instance of such forcing. The mistakes of the early neo-functionalists are being repeated today – in reverse, so to speak – by integrationist leaders, such as German finance minister Schaeuble, who see the crisis of the euro zone as an opportunity to achieve the political unification of Europe: an occasion for centralizing not only monetary but also fiscal policy and key aspects of social policy, such as pensions. Whereas monetary union was originally seen as '*la voie royal vers l'union politique*' (Tsoukalis 1993: 178), now the euro crisis seems to provide the perfect excuse for moving decisively towards full integration. If the early neo-functionalists believed in the possibility of achieving political integration by technocratic methods because of the superiority of such methods, now political integration seems to be achievable precisely because of the breakdown of the same technocratic approach. In either case, the state of public opinion is judged to be completely irrelevant, see the next chapter for more discussion of this paradox.

In one important respect the technocratic view of both the government and the market which underlies neo-functionalist arguments may be compared with the neo-classical view of the firm as a production function: both views completely disregard the existence of transaction costs. As already mentioned, neo-classical economics' view of the firm as a production function fits a world of zero transaction costs. Once the existence and significance of transaction costs is acknowledged, the firm is no longer seen as a mere production function, but as a system of governance of contractual relations. Organizational variety is explained by the fact that transactions differ in their attributes, which means that their governance needs vary. Transaction-cost economies are realized by assigning transactions to governance in a discriminating way (Williamson 1985; see also chapter 2). There is general agreement today that the transaction-cost approach to the study of economic organization has been able to yield new and deeper insights on such issues as vertical integration, non-standard contracting, the organization of work, economic regulation, and the nature of the modern corporation.

As neo-classical economics could view the firm as a production function because of its assumption of a world of zero transaction costs, so the neo-functionalist view of the process of European integration ignored the problems, and the limits, of supranational governance precisely because of its disregard of economic and political transaction costs. While the realization that there are different transaction costs explains the need for different forms of governance, the neo-functionalist unawareness of such costs led to the more or less implicit assumption that there is only one effective method of integration. One recent indication of this monistic view is the invocation of 'more Europe' often repeated as 'the correct answer to a crisis that has brought to light a construction flaw of the European Monetary Union' (Habermas 2012: 486). Of course 'more Europe' is as ambiguous an expression as 'ever closer union'. For Habermas it means primarily 'Social Europe', but the German philosopher does not explain how growing popular resistance to large-scale transfer of national resources to the European level – a resistance made evident by the crisis of monetary union, not only in Germany but in all member states that are net contributors to the EU budget – would allow the development of even a modest welfare state at the supranational level, see chapter 7.

Coming back to Monnet, and to Haas and his followers, it would of course be unfair to criticize them for having failed to anticipate later theoretical developments such as transaction-cost analysis. The fact remains that they never gave much thought to the possible costs of the roundabout strategy they were recommending: to force political integration through ever broader and deeper moves of economic integration. It has already been suggested that the failure to anticipate the negative consequences of the continuous growth of European competences may be largely explained by the neo-functionalists' belief that all important decisions are made by elites, so that popular support is not strictly necessary for the long-term viability of the integration process. As mentioned in a previous chapter, Jean Monnet expressed this philosophy with admirable clarity: 'since the people aren't ready to agree to integration, you have to get on without telling them too much about what is happening' (Ross 1995: 194). Given this belief, it was difficult to imagine that the limited normative resources available to the supranational institutions could one day become a serious constraint on the further expansion of their competences. The error was compounded by the further assumption that the relative advantage of the supranational institutions – their central position, superior information, policy expertise, and their capacity to act as 'honest broker' – were such as to guarantee a high level of effectiveness, and thus a progressive transfer of loyalties and political demands from the national to the supranational level.

Such confidence in the superiority of the supranational institutions may have been induced by the belief that the nation state, as an independent system of governance, was doomed – at least in Europe. Like the federalists of the immediate post-war period, the first students of European integration greatly underestimated the resilience of the traditional state institutions. Today we can see more clearly that neither globalization nor European integration have reduced the role of the nation state: internationalization and regionalism have made the nation state, if anything, even more important (see chapter 10). At any rate, the belief in the superior effectiveness of the supranational institutions had significant implications for neo-functionalist theory since it assured the progressive transfer of loyalties and political demands from the national to the European level. That such an assumption was mistaken is of course much more obvious today than it was in the 1960s or even later. In pre-EMU days, for example, complaints about the disappointing economic performance of the EU could be answered by reminding the critics that Community competences did not include macroeconomic policymaking. Such excuses are no longer possible after the centralization of monetary policy and tightening European constraints on the fiscal autonomy of the national governments.

In many respects monetary union represents the extreme achievement of neo-functionalism, but at the same time it exposes the inability of neofunctionalists to understand the importance of the socio-political context in which 'technocratic' institutions operate. This may be seen most clearly by comparing the supranational ECB with the old Bundesbank. For almost half a century the latter was a model of central bank independence while at the same time enjoying broad popular support, and even becoming an important element of Germany's political culture as the symbol of the rebirth of the country after the war. The ECB, on the other hand, operates in a political and social vacuum – an insularity shared with other European institutions, particularly the ECJ, see the last section of the present chapter. Even the EP, although directly elected, lacks the social embeddedness which makes the national parliaments truly representative of their voters. Treaty after treaty the powers of the EP have been increased, but this expanded role has not produced the hoped-for increase in the political legitimacy of the supranational parliament. Hence the paradox of a parliament which, rather than legitimating the other European institutions, suffers itself from a democratic deficit. Surprising as this paradox may appear, it can be easily explained.

The EP does not differ from the legislatures of parliamentary democracies only because it lacks their power to tax and spend, to initiate legislation, and to validate a government's actions. Another fundamental difference is the absence of the traditional government–opposition dialectic. The consequences of this absence are significant: being denied an appropriate political arena in which to hold European governance accountable, voters are almost pushed into organizing opposition to Europe (Mair 2007). Hence the transformation of popular referendums on new treaties into contests for or against the EU. The *sui generis* nature of the EP is also revealed by the attitude of its members: many MEPs see themselves as policy specialists rather than as partisan politicians, and insist that the Commission should be a neutral institution, and that individual Commissioners should forget their party affiliation, if any (Magnette 2001). This attitude may also account, at least in part, for the fact that the EP has never seriously contested the Commission's monopoly of legislative initiative. But if the EP differs in important respects from national legislatures, non-elected institutions like the ECB and the

ECJ also differ significantly from the homonymous institutions operating at the national level. We explore these differences in the next two sections.

Politically independent but socially embedded: non-majoritarian institutions and democratic government

A significant feature of the governance structure of all contemporary democracies is the delegation of significant powers to institutions that are not accountable to the voters or to their elected representatives: courts, independent central banks, and regulatory authorities operating outside bureaucratic hierarchies. As we saw in the preceding chapter, an important reason for delegating policymaking powers to institutions independent of the electoral cycle is to increase the credibility of long-term commitments. The delegation of powers to such 'non-majoritarian' institutions is meant to restrain the temptation of democratic politicians to assign greater weight to short-run considerations and to default on long-term commitments. At the same time, in a democracy important policy choices are supposed to be made by electorally accountable leaders, so that such delegation inevitably raises problems of democratic legitimacy. How are such problems resolved? The answer is that they have never been satisfactorily resolved in terms of general democratic theory, but that different pragmatic solutions have been worked out, more or less successfully, by different countries according to their own constitutional traditions and political culture. Thus in the US the propriety of delegating quasi-legislative powers to independent regulatory authorities is now regarded as having been settled by the practice of more than one century. In the past, a 'non-delegation doctrine' enjoyed such widespread acceptance that it came to be regarded as the traditional model of American administrative law. The model conceived the regulatory authority as a mere transmission belt for implementing legislative directives in particular cases. Hence when passing statutes Congress should decide all questions of policy, and frame its decisions in such specific terms that administrative regulation will not entail the exercise of broad discretion by the regulators (Stewart 1975).

The non-delegation doctrine had already found widespread acceptance when the first institutionalization of the American regulatory state, the Interstate Commerce Commission, was established by the 1887 Interstate Commerce Act. The Act's detailed grant of authority seemed to exemplify the transmission-belt model of regulation. However, the subsequent experience of railroad regulation revealed the difficulty of deriving operational guidelines from general standards. Thus, when the Federal Trade Commission was established in 1914, it received essentially a blank cheque authorizing it to eliminate unfair competition. The New Deal agencies received even broader grants of power to regulate particular sectors of the economy 'in the public interest'. The last time the Supreme Court used the non-delegation doctrine was in 1935, when in *Panama Refining Co. v. Ryan* (293 US 388) and in *Schecter Poultry Corp. v. United States* (295 US 495) it held the delegation in the National Industrial Recovery Act unconstitutional. The Court has subsequently upheld many delegations of legislative powers that were no more specific than those found wanting in 1935. Hence the suspicion that *Panama Refining* and *Schecter Poultry* are better explainable in terms of the anti-New Deal bias of the Supreme Court in 1935 than in terms of constitutional theory. At any rate, the Supreme Court's reiteration of the non-delegation principle, coupled with its very sparing use to strike down legislation, illustrates a continuing judicial effort to harmonize the modern regulatory state with traditional notions of separation of powers, representative government, and the rule of law (Mashaw *et al.* 1998).

For historical, institutional, and political reasons explained in some detail elsewhere (Majone 1996), the development of statutory regulation by independent agencies is a much more recent phenomenon in Europe, but this mode of regulation quickly became the leading edge of public policymaking. Compared to traditional forms of state intervention, such as public ownership, 'American-style' statutory regulation was increasingly perceived as being less bureaucratic and more independent of party-political influences; more committed to a problem-solving, rather than a bargaining, style of policymaking; and better able to protect the diffuse interests of consumers rather than the concentrated interests of producers. At the same time, the legitimacy and democratic accountability of independent regulatory institutions soon emerged as a significant topic of political discourse in Europe. While European governments acknowledged the importance of policy credibility in an increasingly interdependent world, and thus were prepared to accept the independence of regulators, in practice the prevailing political culture often induced governments to limit regulatory discretion. Thus, even though the German competition regulator – the Cartel Office – has considerably more extensive powers than the competition authorities of most other European countries, the government retains considerable powers of intervention in competition policy, especially in merger cases. In such cases, the Minister of Economics can overrule a negative decision of the Cartel Office. Moreover, in granting exemptions from the prohibition of mergers and cartels, the minister seems to be driven more by political and social considerations than by efficiency criteria (Baake and Perschau 1996).

Also Germany's central bank as it operated before EMU (the old 'Bundesbank') was considered not only the most powerful, but also the most politically independent central bank in Europe, if not in the world. Yet, this independence had only a statutory basis: a law which the German Parliament could have changed overnight if it felt that the policies of the Bank were contrary to the public interest or to the policy preferences of the majority of the voters. Thus, in 1978 Chancellor Helmut Schmidt threatened to have the Parliament limit the independence of the Bundesbank by modifying the 1957 law (*Bundesbankgesetz*) should the Bank continue to oppose the establishment of the EMS (Marsh 1992). That the independence of the Bank in fact has never been limited, despite frequent frictions with both conservative and social-democratic governments, shows that the real foundation of the Bank's legitimacy was not its statute-based independence, but rather the support of a public opinion traditionally averse to inflation. At the same time, Germany's central bankers were well aware that to lose contact with the national government meant to lose the possibility of exerting a significant influence on the economic governance of the country. In sum, despite frequently repeated assertions that the old Bundesbank served as the model for the ECB, the differences between the two institutions are much more significant than the similarities, see the following section.

The US Federal Reserve also enjoys a well-deserved reputation for independence, which is guaranteed by the Federal Reserve Act, a statute originally passed in 1914. However, no Federal Reserve chairman, no matter how independently minded, can safely ignore the vigorously expressed wishes of a strong American President. As Peterson and Rom point out (1989: 155–63), the Federal Reserve knows that its statutory powers, with all the independence and autonomy they confer, can be altered at any time by new legislation. If a strong US President, backed by loyal supporters in Congress, wished to restructure the board of the bank, the Federal Reserve could not prevent him from doing so. Nor does the chairperson of the Federal Reserve often have to guess at what the administration wishes:

Professional and social contacts frequently occur between the executive branch and the Fed. For example, the chairman has lunch at the Treasury every week, and there are frequent exchanges between the Fed's senior staff and the Office of Management and Budget (OMB) as well as the president's Council of Economic Advisers. . .It is not easy to ascertain the direction of influence at such meetings, but Fed policy is usually quite consistent with administration policy and presidential disagreements with the Fed are usually marginal and short-lived.

(Ibid.: 155–6; footnotes omitted)

The Federal Reserve is a creature of Congress, the product of the 1914 statute, and thus technically subject to congressional control. Congress could at any time pass new legislation changing the Federal Reserve's terms of reference, and as Peterson and Rom note, in virtually all sessions of Congress legislation is introduced that would have exactly that effect. But if Congress potentially has the authority to restructure the Federal Reserve, only minor changes in its operating procedures have had any realistic chance of congressional passage. Any major alteration in the workings of the Federal Reserve would require vigorous Presidential support. Lacking that, most efforts to limit the authority of the Federal Reserve or reorganize its operating procedures fail to negotiate the complex congressional maze. Again, the difference with the way in which the ECB operates is striking: at the European level there is no government with which the monetary authority could engage in a productive exchange of opinions.

Independent regulatory authorities and central banks may be the best-known contemporary examples of non-majoritarian institutions. Historically, however, courts of law are the prototype of such institutions. Even in England the complete independence of judges was not fully secured until the early eighteenth century (Georgian period) when the judges, though appointed by the Crown, were no longer subject to its influence in their decisions: they could not be removed except on an address from both Houses of Parliament. The problem of the democratic legitimacy of judicial decisions has been especially felt in the US, where federal courts may strike down a law enacted by Congress, and so presumably expressing the preferences of the majority of American voters. The legitimacy problem is particularly acute when the US Supreme Court engages in 'non-interpretive' review, i.e. when it makes the determination of constitutionality of a given policy by reference to a value judgement other than one embodied, even if only implicitly, either in some specific provision of the Constitution or in the overall structure of government as set up by the Constitution. A rich body of literature deals with the issue of judge-made constitutional law, and with the role and justification of the Supreme Court as a non-majoritarian, or even anti-majoritarian, institution (Ely 1980; Choper 1983; Wolfe 1987; Berger 1997, to mention only some of the best-known works). However divided the opinions about judicial activism are, few observers would deny that the Supreme Court is inescapably a participant in the larger political process of the American democracy. To begin with, US Presidents tend to appoint justices who are not hostile to their own views on public policy, nor could they expect confirmation of a justice whose stance on key issues was flagrantly at odds with that of the dominant majority in the Senate. It is also the case that 'the policy views dominant in the Court will never be out of line for very long with the policy views dominant among the law-making majorities of the United States...it would be most unrealistic to suppose that the Court would, for more than a few years at most, stand against any major alternatives sought by a law-making majority' (Dahl 1972: 206).

The fact is that acting solely by itself with no support from the President and Congress, the Court is almost powerless to affect the course of national policy. In order to come as close as possible to the goal of imposing its policy preferences on society the Court must therefore defer to the preferences of Congress. Nor is it only a question of imposing the preferences of the Court as a privileged interest group. In order to confer legitimacy, the Court must itself possess legitimacy. However, the Court jeopardizes the legitimacy attributed to its interpretations of the Constitution if it flagrantly opposes the major policies of the dominant majority. To the extent that the legitimacy of every political institution in a democratic system of government depends finally on its consistency with democratic principles, the legitimacy of judicial review and the Court's exercise of that power must stem from the presumption that the Court is subject to popular control. Hence Dahl concludes:

> The more the Court exercises self-restraint and the less it challenges the policies of law-making majorities, the less the need or impulse to subject it to popular controls. The more active the Court is in contesting the policies of law-making majorities, the more visible becomes the slender basis of its legitimacy by democratic standards, and the greater the efforts to bring the Court's policies into conformity with those enacted by law-making majorities.

(Ibid.: 209)

In fact, the Supreme Court justices are acutely aware of the limitations of the Court's powers and its dependence on voluntary acquiescence to its decisions. Hence, the Court's concern with its authority makes it reluctant to depart too far or for too long from prevailing public opinion in its decisions. Sophisticated statistical analysis of Supreme Court decisions for the period 1956–1989 indicates that for most of this period 'the Court has been highly responsive to majority opinion. Its decisions not only have conformed closely to the aggregate policy opinions of the American public but have thereby reinforced and helped legitimate emergent majoritarian concerns' (Mishler and Sheehan 1993: 97). The same political scientists go as far as inferring from their data that there is a five-year lag between changes in majority opinion and the reflection of those changes in the Court's decisions. This lag suggests that the Court 'also serves as a temporary buffer against public opinion, shielding the policy process from public caprice and the passions of the moment' (ibid.). Other scholars, using game-theoretic models to study the interactions between the US Supreme Court and Congress, came to the conclusion that Supreme Court justices will frequently defer to preferences of Congress when making decisions, particularly in statutory cases in which it is presumably easy for Congress to reverse the Court. Some legal scholars have gone even further, arguing that a constitutional court cannot run either too far ahead of or too far behind the fundamental political and social currents of a society for any long period without losing its credibility. *Mutatis mutandis*, the same warning applies to any politically independent institution with wide powers but limited normative resources.

Independent but disembedded: non-majoritarian institutions in the EU

As suggested in the preceding section, pragmatic solutions of the legitimacy problem of non-majoritarian institutions depend very much on the legal traditions and the political culture of different countries. However, a common feature of the various national solutions, in addition to the crucial role of public opinion, is the interaction between the independent institutions and the branches of a democratically legitimated government – an interaction which is a mixture of competition and cooperation. Because of the absence, or very limited scope, of such interactions at the European level, the role and behaviour of EU non-majoritarian institutions is quite different from that of their national counterparts. Absent the risk of direct democratic control, and not too concerned about the scarcity of the normative resources at their disposal, such European institutions have few incentives to exercise the kind of self-restraint noted by Robert Dahl in the case of the US Supreme Court. According to this distinguished American scholar, it will be recalled, the more the Court exercises self-restraint the less the impulse to subject it to popular controls. Conversely, the more active the Court is in contesting the policies of law-making majorities, the more visible becomes the slender basis of its legitimacy by democratic standards.

The lack of political incentives for the highest EU Court to exercise self-restraint is strikingly revealed by such cases as *Viking* (Case C-341/05), and *Laval* (Case C-438/05). At about the same time as the French and Dutch voters rejected the draft Constitutional Treaty, revealing the extent of Euro-fatigue even among the founding members of the EC, the ECJ chose to assert categorically the supremacy of the right of free movement and access to the European single market over national labour laws and constitutionally protected social rights. A brief description of the issues involved may help to better appreciate the indifference of the ECJ to the social traditions and political cultures of the member states (for a detailed analysis of these cases see Joerges and Roedl 2009: 10–19). Viking, a Finnish shipping company and its Estonian subsidiary were involved in a legal action against trade union activities. The company owned the ferry *Rosella* registered in Finland and operated by a predominantly Finnish crew. As the *Rosella* was not producing enough profits Viking decided to re-flag the ferry in Estonia, replacing the Finnish crew by lower-paid Estonian seamen. The Finnish Seamen Union then threatened to go on strike. According to the rules of the London-based International Transport Workers Federation (ITF) only Finnish unions were authorized to agree to wage settlements with Viking. Hence, ITF advised its member unions not to enter into collective negotiations with Viking, a suggestion that was also followed by the Estonian union. The shipping company responded with the argument that the threat of collective action by the Finnish union and the coordinating activities of the ITF were incompatible with Viking's right of establishment guaranteed by Article 43 of the EC Treaty. In its judgment the ECJ effectively concluded that European law may set limits on fundamental labour and social rights guaranteed by national laws or protected by the political culture of a member state.

In the *Laval* case the plaintiff was a company incorporated under Latvian law and with a registered office in Riga. Laval's previous Swedish subsidiary had been awarded the contract for building a school in the outskirts of Stockholm. In winning the contract Laval's subsidiary had been helped by the fact that it employed workers from Latvia receiving much lower wages than Swedish workers. The Swedish building and public works union, supported by the electricians' union, responded by blockading the building sites. Laval went to court and the ECJ declared illegal all demands and all supporting activities of the Swedish unions. It interpreted Article 49 TEC (now Article 56 TFEU) on freedom of providing services, as saying that the rights of free movement precluded a trade union from using a blockade of sites to force an employer from another member state to sign a collective agreement containing terms that were more favourable than those laid down in the relevant legislation.

This judgment must be read in the context of the serious problems created by the 'big bang' enlargement of 2004–2007. The migration of workers from the new member states wishing to benefit from higher wages in the richer member states creates a tension between different social-policy regimes coexisting in the same state. This is because migrant workers take with them elements of the social and wage policies of their country of origin. The 1996 Directive on the Posting of Workers represents a major attempt to resolve, or at least to reduce, the severity of such problems, especially by avoiding a race to the bottom in wages. Instead, in *Laval* the ECJ interpreted this same Directive in the sense that it prohibits all union activities beyond those essential working conditions enumerated in Article 3(1) of the Directive; that it prohibits union activities for essential working conditions that are better than those already legally provided; and that it prohibits union activities for all wages higher than the lowest wage group (Joerges and Roedel 2009: 17). In sum, the Court chose to interpret the 1996 Directive as imposing strict limits on the right to strike. In both *Viking* and *Laval*, as well as in the later *Rueffert* case, decided in 2008 (*Rechtsanwalt Dr. Dirk Rueffert v. Land Niedersachsen.* C-346/06 [2008] ECR I-01989), the ECJ reaffirmed the supremacy of economic rights protected by European treaties and secondary legislation over social rights and political norms developed at national level over many years. The Court's position is consistent with its doctrine of the primacy of European law, and with the legal centralism that distinguishes the EU approach to regional integration, see chapter 3. Under present circumstances, however, such a position betrays insufficient appreciation of the fact that the deeper the level of integration, the more difficult it becomes to separate economic and political considerations. In other words, the deeper the level of integration, the higher the cost of operating in a political vacuum, not only in terms of democratic legitimacy but also of policy effectiveness.

The case of the ECB provides a particularly clear illustration of the problems of policymaking in the absence of a fully-fledged democratic government. As we know, the delegation of powers to a politically independent central bank is meant to restrain the temptation of democratic politicians to assign greater weight to short-run considerations and thus to default on long-term commitments. A politically independent central banker does not depend on the electoral cycle, and hence has a longer time horizon and different incentives from those of elected politicians. This does not mean that he or she should only care about inflation. Rather, the 'optimal' central banker must cooperate with the government to strike a balance between credibility and flexibility in case of serious economic shocks, see chapter 4. Let us now consider how the commitment problem has been tackled in the EU. The willingness of integrationist leaders to sacrifice democracy for the sake of deeper integration was revealed once more when it was decided to give quasi-constitutional status (i.e., a treaty basis) to the independence of the ECB. This means that changing the rules under which the ECB operates requires a treaty revision acceptable to all the member states – a complex and politically hazardous procedure. The net result is that the parliaments and governments of the members of the euro zone have lost control over monetary policy, while the EP has no authority in this area. Unlike the US Federal Reserve, which is placed within a political structure where Congress, the President, and the Treasury supply all the necessary political counterweights, the ECB is free (indeed, is supposed) to operate in a political vacuum, without a European government to balance its powers, and in the absence of effective mechanisms to coordinate the fiscal policies of the member states, at least so far.

In this connection it should be noted that the ECB enjoys both 'instrument independence' and 'goal independence'. When a central bank enjoys only instrument independence, it is up to the government to fix the target – say, the politically acceptable level of inflation – leaving the central bank free to decide how best to achieve the target. Because of the grant of both instrument and goal independence to the ECB, some scholars have raised the issue of the democratic deficit of the Bank, arguing that in order to reduce this deficit the ECB should evolve toward a governance model excluding goal independence (Gormley and de Haan 1996). The idea that central bankers, or other economic experts, may know what rate of inflation is in the long-run interest of a country (and, *a fortiori*, of a group of countries at very different levels of socio-economic developments such as the EU) is indeed extraordinary. Politicians and elected policymakers, rather than experts, can be expected to be sensitive to the public's preferred balance of inflation and unemployment. If the public wants to trade some unemployment for a somewhat higher rate of inflation, it can make this preference known by electing candidates who stand for such a policy.

The fact that the EU offers no such possibility to its citizens proves again that the democratic-deficit problem is rooted in the integration methods followed for more than half a century, and hence that no solution can be found without a radical revision of the methods themselves. It is not enough to argue that the democratic accountability of the ECB is poorly organized, and that monetary policy ultimately must be controlled by democratically elected politicians. Such a change in the governance structure of the euro zone would require a treaty amendment, which most likely would face a German veto. Like many other writers on the democratic deficit, Gormley and de Haan do not tell us how their goal of a European monetary policy ultimately controlled by elected politicians could be achieved without jettisoning the traditional approach to European integration – starting with the old strategy of fait accompli which eventually produced monetary union at a time when political union was becoming increasingly unlikely. The decision to pursue monetary integration in the absence of agreement, not only on political union but even on exchange-rate policy and other crucial institutional and policy issues, has produced a level of institutional and policy rigidity unknown at the national level. Without a democratically legitimated European government to counterbalance the central bank, or at least a European finance minister to interact with the monetary policymakers, how could transparent procedures for overriding ECB decisions be designed and enforced? Under present conditions authority over the entire domain of monetary policy will continue to flow, by default, to the ECB – or else be exercised by a handful of member states ready to violate the spirit and the letter of the monetary constitution, including the no-bail-out clause, Article 125(1) of the Lisbon Treaty.

Some forty years ago Samuel Brittan, the well-known British columnist, wrote: 'An attempt to freeze the pattern of [exchange] rates before there is a European political authority or common budget...would threaten the degree of trade and other liberalization already achieved; it would thus be a classic example of putting the cart before the horse'

(Brittan 1971: 46). The prescient quality of Brittan's warning was revealed some ten years after the final decision to go ahead with monetary union, when French President Sarkozy and other EU leaders became convinced that the national governments should have a bigger say in the making of European monetary policy, especially in decisions concerning exchange rates. An excessive appreciation of the euro, these leaders complained, is damaging the national economies. In March 2008, while the euro was reaching new record levels against the dollar, the then managing director of the IMF, Dominique Strauss-Kahn, joined the debate attributing the overvaluation of the European currency to the excessive power of the ECB. According to Strauss-Kahn the ECB fulfils its statutory duty of containing inflation, but the absence of a finance minister of the EU means that at the European level concerns about inflation *de facto* prevail over concerns about growth: the ECB is overpowering precisely because it has no political counterweight (cited in Beuve-Mèry 2008).

Germany, however, is resolutely opposed to any significant change in the existing framework of economic governance, and the ECB itself strongly resists any external interference. Precisely for this reason, for a long time the Bank resolutely opposed any proposal to being named a 'European institution', fearing that having the same legal status as the Council, the EP, the ECJ, or the Commission, could entail commitments – such as expectations of inter-institutional cooperation, and consultations before taking certain decisions – which could threaten the ECB's total independence. As a consequence, until the TFEU was ratified, the ECB was simply a 'body' – free of the 'constitutional glue' that is supposed to hold together those European institutions that are listed as such in the Treaty. Those European scholars who look to the Federal Reserve as the better model – because it is politically more accountable, and not exclusively concerned with price stability – seem to forget that the Federal Reserve operates within the framework of a democratic polity capable of providing all the necessary checks and balances. In a comparative perspective, the well-nigh total independence of the ECB, its supposedly exclusive focus on the goal of low inflation, its mode of operation in a political vacuum, appear to be almost a caricature of how monetary policy is conducted in contemporary democracies.

Ironically, recent research has raised doubts about the relationship between inflation and central bank independence. The available data do indicate a definite inverse correlation between inflation and independence, but of course correlation does not necessarily imply causation. The correlation between low inflation and high levels of central bank independence could be explained by a third factor such as widespread popular support for monetary stability, as in the case of Germany. Indeed, according to monetary economist A.S. Posen (1994), price stability is not a function of the autonomy of the central bank. Rather, monetary policy is driven by a coalition of political interests in society, because a central bank will be prepared to take a strong anti-inflation line only if it can count on a coalition of interests politically strong enough to sustain such a policy stance. Also economists who believe that the relationship between indicators of central bank independence and inflation is quite robust, even after various control variables are included, agree that public opposition to inflation is an important determinant of central bank independence. It follows that 'granting central bank independence, if not widely supported by society, is over the long run unlikely to have the intended counterinflationary effect' (De Haan 1997: 409). In Germany the aversion to inflation has deep historical and cultural roots but many member states of the EU do not share that aversion. This is the reason why the Bundesbank and the German government itself tried to limit membership in the monetary union to countries practising fiscal discipline on the German model. Having failed in this attempt, they hoped to impose fiscal discipline on all members of the monetary union by insisting on the inclusion of various convergence criteria in the Maastricht Treaty and, later, by means of a strict stability pact. This disciplinary approach to monetary integration failed, however, to transmit a culture of monetary stability to all the members of the euro zone. On the other hand, a politically and socially disembedded institution like the ECB is not in the best position to inspire the formation of broad coalitions in support of a strong anti-inflation policy.

Also the European Commission is very much attached to its treaty-based independence from the national governments, but because of its traditional aspiration to become the future government of a politically united Europe, it aspires to a significant degree of political embeddedness. Hence the attraction of the idea of a popularly elected Commission. After his appointment in 1999 as Commission President, Romano Prodi played with this idea for some time. By the summer of 2002, however, he acknowledged that it would be impossible for a single candidate to fight a meaningful election across more than twenty member states (cited in Friedrich 2002). Under a later proposal, the new president would be nominated by the EP and by representatives of the national parliaments, and approved by EU leaders, thus attempting to tap all sources of democratic legitimacy in the EU. But precisely the need to appeal to the legitimacy of the national parliaments is the clearest admission of the difficulty of legitimating an institution with such broad objectives, and mixed competences that include the monopoly of legislative initiative. The idea of an elected Commission president, who would then choose his/her Commissioners, has been recently resurrected, but no satisfactory answer to Prodi's practical concerns has yet been provided.

One final point: since the non-majoritarian institutions operating at European level have no built-in incentives to exercise self-restraint, the only solution open to the member states would seem to be to set clear limits to European competences. Despite growing popular dissatisfaction with the apparently unstoppable growth of EU powers and the steady expansion of its borders, this is more easily said than done. The obstacles to radical reform are not only the unanimity required for treaty revisions, the difficulty of enforcing the principle of subsidiarity, or the web of vested interests developed in more than half a century of negotiations, bargaining, and behind-the-scene bureaucratic politics. Perhaps more than anything else, it is the idea of integration as an infinite process, with no definite goal in view – the open-ended commitment to 'ever closer union of the peoples of Europe' – that creates the impression that there is no effective barrier to the continuous, if incremental, expansion of supranational powers. In 1990 a prominent legal scholar, and member of the European Court of First Instance (now General Court), could write that 'there is no nucleus of sovereignty that the Member States can invoke, as such, against the Community' (Lenaerts 1990: 220). When these words were written, few people appeared to object to them – or even to take notice. The rejection of the draft Constitutional Treaty and the Irish 'No' to the Lisbon Treaty show how much the public mood has changed since 1990. Even more significant may be the long-term effects of the debt crisis of the euro zone on both public and elite opinion. Nevertheless, the idea of 'more Europe' as the only way of resolving the present crisis and moving forward is still advocated by some political and intellectual leaders, see chapter 7.

'Economies are politically embedded, and this is decisive for the way they perform' (Jones 1987: xxiii). Between the fifteenth and the nineteenth century Europe came to outclass Asia and the rest of the world in economic, scientific, technological and, arguably, in cultural terms as well. According to the British historian the essence of this 'European miracle' lies in politics rather than economics: 'in its states system Europe had a portfolio of competing and colluding polities whose spirit of competition was adapted to diffusing best practices' (ibid.: 115). In other words, Europe's hegemony should be attributed to its polycentric, competitive states system; this is what allowed the Old Continent to leave behind such superpowers as the Chinese, the Mogul, and the Ottoman empires. This explanation of the European miracle of the past suggests that the poor results of the European integration of today may be due to the EU's lack of a political embedding corresponding to the scope of its economic powers. What is becoming increasingly evident is that the crisis of monetary union is the consequence of a serious mismatch between economic tasks and political resources, in particular the absence of clear political leadership, as discussed in chapter 8. This mismatch has normative as well as economic consequences. In fact, normative and economic consequences are closely correlated, as we shall see in the next chapter.

6

From the democratic deficit to a democratic default? The normative dimension of the euro crisis

The European Parliament: a formal solution to the EU's legitimacy problems

No country can become a member of the EU unless it is recognized by the other member states as being a true representative democracy. The EU itself, however, is not a fully-fledged democracy: it suffers from a serious 'democratic deficit' – not a total absence but an incomplete development, or even a distortion, of the practices and institutions of representative democracy. For example, legislation can only be initiated by the non-elected European Commission. Hence the jocular paradox: if the EU were a state it could not become a member of the Union! Despite a vast body of literature trying to explain this paradox, and despite the important place the issue of the democratic deficit has occupied in public discourse for the last twenty or so years, few problems of European integration have been so consistently misunderstood, or deliberately misconstrued. I suggest that a correct understanding of the question must start from the realization that the problem of the insufficient democratic legitimacy of the European project only started to attract attention in the late 1980s, and became increasingly visible with the steady growth of European competences, culminating in monetary union.

The standard explanation of the limited democratic legitimacy of the EC/EU has been first the absence of a directly elected EP and then – after 1979 when direct European elections took place for the first time – the inadequate powers granted to the supranational parliament. As already noted in chapter 1, the powers of this body have been expanded treaty after treaty without, however, producing the hoped-for results. According to a knowledgeable student of the EP, the driving force in this expansion of parliamentary powers has been the power of the democratic idea. He writes: 'Governments have found it extremely difficult to resist an increase in the role of the EP, because they have not easily been able to formulate an alternative for addressing the "democratic deficit"' (Shackleton 2012: 145). In fact, it would be more correct to speak of the unwillingness, rather than inability, to formulate alternatives for tackling the question of insufficient democratic legitimacy. An obvious alternative for addressing this particular problem would be to renounce the traditional (Monnet) strategy of fait accompli (see chapter 2), and to expand European competences only in the presence of sufficient popular support. This has not been the practice, however, even in the recent past. The majority of European governments never held a popular vote to decide critical issues arising in the course of integration: whether or not the country should join the Community or Union; adopt the common currency; or accept the harsh conditions imposed by the new 'Fiscal Compact'. The new Fiscal Compact – officially known as the Treaty on Stability, Coordination and Governance in the Economic and Monetary Union – imposes strict fiscal discipline and supranational oversight, as well as economic convergence. In line with German wishes, the Treaty obliges the twenty-five member states that signed it to introduce a legally binding, 'preferably constitutional', balanced-budget rule within one year of its entry into force. The implications of such a rule for domestic, and particularly social, policy can be enormous, but European voters, who were presented with the fait accompli of monetary union in the 1990s, now are required to accept the consequences of that fateful decision. Also the main legal and economic instruments to deal with the crisis, such as the European Financial Stability Mechanism and its successor, the ESM, have largely bypassed the EP as well as the national parliaments.

The truth is that when it comes to European integration, most national governments, as well as the supranational institutions, are wary of public opinion – when not decidedly hostile to it, see the following section. Under these circumstances it is hardly surprising that the directly elected EP failed to reduce the democratic deficit. This failure is revealed by, among other things, the strict correlation between the continuous growth of the powers of the EP and the steady decline of the turnout in successive European elections. Starting with a participation rate of 62 per cent in 1979, this indicator of voters' interest shows a steady decrease: to 61.0 in 1984, 58.5 in 1989, 56.7 in 1994, 49.5 in 1999, 45.5 in 2004, and 43.0 in 2009. Perhaps even more revealing is the comparison between the level of interest that voters exhibit for national politics and their growing indifference, when not outright hostility, towards the EP and the EU. At the European elections of June 2004, for example, the vote in the UK was down by 20 percentage points from the most recent national elections; in Spain by 23 percentage points; Portugal saw a drop of 24 percentage points; Finland, 39 points; Austria, 42 points; and Sweden, 43 points. According to a well-known historian of post-war Europe:

> The pattern is far too consistent to attribute to local circumstances. Moreover – and with more serious implications for the Union's future – it was closely replicated in the new member-states of the East, even though this was their first opportunity in an election to the parliament of Europe that they had waited so long to join. In Hungary the turnout in the June 2004 European elections fell short of the last national elections by 32 percentage points; in Estonia by 31 points; in Slovakia, where the latest national elections had seen a 70 percent turnout, the share of the electorate that bothered to come and vote in the European elections was 17 percent. In Poland the turnout of just 20 percent represented a 26-point decline from the national elections of 2001 and was the lowest since the fall of Communism.
>
> (Judt 2010: 730–1)

In a sense, such differences in the turnout at national and European elections are not at all surprising. As already mentioned in chapter 1, in national elections the voters choose their government, but this is not the case in European elections. Also, some of the most important issues for the voters remain, at least so far, within the competence of the member states. More difficult to explain is the persistent belief that a directly elected and sufficiently powerful EP could eliminate, or at least significantly reduce, the EU's lack of democratic legitimacy. It has been argued that by now most political leaders of the member states probably understand that 'enhancing further the EP's power will not help to solve the EU's legitimacy problems, because these problems are not an issue of formal democracy' (Piris 2011: 13). However, the new Lisbon Treaty contains for the first time a title on democratic principles, and Article 10(1) of the Treaty claims that the EU's functioning is based on the principle of representative democracy: the citizens of the EU are represented directly in the EU Parliament. Thus, regardless of what national leaders may think privately, it is still official doctrine – supported by another significant expansion of the role of the EP in the new treaty – that there is no alternative for addressing the 'democratic deficit', as Shackleton argues. The fact that this unique 'solution' does not seem to work in practice is, again, less surprising than might appear at first sight.

First, the primacy of process over results is, as we know, a key element of the political culture of the EC/EU, and in a strictly procedural perspective 'formal democracy' is deemed to be sufficient for the purpose. Second, the temptation of integrationist leaders to imagine the EU of the future as a traditional state 'writ large' pushes in the direction of identifying European institutions with national institutions – a tendency noted in chapter 2, and which was already apparent in the 1960s, when some German legal scholars claimed that the institutions of the European Communities had been designed with the idea of replicating the model of the Federal Republic of Germany. In fact, the homonymy of national and European institutions is quite misleading, as noted in the preceding chapter.

Coming back to the EP and the EU's legitimacy problems, it may be worthwhile to recall the comment of *The Economist* on the occasion of the rejection of the Constitutional Treaty by the French and Dutch voters in May/June 2005. The referendum results, according to *The Economist* of 11 June 2005, 'cruelly exposed the fantasy that the EP is the answer to the disconnect between political elites and ordinary citizens' (cited in Shackleton 2012: 140). As I have argued at some length elsewhere (Majone 2009: 22–35), this disconnect between elites and citizens is a basic feature of the approach to European integration followed for more than half a century: by its very nature, 'integration by stealth' was, and continues to be, an elitist project. It is difficult to see how even a directly elected European parliament could correct this structural flaw – especially since the EP still lacks some basic prerogatives of national parliaments, such as the power of initiating legislation or of deciding levels of taxation and the size of the public budget. In the immediate post-war period federalists based their idea of the United States of Europe on the mistaken assumption that the age of the nation state was over, at least in Europe. Neo-functionalists drew from this assumption the corollary that European integration was too important to be left to the uncertainty of democratic politics. In fact, the persistent underestimation of the importance of broad popular support for the long-term viability of the integration project has produced consequences that are becoming increasingly evident as the crisis of monetary union deepens.

European law between *thesmos* and *nomos*

'Integration through Law' is the title of one of the earliest and most influential series of books on European integration. Despite the central role assigned to law in the integration process (see chapter 3), the attempt to make 'Europe without Europeans' (Schmitter 2005) led integrationist leaders to blur a basic distinction that was well understood in ancient Greece well before the age of Pericles. At some time about the end of the sixth century BC, the word for law as set down for the people's benefit by the law-giver, *thesmos*, was replaced by *nomos*, the law as approved and enacted by the people itself (Maddox 1989). By confusing the two kinds of law, EU leaders show a remarkable affinity with pre-democratic philosophies of government. One of the most striking features of the Enlightenment of eighteenth century Europe was the faith of the rulers in the possibility of changing the economy and society through legislation. Hence the importance attached to legislation and codification by Joseph II of Austria and Friedrich the Great of Prussia. However, these rulers conceived the law, not as *nomos*, but as law set down for the people's benefit – *thesmos*. The EU leaders of today give the impression that they see themselves as the updated version of the enlightened rulers of a pre-democratic age; hence it is not surprising that even the directly elected EP cannot legitimate a project conceived in terms of pre-democratic norms.

The EU's democratic deficit is a direct consequence of such elitist views of the integration process, and of the consequent failure to convert a majority, or even a significant minority, of Europeans to the cause of political integration. In the absence of popular support for the political integration of the continent, the founding fathers of communitarian Europe, and all integrationist leaders after them, were faced with a fundamental trade-off between democracy and integration – which they consistently resolved in favour of integration. The strategy might have worked if integration had produced the promised economic benefits. In this case the efficient delivery of benefits would have provided the time necessary for legitimacy to develop, as discussed in a later section on effectiveness and legitimacy. But as already pointed out, the myth of fifty years of prosperity made possible by European integration rests on the *post hoc, ergo propter hoc* fallacy: inferring a causal connection from a mere sequence in time. Between 1950 and 1970, Europe was indeed the fastest-growing region in the world, Japan excepted. However, economists and economic historians have shown that this growth was shared in all parts of the continent: in North-Western Europe's industrial core, in the Mediterranean countries, even in Eastern Europe. Hence the EEC (which first reached the stage of a customs union in 1968) could not have played a significant causal role in the impressive economic development of the first two decades after the end of World War II. What is undisputed, at any rate, is that growth in the EC/EU has stagnated or even regressed since the launch of the two most important economic projects: the Single Market and EMU (Majone 2009: 81–7).

With the crisis of monetary union, the risks about which some well-known experts had warned for years finally became evident to all the citizens of both heavily indebted and donor countries. According to the survey conducted by the Pew Research Center in 2012 (see the Introduction) Germany is today the only member of the EU in which most people, 59 per cent, think their country has been helped by European integration. Majorities or near majorities in most countries surveyed now believe that the economic integration of Europe has actually weakened their economies. This is the opinion in Greece (70 per cent), France (63 per cent), Britain (61 per cent), Italy (61 per cent), the Czech Republic (59 per cent), and Spain (50 per cent). The survey data also show that the crisis of the euro has triggered a full-blown crisis of public confidence: in the economy, in the future, in the benefits of European economic integration, in membership in the EU, in the euro and in the free-market system. Again, Europeans largely oppose further fiscal austerity to deal with the crisis; they are divided on bailing out indebted nations; and oppose Brussels' oversight of national budgets. In short, the European project is a major casualty of the ongoing sovereign-debt crisis: we are witnessing the failure of the attempt to integrate Europe through a 'positive' law that has neither produced the promised benefits for the people, nor has it been enacted by the people itself.

The distinction between positive and negative integration (already mentioned in chapter 3), like the corresponding distinction between positive and negative law, goes back to the earliest studies of regional economic integration. The Treaty of Rome itself did not attach any normative connotation to the distinction. The common market was to be achieved by both methods, but in fact by greater reliance on negative law. In this the founding fathers were right. After so many failures of 'positive' law, we may conclude that European law in its 'negative' mode can at least be considered the contemporary equivalent of *thesmos*, the law enacted for the people's benefit by the law-giver.

The 'referendum threat'

Because of the growing difficulty of treaty ratification by popular vote, integrationist leaders tend to see public opinion as the main obstacle to what is assumed to be an on-going process of federalization. Actually, doubts about the wisdom of consulting public opinion had been voiced long before the negative results of the French, Dutch, and Irish referendums in 2005 and 2008. Thus Commission President Romano Prodi, in an interview given to the American journalist Alan Friedman (Friedman 2000), expressed deep scepticism about the usefulness of holding popular referendums on European issues; especially, he pointed out, when all opinion surveys indicate growing opposition to the EU. Prodi's scepticism was revealed even more clearly when he rebuked the Commissioner for Enlargement – that same Guenther Verheugen who had once admitted that the euro had been introduced 'behind the backs of the population' – for saying that Germany (Verheugen's own country) should hold a referendum on future enlargements of the EU (cited in Friedman 2000).

Around the time of the French and Dutch referendums some scholars began to speak of a 'referendum threat', and also of a 'federalist deficit' – i.e., a slowing down or reversal of the federalization process caused by popular votes on European issues. The argument advanced by these scholars is that in an association of twenty-seven (or more) member states whose political, socioeconomic, and cultural heterogeneity is probably greater than in any free association of states which ever came together to form some kind of union, the probability of a negative vote is high. On the other hand, the risks of deadlock are not as high at the level of the EU's summit diplomacy, where Euro-elites are able to deliberate, bargain, trade votes, and coordinate their moves. Also parliamentary ratification does not pose a serious risk: in parliamentary systems majority parties usually support the decisions of their government leaders. In sum, the real threat to European integration is supposed to come mainly from the direct expression of voters' preferences. Given the high risk that popular vote may block the federalization process, '[r]educing or even fully overcoming the federalist deficit might...become of the utmost importance to the future process of European integration' (Trechsel 2005: 410). To reduce this deficit, it is suggested, federalists should be prepared to accept even a worsening of the Union's democratic deficit. These, or similar, arguments have also been used by some political leaders. Hence the angry accusations that in 2008 Ireland was taking the other twenty-six members of the EU 'hostage' by blocking ratification of the Lisbon Treaty. But what could be done, in practice, to meet the referendum threat? The answer favoured by federalists is suggested by a superficial analogy with a crucial moment in American history: eliminate the requirement that all member states must approve a European treaty and subsequent amendments.

Something like a 'federalist deficit' was the problem facing American federalists in the summer of 1787, when they were attempting to amend the Articles of Confederation in the direction of a more centralized federation – something which would have required the assent of all the thirteen former colonies. Unfortunately, some states opposed ratification of the text prepared by the federalists in the Constitutional Convention. The way to get around this obstacle was found by James Madison with his 'invention' of an American People, distinct from, and superior to, the peoples of the thirteen separate states. The direct appeal to the sovereign American People was meant to discredit the states' pretensions of sovereignty, and their insistence on unanimity for all decisions affecting their sovereignty. To many of Madison's contemporaries, and also to later political leaders like John Calhoun, the idea of an American People to whom the constituent power belonged, appeared a myth contrived for political purposes. Nevertheless, the myth had some plausibility: a common language; legal systems derived from, and still very much influenced by, English common law; similar political and administrative systems at state level; a fairly homogeneous population, largely of English, Scottish, or Irish stock; above all, a war fought together for eight years against the former colonial power. As I pointed out some years ago, none of these conditions is even remotely approached in contemporary Europe, so that the Madisonian remedy for the 'federalist deficit' is simply unavailable to today's integrationist elites (Majone 2009: 67–71).

The impossibility of reproducing the 'Madisonian moment' in a European context is made even more evident by an obvious but often overlooked difference between the EU and democratic polities, namely the absence of the traditional government–opposition dialectic at the supranational level. Having been denied an appropriate political arena in which to hold European policymakers accountable, voters are almost forced to transform popular referendums into contests for or against the EU. In his speech to the EP of 23 June 2005, British prime minister Tony Blair expressed his conviction that the most likely explanation of the rejection of the draft Constitutional Treaty by the French and Dutch voters was that the referendum 'became merely the vehicle for the people to register a wider and deeper discontent with the state of affairs in Europe' (Blair 2005: 3). This being the state of public opinion, popular referendums are indeed risky, not just in traditionally Euro-sceptic countries but in all member states. Given the absence of democratic means for sanctioning EU policymakers, however, it seems unlikely that it will be possible to force the referendum genie back into the bottle. After the Irish 'No', demands for popular ratification of future European treaties have been advanced by leaders of different countries and political hues.

As mentioned in chapter 2, in July 2008 Werner Faymann, the Social-Democratic candidate for the Austrian federal election to take place the following September, came out in favour of popular referendums for all future treaty amendments, as well as on other important EU issues. In Italy support for future referendums on Europe was expressed in the national Parliament by the spokesman of the populist Northern League, just as the Parliament in Rome was ratifying the Lisbon Treaty. In 2009, the prime minister of Bavaria, Horst Seehofer, discussed the possibility of having popular referendums on important European issues – a possibility excluded by the two major national parties, CDU and SPD. According to the Bavarian leader, German voters should be consulted whenever important decisions, such as further transfers of sovereignty to the European level, or Turkey's EU membership, are being considered. Like his Social-Democratic colleague in Austria, Seehofer was trying to improve the electoral chances of his party by taking advantage of Euro-fatigue, which was, and still is, at least as widespread in Germany as in Austria.

It is by now pretty clear that in the future major advances in European integration will have to be validated by the explicit approval of the voters. In an article titled 'Fragt das Volk!' ('Ask the People!'), Heinrich Wefing (2011) argued that any significant step towards 'more Europe' should be preceded by a popular referendum even at the risk of a negative result: there is simply no other way of legitimating the integration process. Starting from the opinion of the German Constitutional Court that under the Constitution of 1949 the limits to the transfer of national sovereignty to the EU have been well-nigh reached, Wefing pointed out that the present malaise is not caused by the idea of European integration as such, but rather by the integration method followed so far – an important distinction too often overlooked by both politicians and observers of the European scene. Recently, the idea of a referendum to decide the future shape of Europe has been advocated by three distinguished German scholars: Bofinger, Habermas and Nida-Ruemelin (2012). Their thesis that 'more Europe' is the only possible solution of the euro crisis will be discussed in the following chapter. Here I only wish to call attention to the fact that these scholars also fail to make the important distinction, emphasized by Wefing, between the idea of European integration and the particular method of integration followed for half a century. They seem to assume that what is needed today is a 'deepening' of the received integration method (see chapter 4), rather than a truly different approach to the problem of how to achieve unity in diversity.

Of course, any proposal of a new approach to European integration will have to be submitted to the judgement of the voters. One of the favourite arguments against ratification of new treaties or other important documents by popular referendum is that voters cannot be expected to read and evaluate technical and legally complex texts running into hundreds of pages – 346 pages in case of the Lisbon Treaty. This argument is flawed in several respects. It is not only the average voter who does not have the time, or the motivation, to peruse such documents. The Irish prime minister admitted he had not read the Lisbon Treaty, and Ireland's EU Commissioner at that time, Charlie McCreevy, added that 'no sane person' would. Justice Iarhlaith O'Neill, the High Court judge appointed by the Irish government to provide an impartial treaty analysis, admitted that parts of the text are difficult to understand (Murray Brown 2008: 3). It is reasonable to assume that not only the average citizen but also the average member of a national parliament – the body which would have to ratify a new treaty in the absence of popular referendum – would find it hard to understand what was unclear to a High Court judge. The difference is that the average parliamentarian is likely to vote according to party discipline, while the average voter uses the referendum as a rare occasion to express his or her assessment of the European project – voters' turnouts at referendums are typically much higher than at elections for the EP. In sum, it is far from clear why parliamentary ratification of European treaties should be preferable to ratification by popular vote: it is certainly not more democratic, nor is it somehow more rational or better informed.

Moreover, even in national elections it is rational for the average voter *not* to become fully knowledgeable about public affairs. As we saw in chapter 4, already in the 1950s Anthony Downs had pointed out that for the average voter the cost of becoming informed about the details of political issues generally outweighs the relative benefits to be derived from voting on an informed basis. Instead of trying to become fully informed, rational voters develop methods of cutting down the costs of information acquisition by developing a variety of rules employed to determine what to make use of and what not to. In addition, political entrepreneurs find it convenient to expend resources in order to acquire information and then transmit it to the voters. As a matter of fact, political entrepreneurs seem to have played an increasingly important role in recent referendums concerning the EU. Their importance is enhanced by the fact that the political and economic establishment generally support treaty ratification. All the major political parties – on the left and on the right, in government and in opposition – the vast majority of members of the national parliaments, business leaders (in the Netherlands also trade union leaders), major newspapers and other media, the EP and the Commission – all supported ratification of the draft Constitutional Treaty, and also of the Lisbon Treaty. In the Netherlands, for example, two-thirds of members of Parliament voted for the draft Constitutional Treaty, almost exactly the same proportion of voters rejected it. Also the vast majority of the Irish establishment was on the side of the 'Yes' campaign for the Lisbon Treaty. According to polls, 22 per cent of 'No' voters did so because they rejected the claim of the elites that the treaty, in spite of being complicated, was in the best interest of the people. For many other 'No' voters, their lack of understanding of the treaty was a sufficient reason to reject it.

At any rate, since the rise of mass democracy no political leader has seriously proposed to use the 'ignorance' of the voters – any more than their level of education or the lack of taxable property – as excuses to restrict the right to vote at national or local elections. From the viewpoint of democratic theory, therefore, the arguments of integrationist leaders and their academic supporters against ratification by referendum, are flawed. In refusing to meet the requirements of modern mass democracy, pro-integration leaders are conditioned by a political culture in many respects similar to that prevailing before the great reforms of the franchise in the nineteenth century, when policy was considered a virtual monopoly of cabinets, diplomats, and top bureaucrats. In this as in other respects the political culture of old-regime Europe still influences the supposedly post-modern system of governance of the EU (Majone 2005: 46–51).

Effectiveness and legitimacy

In public discourse, but also in the academic literature, much more attention is given to the issue of the democratic deficit than to the question of the effectiveness of the EU. In fact, the traditional emphasis on process (rather than concrete results, see chapter 3) tends to discourage any serious discussion concerning the effectiveness and efficiency of European institutions and policymaking methods. And yet in case of a new polity like the EU effectiveness and legitimacy, although conceptually distinct, are intimately related, as Martin Lipset clearly understood many years ago, see chapter 2. Starting from the observation that crises of legitimacy typically occur during transitions to a new political system, the American sociologist concluded that if the new system is unable to meet the demands of major groups for a long enough period to develop legitimacy, then a serious crisis may develop. Indeed, 'a breakdown of effectiveness, repeatedly or for a long period, will endanger even a legitimate system's stability' (Lipset 1963: 68). It has rightly been pointed out, in particular by Michael Shackleton (2012), that it is not necessary for the EU to meet the same level of legitimacy as its member states, *provided* the Union delivers a reasonable level of benefits in terms of effectiveness. But this is precisely the problem. All the available evidence suggests that even before the crisis of the euro zone, disappointed expectations were one important reason why the EU and its institutions, instead of progressively attracting the loyalty of its citizens, were becoming less popular and less trustworthy with the years.

At the operational level the process of European integration has been largely driven by law and economics. As we saw in the preceding chapter, the essence of the neo-functionalist approach and of the Monnet method of integration by stealth, consists in pursuing political integration under the guise of economic integration. The major risk inherent in this approach is precisely that unsatisfactory economic performance over a period of years may impede the emergence of new sources of legitimacy, and thus further undermine the normative foundations of the elite-driven integration process. This risk was not sufficiently appreciated in the early stages of the process because the foundational period of the European Communities largely overlapped with the three 'glorious decades' 1945–1975, when Europe experienced an unprecedented period of growth, macroeconomic stability, and high levels of social protection. But then the 'economic miracle' came to an end, and the first doubts about the effectiveness of the 'Community method' began to emerge.

For half a century Euro-elites largely succeeded in presenting integration as a positive-sum game; but since the beginning of the euro crisis even the most inattentive citizen realizes that integration entails costs as well as benefits, and that a positive net balance can no longer be taken for granted. This is why today poor economic performance poses more of a threat to the legitimacy and long-term survival of the EU than in the past. Poor economic performance is not, however, the only threat to the legitimacy and long-term survival of the Union. Another, equally significant, cause of the growing democratic deficit is the continuous expansion of EU powers. The possibility of reducing the democratic deficit by drawing more precise limits on the powers exercised by the supranational institutions is seldom, if ever, mentioned – even though this was the basic reason for inserting Article 3b on the principle of subsidiarity in the Maastricht Treaty. The explication of this principle in terms of comparative efficiency ('[T]he Community shall take action...only if and in so far as the objectives of the proposed action cannot be sufficiently achieved by the Member States and can therefore...be better achieved by the Community') tends to obscure the normative intent of the drafters of the Article. The normative bite of Article 3b is in its first comma – 'The Community shall act within the limits of the powers conferred upon it by the Treaty' – suggesting that in the past the supranational institutions repeatedly made use of their delegated powers in ways not approved of by at least some of their political principals. This comma enunciates the principle of attributed powers, and Professor Dashwood was referring to it when he wrote that after Maastricht '[t]he notion of a Community continuously moving the boundary posts of its own competence is ruled out of court' (Dashwood 1996: 115).

In the euphoria created by the Single European Act and by the highly successful marketing of the 'Europe '92' campaign, it became tempting to imagine that there was no effective barrier to the continuous, if incremental, expansion of Community competences. European lawyers could refer to the broad interpretation given by the European Court to Article 235 of the Rome Treaty, which enables the Council of Ministers to take appropriate measures in cases where, 'in the course of the operation of the common market', action by the Community is found to be necessary to attain one of its objectives, and there is no specific treaty-based power available for that purpose. Since the early 1970s the Council and the Commission have made liberal use of this Article to expand Community competences or to broaden the reach of Community legislation in many policy areas, for example, social and regional policy, energy and environment, scientific and technological research and development, and cooperation agreements with third countries. Article 235 was used to accomplish 'the trick of self-levitation through pulling on its own boot straps' (Dashwood 1996: 123); in other words, the Article was used to amend the treaties without following the normal democratic procedures of ratification and approval by national parliaments or popular referendums. The question whether Community action was actually necessary was considered by the European institutions as a matter within their complete discretion to decide.

Interestingly enough, the European Convention responsible for drafting the Constitutional Treaty considered the possibility of scrapping Article 308 of the EC Treaty (former Article 235), but had to retreat in the face of determined opposition by the Commission and by integrationist groups, which were over-represented among the *conventionnels* (Norman 2003). Actually, the Article has rarely been used in recent years, hence not much would have been lost in discarding it, while the message would have reassured all those who fear that the creeping expansion of Union powers will not abate in the future.

The accountability deficit

The proliferation of international and supranational institutions, but also of non-majoritarian, politically independent, institutions at the national level, suggests that legitimacy problems cannot be reduced to the question of democratic legitimacy, understood as accountability to the voters or to their elected representatives. Some years ago I argued that in the EU the real problem – in the sense of a condition about which something could be done without a root-and-branch reform of the current approach to European integration – is not the democratic deficit, but the accountability deficit: a good accountability framework, rather than a poor imitation of national parliamentary institutions, should be the goal of those who wish to enhance the legitimacy of the Union as presently constituted (Majone 2009: 175–8). In reality, both problems are essentially insoluble under present conditions. The problem of establishing an effective system of accountability, while perhaps less daunting than the elimination of the democratic deficit, has become more urgent since the launching of EMU. In this respect, the EU represents an important special case of the general issue analysed by Ruth Grant and Robert Keohane in an important paper on 'Accountability and Abuses of Power in World Politics' (2005).

The problem discussed by these scholars is how to secure accountability in situations where the traditional standards of democratic accountability are either inapplicable or unenforceable. The first step toward understanding the general issue is to recognize that accountability to the voters, or to their elected representatives, is only one dimension of accountability – important, but not always applicable, or the most relevant one. Also in the context of democratic polities accountability to one's peers, to expert opinion, to stakeholders, or to particular segments of public opinion, may be the best way of explaining the reasons of one's decision and of activating other accountability mechanisms. At the international (or supranational) level, on the other hand, the very meaning of democracy, hence of democratic accountability, is contested. As a consequence, the definition given by Grant and Keohane is quite general: 'Accountability...implies that some actors have the right to hold other actors to a set of standards, to judge whether they have fulfilled their responsibilities in light of these standards, and to impose sanctions if they determine that these responsibilities have not been met' (Grant and Keohane 2005: 29). Whatever the political and institutional context, then, accountability involves two judgements: evaluating the outcome of a decision, and/or the quality of the decision-making process, in terms of a given set of standards; and imposing appropriate sanctions in case the decision-makers did not fulfil their responsibilities under those standards. Using these two parameters, it is not difficult to see why the EU suffers from a serious accountability deficit.

To begin with, European policies are often initiated less to solve concrete problems than to drive forward the integration process, or to facilitate political deals between member states. It follows that there are few incentives to seriously evaluate actual policy outcomes, unless the budgetary costs of the policy become intolerable. This explains why ineffective policies can survive, unexamined and unchallenged, sometimes for decades. In such cases actual policy outcomes play a subordinate role at best, while the politically relevant aims are never spelled out: tacit knowledge replaces public discussion. Evaluation is further complicated by the fact that European policies have to satisfy a variety of national and supranational interests, hence must be sufficiently ambiguous to be open to different interpretations. This allows EU policymakers to reorder policy priorities as they see fit, or to make the means a goal, and the goal a means. As we saw in chapter 1, for example, monetary union was originally seen by many actors as a decisive move towards the goal of political union; now, closer political union, starting with greater centralization of economic, financial, and social policy, is seen as the only means to rescue monetary union. As Bofinger, Habermas and Nida-Ruemelin (2012, my translation) write: 'If we wish to avoid both a return to monetary nationalism and a lasting euro crisis, then we must do now what was not done when the common currency was introduced: we must set in motion a process of political union, starting with the core Europe of the 17 members of the euro zone.'

Moreover, the treaty-based independence of the European institutions implies *inter alia* that many of the traditional modes of sanctioning bureaucracies at the national level are not available at the supranational level. In particular, all European treaties emphasize the apolitical character of the Commission, insisting on its complete independence 'from any government or from any other body'. Up to a point, insulation from the political process makes sense if we think of the Commission as the guardian of the treaties or as an independent regulatory authority. That was indeed what the institution was intended to be originally. In time, this independent institution has become a highly politicized body that takes decisions involving political judgement and a high degree of discretion. In spite of these developments, the framework of political accountability has remained quite weak. Thus, it is quite difficult for the EP to censure the Commission on a question of policy. The conclusion is that the accountability deficit, like the democratic deficit, is also built into the institutional architecture of the EU. It follows that there are only two ways to seriously tackle both kinds of deficit: either a radical transformation of the present system, or a drastic limitation of the powers delegated to the European levels.

The experience of countries that, like the US, rely extensively on non-majoritarian institutions shows quite clearly that the legitimacy of such bodies depends crucially on a precise definition of their responsibilities, making accountability possible. Historically, courts of law were the first, and still are the most important example of non-majoritarian institutions. As mentioned in chapter 5, the problem of the legitimacy of judicial decisions has been especially felt in the US, where federal courts may strike down a law enacted by Congress, and so presumably expressing the preferences of the majority of American voters. The problem becomes particularly serious when the US Supreme Court makes the determination of constitutionality of a given policy by reference to a value judgement other than one embodied, if only implicitly, either in some specific provision of the Constitution or in the overall structure of government as set up by the Constitution. Of the abundant literature dealing with the role and justification of the Supreme Court as a non-majoritarian (or even anti-majoritarian) institution, Jesse Choper's 'functional' analysis of the role of the Supreme Court is particularly relevant to our topic. The thesis of this distinguished constitutional lawyer is that, despite the anti-majoritarian character of judicial review, the Court must exercise this power in order to protect individual rights which are not adequately represented in the political process. At the same time, however, the Court should decline to exercise judicial review in other areas in order to minimize the tension between this formal power and democratic dialectic, and to economize on its own legitimacy resources. What Choper proposes is a plan to use these scarce normative resources only where strictly necessary. The functional justification of judicial review in the area of individual rights is that the judiciary has an essential ingredient for this task, which is lacking in the political branches of government: it is 'insulated from political responsibility and unbeholden to self-absorbed and excited majoritarianism' (Choper 1983: 68). In areas like relations between the states and the federal government, and in questions having to do with separation of powers, on the other hand, the Court's involvement should be drastically restricted. The Supreme Court should be active only in areas where it enjoys, in Choper's phrase, a 'distinctive institutional competence' – where it has a clear comparative advantage with respect to all other institutions. *Mutatis mutandis*, criteria similar to the ones advocated by Choper for the US Supreme Court have been used to justify and discipline the political independence of other American non-majoritarian institutions, such as the independent regulatory commissions, see chapter 5 and Majone 1996: 287–91.

Trying to apply Choper's criterion to the EU context, however, one immediately notices how difficult it is to identify the distinctive competence of an institution like the European Commission. Most EU policies are regulatory in nature, and in this respect the Commission may be considered a sort of super-agency or regulatory commission. However, it has been assigned a variety of other functions: executive, legislative, and quasi-judicial. This multiplicity of functions expands the scope of the Commission's discretionary choices, greatly complicating the task of evaluating the overall quality of the institution's performance. And because of the multiplicity of distinct tasks assigned to this body, it is extremely costly to dismiss it even when there is intense dissatisfaction with how it carries out one particular task. The collegial nature of the European Commission further complicates matters, since the EP has been understandably reluctant to dismiss the entire college in order to sanction a single Commissioner. There is, moreover, the 'problem of many hands' mentioned in chapter 2. This problem arises where responsibility for policy in complex organizations is shared, as is the case in the EU, and it is correspondingly difficult to find out who is responsible for what.

The difficulty of enforcing accountability by results in the EU explains why the resignation en masse of the Santer Commission in 1999 was not caused by dissatisfaction with policy results, but because of serious allegations regarding 'fraud, mismanagement, and nepotism in the European Commission'. The report of the Committee of Independent Experts investigating the situation did note, however, the failure 'of any attempt by the Commission to assess in advance the volume of resources required when new policy was discussed among the Community institutions' (citations in Majone 2005: 150). The obvious explanation of this nonchalance concerning the availability of adequate resources is, once more, the primacy of process over actual results. In addition, the lack of information concerning the volume of resources needed to achieve a given policy objective can facilitate the pursuance of other, less explicit, objectives under a false label. This is how the Commission uses its control of the legislative and policy agenda to pursue objectives of political integration and self-aggrandizement while claiming to solve specific policy problems. On the other hand, the lack of a political culture of accountability explains why so many clear cases of policy failure go practically unnoticed. A recent, striking example of unconcern for actual policy results – as distinct from benefits accruing to particular countries, institutions, or interest groups – is provided by the EU mission in Kosovo. The EU has thousands of soldiers, judges and prosecutors in Kosovo to help it become a constitutional democracy. The so-called EULEX mission, with a staff of about 2,500, has cost more than 1 billion euros since the beginning of the mission in 2008. This makes it the biggest and most expensive aid mission in the history of the EU. Nevertheless, according to press reports levels of organized crime and corruption remain high, while the local judiciary is inefficient and suffers from too much political influence. Nobody in Brussels or in the national capitals, however, seems to be particularly disturbed by the disappointing results of a major EU mission.

Facing a democratic default

In January 2011 the magazine *Der Spiegel* revealed that the German Chancellor was working out plans for an 'economic government' of the euro zone. The first step in the new strategy to further integrate the EU on economic issues was to be the 'Pact for Competitiveness' – a long-term plan intended to provide a permanent solution for the on-going euro crisis, see chapter 2. In short, Frau Merkel proposed that the countries of the euro zone, and perhaps later all EU member states, should 'dovetail' their economic and social policies. Biting criticism of the Pact for Competitiveness came from across the EU: from long-time members of the Union and from the new members of Central and Eastern Europe; from small and large countries; from debt-ridden Southern countries and fiscally virtuous Northern countries; even from the head of the European Commission. The Belgian prime minister Yves Laterme pointed out that coupling wages to price trends has been part of his country's social model for decades. Werner Faymann, the Austrian chancellor, opposed Merkel's pension plans saying: 'I am not willing to tell my countrymen that they have to work longer.' Luxembourg prime minister and chairman of the group of finance ministers of the euro zone, Jean-Claude Juncker, found the idea of eliminating wage increases pegged to inflation no more promising than an earlier proposal to suspend voting rights in the European Council for the countries that violated EU budget deficit rules. Commission President Barroso expressed fears that the Competitiveness Pact would undermine the Single Market, a concern shared by British prime minister David Cameron (Brackmann and Muenchrat 2011). Because of such wide-spread reactions to attempts to use the crisis of the euro to bend the social policies of the member states to the needs of monetary union, Frau Merkel's Pact for Competitiveness – but not the goal of greater central-ization, or tighter harmonization, of national economic, fiscal, and social policies – had to be shelved.

The fact that only one year later most national leaders were prepared to accept even more stringent conditions than those foreseen by the Pact is a clear indication of the steady worsening of the crisis. A new, much stricter, regime of regulation and control of national budgetary and economic policymaking was established in 2012 by the Stability Treaty (signed as an international treaty by all EU member states other than the UK and the Czech Republic), together with a group of regulations, issued in 2011, concerning enforcement of budgetary surveillance in the euro zone; enforcement measures to correct excessive macroeconomic imbal-ances; strengthening of the surveillance and coordination of economic policies; and the prevention and correction of macroeconomic imbal-ances. The aim of the new regime is to ensure that the members of the euro zone fulfil three main duties: to achieve a balanced budget; to avoid an excessive government deficit; and to prevent or correct macroeconomic imbalances – the latter duty being in fact a general obligation of all member states, since it concerns general economic policy rather than monetary and fiscal policy. Under the first duty each euro zone member state must submit a stability programme to ECOFIN and the Commission, setting out, among other things, the budgetary and economic policy measures being taken; government liabilities; and the assumptions made about economic developments. However, the key task of each national government is to set a medium-term budgetary objective (MTBO), with a realistic target and a plan to realize it. This will be assessed by the Council which can 'invite' the government to adjust its programme if it is unhappy with it. The Stability Treaty states that the budget of all signatories of the Treaty must be balanced or in surplus. As mentioned in a previous chapter, the balanced-budget rule is considered so central that it is to be set in a binding and permanent national law, preferably of a constitutional character. Hence, the MTBO is the main norm for all states. Countries that do not have a balanced budget must set out adjustment plans towards reaching their MTBO, and make sufficient progress each year towards achieving this goal. The adjustment plan will set out what needs to be done each year in a very exacting way: 'it is the adjustment plan which moves States into a regime where their budgetary planning is co-governed by the EU institutions' (Chalmers 2012: 679).

The second duty of the member states – to avoid an excessive public deficit, i.e. a situation where there is a planned or actual budget deficit of more than 3 per cent of GDP or total government debt of more than 60 per cent of GDP – requires debt reductions for the majority of euro zone states that do not satisfy these parameters. For states with large public debts this may amount to repaying several percentage points of GDP each year. The Stability Treaty requires each member state found to have an excessive deficit to put in place a 'budget and economic partnership' – to be approved by ECOFIN and the Commission – setting out structural reforms to ensure a durable correction of its deficit. Thus:

> Co-government is not simply. . .about debt reduction but about extensive reform which will limit the State's need to borrow, either because it has smaller expenditure requirements (i.e., a smaller welfare state) or has secured higher tax receipts. The partnership will, therefore, go to the structure and rationale of a State's fiscal and welfare systems.

> (Ibid.: 680)

Concerning the final duty of member states – to correct macroeconomic imbalances, defined as developments which may potentially affect the proper functioning of the economy of a member state, of the euro zone, or of the entire EU – an alert mechanism is established to facilitate early identification and monitoring of such conditions. States identified as experiencing excessive imbalances have to agree a corrective action plan with the Council, spelling out detailed policies, provisions for surveillance, and a timetable: again, a regime of co-management between national governments and European institutions, notably the Commission and ECOFIN. The Commission assesses the possibility of an excessive imbalance (or of an excessive deficit) and ECOFIN then decides about the presence of these conditions. During these procedures the state under investigation is subject to monitoring by the Commission and is expected to provide regular reports on its progress in correcting the imbalances. It is to be noted that ECOFIN includes the finance ministers of both debtor and creditor countries, the latter being consistently in favour of a strict disciplinary approach, so as to minimize the risk of having to offer more financial support to the countries in financial difficulties.

The traditional role of the national parliaments is significantly constrained by these new regimes. Thus member states are supposed to present their budgetary plans to the Commission and to the group of finance ministers of the euro zone no later than 15 October in each year, with the Commission giving its opinion before the 30 November; the opinion is then discussed by the Euro-Group. In other words, the Commission, not the national parliament, is the first institution where the proposed budget of a country in financial difficulties is examined. Moreover, the national legislature has only one month to adopt the budgetary law after the Commission opinion. This is because budgetary laws are supposed to be synchronized across the euro zone so that they are adopted no later than 31 December. The final outcome may well be that '[a] zone of influence dominated by the Commission and ECOFIN is established, with political conflicts taking place within these, but the atrophying of local democracy leads to a hollowing out of domestic processes so that these become little more than administrative containers' (ibid.: 693). At that point the democratic deficit of the EU would turn into a democratic default.

Even under present arrangements the political costs of financial aid for debtor countries are extremely high. The detailed conditions which must be satisfied by a country receiving financial aid are specified in a

'Memorandum of Understanding', which is usually updated quarterly. These Memoranda and their updates cut ever more deeply into details of national legislation. Fritz Scharpf (2011: 19) gives the example of the 2010 Memorandum for Greece. The second update of 22 November 2010 included a commitment to 'comprehensive reform of the health care system', which in the third update of 23 February 2011 was further specified to include detailed targets for the pricing of generics and for the methods by which social-security funds pay doctors. In the Irish case the Memorandum of Understanding of 8 December 2010 'was more detailed on reforms of the banking system but also included precise commitments on labour market and pension reforms, on cuts in public-sector employment and pay, on cuts in social programs and reductions of the statutory minimum wage' (ibid.). If national authorities wish to adopt policies that are not consistent with the Memorandum, they must consult with the European Commission, the ECB, and the IMF. The Irish Memorandum goes on to state that the authorities 'will also provide the European Commission, the ECB and the IMF with all information requested...Prior to the release of the instalments, the authorities shall provide a compliance report on the fulfilment of the conditionality.' Scharpf concludes: 'once an EMU member state has applied for the protection of the European rescue funds, its government will be operating under a form of "receivership"'. This explains the reluctance of countries like Spain and Italy to apply for such funds, despite the insistence of the ECB and the Commission.

Actually, 'receivership' might be too mild a term for the conditions imposed on the borrowers. Max Keiser, a British TV presenter and former Wall Street broker, spoke instead of an 'occupation regime' imposed by the troika (cited in Scharpf 2011: 20), and if some recent reports are correct, the reference to the consequence of military defeat is not inappropriate. For example, in 2011 the Irish budget was sent first to Germany for approval before it was even seen by the Irish Parliament. According to usually well-informed observers, the forty-page document detailing Ireland's budget plans for 2012 and 2013, and the covering letters of intent from Minister of Finance Michael Noonan were sent to the European Commission by the troika following its third quarterly review of the implementation of the austerity measures prescribed by the Memorandum of Understanding. This material was then made available to the finance committee of the German Parliament where it was discussed – presumably to satisfy the requirement of the German Constitutional Court that the Bundestag must be aware of Germany's financial commitments and risks. The paradox is that in order to satisfy its constitutional obligations the German Parliament had to infringe a basic right of the equally sovereign parliament of a fellow member state. It is hard to find a better illustration of the costs, in terms of democratic legitimacy, entailed by the current attempts to resolve the crisis of the euro zone without facing the deeper structural problems of a premature and poorly designed monetary union. As the crisis intensifies, all the proposed ad hoc solutions tend to aggravate the democratic deficit of the EU. It is not only the citizens that are being excluded from the debate about the future of the euro zone; also most national governments are forced to accept the solutions proposed by a few national leaders representing the major stockholders of the ECB.

Unsurprisingly, by summer 2012 the distance between European citizens and EU institutions had reached a level unimaginable only a few years before, as made evident by massive anti-EU demonstrations in Athens, Lisbon, Madrid, and Barcelona. In Hungary burning the EU flag became a proper way of expressing deep dissatisfaction with the perceived indifference of 'Europe' to the severe financial crisis of the country. According to Làzlò Lengyel, a Hungarian economist and publicist, what is happening in Eastern Europe today is in many respects similar to the disenchantment with socialism of the 1970s and 1980s. Hungary was the first country to which the sanctions foreseen by the new regime of supranational regulation and control of national budgetary and economic policymaking were applied. This led to mass demonstrations in Budapest, and also to Prime Minister Victor Orbàn denouncing EU's 'colonialism'. Cristian Parvulescu, a Rumanian political scientist, has explained the change of mood with the fact that the great expectations which East Europeans had linked to the membership of their country in the EU have been largely disappointed. The consequence is what we observe today: a return to populism and nationalism. The developments in Hungary, he concludes, should be an alarm signal. Also the Bulgarian political scientist Iwan Krastew sees the politics of the Hungarian prime minister as serious attempts to find nationalist solutions to the problems of the country, and warns about the risks of dismissing Orbàn as a nut. The EU would be faced with a serious situation if the Hungarian model started to have followers in four or five East European countries. In sum, the EU is no longer perceived as a factor of stability in Eastern Europe: from the Baltic republics to Bulgaria, with the only significant exception of Poland, hardly any of the new member states is firmly behind European projects (citations in Verseck 2012).

An odd consequence of the crisis in some countries of Western Europe has been the revival of the old neo-functionalist faith in the virtues of technocracy. As mentioned in the preceding chapter, Haas and his disciples believed that all crucial decisions are made by elites – policymakers, economic elites, professional associations, experts, etc. – so that a parliamentary majority is not required to make policy. So far the technocratic revival has not produced the expected results, however. In Greece the technocratic government of Prime Minister Papademos, a former central banker, did not have sufficient freedom of action because it had to act under the strict bail-out conditions administered by the troika. Hence the experiment was not repeated after the elections of May and June 2012: the Greeks seem to have concluded that under the tight constraints imposed by the EU and the IMF, the distinction between technocrats and politicians supported by highly variegated majorities, becomes elusive.

In Italy economist Mario Monti headed a government of 'technocrats' – mostly university professors and some managers, supported in Parliament by all the major parties of the left, right, and centre – arguably the first government of this kind since the political unification of the country in 1861. Also in Italy the results were not as good as initially expected. Shortly after Professor Monti formed his government (November 2011), the difference between the interest rates paid by Italian ten-year bonds and the interest paid by the equivalent German bills began to shrink. This was interpreted as a sign of confidence of the markets in the new government, and an over-optimistic prime minister announced publicly that the spread would continue to shrink. Alas, pretty soon the difference between Italian and German ten-year bonds started to grow again, reaching levels not very different from those prevailing under the previous government. Six months after the start of the new government, the German edition of the *Financial Times* could already write about 'The Disappointing Performance of Super-Mario'. The paper reported the opinion of several experts, according to whom Mario Monti's technocratic government was compromising the possibility of Italy's economic recovery through excessive taxation and drastic budget cuts.

A collective responsibility

The legitimacy crisis sparked by the crisis of monetary union is aggravated by the refusal of the larger member states to accept their share of responsibility for the present predicament. A convenient theory has been advanced in order to justify this hypocritical stance. The theory, as summarized by Fritz Scharpf (2011: 21–2), runs something like this: if successive Greek governments had not engaged in reckless borrowing the euro crisis would not have arisen; and if the Commission had not been deceived by faked records, rigorous enforcement of the Stability Pact would have prevented it. So, even though the more 'virtuous' members are now unable to refuse to help the 'sinners', such conditions should never be allowed to occur again. Such arguments, which in the 'rescuer' countries still dominate debate about the origins of the crisis, are used to justify the disciplinary measures discussed in the preceding pages. The emphasis is on continuous, and rapid, reduction of total public-sector debt; on the European supervision of national budgeting processes; on greater harmonization of fiscal and social policy; on earlier interventions and sanctions; and on 'reverse majority' rules for the adoption of more severe sanctions by ECOFIN. As most experts agree, however, the received view on the causes of the euro crisis is only partly correct for Greece and completely wrong for countries such as Ireland and Spain.

At any rate, it should not be forgotten that Greece was admitted in 2001 as the twelfth member of monetary union in spite of the fact that all governments knew that Greek financial statistics were unreliable. The responsibility of *all* the member states for the present situation has been emphasized by the director general of EU's statistical office, Walter Rademacher, in an interview published by the *Sueddeutsche Zeitung* on 25 February 2010 (Winter 2010). Rademacher recalled that doubts about the reliability of the information provided by Athens had become a near certainty by 2003. For this reason Eurostat had asked for more powers to control the way the data were produced. However, the member states rejected the Commission proposal that the competences of Eurostat be expanded to make a serious quality control possible. The head statistician of the Union concluded his interview with the words: 'The member states did not give us the instruments with which we could have prevented the crisis.'

What is true in the case of Greece is true in general: all member states, but especially the larger ones, bear their share of responsibility for the present predicament. Recall that in November 2003 a majority of the members of ECOFIN decided to suspend the procedures for excessive deficit initiated by the Commission against France and Germany. Instead, the Council recommended reductions of the structural deficit of the two countries sufficient to bring the deficit below 3 per cent of GDP by the end of 2005. France and Germany promised to do their best to achieve these goals, but this was a political, not a legally binding, commitment. In January 2004 a badly divided Commission decided to bring the decision of the Council before the ECJ. In July of that year the ECJ overturned the decision of the finance ministers to suspend the sanctions procedure against France and Germany. While the ruling partially vindicated the Commission's challenge before the Court to defend the 1997 SGP, the Brussels executive lost in the second, and more important, part of its case, where it claimed that ECOFIN had a duty to adopt the Commission's recommendations. The reform of the Pact in June 2005 in the end eliminated the elements of automatism in the original agreement and introduced considerable room for intergovernmental margins of manoeuvre.

It is remarkable that only today, and only with a good deal of reticence, European leaders begin to admit that the construction of monetary union was seriously flawed from the very start. Indeed, the determination to go ahead with monetary union even at the cost of evading key issues of monetary governance is at the root of many unintended consequences of EMU. A good illustration is provided by what economist Charles Wyplosz has called the 'dark secret' of monetary union: the fact that nobody is clearly in charge of exchange-rate policymaking, see chapter 1. The ambiguity of Article 111 TEU, Wyplosz pointed out, was intentional. In order to reach agreement on monetary union 'the founding fathers...cheated a bit, and produced an article open to all interpretations' (Wyplosz 2000: 35). An American political economist reached a similar conclusion: 'Prudence might have counselled that the European Union take certain steps well before the creation of the euro area: namely, fill in the holes in external policymaking machinery' (Henning 2000: 41).

As noted in chapter 2 and elsewhere, the fact is that prudential reasoning is foreign to the strategy of fait accompli, and to the entire neo-functionalist approach to European integration. This is the reason why agreements reached at the highest level always leave much room for different, even conflicting, interpretations. Because of this lack of precision everybody can claim victory, but the practical result is that many questions remain unsettled. In the case of the almost twenty summits on the euro crisis held between March 2010 and June 2012, for example, no clear-cut solutions have emerged from so many top-level meetings, but each time the leaders of both creditor and debtor countries could tell their voters that their viewpoints had been accepted, at least in part. The absence of prudential reasoning is also evident in the disregard of such well-known problems of collective action as adverse selection and moral hazard, see chapter 4. The refusal to take these problems into consideration when planning monetary union, as well as the total disregard of the warnings of some of the world's best-known experts, prove beyond doubt that all members of the euro zone are responsible for the present emergency, albeit in different degrees.

As noted above, it had always been suspected that Greece, as well as other countries with large public debts, engaged in various forms of pre-contractual opportunism in order to be admitted to monetary union as soon as possible. Early admission was considered important for reasons of national prestige, but even more in the hope that transferring power over monetary policy to a central bank allegedly modelled on the Bundesbank, would allow the national governments to import, or free-ride on, Germany's reputation for fiscal discipline. Thus, perverse incentives to conceal information on the true condition of public finances ('adverse selection') were present from the very beginning of monetary union. What made the temptation irresistible for some countries was the fact that most national governments supported a 'political' decision concerning the flexible application of the Maastricht parameters. They did this in order to start the monetary union with as large a group of participants as possible. As a consequence, countries like Belgium and Italy, with public debts over 100 per cent of GDP – well over the Maastricht limit of 60 per cent – were allowed to join EMU from the beginning, while the financial data presented by Greece and other countries were accepted without any serious scrutiny.

Even after adoption of the euro in January 2001, the governments of Greece continued to play Russian roulette with the national economy. In addition to concealing the extent of their financial problems, successive governments engaged in various practices of 'creative public finance' such as contract swaps, with the help of international banks Goldman Sachs and JP Morgan – a clear case of post-contractual opportunism. The loose governance of the euro zone provided again the wrong incentives. As already mentioned, in 2003 Eurostat was refused the additional authority which might have averted the present crisis. The failure of monitoring is obvious, but to understand the deeper causes of the crisis it is important to realize that the risks of both adverse selection and moral hazard are inherent in the Monnet strategy of fait accompli, see chapter 2.

The political decision to adopt a common currency for a group of countries with different economic structures and different approaches to public finance was bound to generate perverse incentives for at least some of the contractual partners. Before the final decision on EMU was taken, the president of the Bundesbank tried in vain to convince European leaders that '[m]ore than a single currency, the emerging single European market needs converging policies, which are still not in place in all participating countries. The repeated references to alleged huge savings in transaction costs for the countries of a single currency area are not in the least convincing' (Poehl 1990: 36). But for most political leaders the warnings of the experts counted for little when compared with the immediate advantages of monetary union. As soon as a country adopted the euro, its public debt received the highest rating by the international agencies, and consequently its government could borrow at about the same interest rate as the most virtuous members of the bloc. This meant that countries like Greece, Portugal, Spain, or Italy could borrow at rates well below the double-digit rates they had to pay before adopting the euro. In particular, the possibility of borrowing at low cost in the international financial markets is what made possible the Spanish real-estate boom. As a result of the euro-induced boom, wages and inflation grew much faster in Spain than in Germany or France. At the same time, the ECB, being mainly concerned with the level of inflation in the largest economies of the euro zone – Germany, France, and Italy – allowed the interest rate to remain low – too low for the conditions prevailing in Spain.

This is also what happened in the case of Ireland. For a number of years inflation in this country had been considerably higher than the average inflation in the euro zone. The ECB, however, was mainly concerned with the average level of inflation in the euro zone, which average depended heavily on the price level in the larger economies. As a consequence, it kept the interest level much too low with respect to what would have been appropriate for the booming Irish economy. Naturally enough, Irish families took advantage of what were, in real terms, negative interest rates to engage in their favourite activity, buying property, until the real-estate bubble exploded. In November 2010 the government of Prime Minister Brian Cowen was forced to follow the example of Greece, and accept the financial help of the EU and the IMF – together with the harsh conditions imposed by the rescuers. At the same, the unpopularity of this decision forced the prime minister to announce new national elections as soon as Parliament had passed the new budget law.

In sum, practically everybody connected with the EU in one way or another – national governments and their experts, European and international institutions, international banks, over-optimistic academics and other Euro-enthusiasts – bears some responsibility for the present situation. To blame and punish only the countries now facing serious financial problems is not only unfair but also counterproductive: it prevents a serious analysis of the deeper causes of the current predicament and, what is even worse, it impedes the search for ways to avoid similar catastrophes in the future.

7

'More Europe'

The crisis as opportunity

'"More Europe" is a mindless slogan, not the answer to all problems' wrote Samuel Brittan in the *Financial Times* (2011). The solution to problems, the noted publicist went on, is not more Europe, but less. Integrationist leaders naturally think otherwise. Some of them even see the sovereign-debt crisis of the euro zone as a blessing in disguise – a unique opportunity to complete the process started with monetary union with full political and economic union. In the words of the German finance minister, Wolfgang Schaeuble, as reported by the *International Herald Tribune* (Castle and Erlanger 2011): 'In recent months it has become clear: the answer to the crisis can only mean more Europe...Without... further steps toward stronger European institutions, eventually Europe will lose its effectiveness. We have to look beyond the national state.' Other members of the Berlin government, possibly including the Chancellor herself, seem to share the view that the crisis could, paradoxically, bring the EU much closer to a political union. The crisis, they argue, cannot be resolved without a much tighter coordination of the fiscal and social policies of the members of the euro zone, even if this implies additional limits on national sovereignty. Also the leader of the opposition Social-Democratic Party, Sigmar Gabriel, is of the opinion that the crisis calls for political union.

Some intellectuals are even more radical than the politicians. Sociologist Ulrich Beck claimed that the euro crisis was actually a great opportunity (Beck 2009). Two years later Beck went as far as suggesting that the 'predictable problems' of monetary union without political union were anticipated and even intended by the fathers of monetary union as a way of forcing national governments to move towards closer political integration. In an article in *The Guardian* (Beck 2011) he went as far as hailing the crisis as an 'opportunity for democracy'. Not even the worsening economic conditions of members of the euro zone like

Greece, Portugal, Spain, and Italy have dissuaded Beck from the vision of the euro crisis as the instigator of a Habermasian 'Europe of the Citizens'. But as Nicole Scicluna rightly points out:

> The reality...belies such predictions and exhortations. The onset of Europe's financial crisis has sparked the rise of a very peculiar type of 'cooperation', overwhelmingly intergovernmental rather than supranational and so dominated by French President Nicolas Sarkozy and German Chancellor Angela Merkel as to have earned the collective moniker 'Merkozy'.
>
> (Scicluna 2012: 500)

Though in less flamboyant terms than those used by Ulrich Beck, Bofinger *et al.* (2012) also argue that only a significant expansion of European integration can sustain a common currency without the need for a never-ending series of bail-outs, which in the long term would strain the solidarity of the citizens of the euro zone on both sides – donor countries and recipients – to breaking point. To impose effective fiscal discipline and guarantee a stable financial system, however, a transfer of sovereignty to European institutions is unavoidable. What these scholars advocate is the 'institutional underpinning' of a common fiscal, economic and social policy within the euro zone, and a closer coordination of financial, economic and social policies in the member states; all of this in preparation of the 'Social Europe' of the future. But something more is needed, according to Habermas and co-authors, namely to start moving towards political union, beginning with the core Europe composed of the members of the euro zone.

Commendably, the three authors insist on the need of a broad public debate about the purpose and aim of the unification process. In fact, as we saw in chapter 6, they are in favour of national referenda about the establishment of a politically unified core of countries which other countries, in particular Poland, would be allowed to join. The proposal of a political union, these German scholars continue, requires 'clear thinking about the political make-up of a supranational democracy that would allow collective government without assuming the form of a federal state'. They think that a European federal state is the wrong model, demanding more solidarity than the historically autonomous European nations are willing to contemplate. But once the federal model is excluded and the idea of a confederation not even considered, the notion of political union becomes hazy – probably too hazy to be submitted to the test of a referendum. Incidentally, the silence concerning the confederal solution is somewhat surprising since the new Article 50(1) TEU acknowledges the right of any member state 'to withdraw from the Union in accordance with its own constitutional requirements'. This means that the present EU is already, *de facto*, a confederation, and recognition of this point would help to sketch more precisely, at least by exclusion, the basic features of the political union sought by the authors.

In a short paper in the July 2012 issue of the *European Law Journal*, Juergen Habermas repeated that 'more Europe' 'is the correct answer to a crisis that has brought to light a construction flaw of the European Monetary Union' (Habermas 2012: 486). Presumably, the construction flaw referred to by the German philosopher is the decision to proceed with monetary union in the absence of a clear commitment to political union. In the early 1990s, when the Maastricht Treaty was being discussed, integrationist leaders saw monetary union as a means of forcing political union; now, political union, or at least progress in that direction, is the 'correct answer' to the crisis of monetary union. Whatever a philosopher may think of this inversion of the causal chain, the fact remains that Habermas' programme of 'more Europe' is extremely vague. In this as in his other writings on European integration one only finds references to closer coordination of national economic policies and gradual, or 'sensitive', harmonization of country-specific fiscal and social policies.

The problem is that there are many modes of policy coordination and harmonization, and some of them have even been shown to be counterproductive. For example, efforts to cooperate may deflect the attention of national governments from higher-priority domestic policy choices, or give governments incentives to delay policy actions they ought to be taking regardless of international considerations. Again, international coordination of fiscal policy often creates pressures on those countries that have been more successful in correcting their fiscal imbalances to relax their fiscal policy to bring it more in line with that of countries where less adjustment has taken place. Some game-theoretical models even suggest that international policy coordination may damage third parties. For these and other reasons some analysts maintain that intergovernmental competition, rather than coordination, is more likely to serve the interests of the citizens (Bryant 1995: 65–73). Moreover, when the states concerned are at very different levels of socioeconomic development, even minimum policy harmonization – let alone total harmonization, as in the case of monetary union – will likely reduce aggregate welfare (see chapter 4). The mantra of more Europe as the only way forward does not consider, let alone resolve, any of these potential problems.

Social Europe

As mentioned above, some advocates of more Europe think, or at least wish, that movement in that direction will eventually lead to 'Social Europe'. Many years ago Wilhelm Roepke suggested that 'whenever an intervention is called "social", it would be more exact to replace this fashionable adjective by the word "national". . ."Social insurance" is, in fact, "national insurance". . .and "socialization" reveals itself invariably as "nationalization"' (Roepke 1954: 233). Taken literally, Roepke's suggestion would turn the fashionable expression 'Social Europe' into an oxymoron – a combination of opposite ideas. However, the noted liberal economist goes on to argue that 'the enormously increased quota of national income which is claimed by taxation and spent by the State is a very important factor of national integration and of international disintegration because it involves a comprehensive nationalisation of the use of income. . .' (ibid.: 234). Here Roepke invites us to consider an issue that the advocates of 'Social Europe' prefer to evade: where to find the resources necessary to finance large-scale redistributive programmes at the European level without running the risk of disintegration. This question should be addressed especially to those who, like Habermas, are not prepared to argue for a federal Europe, saying that the federal model demands more solidarity than 'the historically autonomous European nations are willing to contemplate'. The existence of strict limits to transnational solidarity is confirmed by the fact that the largest net contributors to the EU budget – Germany, the Netherlands, and Sweden, all three states characterized by highly developed welfare systems – are the same countries which insist that the EU budget should not exceed 1 per cent of Union GDP, and most strongly oppose the transformation of the EU into a 'transfer union'. This seems to corroborate Roepke's thesis that a high level of national resources devoted to welfare is an important factor of national integration and of international disintegration. The tension between national integration and the risk of supranational disintegration, or at least of worsening Euro-fatigue, is also the dilemma confronting those who argue that only a strong social dimension can legitimate the process of European integration and, at the same time, rescue the national welfare state threatened by globalization.

Some champions of Social Europe assert that the addition of an enveloping social dimension to the integration process would enjoy widespread popular support. After the rejection of the draft Constitutional Treaty in 2005, for example, Belgian prime minister Guy Verhofstadt claimed that the French and Dutch voters had voted against ratification of the treaty, not because it was too ambitious, but rather because it was not sufficiently ambitious: it did not go far enough in the direction of a supranational welfare state. Also Habermas explained the failure of the draft Constitution primarily as an indication of the opposition of the voters to the alleged neo-liberal bias of the document, and as an expression of popular demand for a more welfare-oriented Union. In an article published in the *Sueddeutsche Zeitung*, Habermas (2005) wrote: 'If something can be deduced with certainty from the [French and Dutch] vote, it is this: that not all western nations are willing to accept the social and cultural costs of welfare inequality, costs which the neo-liberals would like to impose on them in the name of accelerated economic growth'. Now that the neo-liberals have achieved all their objectives, he continued, it is time to deepen the social dimension, and in particular to soften the impact of monetary integration by means of the gradual harmonization of fiscal, social, and economic policies. As I have shown elsewhere, the alleged neo-liberal bias of this, as of all other European treaties, is largely a myth (Majone 2009: 128–34). On the one hand, the founding treaties authorized some highly interventionist policies, for example in agriculture and in the coal and steel industries – and interventionism became even more pronounced in later treaties and European policies. On the other hand, those free-market principles that can be found in the treaties were introduced primarily in order to make possible the integration of heavily regulated national markets. It was the *dirigisme* of the national governments that forced the founding fathers to accept, however reluctantly, certain principles of a liberal economic order.

In any case, the available empirical evidence in no way suggests widespread support for delegating to Brussels relevant competences in the social field. On the contrary, the data indicate that, to paraphrase the German philosopher, very few, if any, West European nations are willing to accept the economic and political costs of an ambitious, and necessarily centralized, European social policy. Again, in listing EMU among the neo-liberal measures calling for social compensation, Habermas seems to be unaware of the fact that the motivation behind monetary union was political, not economic. As we know, integrationists saw EMU as a decisive step toward European unification, while different national leaders had different, but in each case political, reasons for supporting it. In contrast, most 'neo-liberal', or simply old-fashioned liberal, economists – from Milton Friedman to Martin Feldstein, from Kenneth Rogoff to Paul Krugman and the majority of German economists – opposed the idea of a centralized monetary policy for structurally diverse economies. After the introduction of the common currency, and even before the debt crisis of the euro zone, most competent economists continued to remain sceptical about the long-term success of the project – for good reasons.

The crisis of the euro has revealed the enormous risks involved in establishing a monetary union without a political union. Would the attempt to set up a European 'welfare state', even on a modest scale, be less risky in the absence of strong popular demand for more political integration? It has been argued that it is unnecessary to invent something new like a fully-fledged European federal state: all that is needed is to rescue the European model of welfare state by projecting it beyond the national borders in a different – supranational – format. In addition to ignoring the obvious question of where to find the necessary resources, such thinking reveals a serious lack of appreciation of the difficulties raised by the lack of socio-political embeddedness of supranational institutions, see chapter 5. Other scholars have evoked the image of the EU as a 'federation of welfare states'. But the level of centralized harmonization of social standards required by such a 'federation' would have been politically difficult to enforce even in the old EU; in the enlarged, post-2004, Union it is simply unfeasible, both politically, and economically. If states have different preferences for social standards, hence different policy priorities, as is to be expected in a highly heterogeneous Union, then standards that maximize aggregate welfare will have to be different. A harmonized European rule, even one that sets a minimum standard and allows the member states to adopt more stringent national standards, will not be optimal – unless the minimum standard is low enough to be exceeded by all the national standards, in which instance it is practically irrelevant. The truth is that a '[European] social state without a common economic, cultural, political project is a nightmare of decline' (Ladeur 2008: 158, footnote omitted). A supranational welfare state decoupled from a common political project would indeed be a bureaucratic nightmare; and given popular resistance to large-scale transnational income redistribution, an authoritarian nightmare as well.

Different, apparently more pragmatic, justifications have also been used to endorse the view that the European 'economic space' should be supplemented by a 'social space', based on the harmonization of national social policies – a thesis espoused by the European Commission since the 1970s, and clearly based on the analogy with the harmonization of the different economic regulations of the member states. But as already suggested, harmonization in the social sphere is considerably more difficult than in the economic sphere. Despite some national variations, market economies operate according to the same basic principles, while there are several, quite different, welfare state regimes. In a well-known book, Esping-Andersen (1990) identifies at least four main types of welfare capitalism: a Scandinavian model; an Anglo-Saxon model; the model of the 'Bismarck countries' of Central Europe; and the welfare systems of the Southern rim of the Union. In the enlarged Union the situation, besides being more complex, is in a state of flux. If the probability was always small of a European welfare state somehow emerging as a transnational synthesis (or 'federation') of national welfare systems, today that probability is close to zero. Furthermore, as Obinger and co-authors pointed out almost a decade ago:

> With the benefit of hindsight, we may conclude that the window of opportunity for the supersession of national social programmes by European schemes has diminished with each enlargement, because each increase in membership has multiplied the number of constituent units and thereby increased the number of possible veto players potentially opposed to greater uniformity of provision.
>
> (Obinger *et al.* 2005: 556)

In the final analysis, the main obstacle to a European welfare state is public opinion. It is not only the national governments that refuse to surrender control over social policy. One of the major strengths of the welfare state is the broad electoral base for core social programmes, as shown by the unpopularity of cutbacks. Naturally enough, the same voters who strongly support the national welfare state also resist any significant transfer of social-policy competences to the European level. Eurobarometer data mapping the responses of citizens in the EU-15 with regard to their preferred level of government for social policymaking, indicate that merely one-third of the population was favourable to a shift of social-policy competence to the Union (Obinger *et al.* 2005: 556). The only countries where a majority of citizens supported social-policy integration were the net receivers of European transfers. If such countries are excluded, then the data show that support for a European social policy has declined among the wealthier member states – precisely the ones which would be the net contributors to the EU budget – at least since the late 1980s. In fact, the time series of Eurobarometer data show that opposition to involving the Union in policies dealing with the personal distribution of income is longstanding.

All this explains why EU policies in the social field have evolved along quite different lines from those followed by the member states. The historical conditions prevailing at national level have created a dense web of welfare institutions covering most citizens 'from cradle to grave', while the EU is a 'welfare laggard' in terms of traditional social policy. In the case of the EU one should speak of social regulation – in such areas as occupational health and safety, environment, and consumer protection – rather than of social policy (Majone 1996). For historical, cultural, and political reasons, the domain of social policy has been effectively pre-empted by the member states. Some stubborn advocates of Social Europe argue that if a fully-fledged European welfare state is now politically and economically unfeasible, it should at least be possible to develop further certain of its present elements. At a later stage these elements could be fitted together to achieve a comprehensive regime. Thus, the CAP effects a considerable transfer of money from consumers and taxpayers to farmers, and for this reason it has been considered by students of EU social policy to form the core of a 'welfare state for farmers', as we saw in chapter 3. However, the CAP is not only an inefficient, but also a perverse type of social policy since financial transfers go disproportionately to well-to-do farmers and to rich landowners. Already in 1992 the European Commission reported that the richest 20 per cent of European landowners and agribusiness companies received 80 per cent of EU farm aid, and it seems that the situation has not changed significantly since then. More shocking still – because it is so contrary to the spirit, if not the letter, of the treaty mandate 'to ensure a fair standard of living for the agricultural community, in particular by increasing the individual earnings of persons engaged in agriculture' (Article 33 EC) – is the fact that among the largest receivers of CAP transfers were some of the most prestigious aristocratic families of Britain and the owners of the large collective farms privatized after the fall of East Germany's communist regime.

Regional policy is another potential candidate as building-block of a future Social Europe. EU regional policy, which aims to complement, rather than replace, the regional policies of the member states, is the most conspicuous component of the so-called cohesion policy – the second largest item in the EU budget, after agriculture, making up about 35 per cent of total expenditure. There is of course an important distinction between reducing inequality among individuals and reducing disparities across regions. The difficulty of targeting regions to achieve a better distribution of individual incomes is well known. Since most regions contain a mix of poor and rich individuals, a programme aimed at redistributing resources to a region whose average income is low may result, for example, in a lower tax rate. The main beneficiaries of the programme would then be rich individuals in poor regions. Thus, regional policy is an inefficient instrument of social policy, but in federal or quasi-federal systems it is quite difficult for the central government to aim redistribution directly at individuals. Even in the US, where the federal government pays three-quarters of the cost of welfare assistance, the states set the benefit levels. States differ in their assessment of what a family needs to achieve a reasonable standard of living, and in the amount they are willing to contribute to help families meet that standard. States also differ in the requirements an applicant must satisfy to be eligible for welfare assistance. As a consequence of these differences, the level of welfare assistance among the American states varies widely (Peterson and Rom 1989). The fact that, in Europe as in America, the member states insist on non-individualized transfers of centrally allocated funds provides additional evidence of the inefficiency of regional policy as an instrument of social policy. In sum, cohesion policy is hardly more entitled than the CAP to be considered a potential candidate as building-block of a future Social Europe – despite the fact that the reduction of economic and social disparities between richer and poorer regions is said to be a fundamental objective of the EU.

More of the same? The obsolescence of the Community method

On the occasion of the celebrations for the fiftieth anniversary of the Rome Treaty in 2007, some speakers attributed the accomplishments of half a century of integration to the invention by the founding fathers of an original institutional setting, having its most significant expression in the Community method. Also many advocates of 'more Europe' as the answer to all the problems of the EU assume, more or less explicitly, that the new powers delegated to the European level would be implemented according to this method. Regrettably, the supporters of more and tighter integration do not raise any question concerning the validity of the traditional integration method under completely new conditions; even less do they question its effectiveness in the past. As defined by the European Commission's 2001 White Paper on *European Governance* (Commission 2001), the Community method rests on three principles: the Commission's political independence; its monopoly of agenda setting, meaning that only the Commission can make legislative and policy proposals; and the role of the ECJ as guardian of the rule of law and of the balance among European institutions. From a normative point of view, the paramount feature of this integration method is the monopoly of agenda setting enjoyed by the non-elected European Commission. The Commission also proposes the legal basis for the measure under discussion, which basis determines the required majority in the Council. It is important to understand clearly what is implied by this exclusive power of legislative and policy initiative. First, other European institutions cannot legislate in the absence of a prior proposal from the Commission. It is up to the latter to decide whether the Community should act and, if so, in what legal form, what the content of the policy should be, and which implementing procedures should be followed. Second, the Commission can amend its proposal at any time while it is under discussion, but the Council can amend the proposal only by unanimity. On the other hand, if the Council unanimously wishes to adopt a measure that differs from the Commission's proposal, the latter can deprive the European legislator of its power of decision by withdrawing its own proposal. Of course, the Council and the EP may advance suggestions for new legislation, but the Commission is under no obligation to follow up the suggestions.

There is a fairly obvious connection between the Commission's monopoly of agenda setting and Monnet's principle of fait accompli. In chapter 1 I quoted Lamy's terse description of this principle: 'Europe was built in a St Simonian way from the very beginning, this was Monnet's approach. The people weren't ready to agree to integration, so you had to get on without telling them too much about what was happening.' In fairness to the founders of the EEC, it must be admitted that the implications of the decision to give priority to integration over democracy are clearer to us today than they could have been to the founding fathers – who expected that the competences of the EEC would remain so narrow that the indirect legitimacy provided by the democratic character of the member states would suffice. Even Robert Schuman, patron of the Coal and Steel Community and 'European

saint', was convinced that the competence of the supranational institutions should be limited to technical problems, and should not extend to
functions involving the sovereignty of the member states (Milward
1992). Also at the national level, after all, certain technical tasks are
delegated to non-majoritarian institutions such as politically independent central banks and regulatory authorities (see chapter 5). To the
comment quoted above, Lamy added: 'Now St. Simonianism is finished.
It can't work when you have to face democratic opinion' (cited in Ross
1995: 194). What has changed since the early stages of the integration
process is, of course, the enormous expansion of the powers delegated to
the European level.

   The founders considered the Commission's monopoly of agenda setting as a means of credibly committing the member states to the common project: if the Council had also been granted an autonomous power
of legislative initiative, then the integration process could be arrested,
and perhaps reversed, in response to changing national preferences, or
for short-run political gains at the domestic level. Yet, this argument can
be wholly convincing only if the scope and purpose of the commitment
are reasonably well defined. Hence the credibility argument underlines
the importance of limiting, rather than extending, the range of application of the Community method. Some time ago a sympathetic American
observer wrote: 'It is unimaginable that Americans would grant such
political power as the Commission staff enjoys to a career bureaucracy.
Not surprisingly, the people of Europe increasingly expect democratic
accountability by Community political and bureaucratic leaders'
(Rosenthal 1990: 303). These words were written a few years after the
Single European Act greatly extended the Community's competences. It
is indeed significant that the issue of the democratic deficit was hardly
ever raised before the Single European Act. The delegation of policymaking powers, even important ones, to a non-elected body could be
normatively justified as long as the Community's competences, hence
the Commission's powers, remained limited. But over the years this
institution has been assigned a variety of executive, legislative, and
quasi-judicial tasks. The multiplicity of functions and objectives
assigned to the Commission expands the scope of its discretionary
choices, complicating the task of evaluating the overall quality of its
performance. The collegial nature of the Commission compounds the
difficulty: in spite of the power of dismissal introduced by the 1997
Treaty of Amsterdam, it has already been pointed out that the EP is
understandably reluctant to dismiss the entire college in order to

sanction a single Commissioner. Since the Commission performs a large number of different tasks, it is extremely costly to dismiss it even when there is intense dissatisfaction with how it carries out one particular task. Thus the real normative issue is not so much the delegation of certain functions to a non-elected body like the Commission, as the scope and open-ended nature of the delegation.

The relationship between effectiveness and legitimacy discussed in the preceding chapter – effectiveness as a necessary, though not sufficient, condition for the legitimacy of new institutions – is relevant also in the present context. If the Community method had achieved even a fraction of the successes ascribed to it by its devotees then it would be difficult to understand the persistent legitimacy problems of the European institutions, and in particular of the Commission as the pivot of the method. Actually, in terms of concrete results, rather than process or mere symbolism, the effectiveness of the method is far from having been convincingly demonstrated. For a realistic assessment of the chances of 'more Europe' as a solution of the current problems, it is therefore important to understand the limits of the traditional approach. Take for example the Single Market project, surely one of the most important undertakings of the European Community. The 1985 Commission White Paper entitled *Completing the Internal Market* (Commission 1985) attempted to identify all existing barriers to the 'four freedoms' – the free movement of goods, services, capital, and people – and listed some 300 legislative proposals (later reduced to 279) necessary to create a unified market. According to estimates made by the Cecchini report – a study sponsored by the Commission to demonstrate the benefits that would accrue to the Community from removing barriers to trade – the Single Market could, over the medium term, boost Community GDP by 4.3 to 6.4 per cent; lead to the creation of millions of new jobs; reduce inflation; and produce large budgetary gains. The critical step in implementing the 1985 White Paper proposals was the adoption of the Single European Act in 1986. Article 13 of the Treaty states:

> The Community shall adopt measures with the aim of progressively establishing the internal market over a period expiring on 31 December 1992. The internal market shall comprise an area without internal frontiers in which the free movement of goods, persons, services and capital is ensured in accordance with the provisions of this Treaty.

More than twenty years after the 1992 deadline, a single European market still does not exist – indeed, it is shrinking in relative terms because of the growing importance of a services sector still largely regulated at the national level, as already noted in chapter 2.

The aim of the Single Market project was to create an economic area within which goods, capital, workers, *and services* would move as freely as within a nation state. Although this aim is presented as having been more or less achieved, the reality, according to a top expert on EU law and policy, is quite different (Piris 2011). Also the report on 'A New Strategy for the Single Market', presented to Commission President Barroso by former Commissioner Mario Monti in May 2010, acknowledges that '[t]he Single Market is Europe's original idea and unfinished business'. In his political guidelines for the present Commission, the Monti report continues:

> President Barroso pointed to the gaps and 'missing links' that hamper the functioning of the Single Market. Echoing this orientation, the European Council of 26 March 2010 has agreed that the new Europe 2020 strategy should address 'the main bottlenecks...' related to the working of the internal market and infrastructure. 'Missing links' and 'bottlenecks' mean that, in many areas, the Single Market exists in the books, but, in practice, multiple barriers and regulatory obstacles fragment intra-EU trade and hampers economic initiative and innovation.
>
> (cited in Piris 2011: 16)

On the basis of the Monti Report, the Commission produced a communication (October 2010): 'Towards a Single Market Act. For a highly competitive social market economy', which introduced fifty proposals, including a number of goals that should have been achieved by 1992 – for example, the removal of obstacles to the internal market in transport; the development of the internal market in services; and even 'a more resolute policy to enforce the rules of the single market'. The services sector is particularly important because, as we know, it represents more than 70 per cent of GDP in all advanced economies. A major effort to establish an internal market in services was made with the draft Services Directive presented in early 2004 by Internal Market Commissioner Frits Bolkestein. The draft aimed to go beyond past sector-specific attempts at building a single market for services, by adopting a horizontal approach which covered services of general interest, including health and social services not directly provided by the state. Bolkestein was convinced that there was only one way to dismantle the many regulatory and bureaucratic obstacles still remaining at the national level: to make access to the market for services as automatic as possible by resorting to mutual recognition through the home-country (also called 'country-of-origin') approach. The most controversial aspects of the draft Directive had to do with the conditions applicable to workers providing cross-border services (say, construction workers). In principle such movement falls under the 1996 Directive on the Posting of Workers, by which *host-country* conditions are always imposed on posted workers, except for social-security dues when the period of posting abroad does not exceed twelve months. Thus, a French firm hiring a Polish construction worker must apply French standards and regulations, and offer a French wage and French working hours. Under these conditions the firm obviously has no incentive to hire Polish or other East European workers; as a result, labour mobility across Europe is severely restricted.

The 2004 Bolkestein draft explicitly stated that the Directive on posted workers would not only remain in force, but in case of conflicting rules it would prevail over the new Directive. The proposed regulation focused instead on the temporary provision of services rendered by self-employed individuals in another EU country. Article 16 of the draft stated: 'Member States shall ensure that [service] providers are subject only to the national provisions of their Member State of origin.' According to economist Kostoris Padoa Schioppa (2007: 741), '[t]his sentence by itself, if adopted, would have implied a true revolution. That was so well understood by trade unions, by protected employees and by their parties in continental Western Europe that they aimed only at its cancellation, after massive demonstrations where they pretended to represent social Europe.' The Services Directive finally approved in December 2006 – against the strong opposition of East European governments – made no reference to the home-country principle, so that the host-country rule now applies to self-employed and to employee workers. As a matter of fact, the new directive does little more than restate the principles that have evolved in the case law concerning the freedom to provide services, and the freedom of self-employed professionals and companies to set up the base of their operations anywhere in the EU (Majone 2009: 120–4).

After passage of the watered-down Services Directive, some economists predicted that it would take a decade, or perhaps more, to have an internal market for services. Also the Organization for Economic Cooperation and Development *Economic Survey of the European Union 2007* (OECD 2007) was moderately optimistic on this score. However, such forecasts were based on the assumption of rapid economic convergence between the new member states and the old

EU-15 – a rather doubtful assumption even then, not only because growth figures can be misleading in the case of poorer countries, whose backwardness provides greater scope for faster economic growth; but especially because the process of Eastern and South-Eastern enlargement of the EU is far from being concluded. Thus Nicolaïdis and Schmidt (2007) report that Solidarność, the Polish trade union, justified its opposition to the Bolkestein draft by pointing to the risk that Polish workers would soon suffer from wage differentials with Ukrainian workers. In sum, the prospect of a true single European market keeps receding into the indefinite future because of the high economic, social, and cultural heterogeneity of the EU; because membership is still expanding; and, certainly not least, because of the growing significance of the services sector. The Community method – devised when the Community included only six, fairly homogeneous, member states – is not robust or flexible enough to deal with such complexity.

Nor has it proved capable of dealing resolutely with serious policy failures. The CAP, which still absorbs about 40 per cent of the Union budget, provides the clearest illustration of the difficulties of the Community method in dealing with policy reform rather than policy initiation. To early students of European integration, the CAP represented a working model of the future federal union. Here, wrote Leon Lindberg in 1963, 'the Community institutions have the power to legislate for the Union as a whole, without being required to refer back to the national parliaments. The progress made in agriculture will be of definite importance for the integrative potential of the EEC' (cited in Rieger 2005: 164). The Commission also repeatedly stressed the 'indispensable role' of the CAP in the process of building a united Europe. Some fifty years later we are more inclined to view agriculture as one of the most divisive issues in the EU, or as 'an isolated relic' of the ambitions of the founding fathers of the EEC (Rieger 2005: 165). As mentioned in the preceding section, it has been suggested that the CAP is best understood as part of a West European welfare state – a 'welfare state for farmers'. Even critics of the welfare state, however, find that the analogy is unfair. Whatever their negative consequences in terms of economic growth and market flexibility, national welfare policies at least succeeded in reducing interpersonal income inequality in Europe to a much greater extent than, for example, in the US. On the contrary the CAP has produced perverse redistributive consequences, as previously noted.

The details of the policy were worked out at a conference held in Stresa in 1958. The CAP was to be guided by three basic principles: a single product market; 'Community preference' – an extreme form of protectionism which did not allow any link between Community and world prices of agricultural products; and, third, financial solidarity among the member states, meaning that they would share the overall costs of intervention. It soon became clear that the policy was seriously flawed. Commissioner Mansholt presented the first reform plans only four years after the policy became fully operational in 1964. Already then prices were well above world levels and several commodity regimes were in surplus, but the proposed reforms were rejected by the national governments and powerful farm lobbies. By the early 1980s problems related to unmarketable stocks and structural over-production became increasingly acute. Also, the CAP was producing consequences that adversely affected international trade negotiations, but all reforms undertaken before 1992 were limited measures of adjustment to the level of prices, or the introduction of additional instruments to mitigate the effect of price support.

The reforms proposed by Commissioner Mac Sharry in 1992 were driven more by international factors than by budgetary considerations. It seems unlikely that the Council of Agriculture Ministers would have been able to agree to the proposed measures without the political pressure emanating from the Uruguay Round of GATT negotiations to establish a more transparent and liberal economic order in the agriculture support system. The tying of the CAP reform to the Uruguay Round helped ensure that it would survive. The main features of the 1992 reform – i.e., cuts in the support prices of key crops, direct income payments to farmers as compensation for the cuts, and a set-aside scheme where farmers were compensated for taking 15 per cent of their land out of production – were the first substantial reductions in support prices in the history of the CAP. Yet, these reforms were considered insufficient by most independent experts because farm incomes were only partially decoupled from production and therefore the incentive for increasing production remained, while the original policy objectives enshrined in the Treaty still remained in place. Also, the reform measures increased the bureaucratization of the CAP since the system of direct payments involved substantial paperwork and on-farm regulation of supply through obligations to set land aside.

The international context – the impending enlargement of the EU to Central and Eastern Europe and the preparation for a new round of WTO negotiations – also shaped the Agenda 2000 proposals. Given the size, nature, and role of agriculture in the new member states, it was obvious that to continue the CAP in its current form would have been prohibitively costly. The idea of at least a partial re-nationalization of agriculture policy, by introducing co-financing for direct payments to farmer, emerged at the time of negotiations on Agenda 2000. As for the Eastern European candidates, the Agenda proposed a transitory period of undetermined length and instead of direct payments, rural development aid. The CAP was again reformed in 2003 and 2008. In November 2008, EU agriculture ministers agreed to abolish arable set-asides and to convert market intervention into a genuine safety net. Since the beginning of the financial and debt crisis, the idea of continuing to allocate a large share of the total EU budget expenditure to the CAP is becoming politically untenable. Hence, the growing conviction that the current system cannot survive to the end of the present decade. What is envisaged, if not a complete re-nationalization of agriculture policy, is a gradual replacement of market and income policy by a strengthened rural policy and a remuneration of farmers for the public services they provide – nature conservation, landscape preservation, or water management – rather than for the commodities they produce. However, the costs of such services would be covered by national, regional, or local budgets, and only marginally co-financed from the EU budget. Thus, the history of the CAP, even under the most benign interpretation, raises serious questions about the ability of the Community method to accomplish fundamental reform other than under extreme pressure.

The growing obsolescence of the method reflects the progressive weakening of its pivot: the European Commission. Despite its enhanced role in the application of sanctions against members of the euro zone in serious financial difficulties (see chapter 6), the Commission has gradually become weaker since the 1990s due to a number of factors including its size and composition, and pressures from the EP and from the largest member states (Piris 2011). In particular, the EP has succeeded in influencing the distribution of portfolios within the Commission, and even its composition. Thus on the occasion of the nomination of the first Barroso Commission in October 2004, the EP, for the first time, managed to oust two of the nominees of the national governments. More generally, the EP's increase in power has been achieved largely at the expense of the Commission, which has been forced to accept a number of new demands in the exercise of its duties – such as to take 'utmost account' of the wishes of the EP in matters of political initiative (Dehousse 2011). Since a broad delegation of powers to the

Commission is the distinctive feature of the Community method, any weakening of this institution necessarily entails a loss of effectiveness for the method. Indeed, the so-called 'Open Method of Coordination' launched at an extraordinary meeting of the European Council in March 2000, was meant to represent a new approach to EU governance – an alternative to the Community method in a number of key policy areas including research and development, structural economic reform, education and training, pensions, health, and better regulation.

The size of the Commission is another problem, with significant consequences for the operations of the method. The rule of one Commissioner per member state – rather than two-thirds of the number of member states with a system of equal rotation, as originally determined – was promised to Ireland after the negative result of the first Irish referendum on ratification of the Lisbon Treaty (June 2008) in order to facilitate the success of the second referendum. If the promise is kept, then the Commission will simply be too large to work effectively as a collegial body. Piris points out that with one Commissioner per member state there is the risk of falling into intergovernmentalism, since the states tend to identify 'their' Commissioner as their representative in the Commission. To avoid conflicts with the national governments decisions tend to be made by consensus, which means that, with twenty-eight or more members, the Commission will hardly be in a position to decide at all (Piris 2011: 8–10). At any rate, it has become increasingly difficult to design common policy solutions for so many, highly inhomogeneous countries, with more to join in the near future. The EU of the future will have to adopt new policy modes, emphasizing flexibility and competitive diversity rather than the centralized, top-down harmonization for which the Community method was devised more than sixty years ago.

But even intergovernmentalism – as an alternative to supranationalism and the Community method – is becoming if not obsolete at least increasingly inoperative. Writing in 1943, David Mitrany, the father of functionalism, warned that 'the closer the union the more inevitably would it be dominated by the more powerful member. That is a first objection to schemes for continental [European] union' (cited in Eilstrup-Sangiovanni 2006: 47). The euro crisis provides the best evidence in support of Mitrany's insight. For a short time it seemed that the future of monetary union would depend, if not on the cooperation of all the governments of the euro zone, at least on that of the two largest member states. It soon became clear, however, that only Germany, if any country, could save the euro and possibly also the EU. This harsh fact has been acknowledged, however grudgingly, by all the other member states, and by the European institutions, including the ECB. Not being a lender of last resort, the EU central bank cannot play the role of the Federal Reserve in the US, and hence can only provide temporary and limited help. The irony is that much of the pressure for monetary union in Europe came from France and other countries which greatly resented the central role of the German national Bundesbank in the EMS: see chapter 1.

As was mentioned at the beginning of the present section, some Euro-optimists have attributed the accomplishments of half a century of integration to the invention of an original institutional setting, having in the Community method its most significant expression. The preceding pages have raised serious doubts concerning the substance of the alleged achievements, but before concluding this part of our discussion something should be said about the institutional setting itself. A high level of institutionalization is what distinguishes most obviously the EU from other models of regional integration. The ambition to transform the Community into something more state-like than a mere association, or even a confederation, of sovereign states, has been evident since the beginning of European integration. In choosing a high level of institutionalization as their approach to integration, however, the founding fathers overlooked an important fact, namely, that '[i]t is not institutions that create a sense of belonging, but a sense of belonging which makes institutional constraints acceptable' (Guéhenno 1993: 79, my translation). Acceptance of institutional constraints is particularly problematic when both the legitimacy and the effectiveness of the institutions are questioned. The economic and normative problems raised by a high level of institutionalization deserve more attention by scholars who, like Bofinger *et al.* (2012), advocate a stronger institutional underpinning for a common fiscal, economic and social policy within the euro zone, and in preparation for the 'Social Europe' of the future.

Closer cooperation

In the hope of making the EU more flexible while preserving key elements of the traditional framework, the 1997 Amsterdam Treaty introduced the possibility that some member states may choose to move to more advanced stages of integration by setting up closer patterns of cooperation. At the same time, by giving quasi-constitutional (i.e., treaty) status to the principle of closer cooperation, the framers of the Treaty acknowledged the growing diversity of national interests and priorities. Serious concerns about the risk of fragmentation persisted, however. The result was a set of conditions so strict as practically to rule out the possibility of establishing patterns of cooperation reflecting the policy preferences of various subsets of member states. In spite of the general lack of interest in taking advantage of the new institutional possibility, the issue of closer (later called 'enhanced') cooperation was the one where most progress was made during the negotiations leading to the Treaty of Nice of 2001. Article 43 of this Treaty provided that 'Member States which intend to establish enhanced cooperation between themselves may make use of the institutions, procedures and mechanisms laid down by this Treaty and by the Treaty establishing the European Community'. This possibility was subject to a number of conditions listed in the remainder of the Article: the proposed cooperation must be aimed at furthering the objectives of the Union and of the Community, at protecting and serving their interests, and at reinforcing the integration process; it must respect the Treaties, the single institutional framework of the Union, and the *acquis communautaire*; it cannot concern the areas of exclusive Community competence; it must involve a minimum of eight member states, be open to all members of the Union, and not constitute a barrier to, or discrimination in, trade between the member states, nor distort competition between them. The following Articles 43a and 43b provide, respectively, that enhanced cooperation should be used only as a last resort when it has been determined that the same objectives cannot be otherwise attained within a reasonable period of time; and that enhanced cooperation should be open to all member states at any stage, under the conditions specified by the treaty, and that as many members as possible should be encouraged to take part. Decisions taken in the framework of enhanced cooperation, on the other hand, are not to be part of the Union *acquis* (Article 44).

Both the Constitutional and the Lisbon Treaties were meant to make the use of enhanced cooperation simpler and more operational. Nevertheless, opinions about enhanced cooperation continued to diverge. An optimistic school of thought tended to focus attention on the potential for enhanced cooperation to regulate diversity in a principled way – in the sense that countries wishing to use this possibility must adhere to the objectives of the Union. A more pessimistic school argued that, far from furthering the objectives of the Union, the various forms of selective inter-state cooperation will in fact undermine the basic assumption of the Community method: that all countries would move together along the same integration path. Thus, the official Communication presented by the Commission to the Constitutional Convention (2002) – titled *A Project for the European Union* – was rather hostile to the whole question of flexibility. It objected, *inter alia*, that the enhanced cooperation provisions offered merely theoretical answers to the problems of diversity, and that it was time for a critical reappraisal of all forms of flexibility. The underlying message was that the enlarged EU needs a strengthened Community method in order to be able to 'exercise the responsibilities of a world power' (see Majone 2009: 211–5 for a more detailed analysis of this document). In fact, the possibility of 'enhanced' cooperation – as distinct from other forms of flexibility such as selective opt-outs and ad hoc intergovernmental arrangements – has never been used, presumably because of the strict conditions imposed on the exercise of this option.

With the worsening of the euro crisis and the growing diversity of EU membership, however, some form of differentiated integration is no longer an option but is generally admitted to have become a necessity. The deepening crisis forces stronger economic and fiscal coordination on the members of the euro zone, while a still expanding membership is transforming the EU into an entirely new entity: Croatia, the latest member of the EU, is likely to be followed by most, if not all, other Western Balkan countries – Albania, Bosnia-Herzegovina, Kosovo, Macedonia, Montenegro, and Serbia – and maybe, eventually, by Georgia, Moldova, even Ukraine; though not, apparently, by Turkey. 'Differentiated integration' is a generic and neutral term used 'to denote variations in the application of European policies or variations in the level and intensity of participation in European policy regimes' (H. Wallace 1998: 137). The label applies to several possible models such as 'multi-speed Europe', 'Europe à la carte', and 'variable geometry', to mention only the most important ones. The model of two- or multi-speed Europe assumes that all member states would do the same things but not necessarily at the same time and at the same pace. As we saw in the Introduction, integration à la carte, on the other hand, presupposes some general rules accepted by everybody but grants freedom of choice to each member state as to whether to participate in some policies. According to this model, there would be common European policies in areas where the member states have a common interest, but not otherwise. Thus integration à la carte diverges significantly from the philosophy of enhanced cooperation which, it will be recalled, allows voluntary associations of member states only to the extent that they 'further the objectives of the Union and of the Community, protect and serve their interests, and reinforce the integration process'.

Different meanings have been attached to the label 'variable geometry'. In the meaning most relevant to the present discussion the label refers to a situation where a subset of member states undertake some project, for instance an industrial or technological project in which other members of the Union are not interested, or to which they are unable to make a positive contribution. Since, by assumption, not all member states are willing to participate in all EU programmes, this model combines the criterion of differentiation by country, as in multi-speed integration, and differentiation by activity or project – as in integration à la carte. Still, all member states are supposed to respect a core of binding rules, as mentioned, but no broader commitments than those implied by the rules. Monetary union (with the British and Danish *de jure* opt-outs) and the Schengen Agreement (with the British and Irish opt-outs, and Denmark's partial opt-out) are cited as concrete examples of variable geometry.

Unfortunately, the precise conditions under which a particular model applies are seldom spelled out. For example, it has been argued (for example, by the Belgian political leader Leo Tindemans (1998)) that the idea of multi-speed Europe has found application in the design of monetary union, but this interpretation only reflects the hope of the architects of EMU, namely that all member states would sooner or later adopt the common currency. In fact, it is far from clear that the countries which opted out of the monetary union, in particular the UK, intend to join the euro zone in the foreseeable future, if ever. To speak in this case of multi-speed Europe is only to express a wish; 'variable geometry', or even integration à la carte, are the more appropriate labels. Except for the UK and Denmark, which have permanent derogations, all other member states are supposed to join the euro zone as soon as they fulfil the required conditions. As we know, Sweden was granted only a temporary derogation, but the country's leaders made participation in monetary union depend on approval by a popular referendum. Given the present state of Swedish public opinion (see chapter 4), a positive result seems highly unlikely; hence in the case of Sweden – and of other countries, such as the Czech Republic, which also plan to consult the voters before joining EMU – it is also doubtful whether one can speak of multi-speed integration in the case of monetary union; 'variable geometry' again seems to be the more appropriate label. In this connection it should be recalled that already in the 1970s Ralf Dahrendorf, while still a member of the European Commission, had severely criticized the European institution for their excessive reliance on the centralized Community method. He argued that integration à la carte – in other words, functional rather than territorial integration, see the Introduction and chapter 3 – should become the general rule rather than the exception.

The need for closer cooperation among the members of the euro zone is explicitly acknowledged by Article 136 TFEU: 'In order to ensure the proper functioning of economic and monetary union. . .the Council shall adopt measures specific to those Member States whose currency is the euro.' The Council will be able to take measures 'to strengthen the coordination and surveillance of their [members of the euro zone] budgetary discipline' and 'to set out economic policy guidelines for them, while ensuring that they are compatible with those adopted for the whole of the Union and are kept under surveillance'. It should be noted that measures adopted on the basis of Article 136 in order to strengthen the coordination and surveillance of budgetary discipline, will become part of the *acquis* and thus will have to be applied to all future members of the euro zone. On the other hand, only the full Council with all its twenty-eight members can take legally binding decisions, on the basis of proposals from the Commission. The ministers of the members of the euro zone can only 'meet informally'. According to Article 138, however, it is up to the members of the euro zone to decide to have a unified representation in all international institutions, including the IMF and the World Bank. According to Piris (2011: 39) 'if euro countries decided to use fully the extensive potentialities offered by Articles 136 and 138 TFEU, this would entail a dramatic change of the EU. . .the establishment of a "two-speed Europe" would not need any other legal text to become a reality'. Presumably, it would be a two-speed Europe with the euro zone as the 'hard core' group. Also other students of European integration see the members of the euro zone as the group which should cooperate more closely in different matters – but not on a case-by-case basis – in order to move faster than the other member states of the EU. Thus, Bofinger *et al.* (2012) stress that in order to avoid both a return to monetary nationalism and a permanent euro crisis, it is necessary to begin the process of moving towards political union, beginning with the core Europe of all the member countries of the euro zone.

This view of the present Euro-Group as the spearhead of deeper integration raises several questions which so far have remained unanswered. To begin with, new institutions may have to be set up since it is not clear how the EP and the Commission, whose composition includes the entire membership of the EU, could exercise their functions for a smaller group of states. Hence a new treaty would be required, but this additional treaty should not establish a new international organization but only establish new forms of cooperation among the participating members. For example, Jean-Claude Piris proposes a new 'European Parliamentary Organ' and a new 'Administrative Authority', but not a new court. The Parliamentary Organ would be established by the national parliaments, rather than being directly elected, but would have something which the EP lacks: the power of legislative initiative. The major task of the Administrative Authority would be to control the correct application of all measures adopted on the basis of the additional treaty, and to bring infringement action against the participating states, if needed. On the other hand, this author is against the establishment of a new court because of the risk of conflicts with the ECJ. However it is not difficult to imagine that conflicts could also arise between the new institutions and the European Commission or the EP. On balance, it might be preferable to work out special arrangements so that the avant-garde group could still rely on the Commission and the EP, perhaps in a different configuration.

But these are technicalities. The real problem with the idea of the members of the euro zone forming the avant-garde of a two-speed Europe is, again, that the member states that presently share the common currency are about as different – economically, politically and socially – as the entire membership of the EU. Also their reasons for joining EMU were, as we know, quite different: most, if not all governments, supported the project not for the sake of more and deeper integration, but in the hope of getting help in solving their own domestic problems. Indeed, it could be argued that the euro crisis has made the heterogeneity within this assumed core group a good deal more evident than the diversity of the other members of the Union. The key principle holding together the avant-garde group is that all participating states should be fully committed to participate in all areas of closer cooperation. The additional legally binding commitments could include: stricter budgetary rules, together with close examinations of draft national budgets by the other members of the group; an enforceable maximum level of budgetary deficits; and a commitment to limit the level of public debt, preferably through an amendment in each national Constitution, with controls by an independent body. Is it realistic to assume that all the members of the euro zone would voluntarily agree on a set of policies in

which they would accept such closer cooperation? Piris himself is
not sure:

> Would Germany, the Netherlands or Finland agree with Greece, Ireland
> or Portugal on a common list of social, fiscal, and economic (legally
> binding) measures to be taken? Would Germany accept common
> endeavours in the military domain, or in EU penal legislation? The thrust
> of the problem is here.
>
> (Piris 2011: 57)

The available evidence suggests the difficulty of finding agreement even
on a more limited list of potential common measures. In chapter 6 we
saw the negative reactions to the 'Pact for Competitiveness', conceived
by Germany in 2011 in an attempt to force all euro zone members to
adhere to sound fiscal and social policies. Biting criticism of the Pact
came from across the EU: from long-time members of the Union and
from the new members of Central and Eastern Europe; from small and
large countries; from debt-ridden Southern countries and fiscally virtuous Northern countries; even from the head of the European
Commission, who expressed concerns that the Competitiveness Pact
would undermine the Single Market. We already noted that because of
the debt crisis countries like Greece, Portugal, Ireland, and Spain adopted tough and legally binding measures of fiscal discipline, but such
measures were forced on them, not freely agreed to, and as such were
deeply resented. Indeed, one has to go back to the years immediately
following the end of World War II to find such levels of mutual resentment between the publics of the Southern and the Northern members of
the would-be core Europe – surely one of the most unintended and
undesirable consequences of monetary union. Moreover, it should
always be kept in mind that monetary union is part of the *acquis*,
which means that in the future the membership of the euro zone – if
EMU survives the present crisis – will be even more heterogeneous than
it is today.

Unanticipated consequences of 'more Europe'

The most evident, but also the most paradoxical, of the unintended
consequences of monetary union has been the segmentation of the EU
produced by the very policy which was supposed to make integration
irreversible. Instead of becoming the visible symbol of the irresistible
advance towards a politically united Europe, the euro has split the EU

into different subsets, perhaps permanently. We already have a Union divided into three groups: the members of the euro zone; the *de jure* (UK, Denmark) and *de facto* (Sweden) opt-outs; and the other member states, which are expected to adopt the common currency as soon as they satisfy the relevant criteria. A fourth group may emerge in the not too distant future: the drop-outs of the euro zone – countries with a large public debt which may be forced to abandon the common currency because rigorous implementation of the discipline imposed by the EU and the IMF could entail social and economic costs too high for their voters to accept. It will be recalled that the well-known American economist, Kenneth Rogoff, had predicted such a development already in 2006. In addition, the possibility has already been mentioned that fiscally virtuous members of the euro zone may also decide that in an increasingly heterogeneous Union the costs of a centralized monetary policy exceed the benefits, as pointed out by De Grauwe (2004).

The project of having a group of 'core countries' move ahead with various measures of deeper integration could further aggravate the divisions wrought by monetary union, to the point of endangering the functioning of the single market – precisely the fear expressed by the president of the European Commission, but also by British leaders, in relation to the 'Pact for Competitiveness', see above. Another unintended consequence is the growing popular hostility towards the European institutions and other member states – a hostility fed by the severity of the sacrifices imposed on the citizens of the countries in serious financial difficulties.

Another important unintended consequence of 'more Europe' may be the anti-competitive consequences of the transfer of increasingly significant responsibilities in economic and fiscal policy from the national to the European level. Since the 1990s there have been several attempts to reduce the scope of harmonization in favour of more flexible methods of coordination and inter-state cooperation. In particular, we saw that the OMC launched in March 2000 was meant to be an alternative to the Community method in a number of key policy areas, from research and development to structural economic reform, pension reform, migration, and health. The philosophy underlying the OMC and related 'soft law' methods is that each state should be encouraged to experiment on its own, and to craft solutions fit to its national context. Unlike the classic Community method, the OMC provides no formal sanctions for member states that do not follow the guidelines. Advocates of the new approach argue that the OMC can be effective despite – or perhaps because of – its open-ended, non-binding, non-justiciable qualities. The critics reply that the OMC is at best a method of national, rather than European, policymaking, pointing out that the ECJ, as well as the EP, are completely left out of the OMC procedure. If allowed to creep into areas of existing legislative competence the new approach would sap the EU's capacity to do what, according to the critics, really needs to be done, namely to pass uniform, binding, and justiciable laws (Hatzopoulos 2007). It is true that the OMC has fallen far short of expectations even in areas where one might have presumed it to have yielded the most significant results. But what is important about OMC in the present context is not what the method could achieve, but what it does reveal: a growing realization that what Europe needs today is not more top-down harmonization but more competition – not only among firms, but also among governments.

Already in the mid-1990s, a well-known Canadian economist, quite familiar with European problems, had identified the need for more inter-jurisdictional competition in the EU:

> I believe that the European Union is quite stable but that the stability has been acquired by the virtual suppression of intercountry competition through excessive policy harmonization. . ..To prevent the occurrence of instability, competition is minimized through the excessive harmonization of a substantial fraction of social, economic, and other policies. . .If one compares the degree of harmonization in Europe with that in Canada, the United States, and other federations, one is impressed by the extent to which it is greater in Europe than in the federations.
>
> (Breton 1996: 275–6)

Breton goes on to observe that in order to enjoy a stable Union structure the member states 'impose on themselves a series of harmonizing measures that transforms them into the simile of a unitary state' (ibid.: 276). There is a very real danger that in the end 'more Europe' will amount to a tightening of the straightjacket of excessive harmonization, and that it will mark the end of all attempts to make inter-jurisdictional competition possible. This would be too high a price to pay for rescuing monetary union since competition is the key discovery procedure not only for consumers and firms but also for governments, as we shall see in chapter 9.

Another important point too often overlooked in the debate about how to rescue monetary union is that governments operating in a common market cannot compete vigorously unless the authority to make economic policy remains largely in their hands, as argued, in particular, by Barry Weingast (1995). Hence current attempts to solve the crisis of monetary union by centralizing economic, fiscal, and even key aspects of social policy, such as pensions, may turn out to be self-defeating. This important issue will be considered in some detail in chapter 10.

8

The limits of leaderless Europe

The principle of equality in the EU

A key element of the ideology of European integration is the basic equality and equal dignity of all the member states, from the smallest to the largest: no leader but a 'collective leadership' as the principle of equality of all member states has sometimes been characterized. This principle of formal and (to the extent possible) substantive equality has inspired all the European treaties and also the day-to-day practice. It is reflected in the design and *modus operandi* of the European institutions. Indeed an important, if tacit, responsibility of the Commission is to ensure that the interests of the smaller member states are sufficiently taken into consideration – which explains why the smaller countries have always been the strongest supporters of the supranational executive. Clear evidence of the importance these member states attach to membership in the Commission is the promise made by the European Council after the failure of the first Irish referendum on the Lisbon Treaty (in June 2008) to abandon the planned reduction of the number of Commissioners – a promise meant to facilitate the success of the second referendum. The price of the concession is not negligible, however: as Piris (2011) points out, a Commission with twenty-seven, or more, members is hardly capable of taking decisions.

A direct consequence of the principle of equality is the fact that nobody can claim to govern the Union and, as a corollary, the absence of the traditional government–opposition dialectic. The European Commission, which many Euro-enthusiasts used to see as the would-be kernel of the future government of a politically united Europe, in fact looks more and more like an international bureaucracy and less and less like a proto-government. Even the European Council – the most likely candidate to provide leadership at the supranational level – is only able to achieve what the member states want it to achieve, with agreements hammered out – often bilaterally – beyond its walls (Peterson and

Shackleton 2012). There are good reasons to believe that, short of a radical transformation, political leadership will always be an extremely scarce commodity in the EU. The belief in the equality of all the member states and in unanimity as the optimal decision rule, at least in the case of politically sensitive decisions, has deep ideological roots. The central elements of the original Community method were fourfold (Pollack 2005: 16; emphasis added):

1. Governments accept the Commission as a bargaining partner and expect it to play an active role in building a policy consensus;
2. Governments negotiate over how to achieve collective decisions, and not whether these are desirable or not;
3. Governments, the Commission, and other participants in the process are responsive to each other, do not make unacceptable demands, and are willing to make short term sacrifices in expectation of longer term gains;
4. *Unanimity is the rule*, necessitating that negotiations continue until all objections are overcome or losses in one area are compensated for by gains in another.

Even after French President De Gaulle precipitated the so-called 'Empty Chair Crisis' in 1965, the EEC – which had been scheduled to move to extensive qualified majority voting in 1966 – continued to take most decisions, *de facto*, by unanimity. It is difficult to find a similar attachment to the principle of unanimity in modern European history. The only somewhat comparable case that comes to mind is that of sixteenth and seventeenth century Poland, where the voting procedure used in the *Sejm* (the lower chamber of the Polish Parliament) made it possible for a single delegate to block a measure approved by the majority by opposing his *liberum veto*. The *liberum veto* was based on the assumption of the political equality of every Polish nobleman, and such was the strength of feeling about the need of unanimity that it was considered improper to continue when a single voice was raised with the words 'Veto' or 'I do not allow it'. All efforts toward increasing the power of the central government were held to be against traditional freedom and were thus opposed. However, the system was used so recklessly that all business was frequently brought to a standstill. What was even worse, foreign powers or native magnates could always find a deputy willing to be bribed to exercise his veto in order to dissolve an inconvenient session. In this way, the *liberum veto*, which in theory was meant to ensure unity and unanimity, in practice ensured the perpetuation of chaos (Davies 1982: 345–8).

The costs of collective decision-making

Fortunately, in the EC/EU the consequences of unanimity have not been so devastating. In fact, the emphasis on consensus benefits the smaller member states and members which, like the UK, oppose the steady expansion of Union competences. It is true, nevertheless, that the search for consensus in the absence of a generally acknowledged leadership exposes the Union to some of the same risks experienced by seventeenth century Poland: institutional drift; high bargaining and influence costs; slow and confused reactions to crisis situations; short-run opportunism; and exposure to various kinds of pressure. On the other hand, it would be wrong to deduce from the disastrous experience of the Polish 'Noble Democracy', or from the constraining effect of the norm of consensus on the ambitions of integrationist EU leaders, that unanimity should be rejected as a decision rule. On the contrary, unanimity can be shown to be the optimal decision rule in a variety of situations. One of the main results of the theory of collective choice as developed by James Buchanan and Gordon Tullock (1962: 63–92) is that decision rules should be tailored to the nature of different interests deserving protection. At the constitutional stage the individual member of a would-be polity can foresee that collective decisions in such areas as human or property rights may impose quite severe costs on that member. For this reason, she may insist that collective decisions in the area of fundamental rights be taken by unanimity or near unanimity. It follows that whether or not a rational individual will support the shift of an activity from the private to the public sector (or, in case of the member states of the EU, a shift from the national to the European level) will depend on the decision rule that is to prevail in collective choices concerning that activity. The individual will choose to shift more activities to the public sector the greater the number of individuals whose agreement is required for collective action, with unanimity as the limiting case.

The important point is that the rational choice of rules for collective decision-making depends not only on the time and resources needed to reach a collective decision – the direct costs of decision-making – but also on the costs which that decision may impose on the individual members of the group. Buchanan and Tullock (1962) refer to the latter costs as the 'external costs' of a collective decision. Under the unanimity rule external costs are zero, but the costs of decision-making may be quite high. Hence, there is a trade-off between the external costs caused by a measure to which a member of the group is opposed, and the direct costs of decision-making. Under unanimity any member may block an agreement until a collective decision emerges which that member feels is the best that can be obtained, or at least one that does not pose an unacceptable threat to its basic interests. At the other extreme we have the case where the leader can decide the issue for the entire group. Here decision-making costs for the group will be close to zero but the expected external costs for all members, except the leader, are potentially quite high. The various possibilities can be represented by means of two curves. One curve, call it C, is the 'external-cost function' representing the expected loss of utility from the victory of a collective decision to which a given member is opposed. The other curve, D, the 'decision-making cost function', represents the cost, in time and other resources, of reaching agreement, as a function of the size of the required majority: 100 per cent in case of unanimity, 85 or 80 per cent in case of a super-majority, 50 per cent+1 in case of absolute majority, etc. The total cost of collective decision-making is C+D, and the optimal decision rule, for a given member of the group, is given by the size of the required majority at which the sum of external and decision-making costs is minimized. The reason why one decision rule cannot be optimal for all issues is that the two types of cost represented by the curves C and D vary considerably from issue to issue. Thus, when issues of basic human rights (or of national sovereignty in case of a group of states such as the EU) are under discussion, decision-making costs pale in comparison with the external costs which a collective decision can impose on an individual or corporate member of the polity. In such cases, something close to unanimity is the optimal rule. Again, if a minority feels more strongly on particular issues than the majority, then any decision rule short of (near-) unanimity may lead to policies that will produce a net loss of aggregate welfare for the group. Constitutional protection of basic rights against majoritarian decisions embodies this logic of collective decision-making. The same analysis also reveals the logical mistake of the advocates of qualified majority voting for all, or almost all, issues of EU interest: they consider only one type of cost – the cost in time and other resources required to reach a collective decision – while overlooking the cost imposed on individual members of the Union by a collective decision of which they disapprove.

However admirable the principle of equality of all the member states and however efficient, under some conditions, may be the rule of unanimity or quasi-unanimity in collective decision-making, the truth is that in most circumstances a group interested in a collective good will provide a less than optimal supply of that good. Moreover, the larger the group the less it will further its common interests. In the concluding section of the present chapter I argue that in the absence of outright coercion only a strong leadership can overcome the intrinsic limitations of collective action. The fact that in the EU both options are precluded is of prime importance for the question of the proper scope of European competences. Before proceeding further, however, it is important to recognize that there are different kinds of leadership, and that these different kinds are fungible only to a very limited extent.

Three kinds of leadership

John Plamenatz (1973: 83–90), distinguishes three activities, all of them leadership in the broad sense of the word, which are important in the sphere of governance and politics: management, government, and leadership in the narrow sense. Managers provide leadership by directing the work of others. Government, as distinct from management, consists, not in directing the work of others, but in making rules for their guidance and applying those rules to them. Finally, leadership in the narrow sense consists in promoting or defining some cause that the people (or a section of them) share, or that the promoter hopes to get them to share. This kind of leadership consists, not in ruling or managing others but in speaking for them. Speaking for people in the sense relevant here means, above all, giving expression to aims, beliefs and feelings that people are willing to endorse, though they may never have thought about them until they were adopted by some trusted leader. To be a leader in this sense is to have a large say in defining goals, principles, and attitudes which are, or are supposed to be, shared. Especially in this narrow sense of leadership, the expression 'collective leadership' is an oxymoron, a combination of contradictory ideas – unless all the members of the collective share exactly the same aims, beliefs, and attitudes, which is obviously not the case in the EU.

Three general conclusions about leadership may be derived from Plamenatz's distinction. First, leadership is a specialized form of activity, a kind of work or function; second, to know the work done by leaders we must know something about the specific situations they are called upon to handle; third, it should be possible to differentiate situations that especially require leadership in the narrow sense, from situations where other types of leadership are sufficient. In his classic study of *Leadership in Administration*, the well-known American sociologist

Philip Selznick points out that when true leadership fails, it is more often by default than by positive error. One, but not the only, type of default is the failure to set goals. Selznick writes:

> Once an organization becomes a 'going concern', with many forces working to keep it alive, the people who run it can readily escape the task of defining its purposes. . .there is the wish to avoid conflicts with those in and out of the organization who would be threatened by a sharp definition of purpose, with its attendant claims and responsibilities.
>
> (Selznick 1957: 25–6)

Much administrative analysis, he adds, takes the goal of the organization as given, whereas in many crucial instances this is precisely what is problematic. It is therefore important to emphasize the leader's responsibility to define the mission of the enterprise. A related type of default of leadership occurs when goals, however neatly formulated, enjoy only a superficial acceptance and do not really influence the total structure of the enterprise and its specific activities: 'Truly accepted values must infuse the organization at many levels affecting the perspectives and attitudes of personnel. . .the distribution of authority, relation with outside groups, and many other matters' (ibid.: 26). It follows that the task of building special values and a distinctive competence into the organization is a prime function of leadership. Selznick's analysis of leadership relies heavily on the distinction between 'organization' and 'institution'. While the term 'organization' refers to an 'expendable tool', an 'institution' is a responsive, adaptive organism, heavily dependent on its social or political embedding, and on its contacts with the outside world. To study a government department as an institution, for example, means paying serious attention to its history and to the way it has been influenced by its political and social environment. Keeping this distinction in mind, it becomes clear why the default of leadership shows itself in an acute form when organizational survival – or even organizational achievement in terms of resources, procedures, and stability – is confounded with *institutional* success. The EU may be the clearest illustration of Selznick's thesis that, for the bare continuity of organizational existence, leadership, in the narrow sense, is often dispensable. On the other hand, leadership is required where the problem is to choose key values and to create a social structure that embodies them.

The crucial problems of institutional leadership arise when goals are not well defined, and when fluid situations require constant adaptation. This key point is that the institutional leader cannot permit any partial viewpoint to dominate decisions regarding the enterprise as a whole. However, 'this control will not be possible unless a clear idea of the nature of the enterprise – its long-run aims as shaped by long-run commitments – is grasped and held. Leadership fails if it permits a retreat to the short run' (ibid.: 81). The need to set goals is a problem set for the leadership of any polity – from large organizations to nation states or unions of sovereign states. It is a task of leadership to assess the extent to which widely held views represent the polity's true commitments. But commitments must be credible, and to be credible they have to be supported by adequate resources – economic, political, institutional, and, not least, normative. Thus the task of the institutional leader is not only to set goals representing the polity's commitments, but also to make sure that ends and means are balanced – that the goals are feasible, or at least that the existing constraints may be relaxed at acceptable cost.

Many of the problems of European governance discussed in the preceding chapters can be traced back to the scarcity of leadership *relative to the scope of the powers transferred to the supranational level* – an obvious point which, like the similar relation between democratic deficit and scope of EU competences, is seldom recognized and hence deserves to be emphasized here. The 1957 Treaty of Rome did not require much leadership since its most important articles were concerned with negative integration, i.e. the removal of obstacles to free movement of people and goods, see chapter 3. Given these limited objectives, the kind of leadership discussed by Plamenatz under the labels of management and government as rule-making was sufficient. The default of institutional leadership became increasingly apparent as successive treaties kept expanding supranational competences without a clear statement of mission, without robust popular support, and even without a corresponding increase in institutional resources. Indeed, the strategy of fait accompli traditionally used to expand the activities of the EC/EU represents the clearest admission of the absence of institutional leadership at the European level. It will be recalled that this strategy consists in pushing ahead with ambitious integration projects, without worrying about either feasibility or democratic legitimacy, see chapter 1. The rationale behind the strategy, as Pascal Lamy clearly perceived, was the realization that the people were not ready to accept the steady expansion of supranational powers. Thus, instead of trying to convince the people of the desirability of 'ever closer union', Jean Monnet and his followers preferred, in Lamy's words, 'to get on without telling them too much about what was happening' (see chapter 1). Such lack of trust is incompatible with institutional leadership.

Leadership and trust

Leadership can be crucially important in solving many problems of collective action. Only a leader with the incentive and the capacity to reward those who contribute their fair share and to punish those who do not can cure the pathologies of collective choice noted by Mancur Olson and other scholars – particularly the tendency to free riding and to elicit sub-optimal levels of effort, see the concluding section of this chapter. Leadership can be fragile and ultimately ineffective, however, if the members of the group do not trust their leaders. It has even been argued that trust should precede the acceptance of leadership rather than the other way around. Hence leadership will function best if a prior basis of trust can be established (Bardach 2006: 356). Also Plamenatz, in defining leadership in the narrow sense, i.e. as the activity of giving expression to aims and beliefs that others are willing to endorse, assumes that the leader enjoys a reputation for trustworthiness among would-be followers. Regardless of whether trust precedes leadership or follows it as a result of the actions of the leader, the two notions are closely connected. This is especially evident in the case of a polity like the EU, composed of states with different traditions and methods of government, different needs, and often conflicting priorities. The default of leadership in the EU is a consequence, not only of the ideology of equality of all the member states, but also of the lack of trust between the member states and the European institutions, and between the member states themselves.

The lack of trust of the member states in the supranational institutions has become increasingly evident since the difficult ratification of the Maastricht Treaty – one of the most controversial documents in the history of European integration, being centralized and radical in its EMU provisions, but committed to greater flexibility and to 'subsidiarity' in its political stipulations. The basic reason for introducing the principle of subsidiarity in Article 3b of the Treaty was less a desire to improve the effectiveness of collective decisions – 'the Community shall take action...only if and in so far as the objectives of the proposed action cannot be sufficiently achieved by the Member States and can therefore...be better achieved by the Community' – than an attempt to set stricter limits to the transfer of powers from the national to the European level. The normative bite of Article 3b is in its first sentence – 'The Community shall act within the limits of the powers conferred upon it by the Treaty' – suggesting that in the past the supranational institutions repeatedly made use of their delegated powers in ways not approved of by at least some member states. This sentence enunciates the principle of limited powers, and Professor Dashwood was referring to it when he wrote that after Maastricht '[t]he notion of a Community continuously moving the boundary posts of its own competence is ruled out of court' (Dashwood 1996: 115).

An even clearer indication of a progressive loss of trust in the supranational institutions are the limitations imposed by the more recent treaties on supranational powers, and in particular on the harmonization of national laws and regulations. The Treaty of Maastricht defined for the first time new European competences in a way that actually limits the exercise of Community powers. For example, Article 126 of the Treaty adds a new legal basis for action in the field of education, but policy instruments are restricted to 'incentive measures' and to recommendations: harmonization of national laws is explicitly ruled out. Likewise, Article 129 creates specific powers for the Community in the field of public health protection, but harmonization is again ruled out. The other provisions of the Treaty – defining new competences in areas such as culture, consumer protection, and industrial policy – are similarly drafted. Unwilling to continue to rely on implicit powers, which seemed out of control, the framers of the TEU opted for an explicit grant that delimits the mode and the reach of action (Weiler 1999). Such has been the approach followed thereafter by the Amsterdam and Nice Treaties, and by the Lisbon Treaty. One reason for the growing mistrust of the member states was the realization that:

> [H]armonization tended to be pursued not so much to resolve concrete problems encountered in the course of constructing the common market as to drive forward the general process of integration. This. . .was bound to affect the judgment of the Commission, inclining it towards maximum exercise of [its] powers and towards solutions involving a high degree of uniformity between national laws.
>
> (Dashwood 1983: 194)

From the early 1960s to about 1973 – the date of the first enlargement of the Community – the Commission's approach to harmonization was characterized by a distinct preference for detailed measures designed to regulate exhaustively the problems under consideration, to the exclusion of previously existing national laws and regulations – the approach known as 'total harmonization', see chapter 1. By the mid-1970s, however, the limitations of this approach had become clear; while mounting opposition to what many member states considered excessive centralization convinced the Commission that harmonization had to be used so as not to interfere too much with the regulatory autonomy of the national governments. This realization may have come too late, however. The failure of the Commission as an institutional leader, to be discussed in the next section, can be traced back to the member states' loss of trust in the supranational institutions – an attitude clearly noticeable long before the ratification of the Maastricht Treaty.

The lack of trust in the European institutions is matched by a mutual mistrust of the member states, which becomes particularly evident in crisis situations. Consider, for example, the confusion reigning in Brussels and in the national capitals after the French and Dutch rejection of the Constitutional Treaty in 2005. The presidents of the Commission, of the EP, and of the European Council met in Brussels, to accomplish nothing more than issuing a joint statement claiming that the Constitutional Treaty was still alive, and vainly urging the other member states to continue with the ratification process. The lack of contingency plans, or even of any idea about what to do next, was actually emphasized by the Commission president's announcement of a 'Plan D', where 'D' stood for democracy, dialogue, and discussion. Also the European summit of 16 and 17 June 2005 proved unable to do anything more than postpone any decision, waiting for the French and Dutch elections in 2007, and in the meanwhile hoping for improvements in the general economic climate. One year later, the European summit of June 2006, under Austrian Presidency, again postponed any decision concerning which parts of the Constitutional Treaty, if any, could be salvaged. In the dramatic European summit of late June 2007 a tentative agreement to move forward could be achieved only by scaling down the Constitutional Treaty to a 'Reform Treaty', by granting to the UK and Poland opt-outs on an important matter like the Charter of Fundamental Rights, and by satisfying Polish demands concerning voting rules in the Council of Ministers.

One of the most disturbing consequences of the French and Dutch rejection of the draft Constitution was the return to brutal methods of defence of the national interest. Of course, national interests always become highly visible in critical situations. Still, an implicit rule had developed over the years according to which the defence of the national interest should not exclude concessions to the other member states, and at least a formal acknowledgment of the existence of a higher common interest. De Gaulle, Chirac, and Mrs Thatcher are the exceptions that confirm the general rule. 'Constructivist' theorists of European integration argue that European rules and norms shape the behaviour and the very preferences of member states: 'European integration has a transformative impact on the European state system and its constituent units. European integration has changed over the years, and it is reasonable to assume that in the process agents' identity and subsequently their interests have equally changed' (Christiansen *et al.* 1999: 529). Alas, no such transformative impact could be detected at the Brussels summit of 16 and 17 June 2005, where the financial framework for the period 2007–2013 was to be defined. On this occasion, the mode of interaction among the national leaders reached a degree of brutality seldom, if ever, experienced before. Thus in his advocacy of a narrowly construed national interest, the Dutch prime minister Jan Balkenende was as irremovable as the British, Spanish, Swedish, and Finnish prime ministers, or the French president. His country was tired, Balkenende effectively said, of being the main paymaster of the Union – on a per capita basis, the Netherlands' net contribution to the EU budget was at the time 120 euros, against the 106 of Sweden, and Germany's 97. Unless the net contribution of the Netherlands was sensibly reduced, there would be no long-term financial framework. This from the leader of a country which used to be considered a champion of European integration. And as we saw in chapter 4, Spain's attitude at the Brussels summit was particularly revealing of the resurgence of naked national-interest thinking in case of a serious crisis.

After the French and Dutch 'No' to the Constitutional Treaty in 2005, and the rejection of the Lisbon Treaty by the Irish voters in 2008, the mistrust of the national governments toward each other and toward the European institutions was extended to the entire body of public opinion. Today popular referendums on European issues are seen as a potential hazard to the integration process, not just in traditionally Euro-sceptic countries but in all member states. Hence the talk of a 'referendum threat', and also of a 'federalist deficit', meaning a slowing down or reversal of the federalization process caused by popular votes on European issues, see chapter 6. The real threat to Brussels-style European integration is now seen to come less from the national governments than from the direct expression of voters' preferences. The most recent, and most striking, demonstration of the fear of popular votes on

European issues is the new regime of regulation and control of national budgetary and economic policymaking established in 2012 by the Stability Treaty. After the refusal of the UK and the Czech Republic to accept it, the treaty was signed by the other member states as an international treaty, hence enjoying the protection from the referendum threat usually granted to diplomatic acts. The referendum genie is already out of the bottle, however. Demands for popular ratification of future European treaties have been advanced by political leaders of different countries and political hues, and it is by now pretty clear that in the future major advances in European integration will have to be validated by the explicit approval of the voters.

But to win the approval of the voters it is necessary to explain to them what has been accomplished so far. The problem is that while voters are typically interested in concrete results, one of the characteristic features of the political culture of the EU is the primacy given to process, see chapter 2. This divergence of evaluative criteria is a serious obstacle to political communication between EU institutions and European voters. What is suggested here, at any rate, is that the primacy traditionally assigned to process over actual results is another indication of the default of leadership. While the true leader needs to legitimate his or her decision by results which everybody can perceive, in case of a 'collective leadership' reaching agreement on a common position is already proof of success, regardless of the actual outcomes of the decision. Hence the early enthusiasm about the decision to proceed with monetary union, even though crucially important questions of monetary policy were left unresolved; and hence, more generally, the total optimism exhibited for more than half a century by the European institutions and by many political leaders.

The European Commission as would-be leader

The Commission is the European institution that, at least in the intentions of the founding fathers, should have provided all three kinds of leadership mentioned by Plamenatz: supranational management; government in the sense of rule-making and policymaking; and political leadership in pushing all the member states towards 'ever closer union'. Indeed, the Commission is, or was meant to be, 'a distinct hybrid: the European Union's largest administrator and main policy manager, as well as a source of political and policy direction' (Peterson 2012: 96). Walter Hallstein, the first president of the Commission (from 1958 to 1967) stressed particularly the political function of this hybrid institution, often referring to himself as the equivalent of a European prime minister. Also Jacques Delors (Commission President from 1985 to 1995) envisioned a politically and economically united Europe, with the Commission as the federal executive. Both Hallstein's and Delors' activism illustrate the pitfalls and risks of a strong leadership of this hybrid body. Hallstein's attempt to turn the Commission into an embryonic government of the European Community put him on a collision course with French President De Gaulle, who bitterly opposed any extension of Commission powers. The showdown came in early 1965, when Hallstein introduced proposals to link completion of the financial arrangement of the CAP with greater executive authority for the Commission and budgetary power for the EP. De Gaulle made clear to his Community counterparts that France would reject the Commission's proposals. In July De Gaulle recalled the French permanent representative in Brussels and announced that French officials would no longer participate in the EC Council of Ministers or its committees, thus precipitating the so-called Empty Chair Crisis. In September of the same year, the French leader gave a press conference in which he attacked the political ambitions of both the Commission and the EP. By the end of January 1966, just before an extraordinary Council session in Luxembourg in which France participated but not the Commission, the British press was evoking the possibility of a break-up of the EC, while some French newspapers regarded recent developments as evidence of a double crisis: an institutional crisis among the six members of the Community, amid fears that Paris might even want to revise the Treaty of Rome; and a political crisis between France and Germany, with the German government, concerned about domestic public opinion and the forthcoming elections in September, insisting that the crisis must not appear to be solved at the expense of the Germans.

The crisis, which paralysed the EC for seven months, was eventually resolved at a foreign ministers' meeting in Luxembourg on 28 and 29 January 1966, where agreement was reached to adopt an interim financial regulation for the CAP, deferring the question of additional powers for the Commission and the EP. Both sides approved a short declaration, the famous Luxembourg Compromise, which maintained the principle of majority voting, but acknowledged that 'when very important issues are at stake, discussions must be continued until unanimous agreement is reached'. In the eyes of some commentators the compromise was a real settlement, while in the eyes of others it consisted of an agreement to disagree. What is certain, at any rate, is that the Commission was in a marginalized position during the crisis and in finding a solution to it, while the Council and the member states were the most important actors throughout. In the words of Piers Ludlow (2006: 90) 'Community crisis and the need for political decisions brought the member states to the fore and minimised the scope for the Commission to use the vast technical expertise it had built up of the EEC's day-to-day operation'. The Commission was not invited to the ministerial discussions among the other five member states, and was even excluded from some of the meetings of the Coreper. The regularity and frequency of such encounters during the period of the French boycott 'did graphically underline how completely the Commission had been pushed to the margins of a dispute it was widely – if rather unfairly – blamed for starting' (ibid.: 91).

Hallstein was practically forced to resign, despite the attempt by Kurt Kiesinger, the German chancellor, to propose him again as Commission president. The veto on Hallstein's reappointment was De Gaulle's revenge. Shortly after the new Commission was installed, with the Belgian Jean Rey as president, the 'economic miracle' of the post-war years came to an end. Europe's convergence with the US in the levels of per capita income and most other economic indicators stopped at the beginning of the 1980s (Majone 2009: 81–7). What was even more alarming from the point of view of European integration was the rapid growth of national non-tariff barriers to the free movement of goods, services, labour, and capital, and the resulting segmentation of what was supposed to be a 'common' market. One of the reasons for the EC's inability to remove such barriers in the 1970s and 1980s had been the pervasiveness of unanimous voting in the Council of Ministers as a consequence of the Luxembourg Compromise. It was against this background of 'Eurosclerosis' and regression that Jacques Delors took over as president of the European Commission in January 1985.

The new president was looking for a key project around which the process of European integration could be relaunched. After rejecting a number of possibilities that might fail to attract the unanimous support of the member states, Delors settled on the completion of the internal market as the central plank of his *rélance* of the EC, and charged his new internal market Commissioner, Lord Cockfield, with the drafting of a White Paper on *Completing the Internal Market*. The document listed the obstacles to free movement within the Community and identified the types of action necessary to overcome these obstacles. The absence of a common market for services was recognized as one of the more important barriers subject to removal. At the same time, a key element of the

Single Market programme was its specific timetable: all the approximately three hundred measures of the legislative programme were to be adopted no later than by the end of 1992. A significant accomplishment of the programme was the revival of 'negative integration', that is, the elimination of national rules that impede economic exchange, see chapter 3. More than twenty years after the 'Europe' 92' target, however, the Single Market is still far from being a reality. According to the Commission's biennial *Single Market Scoreboard* prices for the same products in different member states stopped converging a few years after the 1992 deadline, and price variations remain significantly higher in the EU than in the US, suggesting that significant obstacles to trade remain. The most serious problem area when it comes to completing the Single Market was and remains the services sector.

As we had several occasions to point out, in all modern economies the services sector accounts for at least 70 per cent of GDP and 50 per cent of employment. Also in the EU, between the years 1980 and 2000 the share of services in the economy increased by 13 percentage points, to 72 per cent. Hence the free movement of goods, which has been more or less achieved, is no longer sufficient to ensure market integration: no common market may be said to exist without a reasonably well-integrated services sector. Unfortunately, most services are still regulated at the national level, while socioeconomic conditions vary so much across the Union – income inequality, as measured by the Gini concentration coefficient, is greater in the enlarged Union than in the supposedly arch-capitalist US – that ex ante (centralized) harmonization of national laws and regulations is likely to reduce aggregate welfare, while ex post harmonization (via mutual recognition and regulatory competition) continues to meet strong political opposition from EU institutions and most member states. The aim of Delors' Single Market project was to open the EU internal borders to the free movement of all the factors of production and exchange, as within a nation state. This aim is presented as having been more or less achieved, but the truth is that market integration is far from having been attained, especially, in the services sector: 'In many areas the Single Market exists in the books but, in practice, multiple barriers and regulatory obstacles fragment intra-EU trade and hamper economic initiative and innovation (Piris 2011: 15). This is why proposals for 'the development of the single market in services' and for 'a more resolute policy to enforce the rules of the single market' were still debated in Brussels in 2010. Another, equally important, if implicit, aim of Delors was to advance political integration in

Europe on the back of a programme of market liberalization. This goal has been missed even more patently than the Single Market for services.

'Delors wanted a politically integrated Europe. The first step was the single market, once you have a single market you have a single currency, and then the door is open to political integration.' This is how Alexandre Lamfalussy, at the time general manager of the Bank for International Settlements, summarized the grand strategy of the French President of the European Commission in an interview with David Marsh in May 2007 (Marsh 2010: 122). In 1988 – almost twenty years after the initial announcement of the Werner Plan for achieving economic and monetary union in Europe by 1980, see chapter 1 – Delors began a new campaign for EMU, first persuading the European Council to set up a committee composed of central bankers and economic experts, under Delors' chairmanship. Echoing the proposals of the 1970 Werner Plan, the Delors Committee Report recommended a three-stage move to EMU, starting with closer economic and monetary coordination. Unfortunately, the document left many important questions open, supposedly to be settled by the governments later on. As explained by Delors himself to David Marsh in 2007, 'fundamentally EMU was a political issue that could only be decided by the governments. In the report, I wanted to draw attention to the need for sufficient economic coordination as a precondition for EMU' (ibid.). Unfortunately, the old split between 'economists' and 'monetarists' reasserted itself. Franco-German differences were particularly pronounced on the issue of institution building. As in the discussions of the 1970s, France insisted on building the institutions first and then allowing for convergence to happen after that. But Germany and the Netherlands – the leading members of the 'economist' group – insisted that monetary union required, first of all, a closer coordination of the economic, fiscal, and even social policies of the prospective members of monetary union.

What Delors called the 'acceleration of history' in Central and Eastern Europe in 1989 and 1990 made these differences of opinion concerning monetary union appear relatively unimportant. Germany's attention was now focused on national reunification rather than European affairs, and this fact may have facilitated final agreement on EMU. At the same time, the geopolitical events of those years seemed to revive interest in EPU. An intergovernmental conference on political union was called, to occur simultaneously with the EMU conference. The most visible result of two years of frenetic discussions about the nature, scope, and competences of EPU was the three-pillar 'temple' of the Maastricht

Treaty: the EC; an intergovernmental CFSP; and intergovernmental Cooperation on JHA. Delors had vainly opposed this arrangement in favour of a 'tree' whose different functions would be connected to a common Community 'trunk' (Ross 1995). In fact, the Commission had very little influence over the political union negotiations. Maastricht marked the end of the post-1985 renewal of European integration, rather than the big leap forward that Delors had wanted.

In retrospect, the Delors decade ended in defeat as far as hopes of 'ever closer union' were concerned. Instead of the single Community the French leader had worked so hard to establish as the forerunner of something resembling a European federation, the constitutional structure produced by the Maastricht Treaty resulted in what Professor Curtin famously called a Europe of bits and pieces: 'The result of the Maastricht summit is an umbrella Union threatening to lead to constitutional chaos...at the heart of all this chaos and fragmentation, the unique *sui generis* nature of the European Community, its true world-wide historical significance, is being destroyed' (Curtin 1993: 67). George Ross (1995) has correctly identified the basic flaw in Delors' strategy: the failure of the French leader to realize that the traditional Monnet method of 'integration by stealth' – the attempt to achieve political union through ever closer economic integration – could only work as long as Europe did not impact significantly on the daily lives of ordinary Europeans. After the Single Market, but especially after monetary union, this method could not work anymore, see chapters 1 and 2.

Jacques Delors was followed by Jacques Santer, a former prime minister of Luxembourg, as Commission President. Presiding over an administration that had become inefficient, in some respects even chaotic, the Santer era culminated in the dramatic mass resignation of the entire Commission in March 1999, after the publication of a report of a Committee of Independent Experts, convened by the EP, on charges of fraud, mismanagement, and nepotism (Peterson 2012). Since the resignation of Santer and his Commissioners, the institution that was supposed to drive integration forward has become increasingly weak. Thus the Commission was marginalized first in the negotiations that led to the 2000 Treaty of Nice, and then in the Convention on the Future of Europe that drafted the Constitutional Treaty. Romano Prodi, the new Commission President (1999–2004), proposed without success a constitutional structure in which almost all decisions would be taken by majority vote; closer cooperation among some member states would be excluded; and the Community method would be extended to apply to most policy areas, including the CFSP, where use of this Commission-centred approach has never been seriously considered before.

Unsurprisingly, a former member of the Commission later lamented the Prodi Commission's 'astonishing weakness' (citation in Peterson 2012: 117).

Despite recurrent suggestions of a directly elected Commission president – a proposal recently resurrected by Germany's minister of finance, Wolfgang Schaeuble, in an article in the *Wall Street Journal* (2012) – the Commission has gradually become weaker for a number of reasons, including its composition as well as pressures from the EP and the larger member states. In order to increase the effectiveness of the Commission, the Lisbon Treaty had reduced the number of Commissioners from one per member state to two-thirds of the number of member states, with a system of equal rotation. After the failure of the first Irish referendum on the ratification of the Lisbon Treaty, however, the European Council, in order to facilitate the success of the second referendum, promised to abandon the planned reduction in the number of Commissioners. The problem is that a return to the old rule of one Commissioner per member state would result in too high a number of Commissioners for the institution to work efficiently. Already with a membership of twenty-eight states at very different levels of socioeconomic development and with quite different needs, it is quite difficult to follow the traditional one-size-fits-all approach to policymaking. As a consequence in a number of important policy areas the Council does not receive enough proposals because the Commission itself cannot agree on what is needed or desirable. The problem is aggravated by the fact that the member states, old and new, increasingly see 'their' Commissioner as their own representative in the Commission. To avoid these and other difficulties, decisions are made by consensus, which means that with so many members the Commission can hardly take decisions (Piris 2011). Under such conditions the Commission is unable to use not only its monopoly of legislative and policy initiative, but even to exercise the weaker forms of leadership mentioned in a preceding section. Unsurprisingly, the creation of a High Representative for Foreign and Security Policy who is both Vice-President for External Affairs of the Commission and chair of the Council of Foreign Ministers – a unique combination of supranational and intergovernmental roles – has also in no way enhanced the international status of the EU and its institutions.

The 'common' foreign policy of leaderless Europe

When one speaks of the CAP, the reference is to a European policy established in the 1960s with the aim of replacing the different agricultural policies of the members of the EEC – the first major example of total harmonization. No such meaning can be attached to the label CFSP. By now, all EU member states are convinced (or are resigned to the idea) that the CFSP is only a mechanism for consensus building, and that when national interests clash there is simply no EU foreign policy of any kind. The use of the adjective 'common' in this case may be seen as another expression of the political culture of total optimism discussed in chapter 2, or else as a way of disguising the fact that given the commitment to equality and consensus, it is simply impossible to have a *single* foreign policy in the sense of an EU foreign policy that replaces national policies. As noted in a preceding section, one of the key tasks of leadership is the setting of goals representing the polity's true commitments. In the absence of leadership it is very problematic to achieve credible long-term commitments and, without such commitments, as Walter Lippmann pointed out long ago, it is impossible to think at all about foreign affairs. The EU provides ample evidence that under present conditions 'soft diplomacy' and 'normative power' can also achieve very little.

During the Cold War the member states of communitarian Europe were able to devote considerably more resources to welfare than to warfare – and thus could bask in the illusion of inaugurating a new phase in the history of international relations – because their security was guaranteed by NATO and by the US nuclear umbrella. Hence the attempt to conceptualize the EU as a 'civilian', 'normative', or 'civilizing' power in the international system. The real test of the EU's capacity to manage differences peacefully, however, came after the implosion of the Soviet Union and the end of bipolarity. The limitations of the 'soft-power' approach were never so clearly revealed as in the 1990s – not in distant theatres of marginal interest, but in the EU's 'near abroad', in former Yugoslavia. The inability either to convince the Albanians of Kosovo to postpone a unilateral declaration of independence or to persuade the Serbian government to accept the inevitability of the Kosovar secession of February 2008 were only the latest in a long series of failures of EU diplomacy in the Balkans. Promises of substantial economic aid and of a fast-track procedure for the admission of Serbia to the EU proved insufficient to induce that country's leaders to accept the self-proclaimed independence of a region which they consider the cradle of their nation's identity. The failure of EU soft diplomacy was made complete by the inability of the member states to reach a common position on the issue of secession. At the EU summit of December 2007 the rotating president of the European Council, German Chancellor Angela Merkel, had said that it was essential to present a united front on Kosovo, while the prime minister of Luxembourg warned his colleagues that this question should not be allowed to become 'a permanent problem' for the EU. Despite the entreaties and the warnings, some members of the Union chose to follow the example of the US and France in recognizing Kosovo's independence immediately; others decided to wait and see how the situation would evolve; while Spain, backed by Romania, categorically refused diplomatic recognition at any time. At the meeting of EU foreign ministers of 18 February 2008, the Spanish representative stated in no uncertain terms that the unilateral declaration of independence violated international law. Madrid was of course concerned that the example of Kosovo might be imitated by other secessionist movements like the Basque and Catalan nationalists. Other members of the EU – notably Romania, Bulgaria, Greece, Slovakia, and Cyprus – were similarly concerned about the impact of the Kosovo precedent on their own minorities. In particular, the Greek-Cypriot government feared that recognition of Kosovar independence might bolster the cause of Turkish-Cypriot separatists. Given these precedents, it is not surprising that the EULEX mission already mentioned in chapter 6 – the most expensive aid mission in the history of the EU with thousands of soldiers, judges and prosecutors in Kosovo to help it become a constitutional democracy – has been failing.

In 2003, the divisions within the EU concerning the war in Iraq led US Defence Secretary Donald Rumsfeld to dismiss France and Germany, which opposed the war, as 'old Europe', while praising the 'new Europe' of those countries that backed the US. The leaders of Britain, Italy, Spain, Portugal, Denmark, Poland, Hungary, and the Czech Republic signed a joint Op-Ed piece in the *Wall Street Journal* essentially endorsing the American position. This was followed by an even more explicit statement in support of the US by the 'Vilnius ten' Central and South-East European candidates for NATO and EU accession. Although a CFSP is supposed to have existed since the 1990s, both sets of signatories wrote their declarations behind the backs of their EU partners – and in their own defence accused France and Germany of having themselves launched a diplomatic initiative in the name of Europe without having consulted them (Pond 2004: 69). In the meantime France, Germany, and Belgium held a mini-summit in Brussels to declare a core European 'defence union'. France wanted this avant-garde to become a rival to NATO, but Germany refused to move in that direction, and in the end the 'praline summit' as it was ironically called, ended up by establishing an autonomous planning staff that was too small to do much harm (ibid.: 87). Again, in 2011 the EU played no military role in the UN-backed and NATO-supported action in Libya. France took the lead in military operations against the regime of Colonel Qaddafi while Germany refused to participate, and Italy followed France reluctantly and only to prevent Paris from acquiring too much influence in the former Italian colony. The incoherence of the EU's response to the Libyan crisis shows that the Union remains prone to divisions of the kind it experienced over Iraq in 2003.

The limits of a diplomacy based exclusively on dialogue, negotiations, and economic aid have also been clearly revealed in other contexts. In the Middle East, for example, the EU and its members have provided the largest share of economic aid to the Palestinians, without any tangible influence over Israeli–Palestinian relations, and without winning respect for their humanitarian efforts. After the collapse of the Israeli–Palestinian peace process at the end of 2000, the Israelis did not hesitate to destroy much of the civilian infrastructure the EU had financed. The dominance of US power across the Middle East, William Wallace wrote some years ago, 'left European governments able only to issue diplomatic declarations, to provide core financial assistance to the Palestinian Authority – or to pursue commercial interests' (W. Wallace 2005: 450). American analysts like Robert Kagan concluded that the Europeans' advocacy of multilateralism in international relations is a function of the weakness of a leaderless Europe. Because of this weakness the rational division of labour today is, according to these critics, one whereby 'the US does the fighting, the UN feeds, the EU pays', or, in the shorter variant, 'The U.S. does dinner, and the EU does the dishes' (Pond 2004: 88–9).

It has been said that 'European cooperation in foreign policy has gone far beyond the framework of sovereign state diplomacy, but still remains far short of an integrated single policy, with integrated diplomatic, financial and military instruments' (W. Wallace 2005: 455). The same expert of international relations believes that the greatest inhibitor of further subordination of sovereignty, national traditions, and national expenditures to a common cause is the absence of a 'European public space', meaning 'a shared public debate, communicating through shared media, think tanks, political parties, responding to and criticizing authoritative policy makers' (ibid.: 454). This is reminiscent of the nineteenth century vision of government by discussion, but even the classical 'method of discussion' assigned a role to political leadership. The process of political discussion, according to Ernest Barker (1958: 37–8) begins with the action of political parties, which debate and formulate their programmes as the issues for electoral discussion, and then proceed to select and propose their candidates as the exponents of those programmes. Discussion is then carried forward to the electorate, which eventually chooses a majority in favour of one of the programmes. It is next carried forward to parliament, where the majority, in constant debate with the minority, seeks to translate into legislation the measures prepared by its leaders. 'Finally, the process of discussion is carried forward to the cabinet, a body of colleagues, selected by the accredited leader of the majority, who discuss and settle, under his presidency, the legislative measures to be submitted to parliament and the general lines of administrative action to be taken.'

Clearly, the EU system of governance has not been conceived with anything even distantly related to the liberal model of government by discussion. The truth is that after more than half a century of European integration, 'there still is no "European public space" – there is only a juxtaposition of national public spaces, capped by a jumble of intergovernmental and supranational bureaucracies' (Hoffmann 2000: 198). The EP does not differ from the legislatures of parliamentary democracies only because it lacks their power to tax and spend, to initiate legislation, and to validate a government's decisions. Another fundamental difference is the absence of the traditional government–opposition dialectic with the consequence, noted in chapter 4, that voters, being denied an appropriate arena in which to hold European institutions accountable are almost pushed to transform referenda on new treaties into contests for or against the EU.

Leopold Ranke, the leading nineteenth century German historian, believed in the 'primacy of foreign policy' – the notion that in any state the highest principle of action is derived from its foreign policy. The EU does not pretend to be a state and hence it cannot be said to provide a counter-example of Ranke's principle. What remains unclear, however, is the advantage of pretending the existence of a 'common' European foreign and security policy – a policy which in reality continues to reveal the member states' lack of a common vision and of shared interests concerning the crucially important issues of peace and war.

The euro crisis and the problem of the reluctant hegemon

In his classic study of the 1929–1939 world depression Charles Kindleberger writes: 'for the world economy to be stabilized, there has to be a stabilizer, one stabilizer' (1973: 305). The explanation of the Great Depression proposed by the noted economist and economic historian is that the severity of the crisis was caused by the British inability and the US unwillingness to do what was needed in a timely fashion. Britain had stabilized the world economic system in the nineteenth century and up to 1913. But in 1929 the British could not and the US would not do the same – because of domestic concerns the only country able to provide leadership stood aside. In theory, a joint Anglo-American leadership in the economic affairs of the world would have been possible; but Kindleberger points out that according to most economists arrangements such as duopoly or bilateral monopoly are unstable, and the same seems to be true in politics. The reason: 'With a duumvirate, a troika, or slightly wider forms of collective responsibility, the buck has no place to stop' (ibid.: 299–300). These observations served to lay the foundations of what came to be called the theory of hegemonic stability. The two central propositions of the theory are: (1) that order in world politics is typically created by a single dominant power; and (2) that the maintenance of world order requires continued hegemony (Keohane 1984). Hegemony has been defined as preponderance of material resources: 'a situation wherein the products of a given core state are produced so efficiently that they are by and large competitive even in other core states, and therefore the given core state will be the primary beneficiary of a maximally free world market' (Immanuel Wallerstein, cited in Keohane 1984: 33).

Kindleberger noted that in the 1970s leadership was a word with negative connotations, while participation in decision-making was regarded as more 'aesthetic'. In those years the leadership of the US was beginning to slip, and the American scholar doubted that 'the rising strength of Europe in an enlarged European Economic Community will be accompanied by an assertion of leadership...and assumption of responsibility for the stability of the world system' (Kindleberger 1973: 307–8). As we know, neither the EEC nor the EC nor the EU even tried to assume responsibility for the stability of the world system. However, the crisis of monetary union has made clear that only Germany, within the present Union, could provide the needed leadership – not for the world system but at least for the Old Continent; not necessarily on a permanent basis (see below) but at least in a crisis situation. The attempt to establish a sort of French–German duopoly or diarchy – in the short *Merkozy* interlude – did not work, as Kindleberger would have predicted. Actually, this author could call attention to his discussion of the role of

France in the Great Depression of the 1930s, to point out analogies with the present euro crisis:

> Not big enough to have responsibility forced on it, nor small enough to afford the luxury of irresponsibility the French position in the inter-war period was unenviable. It had the power to be a destabilizer, but was insufficiently powerful to stabilize. . .France could be (and was) blamed for upsetting the system when she had no capacity to take it over and run it in the presence of two larger powers, one feeble [the UK], the other irresponsible [the US].

(Ibid.: 303)

Today's Germany is neither feeble like the UK in the inter-war period nor irresponsible like the US in the same period. In spite of the (limited) leadership it has provided and is still providing in the euro crisis, however, it is extremely reluctant to play the role of the hegemon – for very good reasons having to do with history but also with the ideology of the European integration project. As mentioned at the beginning of the present chapter, a key element of that ideology is the basic equality and equal dignity of all the member states. At any rate, given the level of mutual mistrust especially in crisis situations (exemplified by the disorderly reactions to the crisis caused by the French and Dutch rejection of the draft Constitution in 2005, see chapter 6), it is almost unimaginable that the members of the Union, large or small, would be willing to accept a German hegemony, even though Germany, *de facto*, already conditions the economies of the other member states in important respects. In addition to the general attachment to national sovereignty and historically rooted resentments, Paul De Grauwe has identified a new reason for the widespread suspicion of the largest member state of the EU. According to this distinguished monetary economist, when the Federal Republic in the late 1990s dramatically improved its competitive position within the euro zone, this was at the expense of other members, which saw their competitive position deteriorate. It can be said, he adds, that Germany exported its problem of a lack of competitiveness to other member states. Since 1999 this country has followed a tight policy of wage moderation while the rest of the euro zone maintained more or less constant wage increases of around 3 per cent per year. Thus, each year Germany tended to improve its competitive position vis-à-vis the rest of the euro zone – a trend partly explained by the fact that the power of German labour unions has declined significantly, more so than in other euro zone countries. Other countries with particularly close economic ties to Germany are forced to intensify their policies of wage moderation, inducing the leading country again to restrict wage increases. A vicious circle may result when everybody attempts to improve its competitiveness at the expense of the others. As in the case of the so-called race to the bottom in environmental policy, the final outcome is that these countries will not have improved their relative position, but will have adopted wage policies that do not correspond to the preferences of their citizens. At the same time, the distance between the leading group and the other member states keeps growing. Paradoxically, one of the unanticipated consequences of monetary union has been the extent to which the competitive positions of the members of the euro zone have diverged. Italy, Spain, Portugal, and Greece have lost a significant amount of competitiveness, while Germany, Austria, the Netherlands, and a few other Northern countries have gained a significant amount of competitiveness (De Grauwe 2007: 32–3).

As we saw in chapter 2, the consequences of this state of affairs have been drawn by the Hungarian-born American financier George Soros who, in an essay published in September 2012 (Soros 2012), argued that in order to avoid a definitive split of the euro zone into creditor and debtor countries, and thus a likely collapse of the EU itself, Germany must resolve a basic dilemma: either assume the role of the 'benevolent hegemon' or else leave the euro zone. If Germany were to give up the euro, leaving the euro zone in the hands of the debtor countries, all problems that now appear to be insoluble, could be resolved through currency depreciation, improved competitiveness, and a new status of the ECB as lender of last resort. The common market would survive, but the relative position of Germany and of other creditor countries that might wish to leave the euro zone would change from the winning to the losing side. Both groups of countries could avoid such problems if only Germany was willing to assume the role of a benevolent hegemon. However, this would require the more or less equal treatment of debtor and creditor countries, and a much higher rate of growth, with consequent inflation. These may well be unacceptable conditions for the German leaders, for the Bundesbank and, especially, for the German voters. At any rate, both conditions could be satisfied only with significant progress on the road to a political EU in which Germany accepts the responsibilities implied by its leadership role.

Also some German commentators have recently maintained that their country should agree to play such a role, and not just in the present crisis situation. One of the clearest statements of this view is an essay by Christoph Schoenberger: 'Hegemon wider Willen' ('Unwilling Hegemon') (2012). The author argues that the crisis of the euro zone has made clear what people have been reluctant to acknowledge in the past, namely that Germany has become the hegemonic power in Europe. While this leading role provides a unique possibility to influence the future of the Old Continent, it also entails duties and burdens. German political leaders and public opinion are quite unprepared to meet this challenge, however. In fact, as the old East–West conflicts and the post-war division of Germany pass into history, awareness of the precarious situation of the country, placed as it is at the heart of Europe, seems to recede. And yet, German guidance is precisely what Europe needs in order to face up to the uncertainties and challenges of the twenty-first century, according to Schoenberger. The largest, most populous and economically most powerful member of the EU cannot evade this responsibility. To speak of German hegemony is not to advocate Germany's dominance over the rest of Europe – the German scholar is well aware that the Federal Republic is not strong enough, materially and politically, to play such a role – but only to take cognizance of the fact that there are no strong and democratically legitimated institutions at the European level. Those who criticize the European Commission for its alleged interference in domestic affairs, for example, do not realize that very little can happen in Brussels without the agreement of the governments and the bureaucracies of the member states. Even the EP tends to be ignored by voters who see no connections between domestic and European politics. The steadily decreasing turnouts in EP elections provide the clearest proof of the people's indifference towards the institution that should represent them at the European level. In fact, the crisis of the euro zone, with its sequel of summits of the heads of government following one another, has emphasized the intergovernmental features of the Union. On the other hand, the difficulty of finding a solution to the present crisis at the intergovernmental level can only lead to the conclusion that what the EU needs is a hegemonic power – a need usually concealed by the search for consensus which characterizes decision-making in Brussels.

Unfortunately, the argument continues, Germany is not mentally prepared to assume the burden of a European hegemony, and also its institutions were not designed for such a task. Thus the Bundestag, under the pressure of public opinion and the influence of recent decisions of the German Constitutional Court, has developed a tendency to limit more and more the freedom of action of the federal government in foreign and European affairs, pretending that the decisions of the executive in this area should depend on an explicit parliamentary mandate. What, then, are the alternatives to a German hegemony? The only reasonable alternative, according to Schoenberger, would be a strengthening of the supranational institutions to make them dependent, not on the agreement and directions of the national governments, but only on the support of European voters. Unfortunately, such a solution is impossible since the EU has been designed around an intergovernmental core, as the present crisis has amply demonstrated. Thus we are back to the need of a 'wise' German hegemony – unless we are prepared to accept the break-up of the Union. The exercise of a 'wise' hegemony would imply: renouncing that favourite pastime of the Germans, that is, national introspection; detailed knowledge and close observation of the European neighbours; defining Germany's national interests in a way that takes into account the interests of its partners; finally, planning and thinking for the whole of Europe. This is, after all, what the position of the country at the centre of the continent has always demanded of Germany's elites and public opinion.

It is refreshing to read such a crisp analysis of an issue that most Germans, in all walks of life, prefer to ignore. Unfortunately, the analysis is far from being either convincing or complete. First, the author starts from the traditional notion of hegemony as preponderance of material resources. Other, more refined, notions of hegemony and hegemonic stability do not assert an automatic link between power and leadership, see below. But even the cruder notion does not seem to fit the facts. While it is certainly true that Germany is larger, more populous, and economically more powerful than any of its European partners, its superiority is hardly as clear as in historically undisputed cases of international hegemony. In the nineteenth century the *Pax Britannica* was based, not only on Britain's naval supremacy, but also on Britain's pioneering role in the first industrial revolution, on the higher productivity of its industry, at least until the 1870s, and on the role of London as the financial centre of the world. Also the *Pax Americana* of the 1950s and 1960s was based on the absolute superiority of the US in production, services, research and development, technological innovation, not to mention military might. In fact, even at its peak Britain has never been as superior in productivity to the rest of the world as the US was after 1945. Today Germany does not play any comparable role, even on the modest European scale. In particular, this country is hardly a leader in the services sector which, to repeat a point already made several times in the preceding chapters, accounts for more than 70 per cent of the GDP of all modern economies. Thus in the case of financial services the

European leader is Britain, not Germany. At the other end of the policy spectrum, it is almost an oxymoron to speak of a 'common' European foreign and security policy (see the preceding section), but at least one can say that the most active EU members in this area are Britain and France, rather than Germany.

The more sophisticated notion of hegemony emphasizes the importance of domestic attitudes, political structures, and decision-making processes: 'Decisions to exercise leadership are necessary to "activate" the posited relationship between power capabilities and outcomes' (Keohane 1984: 35). As we saw above, Schoenberger is fully aware that this kind of 'force activation' is still lacking in Germany, but he gives no idea of how this limitation could be overcome, or how hegemonic stability could be maintained once the present crisis of the euro zone is somehow resolved. The most serious flaw in the analysis of the German scholar, however, is the implicit assumption that, barring a total collapse of the EU, European integration will remain stable at the present level, or even resume its march towards 'more Europe'. In fact, we saw that integration is becoming more differentiated, and there are also clear indications of a retrograde movement. Thus, the goal of a single European market appears to be less and less feasible; and it can even be argued that the European market is actually less integrated today than twenty or thirty years ago. This is so not only because of the steady growth of services still largely regulated at national level; but also because growing socioeconomic heterogeneity within the Union makes policy harmonization increasingly problematic. Again, monetary union was originally conceived as a public good, shared by all member states, while it turned out to be a 'club good' – a public good from whose benefits member states may be, or may choose to be, excluded (see chapter 3 and, more generally, chapter 10). Recent demands for two-speed integration go in the same direction. At the end of this process of opting out, making exceptions, and separating avant-gardes and rear guards, we may reach a situation where a hegemon leading the entire membership of the EU, is no longer needed: either the aims of European integration are redefined to include a few, limited, and widely shared goals – a return to the spirit of the Rome Treaty with few, concrete commitments, and collective leadership; or the EU becomes a 'club of clubs', with the supranational level mainly responsible for monitoring competition among different territorial and/or functional clubs, as discussed chapters 9 and 10. As already suggested, it seems to be very doubtful that European integration can remain stable at the present

level. In fact, the crisis of monetary union has already deeply transformed the nature of the EU.

The Union transformed

The essential equality of all member states of the EU is an admirable
principle, very much in line with the history of Europe since the Peace of
Westphalia of 1648, and especially with the nineteenth century code of
state behaviour known as the Concert of Europe – a code that recognized
the legitimacy of the pursuit of the national interest but at the same time
implied a sense of responsibility for the orderly, preferably peaceful,
operation of the European states system. Unfortunately, the difficulty
of adhering to the principle of the essential equality of all the member
states increases with the growing size and socioeconomic diversity of the
Union. Size and diversity also make it increasingly difficult to overcome
the limitations imposed by the logic of collective action, as was argued in
previous chapters. It is commonly assumed that if all the members of a
group (whether composed of individuals, private organizations, or of
sovereign states) agree on some common interest, then there would be a
tendency for the group to seek to further this interest, i.e. the group
would to some extent also act in a self-interested or group-interested
manner. Mancur Olson's distinctive contribution to political economy
has been his proof that this familiar assumption is fundamentally wrong
(Olson 1971). Olson's argument is that the members of the group will
not provide as much of the collective good as it would be in their
common interest to provide. This tendency toward sub-optimality is
due to the fact that by definition a collective good, such as economic or
political integration, is available to all other members once it has been
provided by any member, or by a few members, of the group (see chapter
3 for a more precise definition of collective, or public, goods). Since an
individual member gets only part of the benefit of any expenditure he
makes to obtain more of the collective good, he will discontinue his
purchase of the collective good before the optimal amount for the group
as a whole has been obtained. Naturally, this argument assumes that
there is no group leader with the capacity to reward those who contribute
their fair share and to punish those who do not. In this respect, the
notion of 'collective leadership' or 'collective hegemony' sometimes used
to describe the way the EU functions is meaningless, as already noted.
Without a credible system of reward and punishment, no member of the
group has an incentive to contribute enough to produce the optimal

amount of the collective good – hence the paradox that in the absence of leadership (or coercion) groups will not act in their group interest. The relevance of this paradox in the context of the EU is all too obvious.

The most direct challenge to the equality of all the member states, however, has been launched by the euro crisis. Germany may not be a global power like Britain was for a good part of the nineteenth century, or the US in the first decades following the end of World War II; but it is unquestionably the central power in the EU and by far the main creditor in a highly asymmetric monetary union. In a recent essay that further develops some of the points made in the publication mentioned above, Soros (2013) notes that the euro crisis has already transformed the EU from a free association of states enjoying equal rights to a more or less enduring relationship between debtors and creditors. The creditors risk losing a good deal of money if a member states leaves the union, while the debtors are forced to accept conditions which can only aggravate their economic depression, and place them in a subordinate position for an indefinite period of time. In this way the euro crisis threatens to destroy the EU itself. According to the American financier these are the consequences of the fatal flaw of the European monetary union: in creating the ECB as a fully independent central bank the member states indebted themselves in a currency which they cannot control. As a consequence, when the risk of a Greek default became concrete, the financial markets reacted by reducing the status of all heavily indebted members of the euro zone to that of developing countries with large debts in foreign currencies. In this way, these members of the euro zone were treated as if they alone were responsible for their present condition.

The correct response to this situation, Soros concludes, would be the creation of Eurobonds and a banking union, together with the necessary structural reforms. However, Germany refuses to choose between the two alternatives: either accept the Eurobonds or leave the euro zone. On the other hand, a solution of the crisis would also require a level of centralization of the economic and fiscal policies of the member states that is, most likely, politically unfeasible. Thus the end of monetary union appears to be only a question of time, while the position of the major German parties – pro monetary union but against Eurobonds – is clearly contradictory. The pessimistic conclusion of the Hungarian-born American financier should be taken as an invitation to rethink European integration in a new key. Some ideas pointing in this direction will be developed in the last two chapters of the present book.

9

Integration through cooperative competition

The 'European Miracle'

We normally think of competition as an adversarial process. In the case of economic regulation, for example, adversarial competition is supposed to resolve the contest between different approaches in favour of one particular regulatory regime so as to avoid conflicting rules in a single transaction. But as Paul Stephan (2000) pointed out, regulatory competition can also exist in a cooperative framework that permits different regimes to coexist. Such systems encourage potential subjects of regulation to choose which regime they intend to follow. These choices in turn encourage states or other rule-making bodies to offer regulatory packages that will attract transactions from which they can derive economic and other benefits. The issue then becomes whether competition among regulatory authorities leads to races to the bottom or to races to the top, in the sense of regulations more closely tailored to the specific needs of different parties. This issue will be examined analytically in the next sections. In the immediately following pages I suggest, by way of introduction, that cooperative competition, far from being a new phenomenon, is one of the most characteristic features of European history in the centuries that preceded the rise of nationalism. Unfortunately, such precedents are too often ignored by those who assume that 'ever closer union' can be achieved, not through cooperative competition but only through top-down harmonization of the laws and policies of the member states of the EU.

David Landes, the distinguished economic historian, has even seen in the political fragmentation of the Old Continent one of the roots of its later global dominance. By decentralizing authority, fragmentation made Europe safe from single-stroke conquest – the fate of many empires of the past, from Persia after Issus (333 BC) and Rome after the sack of Alaric (410 AD) to Aztec Mexico and Inca Peru. The American historian concludes his argument with a citation from Patricia Crone's *Pre-Industrial Societies*: 'Far from being stultified by imperial government, Europe was to be propelled forward by constant competition between its component parts' (Landes 1998: 528). These and other scholars stressing the importance of inter-state competition in European history have been inspired by the arguments advanced by Eric Jones in his well-known book *The European Miracle*. The miracle the British historian wished to explain is the fact that one thousand years ago, more or less, nobody would have thought possible that Europe could ever be able to challenge the great empires of the East, but five hundred years later European global dominance was already becoming a reality. According to Jones the essence of this 'European miracle' lies in politics rather than in economics: in its long-lasting system of competing but also cooperating states. Considered as a group, the members of the European states system realized the benefits of competitive decision-making but also some of the economies of scale expected of an empire: 'Unity in diversity gave Europe some of the best of both worlds, albeit in a somewhat ragged and untidy way' (Jones 1987: 110). How Europe managed to form a unity while remaining decentralized, and how that mattered for economic development are the two questions Jones examines. Part of the explanation is that in its states system Europe had a portfolio of competing and colluding polities whose spirit of competition was adapted to diffusing best practice:

> This picture of a Europe which shared in salient respects a common culture, or series of overlapped lifestyles, and formed something of a single market demonstrates that political decentralization did not mean a fatal loss of economies of scale in production and distribution. The states system did not thwart the flow of capital and labour to the constituent states offering the highest marginal return. Princes and governments, with the characteristic short-run goals of politicians, often wished to staunch the flow but were largely unable to do so.
>
> (Ibid.: 117)

Whereas a large empire that monopolized the means of coercion and was not threatened by more advanced neighbours had little incentive to adopt new methods, the states of Europe were surrounded by actual or potential competitors. Thus '[t]he states system was an insurance against economic and technological stagnation. . .by functioning as a set of joint-stock corporations with implicit prospectuses listing resources and freedoms, the nation-states insured against the suppression of novelty and unorthodoxy in the system as a whole' (ibid.: 119).

The British historian considered primarily the period between the Peace of Westphalia (1648) and the French revolution, but medieval

Europe also offers many examples of competing and colluding polities. The diffusion of different models of urban law in the thirteenth and fourteenth century provides a clear example of the importance of competition among cities and the related process of adoption or imitation of various urban models. The laws of a dozen major German cities were replicated in hundreds of new towns that were founded in Eastern Europe between the twelfth and the fourteenth centuries. The laws of Luebeck were adopted by forty-three towns, those of Frankfurt by forty-nine, of Munich by thirteen, of Freiburg by nineteen towns. Most important was the dissemination of the laws of Magdeburg to over eighty new towns. The *Magdeburger Recht* became the predominant basis of written law for Central and Eastern Europe (Berman 1983). Likewise, the laws of the Norman town of Breteuil became the model for Norman settlements in Wales, Scotland, and Ireland. The emergence of a limited number of standard models – which were often updated to reflect new legal developments in the mother town – suggests a competitive process leading to a portfolio of types of urban law, each type offering a different combination of advantages and disadvantages. At the same time, imitation and learning ensured that the everyday rights, privileges, liberties, and immunities of English, French, German, or Polish burghers did not differ essentially from those of burghers in other parts of Europe: a very early example of ex post, competition-driven harmonization.

Another consequence was that in many respects urban communities in different countries had more in common with one another than they had with the respective countries in which they were situated. In some cases judges in the mother town would hear judicial appeals from the courts of a daughter town. Such trans-regional networks of urban judicial authorities were not always favoured by territorial rulers, who considered the existence of an alternative and external jurisdiction a threat to their own position. The aspiration of the princes to have a single hierarchy of judicial authority within their territories is an early manifestation of that striving to achieve legal homogeneity typical of the modern conception of national sovereignty. In the thirteenth century and later, however, 'that aspiration faced the powerful alternative of an international urban network that drew the lines more widely and fluidly from mother city to daughter city along the trade routes and the migratory paths rather than within the tight boundaries of the monarchical domain' (Bartlett 1993: 176). The consequence was a unique feature of medieval law: the individual lived under a plurality of legal systems, each governing one of the overlapping sub-communities of which he was a member. Because none of the coexisting legal systems – canon, feudal, mercantile, urban, and royal law – had a claim to be all inclusive or omni-competent, each had to develop constitutional standards for limiting sovereignty. In medieval Europe 'checks and balances' were provided mainly by competing and cooperating polities rather than by concurrent branches of the same polity, as in modern separation-of-powers systems. In sum, competition, cooperation, and imitation were key features of European history for half a millennium, and as I shall argue in the present and in the next chapter, after the shocking experience of the euro crisis these same features should inspire a new, more flexible approach to European integration.

Cooperative competition

In an important book on politics and public finance the Canadian economist Albert Breton (1996) argued that democratic governments compete with one another because they have to respond to their citizens' interests and preferences. As we saw in the preceding pages, inter-jurisdictional competition has been a key feature of the history of our continent, with the European states system of the early modern age preserving important aspects of the cooperative competition which characterized the Middle Ages. Individuals and whole populations sometimes 'voted with their feet' by shifting their allegiance to that country which was governed best. Hence, the fairly rapid diffusion of policy and institutional innovations throughout the continent in the period preceding the full development of the nation state. Unfortunately, the prophets of European integration were too concerned with the tragic consequences of twentieth century nationalism to pay attention to the earlier history of Europe. Paradoxically, however, they remained heavily conditioned by the model of the sovereign nation state even as they were striving to go beyond it. As a result, their opposition to nationalism did not lead them to explore alternative ways of organizing inter-state relations, but rather to transfer as much as possible of the received national model of statehood to the supranational level. Hence their preference for positive integration, legal centralism, and ex ante harmonization of national policies. Quite revealing in this respect is the preference for total harmonization – i.e., for measures designed to regulate exhaustively a given problem to the exclusion of previously existing national measures – in the early stages of the integration process. As we saw in chapter 3, for a long time even the ECJ supported total harmonization as a foundation stone in the building of the common market. The EU's harmonization bias is evident enough to have caught the attention of scholars not primarily concerned with European integration. Thus André Breton in his well-known work on *Competitive Governments* criticizes the EU for what he calls its excessive policy harmonization:

> I believe that the European Union is quite stable but that the stability has been acquired by the virtual suppression of intercountry competition through excessive policy harmonization. . ...To prevent the occurrence of instability, competition is minimized through the excessive harmonization of a substantial fraction of social, economic, and other policies. . .If one compares the degree of harmonization in Europe with that in Canada, the United States, and other federations, one is impressed by the extent to which it is greater in Europe than in the federations.
>
> (Breton 1996: 275–6)

Today we know that even excessive harmonization has not been sufficient to ensure the stability of the EU. Indeed, one could argue that excessive harmonization has been the immediate cause of the present instability: monetary union is, after all, an extreme form of total harmonization, see chapter 1. At least since the *Cassis de Dijon* judgment in 1979, attempts were made to reduce the dependency on harmonization as the main tool of integration. Indeed, the principle of mutual recognition was supposed to reduce the need of ex ante, top-down harmonization, and to facilitate regulatory competition among the member states. Supposedly a cornerstone of the Single Market programme, mutual recognition requires member states to recognize regulations made by other EU members as being essentially equivalent to their own, thus allowing activities that are lawful in one member state to be freely pursued throughout the Union. In this way a virtuous circle of regulatory competition would be stimulated, which should raise the quality of all regulation and drive out rules offering protection that consumers do not, in fact, require. The end result would be ex post harmonization, achieved through competitive processes rather than by administrative measures. However, the high hopes raised by the *Cassis de Dijon* judgment and by what appeared to be the Commission's strong endorsement of the Court's doctrine were largely disappointed. For political, ideological, and bureaucratic reasons, ex post, market-driven harmonization was never allowed to seriously challenge the dominant position of centralized, top-down harmonization. While the *Cassis* doctrine was greeted enthusiastically at a time when the priority was to meet the deadline of the Single Market ('Europe' 92') project, institutional and political interests militated against wholehearted support of mutual recognition and regulatory competition. Instead of viewing competition as a discovery procedure (Hayek 1984), the tendency has always been to assume that integration can be only one way if one wants to prevent a 'Europe of Bits and Pieces' (Curtin 1993). The reluctance of politicians and bureaucrats to rely on competition – especially inter-country or inter-institutional competition – is understandable, since 'competition is valuable only because, and so far as, its results are unpredictable and on the whole different from those which anyone has, or could have, deliberately aimed at. . .the generally beneficial effects of competition must include disappointing or defeating some particular expectations or intentions' (Hayek 1984: 255).

The OMC, codified and endorsed by the Lisbon European Council in March 2000 was another attempt to add a competitive dimension to the traditional methods of integration. The OMC employs non-binding objectives and guidelines, commonly agreed indicators, benchmarking, and persuasion, in an effort to bring about change in such areas as employment, health, migration, and pension reform – where the Community has limited or no competence. The philosophy underlying the OMC and related 'soft law' methods is that each state should be encouraged to experiment on its own, and to craft solutions fit to its national context. While the classic Community method creates uniform rules that member states must adopt, provides sanctions if they fail to do so, and allows challenges for non-compliance to be brought before the ECJ, the OMC provides no formal sanctions for member states that do not follow the guidelines. Advocates of the new approach argue that the OMC can be effective despite – or even because of – its open-ended, non-binding, non-justiciable qualities (Trubek and Trubek 2005). But as already mentioned, the OMC seems to have fallen far short of expectations even in areas where one might have presumed it to have yielded the most significant results. Because member states appear to use the method in areas where it matches domestic policy priorities, but to ignore it in areas where it conflicts with these priorities, the critics say that the OMC is at best a method of national, rather than European, policymaking. At any rate, the whole OMC procedure is too bureaucratic to stimulate genuine inter-state competition.

The evidence from these two attempts to move beyond harmonization in a deliberate way suggests that the notion of competitive governments is foreign to the ideology of European integration espoused by the founding fathers. It is of course true that rules on market competition have always been a key element of EU law, but a moment's reflection shows that the reason for the importance attached to such rules is strictly utilitarian: not a commitment to a genuine free-market philosophy, but the realistic assessment that it would be impossible to integrate a group of heavily regulated economies without limitations on the interventionism of the national governments (Majone 2009: 96–7). What is at any rate clear is that competition between different national approaches to economic and social regulation – not to mention competition between national currencies as advocated by Hayek and supported by the British government in the 1980s and 1990s – has played hardly any role in the integration process. Indeed, a distinguished specialist of EU law has argued that competition among regulators is incompatible with the notion of undistorted competition in the internal European market to which reference is made in Article 3(g) of the EC Treaty. Hence the UK – the member state which has most consistently defended the benefits of inter-state competition – has been accused of subordinating individual rights and social protection to a free-market philosophy incompatible with the basic aspirations of the EC/EU: 'Competition between regulators on this perspective is simply incompatible with the EC's historical mission' (Weatherill 1995: 180).

In this context it is important to keep in mind a point already made at the end of chapter 7. Governments operating in a common market cannot compete vigorously unless the authority to make economic policy remains largely in their hands, while the supranational institutions must have the instruments for preventing national governments using their regulatory authority to erect trade barriers against the goods and services from other member states. According to Weingast (1995) a common market, national (rather than federal or supranational) responsibility for the economy, monitoring by the higher level of government, and a tight budget constraint are crucial conditions of economic development. In addition to a game-theoretic argument, this American political economist provides interesting historical evidence in support of his thesis. Thus, the enormous expansion of the American economy during the nineteenth century was based on the division of labour between the federal state and the states of the federation. The federal government was responsible for establishing and maintaining the common market, but interfered little in economic affairs before the 1880s; while the states were the promoters and entrepreneurs of economic development. Also Louis Hartz in his classic study of the economic policy of the state of Pennsylvania between 1776 and 1860 writes: 'Despite the significant restrictions which the federal constitution imposed upon the states, it reserved to them, both by implication in the enumerated powers of the [federal] government and by the express provisions of the Tenth Amendment, a large authority to deal with economic issues' (Hartz 1948: 3–4). Even the stunning economic growth of modern China, according to Weingast (1995: 21–4), seems to be due to the central government's acceptance of the loss of political control over regional economic policymaking. The degree of support of decentralization among the Peking authorities led to a variety of experiments in economic development. As these proved successful, and the central government did not revoke them, they were expanded and imitated.

By way of contrast, we saw that Albert Breton came to the conclusion that in the EU inter-country competition has been virtually suppressed through excessive policy harmonization. More generally, the Canadian economist suggests that part of the widespread opposition to the idea that domestic governments, national and international agencies, associations of various kinds, vertical and horizontal networks, and so on, should compete among themselves derives from the notion that competition is incompatible with, even antithetical to, cooperation. He cogently argues that this perception is mistaken. Excluding the case of collusion, cooperation and competition can and generally do coexist, so that the presence of one is no indication of the absence of the other. In particular, the observation of cooperation and coordination does not per se disprove that the underlying determining force may be competition. If one thinks of competition not as the state of affairs neo-classical theory calls 'perfect competition', but as an activity – à la Schumpeter, Hayek, and other Austrian economists who developed the model of entrepreneurial competition – then it becomes plain that 'the entrepreneurial innovation that sets the competitive process in motion, the imitation that follows, and the Creative Destruction that they generate are not inconsistent with cooperative behaviour and the coordination of activities' (Breton 1996: 33). Given the appropriate competitive stimuli, political entrepreneurs, like their business counterparts, will consult with colleagues at home and abroad, collaborate with them on certain projects, harmonize various activities, and in the extreme case integrate some operations – all actions corresponding to what is generally meant by cooperation and coordination.

Competition through exit and voice

As we saw in the first section of the present chapter, the exit option was an important element in the competition among medieval cities and city-states, and remained important in early modern history. With the advent of democracy, voice became another, even more effective, mechanism of inter-state competition and mutual learning. Multiple jurisdictions must exist for competition to work either through exit or voice. In case of the federal states of today, this means allowing lower-level bodies, rather than the federal government, to have primary or exclusive regulatory authority so that economic actors may have the possibility of choosing which jurisdiction should regulate their behaviour. In the domain of private law, many governments have allowed parties to choose which legal regime will govern business relations. They do this primarily by giving force to contractual clauses determining the governing law and/or the appropriate forum for resolving disputes between the parties (Stephan 2000). To cite a well-known example, in the US there is a competitive market for corporate charters, in the sense that managers may incorporate in any state, no matter where the firm's assets, employees, and investors are located, while states compete with each other to attract incorporations. Jurisdictions successful in this competition obtain revenue from franchise fees and taxes, and create demand for legal services provided locally. Notwithstanding its small size, the state of Delaware has been by far the most successful in attracting firms. There seems to be general agreement that the success of Delaware comes from its enabling statute, its large body of precedents and sophisticated corporate bar, and its credible commitment to be receptive to corporate needs because of the large percentage of its revenues derived from franchise fees and taxes. What is disputed is whether the competition for revenue resulting from incorporation leads to a race to the bottom. There are good theoretical reasons to believe that in this case (as in other cases discussed in chapter 3 of this book) such a race cannot exist; and also the empirical evidence seems to indicate that investors benefit when firms incorporate in Delaware (Easterbrook and Fischel 1991: 212–15). At any rate, the incorporation debate in the US is an instructive example of a more general difference of opinion about the merits and demerits of regulatory competition, and of other kinds of competition activated by potential entry and exit mechanisms.

According to the so-called Tiebout hypothesis, inter-jurisdictional competition results in communities supplying the goods and services individuals demand, and producing them in an efficient manner. In Tiebout's model communities below the optimum size seek to attract new residents while those above optimum size do the opposite. As a result, the population distributes itself in such a way that in each community all residents tend to have identical, or at least similar, preferences. The idea of horizontal intergovernmental competition seems to have entered the literature of public finance and public choice with Tiebout's 1956 seminal paper on local public goods (Tiebout 1956). But Breton points out that the effectiveness of the entry and exit mechanism for intergovernmental competition may be quite weak beyond the local level because of the limited mobility of persons across national borders, as well as for other more technical reasons. Therefore, the original hypothesis about inter-jurisdictional competition has to be extended to apply to situations where Tiebout's potential entry and exit mechanisms do not work effectively, for instance because mobility is limited by language and/or cultural and social cleavages, as in the EU. One such extension is Salmon's external benchmark mechanism. This extension consists in assuming that the citizens of a jurisdiction can use information about the goods and services supplied in other jurisdictions as a benchmark to evaluate the performance of their own government; and that the same citizens decide to support or to oppose their government on the basis of that assessment. The first assumption corresponds, more or less, to the idea of information exchange underlying the EU's OMC, but since national parliaments are largely excluded from the OMC process, European citizens are unable in practice to use information about the performance of other member states to induce their own government to improve its own performance. Thus, the stimulus to intergovernmental competition which is assumed by the proposed extension of the Tiebout hypothesis is missing.

Generally speaking, opposition to intergovernmental competition – particularly in the area of regulatory policies, as in the citation from Weatherill in the preceding section – can be traced to the persistence of state-centred thinking even among people who see the EU as the model of post-national Europe. Such thinking pervades all attempts to solve the crisis of monetary union by centralizing at EU level policy competences in key areas, such as fiscal and social policy, now under the control of the national governments. This may turn out to be a serious mistake, fed in part by the notion that in a globalizing world the nation state is becoming increasingly irrelevant. A critique of this mistaken notion will be presented in the next chapter. Here it is sufficient to point out the obvious fact that domestic regulatory choices in such areas as production methods and product safety must have an international, not just a European, perspective in what is by now a global marketplace. Hence the opposition to regulatory competition within the EU may be seen as a manifestation of Euro-centricity: the exclusive focus on the European dimension of issues, even where a broader (or, in some cases, narrower) perspective would be more appropriate. A good illustration of the limits of such parochial attitude is the failure of the European Commission to have the Precautionary Principle – an extremely conservative form of risk regulation – accepted as a general principle of international economic law. The EU's commitment to, and application of, this principle has been repeatedly criticized by the WTO, by the US, and by many other developed and developing countries. What international organizations and third countries fear is that something as poorly defined as the PP may be too easily misused for protectionist purposes.

Euro-centricity may have undesirable consequences not only for third countries, but for the member states of the EU as well. One of the reasons for the declining influence of the European institutions on national authorities is the rejection of regulatory diversity and competition in favour of an exclusive focus on EU-mandated rules. For example, already in the 1990s, a Commission's Green Paper on the development of European standardization was strongly criticized by some national standardization bodies because of its exclusive focus on EC-mandated standards, neglect of international standardization, and, in the words of the Dutch Interdepartmental Committee for Standardization, 'an almost cavalier disregard of all interests other than the Community's' (Majone 2009: 79–81). What the Brussels authorities seem to forget is that regulation has become an international activity, subject to peer review and scholarly criticism, and open to comparisons with best international practice. National regulators are increasingly critical of European rules precisely for this reason. They are aware that their reputation depends on conceptual innovation and the ability to discover (or to imitate domestically) efficient solutions to concrete regulatory problems, rather than on their commitment to political objectives related to European integration.

Competitive stability needs monitoring: a new role for the supranational institutions

Inter-state or inter-jurisdictional competition does not necessarily produce stable outcomes. As we saw in chapter 3, already in the 1950s fears were expressed that differences in social conditions among the member states of the EEC could represent a form of 'unfair' competition, so that positive integration (harmonization) was needed in order to prevent 'social dumping' or a 'race to the bottom'. Indeed many, perhaps most, measures of positive integration in the areas of health, safety, and environmental regulation, were justified by the argument that without EU-level harmonization member states would engage in a competitive 'race to the bottom' in order to attract foreign investments. We have shown in chapter 3, however, that race-to-the-bottom arguments are seriously flawed since at the end of such a race, two states starting with equally high standards would have adopted sub-optimally lax standards, but have about the same level of industrial activity as before engaging in the race. In chapter 3 it was also pointed out that if harmonization prevents competition on, say, environmental quality, then states would presumably try to compete over other variables, such as worker safety, minimum wages, or taxation of corporate profits. To avoid these alternative races to the bottom, and the resulting instability, the central regulators would have to harmonize all national rules, so as to eliminate the possibility of any form of inter-state competition altogether. But this would amount to eliminating any trace of national autonomy, so that race-to-the-bottom arguments are, in the end, arguments against subsidiarity.

The fact that in the long run a 'race' would produce sub-optimal results for all competitors does not imply that intergovernmental (horizontal) competition may not produce short-run gains for some of the competitors. At any rate, what the above discussion suggests is that competition should be assessed not only in terms of efficiency, but also in terms of stability. The two questions – efficiency and competitive stability – are related but distinct. Thus, 'intergovernmental price competition may be shown to be efficient or inefficient, but that matter is clearly different from the question of whether intergovernmental price competition degenerates into unstable price war' (Breton 1996: 240). What interests us here is less questions of efficiency than the implications of horizontal (inter-state or inter-jurisdictional) and vertical competition in terms of institutional stability or instability.

Take the case of income redistribution. Economists have traditionally argued that the power to redistribute income among individuals should be assigned to the central government because competition between jurisdictions in this policy area is unstable: income redistribution at the sub-national level would create strong incentives for the wealthy to move out to neighbouring jurisdictions and for the poor to migrate into the socially minded community. However, the empirical evidence contradicts the thesis that centralization is the solution to the problem of competitive instability in the provision of income redistribution among individuals: in most federal states, and increasingly also in unitary states, redistributive policies are implemented by lower-level governments. Even in the US, where the federal government pays three-quarters of the cost of welfare assistance, states insist on defining the standards of need and setting the benefit levels. As a consequence, the level of welfare assistance among American states varies widely, more so than inter-state disparities in wage rates or cost of living (Peterson and Rom 1989). In Europe, too, the countries which benefit most from EU regional aid are strongly opposed to individualized transfers of European funds. In normative terms, this suggests that politically acceptable levels of income redistribution cannot be determined centrally, but only within polities where the people can better control the policy agenda (Majone 2005). Since the theoretical argument about assigning to the central government the power to redistribute income among individuals is correct, Breton interprets the empirical evidence to suggest that there must be institutions that stabilize competition in this policy area.

Concerning competition between the levels of multi-level systems of government, i.e. vertical competition, a comparison of the stability of unitary states, confederations, and federations is of particular interest for our discussion. The many confederations that have existed in the past have now all disappeared, while unitary states of medieval origin are still in existence. The reason, according to Breton, is that unitary states – even those with many jurisdictional tiers – are better able than confederations to adjust to exogenous shocks and ensure that the rules of competition between different jurisdictions are implemented. It is true that some confederations have survived for long periods – for instance, the Swiss Confederation which lasted from the thirteenth century to 1848 or, according to some historians, even until the constitutional reform of 1874, when it was transformed into a federal state. In such cases, however, the confederation had only one central task: the defence of the member states against foreign aggression. It is only when a significant number of powers is assigned to the centre, as in the American Confederation of 1781, that competition between jurisdictional tiers can cause instability – as Tocqueville had clearly understood: in Part I, chapter 8, of *Democracy in America* (1948 [1835]) he wrote that the weakness of confederal governments almost always increases in direct proportion to the extent of their nominal powers. Federal states, on the other hand, tend to be stable because they have the constitutional authority to monitor the behaviour and functional performance of the members of the federation. In many respects, they are even more stable than unitary states because they are in a better position to respond to the different needs and preferences of various segments of the population and of different jurisdictions (Breton 1996: 247).

As long as the member states retain their sovereignty the EU is, at best, a confederation. Instead of concentrating on a central task, such as the integration of the national markets, however, the Union attempts to mimic a federal state, not only by steadily striving to expand its own competences, but also by using the symbols of statehood: flag, 'national' anthem, EU citizenship, passport, even official titles such as president of the European Council and foreign minister of the EU – the latter title renamed, more modestly, High Representative for the Common Foreign and Security Policy after the rejection of the draft Constitutional Treaty. As was noted in previous chapters, this mimicking of statehood has been evident since the early stages of integration. In spite of the high-sounding titles, however, European institutions have neither the resources nor the authority to act decisively in case of a serious shock like the current debt crisis of the euro zone. Only the most powerful member state can credibly attempt to meet the emergency by acting, however reluctantly, as a (temporary) hegemon, see chapter 8. There is no more compelling evidence of the instability of the governance structure of the present EU.

Rather than aspiring to the status of a quasi-federation, the EU should concentrate on the task of monitoring the member states to insure that the national governments, as well as other territorial or functional associations (or 'clubs', see chapter 3), follow the rules adopted in order to prevent competitive instability. The instruments to monitor horizontal competition are numerous, and the precise subset to be used in any particular context will vary as circumstances change. Some instruments are already part of EU law, such as the prohibition of tariff and non-tariff barriers to the movement of goods, services, and factors of productions, or the prohibition of the exportation of environmental and other negative externalities from one state to another. Another already available tool to stabilize horizontal competition is the prohibition of state aid to business, whether private or state-owned, which, if it distorts competition, is deemed to be 'incompatible with the common market' (Article 92 EEC). The prohibition applies not only to direct state subsidies to firms, but to all forms of assistance, including tax breaks, preferential purchasing, loans, and even to loan guarantees. As recently as the 1980s some forms of state aid, and especially large subsidies, were considered a major tool of industrial policy in most member states, but many have been eliminated under the tightening state aid rules. More rules to stabilize inter-state competition are certainly needed, such as rules to prevent conspiracies of some governments directed at outbidding another government that is seeking to attract investments to its jurisdiction.

Presently EU competition policy is managed by the Commission's Directorate-General for Competition, DG COMP, which is increasingly challenged by the competition authorities of the member states. In many cases these national authorities offer a viable alternative to DG COMP, by offering superior analytical abilities based on more effective national law (Wilks 2005). However, monitoring inter-state competition is a task which only a supranational body can perform. In addition to competition policy, other EU policies could also be used in order to stimulate inter-state competition. Cohesion policy, for example, could be implemented not only to reduce regional disparities and support territorial cooperation but also, and perhaps mainly, to allow all governments to compete with one another on a more equal footing than they could without some financial help. Already some years ago the semi-official Sapir Report had suggested that the new EU convergence policy should focus on low-income countries rather than low-income regions, using national per capita GDP (measured in purchasing power parity) as an eligibility criterion. Such refocusing of the convergence policy should help the new member states to compete on more equal terms with the older members of the EU. The Report acknowledged that during the catch-up process, increasing regional disparities within these poorer countries could emerge. However, this phenomenon could be mitigated by national growth, and should anyhow be eased by national, rather than EU, policies (Sapir *et al.* 2004).

Competing models of regional integration

It will be recalled from the section on competition by exit or voice that Salmon's model assumes that citizens in a jurisdiction assess their government's performance by comparing it to that of governments in other jurisdictions. In this and in the next section I argue that the citizens of the EU and their democratic representatives would benefit from a comparison between the European centralized and heavily institutionalized model of regional integration and other, less ambitious, more flexible, and especially cheaper, regional models. As mentioned in the Introduction, the revival of regional integration agreements in the 1980s – primarily free trade areas, customs unions, and common markets – has been labelled the 'Second Regionalism', in contrast to the 'First Regionalism' of the 1960s. In the earlier period regionalism was especially popular among developing countries: the Greater Columbia Economic and Customs Union established in 1948 and including Columbia, Ecuador, Panama, and Venezuela; the Central American Common Market (1960); the Latin American Free Trade Association (1960), including Mexico and almost all South American countries; the Andean Pact (1969) among Bolivia, Ecuador, Columbia, Peru, and Venezuela. Regional integration schemes were also popular in Africa and Asia (Mattli, 1999). The notable exception, and practically the only surviving specimen of the first wave of regional integration, was the EEC established in 1957.

The interest in free trade and common market agreements among developing countries in the first wave of regionalism is thought to have been stimulated by the European examples – the EEC and the European Free Trade Area (EFTA), established in 1960 and including most European countries which were not part of the EEC at the time. In fact, these early attempts at forming Free Trade Areas and Custom Unions outside Europe were motivated by the altogether different rationale of import-substituting industrialization. Developing countries with their small markets thought they could reduce the costs of this mode of industrialization by exploiting economies of scale through preferential opening of markets with one another. By the end of the decade, however, the attempt to form customs unions or free trade areas along these lines had collapsed. Of major significance among the causes of the resurrection of regionalism since the 1980s was the conversion of the US to geographically restricted forms of economic cooperation. As the former key advocate of multilateralism (i.e. free trade for all) the US decision to travel the regional integration route seems to have tilted the balance from multilateralism to regionalism, suggesting that this time regionalism is likely to endure (Bhagwati 1993).

A second important factor in the revival of regionalism was the widening and deepening of the EC/EU. Thus the fear that European investments would be diverted to Eastern Europe was cited by President Salinas of Mexico as a factor decisively pushing him toward NAFTA. He felt that a free trade area embracing all of North America would enable Mexico to get the investments needed from the US and Canada, as well as from Japan (Vega Cànovas 2010). As mentioned in the Introduction, some European economists considered the likelihood of a gradual enlargement of NAFTA to include a number of other Latin American countries. One reason for this enlargement, it was thought, 'would be the growing influence of the European Community in trade, macroeconomic and foreign policy matters. U.S. political and economic leaders may adopt the view that it is necessary to expand [NAFTA] in order to match the increasing political and economic power of the Community' (Baldwin 1993: 54). An overly optimistic view of Brussels-style European integration, as it turned out.

A distinguishing characteristic of the new regionalism is the movement from shallow integration – integration based on the removal of barriers to trade at the border, and limited coordination of national policies – to deeper integration, concerned with behind-the-border issues (see chapter 3). This feature of the new regionalism has tempted some American analysts also to envisage a 'European' model of the future of regional integration. According to this model 'intensified economic integration implies stronger, more formal institutions that become wider and wider in scope. Institutions become more effective as they become more "state-like"' (Kahler 1995: 19). In reality, far from adopting the EC/EU model, or adapting it to their needs, the new or revived regional groups are seldom supported by significant supranational institutions or elaborate mechanisms for common decision-making. This is also true of regional organizations designed to be more than free trade areas or customs union such as MERCOSUR and ANZCERTA. As mentioned in the Introduction, executive power within MERCOSUR is with the governments of the member states rather than with a European-style Commission; while the Australia–New Zealand trade agreement 'is almost defiantly lacking in formal institutional development' (Kahler 1995), despite its ambitious aims of deep integration, including full liberalization of trade in services and harmonization of regulatory practices. Indeed, ANZCERTA is the clearest example of a model of regional integration that is explicitly alternative to the European model. As such, it provides strong support for the thesis, espoused by a number of distinguished economists, that ambitious programmes of trade liberalization, including the elimination or reduction of behind-the-border obstacles, do not require the support of significant supranational institutions or elaborate mechanisms for common decision-making. By 1990 nearly all barriers to a single market between Australia and New Zealand were removed. Yet, despite the single market and extensive legal and policy harmonization (or mutual recognition), monetary union was not deemed to be at all necessary. Even moves towards closer exchange-rate coordination were resisted, especially by Australia, proving that a single market does not require a single currency.

NAFTA provides additional evidence in support of the thesis that the development of intensive economic relations is possible without heavy investments in institutional infrastructure. The key NAFTA institution is the trilateral North American Free Trade Commission, composed of cabinet-level representatives from each country, to administer the agreement and adjudicate disputes over the interpretation or application of NAFTA rules. As discussed in the following section, the dispute-resolution mechanisms are the most interesting elements of NAFTA's institutional architecture. The active role assigned to panels of experts and to the member states themselves, rather than to supranational bodies, makes it possible for NAFTA to operate effectively with a minimum of institutional infrastructure. Even before the establishment of NAFTA the economic relations between Canada and the US represented the largest bilateral trade relationship in the world: by the late 1980s two-thirds of Canada imports came from the US and three-quarters of its exports went to its Southern neighbour, while about one-fifth of US imports came from Canada and one-quarter of US exports went to Canada (Trebilcock and Howse 1995). In spite of such close economic relations, the institutional provisions of the far reaching 1988 Canada–US Free Trade Agreement were kept to a minimum – essentially, a Trade Commission in which both countries were represented equally by their trade ministers – while monetary union between the two countries was never seriously considered. In sum, despite repeated suggestions that 'the study of economic integration has been inspired if not dominated, by the European example' (Pelkmans 1997: 2), the available empirical evidence points unmistakably to the fact that the European example has elicited defensive reactions rather than emulative responses. To repeat the conclusion reached in the Introduction, in terms of comparative regionalism the EU seems to be the outlier rather than the model.

The diffusion of regionalism in recent years, with the variety of institutional solutions adopted, provides abundant empirical material for comparing the transaction costs and net benefits of different models of regional integration. In this connection it should be pointed out that although transaction costs – especially political transaction costs – are often difficult to quantify, the difficulty can be mitigated by assessing such costs in comparative terms. As Williamson (1985: 22) has argued, it is the difference between, rather than the absolute magnitude of, transaction costs that matters; empirical research on the incidence of transaction costs almost never attempts to measure such costs directly. Particularly significant, for a comparative analysis of different models of regional integration, are not only bargaining costs, but also influence costs. Bargaining costs were defined in chapter 4 as the transaction costs involved in negotiations among different parties. They include the opportunity costs of bargainers' time, as well as resources expended trying to improve one's bargaining position, the costs of monitoring and enforcing the agreement, and the losses from failure to reach an agreement. A most important source of bargaining costs, I pointed out in the earlier chapter, is the opportunistic behaviour of bargainers mainly interested in private (rather than aggregate) benefits and costs – a behaviour that makes it impossible to resolve satisfactorily the inescapable tension between cooperative moves to create value jointly (expanding the pie) and competitive moves to gain individual advantage (dividing the pie). As the examples given there and in following chapters show, in the EU context opportunistic behaviour becomes particularly evident in crisis situations.

Influence costs were defined in the same chapter 4 as the costs incurred in attempts to bias the decision of the central institutions in a self-interested fashion, in attempts to counter such influence activities by others, and in the resulting degradation of the quality of decisions. There we quoted Milgrom and Roberts (1992) to the effect that the opportunities for influencing governmental decisions grow with the size and scope of government. Relative to other regional organizations, the EU is indeed 'big government' in both size and scope: as already mentioned in the Introduction, there is pretty general agreement that by now the EU's policymaking powers touch 'almost every imaginable public policy objective' (Curtin *et al.*, 2013: 1). Hence it is reasonable to infer that influence costs – as well as many other political transaction costs, including administrative costs – are much higher in case of the EU than in smaller, more focused, and less institutionally developed regional organizations. Indeed, with its current twenty-eight member states (including Croatia), and perhaps as many as ten more to come in the not too distant future, the EU is unique among contemporary regional organizations: ANZCERTA has only two members; NAFTA, three; MERCOSUR, four member states. Early expectations that NAFTA would expand into a free trade area of the Americas including most countries of Latin America were disappointed, as already mentioned. Apparently the US government prefers to sign bilateral free trade agreements with other countries of Latin America rather than extending regional integration beyond North America.

Size of membership matters not only because a small organization economizes on various transaction costs, but also because small size facilitates the development of a system of reputations based on mutual trust. In turn, such a system facilitates the enforcement of agreements among the members of the organization, in particular by mitigating problems of moral hazard, see again chapter 4. Besides affecting transaction costs and the development of mutual trust, size and scope have a number of other consequences that deserve attention.

Private ordering vs. legal centralism

In a comparative perspective the EU is an outlier, not only in terms of size of membership and scope of competences but also in the sense that most other regional organizations have deliberately minimized recourse to formal legal institutions. It will be recalled from chapter 3 that in the EU context legal centralism implies the supremacy of European law, so that disputes over trade and investment must be resolved by the European courts applying European law. The advocates of private ordering, on the other hand, maintain that arbitration mechanisms are much more efficient for settling disputes between contractual partners than court ordering. Most new regional organizations have expressed a clear preference for approaches to dispute resolution that depend much less on legal centralism and court ordering than the corresponding arrangements in the EU, and for this reason are likely to be more cost-effective, as well as more transparent, than the state-like mechanisms adopted by the Union. The expression 'Integration Through Law' acknowledges the preference for the legalistic approach which has characterized European integration since the 1950s.

Article 169 of the Treaty of Rome enabled the European Commission to invoke the compulsory jurisdiction of the ECJ against a defaulting member state. Joseph Weiler has identified four 'glaring weaknesses' of this system: first, the procedure is, in practice, political in nature – the Commission may have non-legal reasons not to initiate a prosecution; second, a centralized body with limited human resources is unable adequately to identify, process, and monitor all possible member states' violations and infringements; third, Article 169 may be inappropriate to apply to small violations: dedicating limited Commission resources to infringements that do not raise an important principle or create a major economic impact, is wasteful; finally, no real enforcement mechanisms existed at the time (Weiler 1999: 27). These weaknesses are remedied, to some extent, by the cooperation between the European Court and national courts established by means of the preliminary ruling reference to the ECJ. Preliminary ruling references soon became the largest source of the Court's cases, and many of its landmark decisions have been made in preliminary rulings decisions. Individuals do not have a right of appeal to the ECJ – only a national court can make the decision to defer. Nevertheless, individuals have raised legal questions that the national courts and the European Commission would never have asked, allowing the Court greatly to expand the reach and scope of European law at the national level.

As much as anything else, the existence of an exclusive forum for adjudicating disputes sets the EU apart from other regional and international organizations – a clear indication of the EU's aspiration to a state-like role. As already noted, most new regional organizations have deliberately minimized recourse to legal and bureaucratic institutions. Take for example the CUSTA, which was ratified in 1988. In addition to aiming for the complete elimination of tariffs and the prohibition or restriction of non-tariff barriers, this agreement exempted Canada from any US trade-restricting law unless Canada was mentioned explicitly in the legislation. Even more remarkably, any legislation affecting Canada had to be discussed bilaterally before passage. Prospective trade conflicts were to be treated by consultations and a variety of dispute-settlement mechanisms (DSMs). Of these DSMs, those introduced under Chapter 19 of the Agreement have attracted most attention because of their innovative character:

> Rather than attempting to harmonize rules on dumping and state subsidies – topics of irreducible disagreement between Canada and the U.S. in the past–dispute settlement under chapter 19 was carried out by using each side's national trade laws as benchmarks. When an initial decision by a domestic administrative agency was contested, review would not take place in the national courts but before a bi-national panel of five persons. The panel would assess only whether the administrative agency applied the relevant national law appropriately, it would not apply a new standard.
>
> (Kahler 1995: 100–1)

Thus CUSTA provides an early, possibly the earliest, indication of the rejection of legal centralism by the newer regional organizations, in favour of more efficient methods of dispute resolution. The other institutional provisions similarly minimized the use of legal means, favouring instead recourse to mediation and arbitration, supported by the appropriate kind of expertise and, if necessary, by the threat of retaliation. The Agreement established the Canada–US Trade Commission in which both countries are represented by their trade ministers. Where disputes arise about the interpretation or application of provisions of the Agreement to actual or proposed measures of either party, the party complaining that such a measure will cause impairment of any benefit reasonably expected under CUSTA can refer the matter to the Commission. The Commission may appoint a mediator and if this fails to result in agreement, the Commission may refer the dispute to a binding arbitration panel, but only if the two parties agree on such a reference. In the absence of agreement the aggrieved party may retaliate. Despite (or rather because of) the absence of elaborate institutions, the DSMs worked – at much lower costs than the dispute-resolution methods used by the EU. According to Kahler, the success of the intergovernmental dimensions of CUSTA can be measured by the absence of new trade conflicts between the parties outside the CUSTA procedures and the transfer of both Chapter 18 and 19 procedures to NAFTA.

In fact, many of the novel features of CUSTA were retained in the design of NAFTA. In particular, NAFTA's DSMs closely resemble those of CUSTA in most respects, while moving beyond them in others. Thus Chapter 20 of the Agreement obliges the contracting parties to notify any measure that may affect trade and investment, and to provide information concerning such measures when requested by another party, whether or not the measure had been notified. If one of the parties thinks that an existing measure is incompatible with obligations under the Agreement it can request consultations in order to reach a mutually satisfactory solution. If the consultations do not produce a solution, any one of the other two members can call for a meeting of the Trade Commission – the institution established to supervise the implementation of NAFTA and mediate in any dispute that may arise – with the exception of cases relating to antidumping and countervailing duties, state aid, investments and financial services – politically sensitive areas for which separate DSMs are provided in Chapter 19 of the Agreement as discussed below. If the Trade Commission cannot find a satisfactory solution, the country that initiated the proceeding can request the establishment of a panel including independent experts, with the task of re-examining the dispute and recommending a solution to the Commission. If this body is still unable to reach a satisfactory solution, and one of the parties thinks that its fundamental rights under the Agreement have been violated, or its interests damaged, by the disputed measure, then the affected party is free to withhold from the other party benefits of equivalent worth, until the moment when the parties reach a satisfactory solution.

The system of dispute resolution under Chapter 19 is guided by two key principles. First, each member of NAFTA maintains the unrestricted right to apply its own trade legislation and to implement its normal administrative procedures with respect to the products of the other two members. At the same time, each member agrees that any legislative or administrative change must be previously submitted to the other two members. The parties also agree to submit any legal changes they may contemplate to a panel of experts to obtain their opinion whether the proposed measures are consistent with duties under NAFTA (and WTO) rules. Second, the member states agree to establish ad hoc panels for a quasi-judicial review of antidumping and countervailing duties measures enacted by the competent national administrative agencies. The idea is, again, to replace courts by bi-national panels of independent experts chosen by the national governments from lists of experts in trade law. However, anybody entitled to invoke judicial review may insist that the case be examined by a national court rather than by a panel.

When bi-national panels adjudicate disputes between two member states, the third member of NAFTA has the option of either participating in the proceedings or pursuing its own process of consultation and dispute resolution. Where complaints procedures are open to a NAFTA member either under the GATT/WTO or NAFTA, the complainant country is entitled to choose which regime it pursues its complaints under, except where the complaint pertains to health, safety, or environmental standards, where the respondent country can insist on dispute resolution under NAFTA rules. In such a case the Agreement provides for the creation of scientific boards to provide expert evidence to panels adjudicating on questions pertaining to such standards. Some experts in trade law have concluded that the NAFTA system of bi-national dispute-settlement panels is preferable to the EU approach, especially in terms of transparency. For example, the distinguished Canadian legal scholars Trebilcock and Howse (1995: 112) have argued that '[t]he EU antidumping system is characterized by discretion and secrecy: the reluctance of the [CJEU] to review the Commission's decisions increases the appearance (at least) of unfairness of the system's administration'.

Subsequent to the negotiation of NAFTA, the US Administration initiated a further set of negotiations on environmental and labour standards that resulted in trilateral side-accords setting up institutional machinery to ensure that existing environmental and labour laws in each of the three countries are effectively enforced by the national authorities, with the possibility of fines and trade sanctions as penalties for non-compliance. The accords also provide for consultative mechanisms designed to promote a higher degree of harmonization of standards in this area in the future. Any member of NAFTA can initiate consultations if it believes that another member government is not enforcing its *national* environmental or labour law. If such consultations do not reach a mutually satisfactory resolution, then further procedures that resemble those under Chapters 19 and 20 can be instituted, including an arbitral panel, the assessment of fines, and ultimately the suspension of benefits under NAFTA. The savings in transaction and other costs of the NAFTA approach, in comparison with the centralized procedures followed by the EU in similar cases, appear to be quite significant.

Incidentally, a comparison between the EU and CUSTA/NAFTA is instructive not only in terms of alternative methods of dispute resolution, but also the relation between economic integration and monetary union. One of the standard arguments used in the 1990s to justify the introduction of a common European currency was that exchange-rate instability would disrupt trade in the common market. A monetary union between Canada and the US, however, has never been seriously considered even though the trading relationship between these two countries is the largest bilateral trading relationship in the world, see the preceding section. The fact that Canadian and US traders continue to operate, apparently with success, using their own currencies shows that the argument about currency swings dampening inter-state trade is far from convincing. Trade is also booming between Canada, Mexico and the US, the three members of NAFTA, in spite of the coexistence of three national currencies (Vega Cànovas 2010).

Commitments and resources

Beyond the issue of the transaction costs and net benefits of different models of regional integration looms the more fundamental question concerning the credibility of the commitment to some particular model;

more precisely, the question of the resources needed to honour that commitment. As I argued in chapter 8, a basic responsibility of the institutional leader is to make sure that ends and means are balanced. In that context it was noted that many of the problems of European governance have their roots in the scarcity of leadership – in relation to the scope of the powers transferred to the supranational level. A comparison of the EC/EU with other models of regional integration allows us to appreciate the importance of this qualification. Under the 1957 Treaty of Rome establishing the EEC, European leaders committed themselves to the removal of obstacles to the free movement of people, goods, and capital – negative integration; to a customs union with common external tariffs; and to a small number of common policies. These were limited and well-defined goals – not much more ambitious, aside from the CAP, than the goals of such regional organizations as MERCOSUR, ANZCERTA and, in perspective, even NAFTA. The commitment of the European leaders was credible because the material, institutional, and normative resources available were certainly sufficient for the task. In fact some of the most important goals, such as the customs union, were attained ahead of schedule, proving that the kind of 'collective leadership' implied by the principle of equality of all the member states was sufficient for tackling these important but limited tasks. Actually, compared to the institutional and political resources available to the other regional organizations, the EEC suffered from an embarrassment of riches.

The gap between growing commitments and inadequate resources – including the scarcity of true leadership noted in chapter 8, and the lack of broad popular support – became increasingly problematic as successive treaties kept raising the level of aspiration, but without a clear statement of the final goal, without adequate increase in institutional resources, and in the absence of sufficient popular support. Today political integration of Europe seems to be too remote a goal to have any practical meaning; but even the commitment to full economic integration is becoming less and less credible in a greatly enlarged and increasingly heterogeneous EU. The signs of a retreat from the original commitments have been evident for some time. In November 2005, for example, the European Commission decided to withdraw its draft Directive for the liberalization of port services. Initially acclaimed as the most important liberalization measure in the area of transportation, the draft proposed to eliminate cargo-handling monopolies by allowing shipping companies to use their own staff to unload cargo, to set limits to permissible state aid in this sector, and generally to stimulate competition among the ports of the EU. Faced by the opposition of the EP and the trade unions, the first Barroso Commission progressively softened many of the draft measures, to the point of making the revised text, in the opinion of some analysts, practically useless. In the end the Commission decided to withdraw the watered-down version of the Directive, implicitly admitting that it considered itself politically too feeble to face the combined opposition of the EP and of the port workers, one of Europe's most protected labour forces.

'Is Europe still capable of moving forward?' asked the editorial of *Le Monde* of 16 February 2006. The topic was the draft Services Directive then being considered by the EP. The editorialist of the influential French newspaper stated very clearly the dilemma facing the EU. On the one hand, integration of the market for services is indispensable: with agriculture and industry no longer creating new jobs, only the services sector could contribute decisively to a reduction of the high level of unemployment in the euro zone. On the other hand, in a socially and economically linked Union, such integration implies serious social problems, especially with respect to wages (Editorial, *Le Monde*: 2006). In fact, the Services Directive 2006/123/EC, seeking to facilitate the exercise of the freedom to provide services – a freedom enshrined in all European treaties – became one of the most controversial pieces of EU legislation in recent history, see chapter 7. The Services Directive, finally approved in December 2006 – against the strong opposition of the East European governments that had supported the original Bolkestein draft – does little more than restate the principles that have evolved in the case law concerning the freedom to provide services, and the freedom of self-employed professionals and companies to set up the base of their operations anywhere in the EU.

There are many other indications of the growing inability of the European model of regionalism to achieve the goal of full market integration – despite its uniquely robust legal and institutional foundations. Thus, the Commission has admitted its inability to enforce a common regime for the use of genetically modified organisms in agriculture. In a highly unusual move, Brussels gave up its competence in this area, proposing that from now on each national government should decide for its own territory. In this connection, *Financial Times Deutschland* of 14 July 2010 titled its editorial 'Bankruptcy [Bankrott] in Brussels'. According to the editorialist, the Commission 'capitulated because the ideological differences among the member states are too deep to make agreement possible'. In case of negative externalities – such as the release into the environment of genetically modified micro-organisms – the only possibility now available is direct discussions between neighbouring countries. But, the editorialist added, the EU was established precisely in order to make unnecessary such time-consuming bilateral negotiations. 'If the Commission itself now begins to cast aside this founding idea of the Union', the article concluded, 'how can it hope to convince its citizens of the need of stronger European institutions?'

The clearest indication of the difficulty of honouring the commitment to full economic integration under the conditions today prevailing in the EU, is the renewed interest in the old notion of a two-speed Europe – a type of differentiated integration discussed in chapter 7. The advocates of this approach start from the observation that the crisis of monetary union cannot be resolved without closer cooperation among the member states of the EU. The two possible options for the future are closer cooperation, either among all the member states of the Union, or among a subset of the EU membership. In the first case, one could continue on the current path, which already allows a number of possibilities of differentiated integration, opt-outs, and enhanced cooperation. However, 'a greatly expanded EU could not work efficiently on the basis of a system conceived for six Member States of a comparable degree of economic development and with the same political desire to integrate' (Piris 2011: 37). Besides, the unprecedented seriousness of the present crisis makes it highly unlikely that a solution could be found using more or less traditional policy instruments. The only promising, and politically realistic option, therefore, seems to be much closer integration among a subset of member states willing to play the role of an avant-garde. The 'bolder' option proposed by Piris to reach this goal is a new treaty applying only to the members of the euro zone. The basic principle of this avant-garde would be that all participating states should be fully committed to participate in all domains of cooperation – no more opt-outs, derogations, or looser forms of differentiated integration! Possible candidates for such closer cooperation: security and defence policy; areas of JHA; and especially the economic and fiscal components of monetary union. In chapter 7 I already discussed some of the problems raised by the view of the Euro-Group as the spearhead of deeper integration. The most obvious difficulty is that the present members of the euro zone are almost as different – economically, politically, and socially – as the entire membership of the EU. Indeed, it can be argued that the euro crisis, by revealing the misbehaviour of some members of monetary union, has made the heterogeneity within this assumed core group a good deal more evident than the diversity of the other members of the Union. At any rate, the main problems facing Piris' and similar proposals are political. It is unrealistic to assume that all the members of the euro zone would be willing to accept the kind of close cooperation and policy coordination which Piris has in mind. He himself is not sure that the requisite level of cooperation could in fact be achieved, as may be seen from his rhetorical question: Would Germany, the Netherlands or Finland agree with Greece, Ireland or Portugal on a common list of social, fiscal, and economic (legally binding) measures to be taken?

Moreover, the fact that monetary union is considered to be part of the *acquis communautaire* means that all future members of the EU would have to adopt the common currency, sooner or later, making the euro zone even more heterogeneous than it is today. But the most fundamental obstacle to the notion of a two-speed Europe is the deep-rooted principle of the basic equality and equal dignity of all the member states. As noted in chapter 8, this principle of formal and (to the extent possible) substantive equality of the members of the Union has inspired all the European treaties, and is reflected in the design and *modus operandi* of the European institutions. It is true that the kind of differentiated integration advocated by Piris and other experts assumes that the rear guard would eventually join the avant-garde. The politically crucial questions, however, are: when and how? Admission to the EU is decided unanimously by all the states already members of the Union, but who is going to decide whether a member state is now ready to move from the rear to the forefront of integration? So far, such questions have been evaded by the proponents of two-speed Europe, but the leaders of the new member states certainly understand the potential implications. They realize that the principle of equality of all member states cannot be easily reconciled with any form of differentiated integration. This mental reservation probably explains why the new Stability Treaty was signed, not just by the members of the euro zone but by all member states other than the UK and the Czech Republic.

This near unanimity suggests that the vast majority of member states reject any differentiation based on the speed of movement towards an unknown final destination. At the same time the exceptional circumstances under which the Stability Treaty was signed, as an international rather than a European agreement, seems to indicate that few, if any, member states are prepared to sacrifice the core of national sovereignty on the altar of European integration. If this is the case, then it is important to understand which role the national state will continue to play in the future, in spite of the constraints set by globalization, on the one hand, and by the rising tide of regional integration, on the other. This is the question to be examined in the next, and final, chapter.

10

The nation state between globalization and regional integration

As globalization of competition has intensified, some have begun to argue a diminished role for nations. Instead, internationalization and the removal of protection and other distortions to competition arguably make nations, if anything, more important. National differences in character and culture, far from being threatened by global competition, prove integral to success in it.

(Porter 1990: 30)

Efforts at European unification are raising questions about whether the influence of nations on competition will diminish. Instead, freer trade will arguably make them more important While the effective locus of competitive advantage may sometimes encompass regions that cross national borders. . .Europe is unlikely to become a 'nation' from a competitive perspective. National differences in demand, factor creation, and other determinants will persist, and rivalry within nations will remain vital.

(Ibid.: 158–9)

Nations can reconcile social purpose with individual aspirations and initiatives and enhance performance by their collective synergy. The whole is more than the sum of the parts. Citizens of a nation will respond better to state encouragement and initiatives; conversely, the state will know better what to do and how, in accord with active social forces. Nations can compete.

(Landes 1998: 219)

Farewell to the nation state?

According to the federalists of the immediate post-World War II period, it was impossible to rebuild a democratic, prosperous and powerful Europe starting with the nation states: only a strong federation could solve the great problems of the post-war period. The establishment of a federal super-state, the Italian federalist Altiero Spinelli argued, would have to precede the political and economic reconstruction of the national states, the former being the necessary foundation of the latter. The government of the future European federation was supposed to be responsible not to the national governments but directly to the peoples of the states of the federation. Indeed, since the construction of a European federal state was supposed to precede the reconstruction of the national governments, the federalist ideology would necessarily supersede the ideological divisions of the past. In turn, the European federation would open the way to a world federation. It is of some interest that the majority of the thirty or so federalist movements existing in Europe at the time also claimed to be working toward a world federation. The idea of an eventual world government was more than an exercise in utopian thinking; it was needed in order to meet the telling argument that a purely European federation would simply reproduce, on a larger scale, the geopolitical ambitions and aggressive tendencies of the traditional nation states.

This was not the vision of Alexandre Kojève, even though he shared the view that the age of the national polities had passed. In an essay written in 1945 and titled 'Outline of a doctrine of French policy' (Kojève 1945) the Russian-born French philosopher took for granted the irreversible crisis of the national idea and the demise of the European nation states. Historical nations such as France, Spain, and Italy, he argued, were no longer capable of surviving politically as independent sovereign states. However, they could rescue themselves not by joining a European, much less a world, federation, but by merging, together with their colonies, in a more homogeneous supranational political structure, under French leadership: a Latin 'empire' based on linguistic, cultural, and mental affinities, as well as on the identity of religious beliefs. The term 'empire' was used by Kojève in the sense of a hegemonic sphere of influence, and the hope was that such a Latin empire could not only play an autonomous role between the US and the Soviet Union, but also prevent a German economic domination of Europe in the future.

More ambitiously, the Spanish philosopher Ortega y Gasset had argued, in *The Rebellion of the Masses* published before World War II, that only a US of Europe would make it possible for the Old Continent to play again a commanding role in the world (Ortega y Gasset 1933). In the same year in which Ortega y Gasset's well-known book appeared, and in a somewhat similar vein, the French writer Julien Benda in his *Discours à la nation européenne* expressed the hope that a European nationalism might replace the nationalism of the different nation states. The symbols of a European nation, he maintained, must supplant the myths of the individual nations (cited in Holmberg 1994: 98–9). In later writings, in particular in a conference held in Berlin in 1954, Ortega was more modest, arguing that the nations of Europe could survive only if they understood that the idea of the nation as the best form of collective life was anachronistic, and had no useful suggestions for the future: it had become an historical impossibility (Campi 2004). Also the majority of the federalist movements active in Western Europe after the end of World War II started to view the future European federation no longer as a would-be world power, but at most as a third force between the two superpowers, America and the Soviet Union.

Already by the late 1940s, at any rate, the prediction that the nation states of continental Europe would all collapse, leaving the people free to design their political future on a clean slate, had been conclusively refuted. The federalists attributed the responsibility of this failure to the interests of the superpowers in preserving the old state structures, except in the case of Germany. The truth is that Spinelli like many other intellectuals, then as now, underestimated both the amazing ability of the European nation state to react to the catastrophes of the twentieth century, and the depth of popular attachment to national sovereignty. Also the authors of the first social-scientific analyses of the European integration process, Ernst Haas and his neo-functionalist school, assumed that the national state would be made increasingly irrelevant by the progress of integration. The superior problem-solving capacity of the supranational European institutions was supposed to produce a sufficient normative basis for the integrationist project by inducing the progressive transfer of the loyalties and political demands of social groups from the national to the European level. According to Haas political integration 'is the process whereby political actors in several distinct national settings are persuaded to shift their loyalties, expectations and political activities to a new centre, whose institutions possess or demand jurisdiction over pre-existing national states' (Haas 1958: 16). Thus, as Milward and Sørensen (1994) noted, neo-functionalists effectively assumed away the nation state from the very start. Like the federalists of the immediate post-war period, the first academic students of European integration greatly underestimated the effectiveness of the nation state and of its institutions. The progressive transfer of loyalties and political demands from the national to the European level was predicated precisely on the basis of the superior problem-solving capacity of the supranational institutions.

What happened in fact was that in the years following the end of the war, popular attachment to the national institutions was enhanced by the enormously successful reconstruction of the national economies of continental Europe. In the same years the British government developed such an extraordinary activism in the social sphere that historians writing some thirty years later considered the foundation of the welfare state Britain's greatest post-war achievement (Sked and Cook 1979). As soon as the work of economic reconstruction was completed, the British model was imitated, more or less closely, by all democratic states of Western Europe. By the mid-1950s perceptive analysts could already see that throughout the Western part of the Old Continent the nation state, far from withering away, was in the process of becoming the omnicompetent welfare state of later decades. The brilliant economic performance of the 1950s and 1960s – that is to say, even before the integration of the national markets of communitarian Europe could make its effects felt – disproved conclusively the federalists' claim that it was impossible to reconstruct a democratic and prosperous Europe starting with the nation states. Far from being a relic of the past, the European nation state proved to be not only highly resilient, but also quite capable of rebuilding the national economies and starting a process of intense economic integration in the Old Continent.

In order to start the integration process, however, it was necessary to get rid of all traces of the nationalism of the past, and the 1957 Treaty of Rome imposed the necessary discipline, at least in the economic domain. Hence the importance of the articles of the treaty dealing with the elimination of customs duties and of quantitative restrictions to intra-Community trade; with the free movement of persons, services, and capital; and with distortion of competition, see chapter 6 above. There is no doubt that European integration, even if limited to the economic sphere, required a significant restriction of the scope of national sovereignty. But here, as Wilhelm Roepke pointed out long ago, it is necessary to make the right distinction between such sovereign rights as correspond to the genuine sphere of government, such as order and justice, and others which do not, such as a regime of detailed economic regulation. To diminish national sovereignty is one of the urgent needs of our time, he argued:

> But the excess of sovereignty should be abolished instead of being transferred to a higher political and geographical unit. Not to grasp this truth is one of the many fallacies behind many current discussions on the economic integration of Europe. In order to correct it let us stress again that 'sovereignty' means not only unimpeachable rights of one

government vis-à-vis other governments but also vis-à-vis its own nationals. . .It is in the second sense that it has become the great problem of our time. A mere shift in the seat of sovereignty not only leaves the problem of its over-dose unsolved, but it even makes it worse.

(Roepke 1954: 250)

It is interesting to note that for Roepke European political integration was possible, if at all, only as a federation, but a federation which would give 'the largest possible scope to the national way of life' (ibid.: 243). What this liberal German economist apparently had in mind was something like what the American political economist Barry Weingast – whose ideas have already been mentioned in chapters 7 and 9 – would later call 'market preserving federalism'. A federal system is market preserving if it satisfies three conditions: (1) the member states (not the federal level of government) have primary regulatory responsibility over the economy; (2) a common market is insured, preventing the member states from using their regulatory authority to erect trade barriers against goods and services from other members; and (3) the member states face a hard budget constraint, that is, they have neither the ability to print money nor access to unlimited credit; in other words, the federal government cannot bail out a member state facing serious fiscal problems (Weingast 1995). According to Weingast the nineteenth century US was such a market-preserving federation, while the US of today is simply a very large nation state. In the context of European integration we may note that the condition concerning the hard budget constraint was not present in the Rome Treaty but was eventually introduced by the Maastricht Treaty. The first condition, on the other hand, has been repeatedly violated since the Single European Act, and the various measures proposed to solve the euro crisis amount to an almost complete reversal of roles, with the higher-level government assuming control of the economy of the members of the euro zone in serious financial difficulties. Thus the only form of federalism which Roepke judged to be compatible with the complexity of European history and the variety of its political cultures is effectively rejected by the very supporters of ever closer integration.

The competitive advantage of nations

If in the 1930s Ortega y Gasset could argue that a united Europe might still rule the world, today's integrationist leaders tend to see the EU, more modestly, as a protecting wall built around a group of countries that are said to be too small to count on a world scale, and economically and demographically too weak to take care of themselves. Three noted scholars recently expressed their concern over the international role of Europe and, even more, over the future of the European welfare state:

> The peoples of Europe must learn that they can only preserve their welfare-state model of society and the diversity of their nation-state cultures by joining forces and working together. They must pool their resources if they want to exert any kind of influence on the international political agenda and the solution of global problems. To abandon European unification now would be to quit the world stage for good.
>
> (Bofinger *et al.* 2012)

As we saw in chapter 7, the standard formula to overcome the present difficulties is 'more Europe' – pretty much along the lines that have been followed for more than half a century. Such an approach diverts attention from the structural flaws of the European construction and the many errors of the past. It also attaches too much importance to formal powers, and not enough to flexibility, to the benefits of institutions and policies tailored to specific national needs, to shared values and common traditions. Joining forces and working together can produce results only if there is general agreement about the goals and the best means for achieving them, which is certainly not the case in the EU of today. Above all, the advocates of 'more Europe' ignore Tocqueville's warning that the real weakness of confederal governments increases in direct proportion to the growth of their nominal powers, see chapter 9. This being the situation, as long as the peoples of Europe are not willing to support something like a fully-fledged federal solution, we must still rely on the problem-solving capacity of the national states and hence must avoid too rigid limits on their freedom of action.

Indeed Michael Porter, of the Harvard Business School, has convincingly argued that neither globalization nor European integration have reduced the central role of the national state in economic development and innovation. To support his thesis, Porter starts from the empirical observation that the leaders in particular industries and segments of industries tend to be concentrated in a few nations and sustain their competitive advantage for many decades. This competitive advantage is created and sustained in a highly localized (national or even subnational) process:

Differences in national economic structures, values, cultures, institutions, and histories contribute profoundly to competitive success. . .While globalization of competition might appear to make the nation less important, instead it seems to make it more so. With fewer impediments to trade to shelter uncompetitive domestic firms and industries, the home nation takes on growing significance because it is the source of the skills and technology that underpin competitive advantage. . .The home base [for successful global competitors] is the nation in which the essential competitive advantages of the enterprise are created and sustained. It is where a firm's strategy is set and the core product and process technology (broadly defined) are created and maintained.

(Porter 1990: 19)

These propositions are supported by an impressive amount of statistical and descriptive material showing how a nation provides the environment in which its firms in a particular industry are able to improve and innovate faster than foreign rivals. The sample includes ten important trading nations – from Asia (Japan, Singapore, Korea), Europe (the UK, Germany, Italy, Denmark, Sweden, Switzerland), and the US – and over one hundred industries. The theoretical core of Porter's approach is a critique of the static (neo-classic) view of competition in which a nation's factors of production are fixed and firms deploy such factors in industries where they will produce the greatest return. In actual competition, Porter points out, the essential character is innovation and change: 'Instead of simply maximizing within fixed constraints, the question is how firms can gain competitive advantage from changing the constraints' (ibid.: 21). To expand the range of feasible choice, however, both firms and national governments must enjoy a considerable freedom of action. Given sufficient freedom of action, even small countries can achieve extraordinary economic results.

Thus, by the early decades of the twentieth century Switzerland, with a population of about seven million, had emerged as an industrial country of importance far beyond its small size, and in the post-World War II period it became one of the richest industrialized countries. By some measures it actually had the highest per capita income in the world by the 1960s. Swiss companies, among them Nestlé, Sandoz, Ciba-Geigy, and Lindt are among the most global of any country, and generally employ far more people outside the country than in Switzerland. The Swiss case, writes Porter (1990: 307–8), 'vividly illustrates how a small nation, without a large home market as in Japan or America, can nevertheless be a successful global competitor in many important industries. Switzerland is also an economy that has continuously upgraded itself to support a rising standard of living.' Also Sweden, not significantly larger than Switzerland in terms of population, is the home base of a striking number of large, global companies. Its economy supports a very high standard of living, as well as one of the most highly developed welfare states in the world.

This American business economist reaches the conclusion that nations enjoy a competitive advantage in industries that draw most heavily on unique elements of their histories and characters. Moreover, the influence of the national environment becomes even more vital as competition becomes more knowledge based. This environment shapes the way opportunities are perceived, how specialized skills and resources are developed, and the pressures on firms to mobilize resources in rapid and efficient ways: 'It is the creation of knowledge and the capacity to act, which are the result of a process that is highly localized, that determines competitive success.' In sum, 'globalization makes nations more, not less, important' (ibid.: 736). Such a view of the competitive advantage of nations contradicts the one-size-fits-all philosophy and the emphasis on the harmonization of national policies, which have characterized the process of European integration since the 1950s. More recent research provides additional support for the thesis that economic development is possible only by preserving and even strengthening the policymaking autonomy of the national governments.

As Dani Rodrik, an economist teaching at Harvard's Kennedy School of Government, writes: 'Markets are most developed and most effective in generating wealth when they are backed by solid governmental institutions. *Markets and states are complements*, not substitutes, as simplistic economic accounts would have it' (Rodrik 2011: 16; italics in the original). Analysing a huge set of economic data from both advanced and developing countries Rodrik found a strong positive correlation between a country's exposure to international trade and the size of its government. In other words, 'governments had grown the largest in those economies that were most exposed to international markets' (ibid.: 17). Thus countries heavily engaged in international trade, like Sweden or the Netherlands, devote the highest proportion of their resources to the public sector – between 55 and 60 per cent of GDP. How to explain this rather counterintuitive finding? Rodrik considers many possible explanations and in the end concludes that the evidence points strongly towards the social insurance motive: 'People demand compensation against risk when their economies are more exposed to international economic forces; and governments respond by erecting broader safety nets. . .If you want markets to expand, you need governments to do the same' (ibid.: 18). In the decades following the Great Depression of the 1930s, industrial states have erected a wide array of social protections – unemployment compensation and other labour markets interventions, health insurance, family support, etc. – that mitigate demand for cruder forms of protection such as sheltering the economy behind high tariff walls, as was done during the Great Depression. This is the reason why today protectionism can be kept under control, in America as in Europe.

However, at the European level we have the paradox that while the EU does not have either the financial resources or the legal powers to provide similar compensations against the risks of globalization, at the same time it pretends to limit the autonomy of the member states by imposing increasingly stringent constraints on national policymaking. Since the very beginning of European integration the emphasis has been on the top-down harmonization of the laws and policies of the member states rather than on a healthy competition between different national approaches to problem-solving. As a consequence, inter-jurisdictional competition has hardly played a role in the integration process. Indeed, a well-known expert of European law like Stephen Weatherill could maintain that competition among national regulators is incompatible with the notion of undistorted competition in the internal European market, see chapter 9.

The race to deeper integration

The first half of the 1990s saw the start of two parallel races towards deeper integration: at Maastricht, in 1992, it was decided that the EU should proceed to economic and monetary union by 1999 at the latest; on 1 January 1995 the WTO, an international body pursuing a new, much more ambitious kind of economic integration than the old GATT, came into being. In chapters 3 and 4 we distinguished between 'shallow' and 'deep' integration and discussed the most important consequences of deep integration in the context of the EC/EU. However, the establishment of the WTO shows that both the distinction and the consequences are significant not only in the European context but globally. 'Shallow' integration, as we know, is integration based on the removal of barriers to exchange at the border but imposing very few restrictions on domestic policies; while under deep integration the distinction between domestic and international economic policies (in particular, trade policy) tends to disappear. Under shallow integration, policies about competition and antitrust rules, corporate governance, product standards, worker safety, regulation and supervision of financial institutions, and the government's budget, are considered domestic policies and, as such, matters to be determined by the preferences of the nation's citizens and their political institutions, without regard for other countries. For the first three decades following the end of World War II international economic integration was of the 'shallow' variety. The regime introduced by the 1944 Bretton Woods Agreement made significant progress towards trade liberalization, but left national governments largely free to respond to social and economic needs at home. International economic policy was supposed to be subservient to domestic policy objectives, and not the other way around. The goal was a limited version of economic globalization, not what Rodrik (2011) calls 'hyper-globalization' – a regime under which trade agreements extend beyond their traditional focus on import restrictions and impinge on domestic policies; controls on international capital markets are removed; and developing countries are under severe pressure to open their markets to foreign trade and investment.

Multilateralism was a distinctive feature of the post-war international economic system, and the institutional embodiment of multilateralism in trade was the GATT, one of the core international economic institutions of the post-1945 era together with the World Bank and the IMF. After a slow start, successive rounds of multilateral trade negotiations managed to eliminate a substantial part of the import restrictions in place since the 1930s and reduce tariffs from their post-war heights. The volume of world trade grew at a yearly average of almost 7 per cent between 1948 and 1990, considerably faster than anything experienced to date. Output also expanded at a higher rate than ever before in rich and poor countries alike. In terms of the breadth and depth of economic progress, writes Dani Rodrik (2011: 71) 'the Bretton Woods regime eclipsed all previous periods, including the gold standard and the era of free trade during the nineteenth century. If there ever was a golden era of globalization, this was it.' GATT policies did not aim at free trade in all areas. Rather, general economic growth facilitated globalization because it helped national governments to manage the distributional impacts of international trade. In this as in other respects the parallelism between the early stages of globalization in the post-war period and the early stages of European integration is remarkable. Also in the European case the unprecedented economic development of the two decades following the end of World War II made the idea of economic integration attractive, or at least plausible – rather than European integration, then still in its infancy, having produced economic prosperity (Majone 2009: 81–7). And as the objectives of the founding Treaty of Rome were rather limited – a customs union, with an unspecified common market as a distant goal – so GATT's purpose was not to maximize free trade, but to achieve the maximum amount of free trade compatible with national autonomy. Trade became free only where it posed little challenge to national preferences, institutions, or values. What were later viewed as derogations from the principles of free trade were in fact, in Rodrik's phrase 'instances of regime maintenance…Under GATT priorities rested solidly in the domestic policy agenda, and this produced both its success and its endless departures from the logic of free trade' (Rodrik 2011: 75–6). In the case of the EEC the principal derogation from the principle of market liberalization was, of course, the CAP, written into the Treaty of Rome at French insistence.

If we take the above definition of 'shallow' integration literally, then it appears that European integration was from the beginning of the deep, rather than the shallow, variety, see chapter 3. The Rome (EEC) Treaty was concerned with such behind-the-border matters as national monopolies, both public and private, the social-security regime for migrant workers, and equal treatment for male and female workers. As noted in previous chapters, some of these measures, *in primis* those concerned with the discipline of national monopolies and the principle of non-discrimination on the basis of nationality, were simply necessary preconditions of a European common market. A closer reading of the treaty reveals, however, that the opening of the national markets to economic actors from other member states was to be achieved without endangering the capacity of each member state to decide on the appropriate mix of regulatory and fiscal policies. Hence the importance attached to the Directive as a legislative instrument binding with regard to the result to be achieved but allowing member states to choose the means to achieve that result.

Part Two of the EEC Treaty, setting out the foundations of the Community, deals with the free movement of goods, persons, services and capital, as well as with agriculture. However, attention has been called to the fact that the free movement of goods is treated separately from the other three economic freedoms: Articles 38–47 of Title II on agriculture separate Title I on free movement of goods from Title III on the free movement of the other factors. This separate treatment of the economic freedoms, together with the modest goals concerning the free movement of capital, and with the early VAT Directives, which acknowledged the full autonomy of the member states in setting the rates of the Value Added Tax, lead to the conclusion that the drive to a common market consisted in the removal of obstacles *at the border* to goods, services, and people from other member states, and not in a general reconfiguration of national regulatory and taxation norms (Menéndez 2013: 17). It may also be pointed out that it was the ECJ in the *Cassis de Dijon* decision of 1979 that moved from the principle of non-discrimination to that of non-impediment in its definition of non-tariff barriers. The broader principle made all national rules vulnerable to be challenged as violations of European economic liberties, especially after the principle was applied not only to the movements of goods but also to the movement of capital and freedom of establishment (Fritz Scharpf, personal communication).

The coming into force of the TEU and the creation of the WTO – the latter superseding and incorporating not only GATT but also the other agreements and protocols that had been negotiated in the Uruguay Round and in earlier negotiations – ushered in quite a different understanding of both European integration and globalization. Together with the onset of financial globalization in the early 1990s, 'the WTO marks the pursuit of a new kind of globalization that reversed the Bretton Woods priorities: hyper-globalization...The WTO envisaged both a significant ramping up of ambitions with respect to economic globalization and a dramatic rebalancing of nation states' domestic and international responsibilities' (Rodrik 2011: 76–7). The WTO is unique among international organizations both in the extent of the legally binding obligations on its members and in the enforcement mechanisms built into its system for resolving disputes. As we saw in chapter 3, the new dispute-settlement process is a striking contrast to the early days of the GATT, when the 'working parties' set up to report on disputes between member states were really a forum for encouraging negotiation, not a third-party investigation for the purpose of coming to objective conclusions on the merits of the case. If evading the trade regime's judicial verdict had been child's play under the GATT, under the new rules this has become almost impossible. This critically important feature of the new regime colours virtually everything that occurs in the WTO context.

A good example of the effectiveness of the new system is the *Beef Hormones* controversy, which has involved the EU and WTO in a long dispute concerning the appropriate use of the PP in risk regulation. As was mentioned in chapter 3, the WTO Appellate Body ruled that the

EU's prohibition of hormone-treated beef violated international trade rules because it was not based on scientific risk assessment – implying that something as poorly defined as the PP may be too easily misused for protectionist purposes. An EU moratorium on genetically modified products was also successfully challenged on grounds similar to *Beef Hormones*. US fuel emission standards; a US ban on shrimp caught without using turtle-excluder devices; patent rules on pharmaceuticals and agricultural chemical products in India; credit subsidies for the aircraft industry in Brazil: these and other national policies were found to be inconsistent with WTO rules. As these examples suggest, under the 'deep' version of global integration, the distinction between domestic and international trade policy tends to disappear since any discretionary use of domestic regulations can be construed as posing an impediment to international trade. The effectiveness of the new system of rules does, however, raise some troubling questions: How can we ensure that the rules of the WTO are designed and implemented to benefit all rather than the few? What happens when different countries desire or need different rules? Can any model of deep integration prove sustainable when democratic politics remain organized along national lines? (Rodrik 2011: 83).

The second and third questions raised by the Harvard economist are particularly relevant in the European context. The problems raised by the harmonization bias and the traditional one-size-fits-all approach of the EC/EU have been discussed in chapter 1 and elsewhere in the present book. The third question may be restated in the following form: Can a federalized and depoliticized monetary union prove sustainable when democratic politics remain organized along national lines? Apparently such a doubt never crossed the minds of the architects of monetary union, but as the crisis of the euro zone deepens it can no longer be dismissed. In chapter 6 I mentioned the strict regime of regulation and control of national budgetary and economic policymaking established in 2012 by the Stability Treaty. The aim of the new regime is to ensure that the members of the euro zone fulfil three main duties: to achieve a balanced budget; to avoid an excessive government deficit; and to prevent or correct macroeconomic imbalances – the latter duty being in fact a general obligation of all member states, since it concerns general economic policy rather than monetary and fiscal policy.

The new Treaty states that the budget of all signatories of the document must be balanced or in surplus. The balanced-budget rule is considered so central that it is to be set in a binding and permanent national law, preferably of a constitutional character. Countries that do not have a balanced budget adopt an adjustment plan setting out what needs to be done each year in a very exacting way. In such a case national governments move into a regime where their budgetary planning is co-managed by the EU institutions. Also the traditional role of the national parliaments is significantly constrained by the new regime In other words, this process of 'co-management' of the national economies goes to the structure and rationale of a state's fiscal and welfare systems. It represents an unprecedented interference with national sovereignty, at a moment when popular hostility towards the EU and its institutions has reached an intensity never experienced before. To quote Damian Chalmers (2012: 693) again, the final outcome may well be that '[a] zone of influence dominated by the Commission and ECOFIN is established, with political conflicts taking place within these, but the atrophying of local democracy leads to a hollowing out of domestic processes so that these become little more than administrative containers'.

Indeed, tight constraints on national budgetary autonomy have been introduced, not only by the new Stability Treaty but also by the so-called Six-Pack Regulations. Some of these regulations have tightened the Excessive Deficit Procedures of the Stability Treaty by introducing stringent European supervision and quasi-automatic sanctioning mecha-nisms in case of non-compliance. A new Excessive Imbalances Procedures will also allow the Commission to control a wide range of national eco-nomic and social choices. Instead of using the crisis of the euro zone as an occasion to re-examine the political and economic assumptions of mone-tary union, European policymakers have continued to ignore the risks inherent in a one-size-fits-all monetary policy, finding it more convenient to blame the crisis on national policy failures. In effect, writes Fritz Scharpf (2012: 24) 'they seem to have convinced themselves that democratically accountable national governments and parliaments simply cannot be trusted to adopt and implement the kind of policies that would make the euro work'.

The trilemma of hyper-integration

Students of international relations point out that greater interdepend-ence among nations may improve the quality of policymaking by, among other things, making national leaders more aware of the international impacts of their decisions, more willing to engage in international cooperation, and more sensitive to international comparisons. Another indirect benefit of greater economic integration is the added incentive to make the political and bureaucratic systems of trading nations more open and accountable, as well as more efficient. Robert Keohane and co-authors (2009) add that multilateralism may enhance the quality of democratic practices by favouring the use of relevant economic and scientific evidence in public deliberation, facilitating minority representation, and by making capture by interest groups more difficult. Such benign views of economic integration, like traditional views of international cooperation and policy coordination, tend to emphasize potential benefits while ignoring undesirable consequences, see chapter 4.

An important result of international economics known as the Mundell-Fleming Theorem or, more informally, the 'open-economy trilemma', has inspired a more realistic, and analytically more satisfactory, approach to the study of the relations between economic integration and democracy. According to the Mundell-Fleming Theorem, countries cannot simultaneously maintain an independent monetary policy, capital mobility, and fixed exchange rates. If a government chooses fixed exchange rates and capital mobility it has to give up monetary autonomy. If it chooses monetary autonomy and capital mobility it has to go with floating exchange rates. Finally, if it wishes to combine fixed exchange rates with monetary autonomy it has to limit capital mobility. In a paper published in 2000, Rodrik argued that the open-economy trilemma can be extended to what he called the political trilemma of the world economy. The elements of Rodrik's political trilemma, in its more recent (2011) version, are: hyper-globalization, the nation state, and democratic politics. The claim is that it is possible to have at most two of these things, as in the standard trilemma of international economics. If we want deep globalization ('hyper-globalization'), we have to go either with the nation state, in which case the domain of democratic politics will have to be significantly restricted, or else with democratic politics. In the latter case we would have to give up the nation state in favour of global federalism. If we want democratic legitimacy we have to choose between the nation state and deep globalization. Finally, if we wish to keep the nation state, we have to choose between democratic legitimacy at home and deep globalization internationally.

Democratic politics would not necessarily shrink under global federalism as long as economic power and political power remain aligned, meaning that all important political and policy issues would have to be treated at the global level. Unfortunately, a world government is not in the domain of the politically possible, now or in the foreseeable future.

Hence, the price of maintaining national sovereignty while markets become international is that politics has to be exercised over a much narrower range of issues. In order to appear attractive to international markets national regulations and tax policies would have to be harmonized according to international standards, or else structured so as to pose the least amount of hindrance to international economic integration. The only services provided by governments would be those that reinforce the smooth functioning of international markets (Rodrik 2011: 201–6). Naturally, economic integration on a global scale has not yet proceeded as far as is implied by the trilemma of the world economy. For example, some radical critics of globalization claim that under WTO rules a government cannot protect from import competition those domestic industries that have to bear the costs of environmental or other social regulations not applied by other countries. This is not quite true, however. As Roessler (1996) has convincingly argued, WTO rules do permit member states to take a domestic regulatory measure raising the cost of production in combination with subsidies or tariffs that maintain the competitive position of the domestic producers who have to bear these costs. The only restriction is that if the compensatory measures adversely affect the interests of other WTO members, procedures designed to remove the adverse effects of those measures on third countries must be observed. A clear demonstration of the autonomy of national policymakers in politically sensitive matters is provided by the WTO Agreement on SPS Measures, see chapter 3. Under this agreement, it will be recalled, each signatory has the right to set its own standards in the health field. This presumption of national autonomy can be challenged only by showing that a measure lacks a scientific justification. If a health measure has a scientific basis there is little other countries can do to oppose it. The combination of rigid rules with flexible safeguards has permitted the liberalization of international trade to proceed so far without any domestic policy harmonization. This subtle compromise, according to Roessler, makes possible the coexistence of the two apparently opposing principles of domestic policy autonomy and the globalization of trade. Still, Rodrik has identified a very important trend in economic integration, the effects of which are today more clearly visible at the regional, European, level than at the global level.

Before the onset of the euro crisis it could be argued, and it has been argued, that it was possible to integrate national economies while preserving (perhaps even enhancing) the quality of democratic processes at national level. This possibility was allegedly demonstrated by the EU, which has gone further on the road of deep integration than any other group of nation states without making it necessary to surrender either national sovereignty or democracy. But recent attempts to find permanent solutions to the current crisis show how difficult it is to reconcile democratic practice with hyper-integration – that is to say, monetary union, banking union, and the 'co-management' of the economies of debtor countries, to the point of affecting the structure and rationale of a state's fiscal and welfare system. As pointed out in chapter 6, moreover, the legitimacy problem cannot be reduced to the question of democratic legitimacy. For reasons discussed there, in the EU the accountability deficit was always at least as serious as the democratic deficit. The problem of establishing an effective system of accountability, while perhaps less daunting than the elimination of the democratic deficit or averting a possible democratic default, has become more urgent since the launching of EMU, see the following section. Accountability involves two judgements: evaluating the outcome of a decision, and/or the quality of the decision-making process, in terms of a given set of standards; and imposing appropriate sanctions in case the decision-makers did not fulfil their responsibilities under those standards. In our case, neither the European institutions nor the national governments are prepared to accept their share of responsibility for the present predicament. It is much easier to shift the blame onto small countries like Greece or Cyprus, and to insist on a rapid and continuous reduction of total public-sector debts, on European supervision of national budgeting processes, and on greater harmonization of fiscal and social policy. The truth, however, is that all the member states are responsible for the present situation. As we saw in the preceding chapter, this collective responsibility has been clearly established by the director general of the EU's statistical office when he recently acknowledged that doubts about the reliability of the information provided by Athens had become a near certainty already by 2003. For this reason, it will be recalled, Eurostat had asked for more powers to control the way the data were produced, but the member states rejected the Commission proposal that the competences of Eurostat be expanded to make possible a serious quality control of national data.

In conclusion, Rodrik is right when he argues that the EU's own dilemma is no different from that facing the world economy as a whole. Economic integration, if it is sufficiently deep, requires erecting an extensive supranational governance structure to support it, but the governance gaps in the EU have become quite obvious during the euro crisis. Thus, either the EU is prepared to 'bite the political bullet' and start moving towards political union, or resign itself to a more limited economic union. As we saw in chapter 7, the advocates of 'more Europe' do not even consider the possibility of rolling back the present level of economic integration, and hence see the sovereign-debt crisis of the euro zone as a unique opportunity to complete with a political union the process started with monetary union. They invite us to 'look beyond the national state', to use the words of the German finance minister, Wolfgang Schaeuble. Indeed, some eager supporters of political integration go as far as suggesting that the predictable problems of monetary union without political union were anticipated and even intended by the fathers of monetary union, as a way of forcing national governments to move towards closer political integration. In reality, perceptive observers of the European scene have pointed out that the euro crisis has favoured the rise of a very peculiar type of 'cooperation', overwhelmingly inter-governmental rather than supranational and very much dependent on half-hearted German leadership. The result is that the political integration of Europe, in the sense of a voluntary transfer of sovereignty from the national to the supranational level, has never seemed as remote as at present. The disappointments and hardships created by the euro crisis are an important but not the only reason for this result. Other reasons are the steady expansion of the geographical boundaries of the Union, with the corresponding increase in socioeconomic and political diversity, as discussed in previous chapters; and the growing concern of the older member states about the creeping loss of national sovereignty.

Thus in June 2009 the German Constitutional Court ruled that before the Lisbon Treaty could be ratified a new law would have to be passed in Berlin stipulating a far greater role for the national parliament and the upper legislative chamber in decision-making at EU level. According to the members of the highest German court primary responsibility for the integration process lies with the national legislatures – not with the EP, which is said to suffer from a 'structural democratic deficit'. Because of the persistent problem of democratic legitimacy at the European level, the judges concluded that European integration must not be allowed to undermine the democratic system of the member states. The decision of the Constitutional Court was greeted enthusiastically by all political parties represented in the Bundestag and, perhaps more surprisingly, also by many East Europeans. German commentators interpreted the reaction of the new member states as expressing their hope that in the future the German chancellor would no longer be able to tell them how they should decide on European issues. For years Germany has been considered by her Eastern neighbours as a surcharged engine of integration pushing them to surrender parts of the national sovereignty they had just recovered.

The accountability problem after monetary union

As noted above and in chapter 6, the EU's 'accountability deficit' is at least as serious as the 'structural democratic deficit' criticized by the German Constitutional Court. Monetary union has further aggravated this deficit in two important respects. First, as we know from chapter 2 and from the evidence presented in later chapters, the evaluative criteria traditionally used in the EU emphasize process, including deepening integration and institution building, rather than concrete results. Monetary union is so significant from the point of view of accountability precisely because the outcomes of decisions taken by the monetary authorities are much more immediate and visible than the consequences of most policy decisions taken in earlier stages of the integration process. Unlike decisions taken in Brussels, those taken in Frankfurt by the ECB are widely advertised, and their consequences have a direct impact on the welfare of all inhabitants of the euro zone, indeed of the entire EU. Furthermore, since the beginning of the crisis of monetary union everybody realizes that European integration entails costs as well as benefits, and that a positive net balance of benefits over costs can no longer be taken for granted. This new awareness, I argued in chapter 6, is likely to generate a much stronger demand for accountability by results – precisely what is foreign to the political culture of total optimism of EU leaders. Once results become clearly visible, the normative consequences of a failure to satisfy promises or to meet expectations may be quite serious. This is particularly true in the case of new institutions and new policies. Recall Martin Lipset's warning: 'After a new social structure is established, if the new system is unable to sustain the expectations of major groups (on the ground of "effectiveness") for a long enough period to develop legitimacy upon the new basis, a new crisis may develop' (Lipset 1963: 65). The general notion of legitimacy involves the capacity of a political system to engender and maintain the belief that its institutions are capable of resolving the major problems facing society. It is precisely the connection between effectiveness, legitimacy, and systemic stability that makes so worrisome the unsatisfactory economic performance of the last decades, and especially the deep crisis of the euro zone.

A second, even more important, reason why monetary union has aggravated the already serious accountability problem of the EU is the fact that responsibility for decisions on monetary policy is not shared between the national governments and the European institutions, as in the other areas of EU policymaking. In principle, responsibility for such decisions rests exclusively with the ECB, which is not only politically independent but also democratically unaccountable. As we saw in chapter 5, the ECB – unlike, say, the US Federal Reserve which is placed within a political structure where Congress, the President, and the Treasury supply all the necessary political counterweights – is free (indeed, is supposed) to operate in a political vacuum: the parliaments and governments of the members of the euro zone have lost control over monetary policy, while the EP has no authority in this area. Moreover, the ECB enjoys not only 'instrument independence' but also 'goal independence'. When a central bank enjoys only instrument independence, it is up to the government to fix the target – say, the politically acceptable level of inflation – leaving then the central bank free to decide how best to achieve the target. In the case of goal independence, the discretionary power of the central banker is much larger. The idea that central bankers, or other economic experts, may know what rate of inflation is in the long-run interest of a country (and, *a fortiori*, of a group of countries at very different levels of socioeconomic developments such as the EU) is indeed extraordinary. Politicians and elected policymakers, rather than experts, can be expected to be sensitive to the public's preferred balance of inflation and unemployment. If the public wants to trade some unemployment for a somewhat higher rate of inflation, it can make this preference known by electing candidates who stand for such a policy; but no such possibility is given to the citizens of the euro zone or to their political representatives. The conclusion drawn in chapter 6 was that the decision to pursue monetary integration in the absence of agreement, not only on political union but even on exchange-rate policy and other crucial institutional and policy issues, was doomed to produce a level of institutional and policy insularity that would be simply unacceptable in a democratic state. While in other policy areas the EU is to some extent accountable to its citizens – indirectly through the national representatives in the Council of Ministers and more directly, at least in theory, through the EP – democratic accountability is almost totally absent in the critically important area of monetary policy. Here we are facing no longer a deficit of accountability but rather a total absence of it.

In his recent paper mentioned above, Fritz Scharpf has produced one of the most perceptive analyses of this striking consequence of monetary union and the euro crisis. He points out that while in the past the moderating influence of national governments on EU legislation, and their continuing accountability for its implementation, kept the democratic and accountability deficits of the Union within more or less acceptable limits, in the present euro crisis 'the shield of legitimacy intermediation has been pushed aside as citizens are directly confronted with the massive impact of European policies – and with their manifest lack of democratic legitimacy' (Scharpf 2012: 19). At the national level, the independence of central banks and other non-majoritarian institutions is supported, and can be modified if necessary, by democratically legitimated governments and parliaments. Even the legitimacy of judicial review depends in the final analysis on the embeddedness of the courts in a well-defined political and social context. As was mentioned in chapter 5, even such an ancient and influential institution as the US Supreme Court is aware of how slender is the basis of its democratic legitimacy, and thus is reluctant to depart too far or for too long in its decisions from prevailing public opinion. In the EU, by contrast, both the ECJ and the ECB are almost completely removed from the influence of democratically accountable institutions, and do not need to bother about accountability to a non-existent European demos.

The result, Scharpf concludes, is that monetary union, a major step in European economic integration, at the same time has deprived democratic member states of the instruments of macroeconomic control over their national economies. Debtor states have completely lost fiscal autonomy, while the exercise of significant parts of their economic, social, and labour-market competences has been subjected to direct European controls:

> The Monetary Union, the euro crisis and the policies defending the euro have created an institutional constellation in which the control of democratic member states over their economic fate has been largely destroyed. Since the effective instruments have been removed, the loss cannot be compensated by ever more intense European controls of the remaining national options. Instead, effective macroeconomic control at the European level would require the capacities of a federal state with a large central budget, centralized capital taxation and social and employment policies – and with the capacity for democratically legitimated majoritarian policy-making.
>
> (Ibid.: 29)

Unfortunately, the days have long past when even responsible political leaders could use the slogan 'Europe must federate or perish'. As already mentioned, the prediction that the nation states of Europe would collapse, and the federalists' claim that it was impossible to reconstruct a democratic and prosperous Europe starting with the nation states had both been conclusively refuted by the late 1940s. Far from being a relic of the past, the nation state proved to be not only highly resilient, but also quite effective (Majone 2009: chapter 2). Of course, belief in the continued vitality of this epoch-making political invention of the old continent does not exclude the need of significant changes in organization and range of activities if the nation state is to meet the challenges of globalization. The EU is much more fragile than the nation states which compose it, and for this reason it will have to undergo more radical transformations if the very idea of European integration is to survive the present general crisis: not only the euro crisis, but also a crisis of legitimacy, of dysfunctional institutions, and of integration methods. What needs to be questioned, then, is the very nature and the aims of the integration process.

European integration: from collective good to 'club good'

As we saw in chapter 8, the cost of adhering to the principle of the basic equality and equal dignity of all the member states keeps growing as the membership expands and more and more competences are transferred to the European level. This is because without strong leadership and sufficient mutual trust it becomes increasingly difficult to overcome the limitations imposed by the logic of collective action. As Mancur Olson proved long ago, the incentive for group action diminishes as group size increases, so that larger groups are less able to act in their common interest than small ones: 'The larger the group, the farther it will fall short of providing an optimal amount of a collective good' (Olson 1971: 35). This tendency towards sub-optimality follows from the definition of a collective good as a good such that other members of a given group cannot be kept from consuming it once any individual in the group has provided it for himself. An individual member gets only part of the benefit of any expenditure he makes to obtain more of the collective good, hence he will discontinue his purchase of the collective good before the optimal amount for the group as a whole has been obtained. Moreover, the amounts of the collective good that a member of the group receives from other members will further reduce his incentive to provide more for the group at his own expense.

This sub-optimality, Olson points out, tends to be somewhat less serious in groups composed of members of greatly different size or interest in the collective good. But in this case there is a systematic tendency toward an unequal sharing of the burden of providing the good, as discussed in chapter 2. The member who would on its own provide the largest amount of that public good bears a disproportionate share of the burden of providing the good, while smaller members have less incentive to provide additional amounts of the same good. Hence the tendency for the 'exploitation' of the great by the small. Given the incentives to free-ride, behaviour that is consistent with the collective interest may depend on the availability of rewards or the application of sanctions. In fact, Olson found that participation in large voluntary organizations, such as trade unions or professional associations, depends less on the collective benefits these organizations provided for all their members, than on the individualized incentives – selective benefits or individualized sanctions – they provide. For the EU, however, it is increasingly difficult to provide selective incentives since its resources do not grow in proportion to its expanding membership and scope of competences. At the same time, narrow political limits make the use of strict sanctions extremely difficult, as shown by the refusal to apply the no-bail-out clause of the Maastricht Treaty in the case of members of the euro zone in serious financial difficulties, but also by the watering down of the SGP in 2005, see chapter 1. The use of strict sanctions can also be counterproductive, by increasing popular resentment against the EU while, at the same time, compromising the legitimacy of the national governments.

If neither the incentives nor the sanctions that make collective action possible are available, then one has to question the very existence of something that may be properly called a European collective good. So far this basic question has been evaded with the help of vague formulas such as 'ever closer union'. But as Edward Carr wisely put it, '[t]he conception of politics as an infinite process seems in the long run uncongenial or incomprehensible to the human mind' (1964: 89). Just as the development of a true European political identity has been made impossible by the absence of well-defined and stable geographical boundaries (Majone 2009: 64–7), so the absence of widely shared political, or even economic, goals has made the development of collective projects increasingly problematic. Thus monetary union, initially conceived as a collective good to be shared by all the member states of the EU, was quickly transformed into a 'club good' by the British and Danish *de jure* opt-outs and Sweden's *de facto* opt-out.

Let us recall some definitions given in chapter 3. A 'club good' is a collective good from whose benefits individuals may be (or may choose to be) excluded; an association established to provide an excludable public good is a 'club'. The same definitions apply if instead of individuals we consider independent states. Associations of independent states, such as alliances or leagues, are typically voluntary, and their members are exclusively entitled to enjoy certain benefits produced by the association. The club goods in question could be collective security, policy coordination, common technical standards – or a monetary union limited to a subset of members of the association. In these as in many other cases, countries unwilling or unable to share the costs are usually excluded from the benefits of inter-state cooperation in a particular project. The important point, in the present context, is that as an association of states expands, becoming more diverse in its preferences and its socioeconomic conditions, the cost of uniformity in the provision of collective goods can escalate dramatically. The economic theory of clubs predicts an increase in the number of voluntary associations to meet the increased demand for goods more precisely tailored to the different requirements of various subsets of more homogeneous states. Aggregate welfare is maximized when the variety in preferences is matched by a corresponding variety of institutional arrangements.

In chapter 3 we also noted that the theory of clubs provides a good conceptual foundation for the functional (rather than territorial) approach to international governance – an approach advocated by Mitrany in the 1940s and by Dahrendorf in the 1970s. A territorial union, to quote again Mitrany's words, 'would bind together some interests which are not of common concern to the group, while it would inevitably cut asunder some interests of common concern to the group and those outside it'. To avoid such 'twice-arbitrary surgery' it is necessary to proceed by 'binding together those interests which are common, where they are common, and to the extent to which they are common'. Thus the essential principle of a functional organization of international activities 'is that activities would be selected specifically and organized separately, each according to its nature, to the conditions under which it has to operate, and to the needs of the moment' (citations in Eilstrup-Sangiovanni 2006: 57–8). At the same time, Mitrany was sceptical about the advantages of political union. His main objection to schemes for continental unions was that the closer the union the more inevitably would it be dominated by the more powerful member. This point, which has hardly been considered by later writers on European integration, is directly linked to the discussion of Germany as a potential (if reluctant) hegemon, see chapter 8.

Thus the economic theory of clubs emphasizes the advantages of institutional pluralism, and implies that an efficient assignment of tasks between different levels of governance need not coincide with existing national boundaries: there may be significant externalities and a need for coordination between some, but not all, regions within a country or group of countries. For instance, the existence of transboundary externalities is often cited as a justification for EU-wide harmonization. The Commission has affirmed that where there is a potential for transboundary pollution there is often justification for the EU to act. This is far from being generally true. Thus for most environmental problems the EU is not an optimal regulatory area, being either too large or too small. In a number of cases – for example, the Mediterranean, the Baltic Sea, or the Rhine – the scope of the problem is regional rather than EU-wide, and is best tackled through regional arrangements tailored to the scope of the relevant environmental externality. Self-regulatory organizations encompassing only some states ('regional compacts', such as the Delaware River Basin Commission or the Appalachian Regional Commission) have been used in the US since the 1960s, and in a few cases even earlier. The central government is represented by a federal coordinator who sometimes is appointed jointly by the US President and by the governors of the states making up the particular inter-state compact (Derthick 1974). More recently, organizations including some US states and Canadian provinces have been created in order to control pollution in the Great Lakes region. By pooling their financial, technical, and administrative resources, these consortia are in a better position to deal effectively with their regulatory problems than each jurisdiction either acting alone or relying exclusively on centralized regulation which could not be closely tailored to their specific needs.

Again, the theory of clubs explains why a number of tasks which used to be assigned to central governments are today performed by private, increasingly transnational, organizations. Although there is a strong historical correlation between standardization and the emergence of the sovereign territorial state (Spruyt 1994), current views on standardization have changed radically as a result of the advance of globalization, the development of technology, and the growing variety and sophistication of technical standards. As far as a given community of users is concerned, standards are collective goods – in that they fulfil specific functions deemed desirable by the community that shares them – but this does not mean that they must be established by government fiat. A good standard must reflect the needs, preferences, and resources of the community of users, rather than some centrally defined vision of the 'common interest'. As Alessandra Casella (1996) has argued, the fact that in today's integrating world economy the relevant community of standards users need not be territorially defined, distinguishes the traditional approach from the contemporary understanding of standards as a special class of club goods. Moreover, as the complexity of a society increases, perhaps as the result of integration of previously separate markets, the number of clubs tends to increase as well. This is because greater diversity of needs and preferences makes it efficient to produce a broader range of club goods, such as product standards. The general implication of Casella's argument is that top-down harmonization may be desirable when the market is relatively small and homogeneous. In a large market, on the other hand, harmonization tends to be brought about by the recognition of similar demands or needs, rather than by a policy imposed from the top. Hence a multiplicity of club goods replaces policy harmonization. This conclusion is supported by empirical evidence. Already some years ago the OECD noticed that all industrialized countries tend to converge towards a greater emphasis on self-regulation and non-mandatory standards – that is, towards a plurality of standards and standard-setting organizations.

As noted in chapter 9, a Europe of clubs organized around functional tasks would not exclude the possibility of large projects supported by all the member states – as long as there is clear evidence (through referenda, supermajorities in national parliaments, etc.) of sufficient popular support. This is precisely the point Dahrendorf wished to emphasize. The Single Market project, for example, seems to enjoy broad support even in so-called Euro-sceptic countries. Hence, it would be a natural starting point for assessing the extent of popular support in favour of further movement in the direction of closer integration. Once decisions about the extent of integration are no longer taken *in camera* but are submitted to the decision of the voters, however, the provision of correct information – about the expected benefits and costs of new advances, and about successes and failures of past policies – becomes truly indispensable. Even in case of a project like the Single Market, for example, the general public should know that the promise of reaching that goal by

1992 is still far from being fulfilled, and should also be informed about the reasons for the delay.

The view of Europe as a 'club of clubs', far from being new, has deep roots in the history of the Old Continent. As several distinguished historians have argued, the European global dominance of the past was made possible not by centralization, but by fragmentation and by the competition stimulated by fragmentation:

> Europe's great good fortune lay in the fall of Rome and the weakness and division that ensued...The Roman dream of unity, authority, and order (the *Pax Romana*) remained, indeed has persisted to the present. After all, one has usually seen fragmentation as a great misfortune, as a recipe for conflict; it is no accident that [the] European union is seen today as a cure for the wars of yesterday. And yet, in those middle years between ancient and modern, fragmentation was the strongest brake on wilful, oppressive behaviour. Political rivalry and the right of exit made all the difference.
>
> (Landes 1998: 37–8)

In turn, political rivalry facilitated the commercial revolution of the Middle Ages by making it possible for the mercantile community to bypass, where necessary, the rules of this or that city or state, and creating 'a world of its own like an overlay on the convoluted, inconvenient mosaic of political units' (ibid.: 44). The Hansa, which has been viewed by some scholars as a major unifying force in Northern Europe, developed from being an association of merchants to a league of towns in the Baltic and the North Sea. One of the tasks of the league was to facilitate the exchange of information between merchants, but the Hansa was not merely an economic association. Like states, it waged wars, and on occasion it could make or break kings. In fact, the Hansa was an alternative to the sovereign state (Spruyt 1994: chapter 6).

The 'European miracle' made possible by a unique combination of competition and cooperation continued in later centuries. The states of early modern Europe were surrounded by actual or potential competitors. Hence the fairly rapid diffusion of policy and institutional innovations throughout the continent in the period preceding the full development of the nation state. In its state system, writes Eric Jones (1987: 115) 'Europe had a portfolio of competing and colluding polities whose spirit of competition was adapted to diffuse best practice'. But as the European nation states became more self-conscious they began to impede the movement of capital and people by closing their borders and enforcing cultural and legal homogeneity on their people. The long century of nationalism that followed was an aberration in European history, and the integration process that followed the end of World War II, was a healthy, indeed a necessary, reaction to the catastrophic consequences of nationalist ideology. In the early stages of the integration process it was not unreasonable to assume that the EC would evolve, sooner or later, into a politically integrated bloc, perhaps even into something like a federation. That assumption is no longer tenable in a Union of twenty-eight members at vastly different stages of socioeconomic development, with different geopolitical concerns, and correspondingly diverse policy priorities. As I pointed out some years ago (Majone 2009: 204–11), the mistake of integrationist leaders was to assume a unilinear development from the nation state to something fulfilling much the same functions, on a grander scale and allegedly more effectively. European history suggests that there is something unnatural in this approach, as far as our continent is concerned. European unity has never been the unity of empire or even of a large transnational federation, but a much subtler unity in diversity achieved through a unique mixture of competition, cooperation, and imitation. In this perspective contemporary European integration, as practised since the 1950s, has not gone far enough: what is needed today is something richer and at the same time more flexible than a simple linear extrapolation of the traditional nation state model.

BIBLIOGRAPHY

Alesina, A. and V. Grilli (1994) 'The European Central Bank: Reshaping Monetary Politics in Europe', in T. Persson and G. Tabellini (editors) *Monetary and Fiscal Policy*, Vol. 1, Cambridge, MA: The MIT Press, 247–78.

Alter, K. (2001) *Establishing the Supremacy of European Law*, Oxford and New York: Oxford University Press.

Amann, M. and U. Kloepfer (2011) 'Noch mehr Europa laesst das Grundgesetz kaum zu' ('Still more Europe is Hardly Allowed by Our Constitution'), interview of the President of the German Constitutional Court, *Frankfurter Allgemeine Zeitung*, 25 September 2011, 37–8.

Attali, J. (2011) 'The crisis is in Brussels, not just Athens', *International Herald Tribune*, 20 June 2011, 21.

Baake, P. and O. Perschau (1996) 'The Law and Policy of Competition in Germany', in G. Majone, *Regulating Europe*, London: Routledge, 131–56.

Bailer, S. and G. Schneider (2006) 'Nash versus Schelling? The Importance of Constraints in Legislative Bargaining', in R. Thompson, F. N. Stokman, C. H. Achen and T. Koenig (editors) *The European Union Decides*, Cambridge University Press, 153–77.

Balassa, B. (1961) *Theory of Economic Integration*, Homewood, IL: Irwin.

Baldwin, R. (1993) 'Comments on Bhagwati "Regionalism and Multilateralism: an Overview"', in J. De Melo and A. Panagariya (editors) *New Dimensions in Regional Integration*, Cambridge University Press, 54–6.

'Bankrott in Brussels' (2010) *Financial Times Deutschland*, 14 July 2010, 1.

Bardach, E (2006) 'Policy Dynamics', in M. Moran, M. Rein and R. Goodin (editors) *The Oxford Handbook of Public Policy*, Oxford University Press, 336–66.

Barker, E. (1958) *Reflections on Government*, New York: Oxford University Press.

Bartlett, R. (1993) *The Making of Europe*, London: Penguin Books.

Beck, U. (2009) 'This Economic Crisis Cries Out to be Transformed into the Founding of a New Europe', *The Guardian*, 13 April 2009.

   (2011) 'Europe's Crisis Is an Opportunity for Democracy', *The Guardian*, 28 November 2011.

Berger, R. (1997) *Government by Judiciary*, Indianapolis, IN: Liberty Fund.

Berman, H. J. (1983) *Law and Revolution*, Cambridge, MA.: Harvard University Press.

Beuve-Mèry, A. (2008) 'La strategie de Berlin en question', *Le Monde*, 16 March 2008.

Bhagwati, J. (1993) 'Regionalism and Multilateralism: an Overview', in J. De Melo and A. Panagariya (editors) *New Dimensions in Regional Integration*, Cambridge University Press, 22–50.

Bhagwati, J. N. and R. E. Hudec (editors) (1996) *Fair Trade and Harmonization*, Cambridge, MA: The MIT Press.

Blair, W. (2005) 'Full text: Blair's European speech' *BBC News/Politics/Full text: Blair's European Speech*, 23 June, 1–6, available at http://news.bbc.co.uk/1/hi/uk_politics/4122288.stm.

Bofinger, P. (2010) 'Dem Euro-Raum eine Chance' ('A chance for the euro zone'), *WirtschaftsWoche*, 22 May 2010, 40.

Bofinger, P. J., J. Habermas and Nida-Ruemelin (2012) 'Einspruch gegen die Fassandendemokratie' (Protest against a would-be democracy), *Frankfurter Allgemeine Zeitung*, 4 August 2012.

Brackmann, J. and J. Muenchrat (2011) 'Wer regiert Europa?' ('Who rules Europe?'), *Handelsblatt*, 17 February 2011.

Breton, A. (1996) *Competitive Governments*, Cambridge University Press.

Brewer, J. (1989) *The Sinews of Power*, London: Unwin Hyman.

Brittan, S. (1971) *Government and Market Economy*, London: The Institute of Economic Affairs, Hobart Paperback.

Brittan, S. (2011) 'Last Chance to Save the Euro', *Financial Times*, 16 December 2011.

Bryant, R. C. (1995) *International Coordination of National Stabilization Policies*, Washington, DC: The Brookings Institution.

Buchanan, J. M. (1965) 'An Economic Theory of Clubs', *Economica*, Vol. 32, No. 1, 1–14.

Buchanan, J. M. and G. Tullock (1962) *The Calculus of Consent*, Ann Arbor, MI: The University of Michigan Press.

Campi, A. (2004) *Nazione*, Bologna: Il Mulino.

Carr, E. H. (1964 [1939]) *The Twenty Years' Crisis, 1919–1939*, New York, NY: Harper & Row.

Casella, A. (1996) 'Free Trade and Evolving Standards', in J. N. Bhagwati and R. E. Hudec (editors) *Fair Trade and Harmonization*, Vol. 1. Cambridge, MA: The MIT Press, 119–56.

Castle, S. (2007) 'EU Leaders Want to Try Again with Subsidies – Wealthy Landowners Stand to Lose Most From Suggested Cuts', *International Herald Tribune*, 8 November 2007, 1 (continued on 8).

Castle S. and S. Erlanger (2011) 'At the End of the Euro Tunnel', *International Herald Tribune*, 3 October 2011.

Chalmers, D. (2012) 'The European Redistributive State and a European Law of Struggle', *European Law Journal*, Vol. 18, No. 5, 667–93.

Choper, J. H. (1983) *Judicial Review and the National Political Process*, Chicago, IL: The University of Chicago Press.

Christiansen, T., K. E. Joergensen and A. Wiener (1999) 'The Social Construction of Europe', *Journal of European Public Policy* special issue, Vol. 6, No. 4, 528–44.

Coase, R. H. (1988) *The Firm, The Market and the Law*, Chicago, IL: The University of Chicago Press.

Commission of the European Communities (1985) *Completing the Internal Market: White Paper from the Commission to the European Council*, COM (85) 310 final.

   (1990) *One Market, One Money*, (European Economy 44).

   (2000) *Communication from the Commission on the Precautionary Principle*, COM (2000) 1.

   (2001) *European Governance*, Luxembourg: Office for Official Publications of the European Communities.

Communication from the Commission to the Constitutional Convention (2002) *A Project for the European Union*, Brussels, CONV. 636/02.

Communication from the Commission to the European Parliament, the Council, the Economic and Social Committee and the Committee of the Regions (2010) 'Towards a Single Market Act For a Highly Competitive Social Market Economy: 50 Proposals for improving our work, business and exchanges with one another', doc. COM (2010) 608, 7 October 2010.

Craig, P. and G. de Búrca (2003) *EU Law: Text, Cases, and Materials* (3rd edition) Oxford University Press.

Curtin, D. (1993) 'The Constitutional Structure of the Union: A Europe of Bits and Pieces', *Common Market Law Review*, Vol. 30, No. 1, 17–69.

Curtin, D., H. Hofmann and J. Mendes (2013) 'Constitutionalising EU Executive Rule-Making Procedures: A Research Agenda', *European Law Journal*, Vol. 19, No. 1, 1–21.

Dahl, R. A. (1972) *Democracy in the US*, Chicago, IL: Rand McNally.

Dahrendorf, R. (1973) *Plaedoyer Fuer die Europaische Union* ('Plea for the European Union'), Munich: R. Piper & Co.

Dani, M. (2009) 'Constitutionalism and Dissonances: Has Europe Paid Off Its debt to Functionalism?', *European Law Journal*, Vol. 15, No. 3, 324–50.

Dashwood, A. (1983) 'Hastening Slowly: The Communities' Path towards Harmonization', in H. Wallace, W. Wallace and C. Webb, (editors) *Policy-Making in the European Community* (2nd edition) Chichester: Wiley, 177–208.

   (1996) 'The Limits of European Community Powers', *European Law Review*, Vol. 21, No. 1, 113–28.

Davies, N. (1982) *God's Playground – A History of Poland*, New York, NY: Columbia University Press.

De Grauwe, P. (2004) 'Challenges for Monetary Policy in Euroland', in F. Torres, A. Verdun, C. Zilioli and H. Zimmerman (editors) *Governing EMU*, Florence: European University Institute, 363–88.

(2007) *Economics of Monetary Union* (7th edition) Oxford University Press.

De Haan, J. (1997) 'The European Central Bank: Independence, Accountability and Strategy: A Review', *Public Choice*, 93, 395–426.

Dehio. L. (1962) *The Precarious Balance*, New York, NY: Vintage Books.

Dehousse, R. (2011) 'Conclusion: Obstinate or Obsolete?', in R. Dehousse (editor) *The 'Community Method' – Obstinate or Obsolete?* London: Palgrave MacMillan, 199–204.

Delors Report (1989), Committee on the Study of Economic and Monetary Union (the Delors Committee) (1989) *Report on Economic and Monetary Union in the European Community*, Luxembourg: Office for Official Publications of the European Communities.

Derthick, M. (1974) *Between State and Nation: Regional Organizations of the US*, Washington DC: The Brookings Institution.

De Schoutheete, Ph. (2006) 'The European Council' in J. Peterson and M. Shackleton (editors) *The Institutions of the European Union* (2nd edition) Oxford University Press, 37–59.

De Witte, B. (1999) 'Direct Effect, Supremacy, and the Nature of the Legal Order', in P. Craig and G. De Búrca (editors) *The Evolution of EU Law*, Oxford University Press, 177–213.

Dixit, A. K. (1996) *The Making Of Economic Policy*, Cambridge, MA: The MIT Press.

Dixit, A. K. and Nalebuff, B. J. (1991) *Thinking Strategically*, New York, NY: W.W. Norton.

Dougan, M. (2006) '"And Some Fell on Stony Ground..." – A Review of G. Majone's Dilemmas of European Integration', *European Law Review*, Vol. 31, No. 4, 865–72.

Downs, A. (1957) *An Economic Theory Of Democracy*, New York, NY: Harper & Row.

Easterbrook, F. H. and D. R. Fischel (1991) *The Economic Structure of Corporate Law*, Cambridge, MA: Harvard University Press.

Eichengreen, J. and J. A. Frieden (1995) 'The Political Economy of European Monetary Unification: An Analytical Introduction', in J. A. Frieden and D. A. Lake (editors) *International Political Economy* (3rd edition) London: Routledge, 267–81.

Eilstrup-Sangiovanni, M. (2006) *Debates on European Integration*, New York, NY: Palgrave.

Ely, J. H. (1980) *Democracy and Distrust*, Cambridge, MA: Harvard University Press.

Epstein, D. and S. O'Halloran (1999) *Delegating Powers*, Cambridge University Press.

Esping-Andersen, G. (1990) *The Three Worlds of Welfare Capitalism*, Cambridge: Polity Press.

Feldstein, M. (1992) 'The Case against EMU', *The Economist*, 13 June 1992, 19–22.

Fischer, J. (2000) 'Vom Staatenverbund zur Foederation – Gedanken ueber die Finalitaet der europaeischen Integration' ('From Confederation to Federation: Thoughts on the Finality of European Integration'), speech given at the Humboldt University, Berlin, 12 May 2000.

Friedman, A. (2000) 'The New President of the European Commission', *The Wall Street Journal*, 30 April 2000.

Friedrich, H. (2002) 'Fragen an den Praesident der Europaeischen Kommission, Romano Prodi', *Frankfurter Allgemeine Zeitung*, 7 March 2002.

Furubotn, E. G. and R. Richter (2000) *Institutions and Economic Theory*, Ann Arbor, MI: The University of Michigan Press.

Galanter, M. (1981) 'Justice in Many Rooms: Courts, Private Ordering, and Indigenous Law', *Journal of Legal Pluralism*, No. 19, 1–47.

Gerards, J. (2011) 'Pluralism, Deference and the Margin of Appreciation Doctrine', *European Law Journal*, Vol. 17, No. 1, 80–120.

Geyer, C. (2012) 'Anatomie einer Hintergehung' ('Anatomy of a Deception'), *Frankfurter Allgemeine Zeitung*, 21 June 2012, 29.

Gordon, P. H. and J. Shapiro (2004) *Allies At War*, New York, NY: McGraw-Hill.

Gormley, L. and J. de Haan (1996) 'The Democratic Deficit of the European Central Bank', *European Law Review*, Vol. 21, 95–111.

Grant, R. W. and R. O. Keohane (2005) 'Accountability and Abuses of Power in World Politics', *American Political Science Review*, Vol. 99, No. 1, 29–43.

Guéhenno, J. M. (1993) *La fin de la démocratie*, Paris: Flammarion.

Haas, B. (1958) *The Unity of Europe: Political, Social and Economic Forces 1950–1957*, Stanford, CA: Stanford University Press.

Habermas, J. (2005) 'Europa ist uns ueber die Koepfe hinweggerollt' ('Europe has Moved Away Over Our Heads'). *Suddeutsche Zeitung*, 9 June 2005.

(2012) 'Bringing the Integration of Citizens into Line with the Integration of States', *European Law Journal*, Vol. 18, Issue 4, 485–8.

Hartz, L. (1948) *Economic Policy and Democratic Thought*, Cambridge, MA: Harvard University Press.

Hatzopoulos, V. (2007) 'Why the Open Method of Coordination Is Bad For You: A Letter to the EU', *European Law Journal*, Vol. 13, No. 3, 309–42.

Hayek, F. A. (1948) [1939]) 'The Economic Conditions of Interstate Federalism', in F. A. Hayek, *Individualism and Economic Order*, Chicago, IL: University of Chicago Press, 255–72.

(1960) *The Constitution of Liberty*, London: Routledge and Kegan Paul.

(1984 [1978]) 'Competition as a Discovery Procedure', in C. Nishiyama and K. R. Leube (editors) *The Essence of Hayek*, Stanford, CA: Hoover Institution Press, 254–65.

Hayes-Renshaw, F. (2002) 'The Council of Ministers', in J. Peterson and M. Shackleton (editors) *The Institutions of the European Union*, Oxford University Press, 47–70.

Hayes-Renshaw, F. and H. Wallace (1997) *The Council of Ministers*, London: Macmillan Press.

Heipertz, M. and Verdun, A. (2010) *Ruling Europe: The Politics of the Stability and Growth Pact*, Cambridge University Press.

Henning, C. R. (2000) 'US-EU Relations after the Inception of the Monetary Union: Cooperation or Rivalry?', in C. R. Henning and P. C. Padoan (editors) *Transatlantic Perspectives on the Euro*, Washington DC: The Brookings Institution, 5–63.

Hirschman, A. O. (1981) 'Three Uses of Political Economy in Analyzing European Integration', in A. O. Hirschman, *Essays in Trespassing*, Cambridge University Press, 266–84.

Hoffmann, S. (2000) 'Towards a Common Foreign and Security Policy?', *Journal of Common Market Studies*, Vol. 38, No. 2, 189–98.

Holmberg, A. (1994) 'The Holy European Empire', in E. Loennroth, K. Molin, R. Bjoerk (editors) *Conceptions of National History*, Berlin: Walter de Gruyter, 98–113.

Howarth, D. and P. Loedel (2004) 'The ECB and the Stability Pact: Policeman and Judge?', *Journal of European Public Policy*, Vol. 11, No. 5, 832–53.

Ipsen, H. P. (1972) *Europäisches Gemeinschaftsrecht*, Tuebingen: J. C. B. Mohr/ Paul Siebeck.

Ipsos-Publicis (2013) 'Europeans and the End of the Crisis', 30 May 2013, available at www.ipsos-mori.com/newsevents/blogs/thepoliticswire/1406/ The-End-of-the-Crisis-The-Mood-in-Europe.aspx.

Issing, O. (2008) *The Birth of the Euro*, Cambridge University Press.

Jackson, J. H. (1999) *The World Trading System*, Cambridge, MA: The MIT Press.

Joerges, C. and F. Roedl (2009) 'Informal Politics, Formalized Law and the "Social Deficit" of European Integration: Reflections after the Judgments of the ECJ in Viking and Laval', *European Law Journal*, Vol. 15, No. 1, 1–19.

Johnson, H. G. (1972) *Aspects of the Theory of Tariffs*, Cambridge, MA: Harvard University Press.

Jones, E. L. (1987) *The European Miracle: Environments, Economies and Geopolitics in the History of Europe and Asia* (2nd edition) New York, NY: Cambridge University Press.

Judt, T (2010) *Postwar*, London: Vintage Books.

Jung, A., A. Mahler, C. Pauly, C. Reiermann, M. Sauge (2010) 'Der augehoelte Euro' ('The diminished euro'), *Der Spiegel*, 17 May 2010, 72–6.

Kahler, M. (1995) *International Institutions and the Political Economy of Integration*, Washington DC: The Brookings Institution.

Keohane, R. O. (1984) *After Hegemony*, Princeton, NJ: Princeton University Press.

Keohane, R. O., S. Macedo and A. Moravcsik (2009) 'Democracy-Enhancing Multilateralism', *International Organization*, Vol. 63 (Winter 2009) 1–31.

Kindleberger, C. P. (1973) *The World in Depression*, Berkeley and Los Angeles: University of California Press.

Knudsen, J. S. (2005) 'Is the Single European Market an Illusion? Obstacles to Reform of EU Takeover Regulation', *European Law Journal*, Vol. 11, No. 4, 507–24.

Kojève, A. (1945) 'Outline of a Doctrine of French policy', available at www. hoover.org/publications/policy-review/article/7750.

Kostoris Padoa Schioppa, F. (2007) 'Dominant Losers: A Comment on the Services Directive from an Economic Perspective', *Journal of European Public Policy*, Vol. 14, No. 5, 735–42.

Kumm, M. (2005) 'The Jurisprudence of Constitutional Conflict: Constitutional Supremacy in Europe before and after the Constitutional Treaty', *European Law Journal*, Vol. 11, No. 3, 262–307.

Ladeur, K.-H. (2008) 'We, the European People...Relâche?', *European Law Journal*, Vol. 14, No. 2, 147–67.

Lakoff, G. and M. Johnson (1980) *Metaphors We Live By*, Chicago, IL: The University of Chicago Press.

Lammer, N. (2012) 'Da hapert's an allem', ('There are blocks everywhere'), *Die Welt am Sonntag*, 14 October 2012, 13.

Landes, D. S. (1998) *The Wealth and Poverty of Nations*, New York, NY: W.W. Norton.

Lawson, N. (2012) 'The Prime Minister Says He Wants a Stable Eurozone: It is Complete Nonsense', *The Mail on Sunday*, 20 May 2012, 7.

Le Monde – Éditorial (2006) 'Test européen', 15 February 2006, 2.

Lenaerts, K. (1990) 'Constitutionalism and the Many Faces of Federalism', *American Journal of Comparative Law*, Vol. 38, 205–63.

Lévy, M. (2012) 'Deutschland sollte uns Vorbild sein' ('Germany should be our model'), *Sueddeutsche Zeitung*, 26 September 2012, 20.

Lewis, J. (2002) 'National Interests: Coreper', in J. Peterson and M. Shackleton (editors) *The Institutions of the European Union*, Oxford University Press, 277–98.

Lipset, S. M. (1963) *Political Man*, Garden City, NY: Anchor Books.

Maddox, G. (1989) 'Constitution', in T. Ball, J. Farr and R. L. Hanson (editors) *Political Innovation and Conceptual Change*, Cambridge University Press, 50–67.

Magnette, P. (2001) 'Appointing and Censuring the Commission: The Adaptation of Parliamentary Institutions to the Community Context', *European Law Journal*, Vol. 7, No. 3, 292–310.

Mair, P. (2007) 'Political Opposition and the European Union', *Government and Opposition*, Vol. 42, No. 1, 1–17.

Majone, G. (1989) *Evidence, Argument & Persuasion in the Policy Process*, New Haven, CT: Yale University Press.

(1996) *Regulating Europe*, London: Routledge.

(2005) *Dilemmas of European Integration*, Oxford University Press.

(2009) *Europe as the Would-be World Power: The EU at Fifty*, Cambridge: Cambridge University Press.

Marsh, D. (1992) *The Bundesbank: The Bank that Rules Europe*, London: Heinemann.

(2010) *The Euro*, New Haven, CT and London: Yale University Press.

Martens, M. (2009) 'Operation Maastricht', *Frankfurter Allgemeine Zeitung* 16 November 2009, 10.

Mashaw, J. L., R. A. Merrill and P. M. Shane (1998) *Administrative Law*, (4th edition) St Paul, MN: West Group.

Mattli, W. (1999) *The Logic of Regional Integration*, Cambridge University Press.

McNamara, K. R. (2006) 'Managing the Euro', in J. Peterson and M. Shackleton (editors) *The Institutions of the European Union* (2nd edition) Oxford University Press, 169–89.

Meardi, G. (2007) 'More Voice After More Exit? Unstable Industrial Relations in Central Eastern Europe', *Industrial Relations Journal*, Vol. 38, No. 6, 503–23.

Meier, G. M. (1982) *Problems of a World Monetary Order*, New York, NY and Oxford: Oxford University Press.

Menéndez, A. J. (2013) 'The existential crisis of the European Union', Paper presented at the ARENA Conference 'Europe in Crisis: Implications for the EU and Norway', *Oslo*, 14–15 March 2013.

Milgrom, J. and P. Roberts (1992) *Economics, Organization and Management*, Englewood Cliffs, NJ: Prentice-Hall.

Milward, A. S. (1992) *The European Rescue of the Nation State*, London and New York, NY: Routledge.

Milward, A. S. and V. Soerensen (1994) 'Interdependence or integration?', in A. S. Milward, M. B. Lynch, F. Romero, R. Ranieri and V. Soerensen (editors) *The Frontier of National Sovereignty*, London and New York, NY: Routledge.

Mishler, W. and R. S. Sheehan (1993) 'The Supreme Court As A Countermajoritarian Institution?', *American Political Science Review*, Vol. 87, No. 1, 87–101.

Monti, M. (2005) 'Lo Stato dell'Unione', *Sole-24 Ore*, 24 November 2005, 3.

(2011), 'The Real Problem is Excessive Deference', *Financial Times*, 21 June 2011, 11.

Moravcsik, A. (2005) 'The European Constitutional Compromise and the Neofunctionalist Legacy', *Journal of European Public Policy*, Vol. 12, No. 2, 349–86.

Mueller, H. (2006) 'Dann wird die Eurozone explodieren' ('Then the euro zone will explode'), *Spiegel On Line*, 20 December 2006.

Muenchau, W. (2012a) 'Ordnungspolitik, was ist das?' ('Ordnungspolitik', what's that?'), *Spiegel On Line*, 15 February 2012.

(2012b) 'Warum schon die deutsche Einheit ein Fehler war' (Why German unification was already a mistake), *Spiegel On Line*, 26 September 2012.

Murray Brown, J. (2008) 'Businessman Proves a Thorn in the side of the Irish Yes Vote Campaign', *Financial Times*, 7/8 June 2008.

Nicolaïdis, K. and S. K. Schmidt (2007) 'Mutual Recognition "On Trial": The Long Road to Services Liberalization', *Journal of European Public Policy*, Vol. 14, No. 5, 717–34.

Norman, P. (2003) *The Accidental Constitution*, Brussels: EuroComment.

North, D. C. (1990) 'A Transaction Cost Theory of Politics'. *The Journal of Theoretical Politics* Vol. 2, No. 4, 355–67.

Obinger, H., S. Leibfried and F. G. Castles (2005) 'Bypasses to a Social Europe? Lessons from Federal Experience', *Journal of European Public Policy*, Vol. 12, No. 3, 545–71.

OECD (2007) *Economic Survey of the European Union*, Paris: OECD.

Olson, M. (1971) *The Logic of Collective Action*, Cambridge, MA: Harvard University Press.

Ortega y Gasset, J. (1993 [1933]) *La Rebellión De Las Masas*, Madrid: Espasa Calpe.

Ostner, I. and J. Lewis (1995) 'Gender and the Evolution of European Social Policies', in S. Leibfried and P. Pierson (editors) *European Social Policy: Between Fragmentation and Integration*, Washington DC: The Brookings Institution, 159–93.

Otsuki, T., J. S. Wilson and M. Sewadeh (2000) *Saving Two in a Billion: A case study to quantify the trade effect of European food safety standards on African exports*, Washington DC: The World Bank (mimeo).

Parker, G. (1998) *The Grand Strategy of Philip II*, New Haven, CT and London: Yale University Press.

Pelkmans, J. (1997) *European Integration*, London: Longman.

Peterson, J. (2012) 'The College of Commissioners', in J. Peterson and M. Shackleton (editors) *The Institutions of the European Union* (3rd edition) Oxford University Press, 96–123.

Peterson, J and M. Shackleton (2012) 'Conclusion', in J. Peterson and M. Shackleton (editors) *The Institutions of the European Union* (3rd edition) Oxford University Press, 382–402.

Peterson, P. E. and M. Rom (1989) 'Macroeconomic Policymaking: Who Is in Control?', in J. R. Chubb and P. E. Peterson (editors) *Can The Government Govern?*, Washington DC: The Brookings Institution, 139–82.

Pew Global Attitudes Project (2012) *European Unity on the Rocks, Greeks and Germans at Polar Opposites*, Washington DC: Pew Research Center.

Piers Ludlow, N. (2006) 'De-Commissioning the Empty Chair Crisis: The Community Institutions and the Crisis of 1965–66', in J.-M. Palayret,

H. Wallace and P. Winand (editors) *Visions, Votes and Vetoes*, Brussels: P.I. E.-Peter Lang, 79–96.

Pinzer, P. and J. Fritz-Vannahme (2003) 'Geht's nicht auch eine Nummer kleiner?' ('Europe: couldn't we have it one size smaller?'), *Die Zeit*, 4 December 2003, No. 50, 3.

Piris, J.-C. (2011) *It is Time for the Euro Area to Develop Further Closer Cooperation Among its Members*, New York, NY: Jean Monnet Working Paper 05/11, NYU School of Law, The Jean Monnet Center for International and Regional Economic Law & Justice.

Plamenatz, J. (1973) *Democracy and Illusion*, London: Longman.

Poehl, K. O. (1990) 'Towards Monetary Union in Europe', in Institute of Economic Affairs, *Europe's Constitutional Future*, London: Institute of Economic Affairs, 35–42.

Polanyi, M. (1951) *The Logic Of Liberty*, London: Routledge and Kegan Paul.

Pollack, M. A. (2005) 'Theorizing EU Policy-Making', in H. Wallace, W. Wallace and M. A. Pollack, *Policy-Making in the European Union*, (5th edition) Oxford University Press.

Pond, E. (2004) *Friendly Fire*, Washington DC: Brookings Institution Press.

Porter, M. E. (1990) *The Competitive Advantage Of Nations*, New York, NY: The Free Press.

Posen, A. (1994) 'Is Central Bank Independence the Result of Effective Opposition to Inflation? Evidence of Monetary Policy Institutions', mimeo, Cambridge, MA: Harvard University.

Report to the President of the European Commission, José Manuel Barroso (2010) 'A new strategy for the Single Market at the service of Europe's economy and society', 9 May, available at http:// ec.europa.eu/bepa/pdf/monti.

Reiermann, C. (2009) 'Support for Wobbly Euro Economies', *Spiegel On Line International*, 20 February 2009.

Revesz, R. L. (1992) 'Rehabilitating Interstate Competition: Rethinking the "Race-to-the-Bottom" Rationale for Federal Environmental Regulation', *New York University Law Review*, Vol. 67, 1210–54.

Rhodes, R. A. W. (2006) 'Policy Network Analysis' in M. Moran, M. Rein, R. E. Goodin (editors) *The Oxford Handbook of Public Policy*, Oxford University Press, 425–47.

Rieger, R. (2005) 'Agricultural Policy', in H. Wallace, W. Wallace and M. A. Pollack (editors) *Policy-Making in the European Union* (5th edition) Oxford University Press, 161–90.

Rodrik, D. (2000) 'How Far Will International Economic Integration Go?', *Journal of Economic Perspectives*, Vol. 14, No. 1, 177–86.

(2011) *The Globalization Paradox*, Oxford University Press.

Roepke, W. (1954) 'Economic Order and International Law', *Recueil des Cours*, Vol. 86, Leiden: University Press, 218–50.

Roessler, F. (1996) 'Diverging Domestic Policies and Multilateral Trade Integration', in J. N. Bhagwati and R. E. Hudec (editors) *Fair Trade and Harmonization*, Vol. 2, Cambridge, MA: The MIT Press, 1–56.

Rogoff, K. (1985) 'The Optimal Degree of Commitment to an Intermediate Monetary Target', *Quarterly Journal of Economics*, Vol. 100, 1169–90.

Rosenthal, D. E. (1990) 'Competition Policy', in G. C. Hufbauer (editor) *Europe 1992: An American Perspective*, Washington DC: The Brookings Institution, 293–344.

Ross, G. (1995) *Jacques Delors and European Integration*, London: Polity Press.

Sapir, A. (1996) 'Trade Liberalization and the Harmonization of Social Policies: Lessons from European Integration', in J. N. Bhagwati and R. E. Hudec (editors) *Fair Trade and Harmonization*, Vol. 1, Cambridge, MA: The MIT Press, 543–70.

Sapir, A., P. Aghion, G. Bertola, M. Hellwig, J. Pisani-Ferry, D. Rosati, J. Vinals and H. Wallace (2004) *An Agenda for a Growing Europe*, Oxford University Press.

Sarrazin, T. (2012) *Europa Braucht Den Euro Nicht* ('Europe does not need the Euro'), Munich: Deutsche Verlags-Anstalt.

Schaeuble, W. (2012) 'Building a Sturdier Euro', *Wall Street Journal*, 13 December 2012, 17.

Scharpf, F. (2011) 'Monetary Union, Fiscal Crisis and the Preemption of Democracy', *Zeitschrift fuer Staats- und Europawissenschaft*, 9, 163–98.

(2012) 'Legitimacy Intermediation in the Multilevel European Polity and its Collapse in the Euro crisis', Cologne: *Max Planck Institute for the Study of Society, Discussion Paper 12/6*.

Schmitter, P. C. (2005) 'Ernst B. Haas and the Legacy of Neofunctionalism', *Journal of European Public Policy*, Vol. 12, No. 2, 255–72.

Schoenberger, C. (2012) 'Hegemon wider Willen' ('Unwilling Hegemon'), *Merkur*, January 2012, Vol. 66, No. 1, 25–33.

Scicluna, N. (2012) 'EU Constitutionalism in Flux: Is the Eurozone Crisis Precipitating Centralisation or Diffusion?', *European Law Journal*, Vol. 18, No. 4, 489–503.

Sedelmeier, U. and H. Wallace (2000) 'Eastern Enlargement', in H. Wallace and W. Wallace (editors) *Policy-Making in the European Union* (4th edition) Oxford University Press, 427–60.

Selznick, P. (1957) *Leadership in Administration*, New York, NY: Harper & Row.

Shackleton, M. (2012) 'The European Parliament', in J. Peterson and M. Shackelton (editors) *The Institutions of the European Union* (3rd edition) Oxford University Press, 124–47.

Shore, C. (2006) 'Government Without Statehood? Anthropological Perspectives on Governance and Sovereignty in the European Union', *European Law Journal*, Vol. 12, No. 6, 709–24.

(2011) '"European Governance" or Governmentality? The European Commission and the Future of Democratic Government', *European Law Journal*, Vol. 17, No. 3, 287–303.

Sked, A. and C. Cook (1979) *Post-War Britain – A Political History*, Harmondsworth, Middlesex: Penguin Books.

Skrzypek, S. (2010) 'Poland Should Not Rush to Sign Up to the Euro', *Financial Times*, 13 April 2010, 11.

Smith, M. (2012) 'Developing Administrative Principles in the EU: A Foundational Model of Legitimacy?', *European Law Journal*, Vol. 18, Issue 2, 269–88.

Soros, G. (2012) 'Deutschland muss fuehren oder aus dem Euro austreten' ('Germany must lead or else give up the euro'), *Spiegel On Line*, 9 September 2012.

(2013) 'Falls Jemand den Euro verlaesst, sollte es Deutschland sein' ('If anybody should leave the euro it ought to be Germany'), *Spiegel On Line*, 9 April 2013.

Spruyt, H. (1994) *The Sovereign State and Its Competitors*, Princeton, NJ: Princeton University Press.

Stephan, P. B. (2000) 'Regulatory Cooperation and Competition: the search for virtue', in G. A. Berman, M. Herdegen and P. L. Lindseth (editors) *Transatlantic Regulatory Co-Operation*, Oxford University Press, 167–202.

Stone Sweet, A. and T. Caporaso (1998) 'From Free Trade to Supranational Policy', in W. Sandholtz, and A. Stone Sweet (editors) *European Integration and Supranational Governance*, Oxford University Press, 92–133.

Stewart, R. B. (1975) 'The Reformation of American Administrative Law', *Harvard Law Review*, 88, 1667–813.

Szyszczak, E. (2006) 'Experimental Governance: The Open Method of Coordination', *European Law Journal*, Vol. 12, No. 4, 486–502.

Tiebout, C. M. (1956) 'A Pure Theory of Local Expenditures', *Journal of Political Economy*, Vol. 64, No. 5, 416–24.

Tindemans, L. (1998) 'Dreams Come True, Gradually: The Tindemans Report a Quarter of a Century Later', in L. Westlake (editor) *The European Union Beyond Amsterdam*, London: Routledge, 131–44.

Tocqueville, A. (1948 [1835]) *Democracy in America*, edited by P. Bradley, 2 vols. New York, NY: Holt, Rinehart and Winston.

Trebilcock, M. J. and R. Howse (1995) *The Regulation of International Trade*, London and New York, NY: Routledge.

Trechsel, A. H. (2005) 'How to Federalize the European Union. . .and Why Bother', *Journal of European Public Policy*, Vol. 12, No. 3, 401–18.

Troesken, W. (1996) *Why Regulate Utilities?*, Ann Arbor, MI: The University of Michigan Press.

Trubek, D. M. and L. G. Trubek (2005) 'Hard and Soft Law in the Construction of Social Europe: the Role of the Open Method of Co-ordination', *European Law Journal*, Vol. 11, No. 3, 343–64.

Tsoukalis, L. (1993) *The New European Economy* (2nd revised edition) Oxford University Press.

(2003) 'Economic and Monetary Union', in H. Wallace and W. Wallace (editors) *Policy-Making in the European Union* (4th edition) Oxford University Press, 149–78.

Uri, P. (1989) 'Réflexion sur l'approche fonctionaliste de Jean Monnet et suggestions pour l'avenir', in G. Majone, E. Noël and P. Van den Bossche, (editors) *Jean Monnet et l'Europe d'aujourd'hui*, Baden-Baden: Nomos, 75–82.

Vauchez, A. (2010) 'The Transnational Politics of Judicialization: Van Gend en Loos and the making of EU polity', *European Law Journal*, Vol. 11, No.1, 1–28.

Vega Cànovas, G. (2010) *El Tratado De Libre Comercio En America Del Norte*, Mexico DF: El Colegio de Mexico.

Verseck K. (2012) 'Europas Osten rueckt nach rechts' ('Eastern Europe moves to the right'), *Spiegel On Line*, 17 January 2012.

von der Groeben, H. (1987) *The European Community – The Formative Years*, Luxembourg: Office for Official Publications of the European Communities.

Wallace, H (1998) 'Differentiated Integration', in D. Dinan, (editor) *Encyclopedia of the European Union*, Boulder, CO: Lynne Rienner Publishers, 137–40.

Wallace, W. (2005) 'Foreign and Security Policy', in H. Wallace, W. Wallace and M. A. Pollack (editors) *Policy-Making in the European Union* (5th edition) Oxford University Press, 429–56.

Weatherill, S. (1995) *Law and Integration in the European Union*, Oxford: Clarendon Press.

Wefing, H. (2011) 'Fragt das Volk!' ('Ask the people!'), *Die Zeit*, 29 September 2011.

Weingast, B. R. (1995) 'The Economic Role of Political Institutions: Market-Preserving Federalism and Economic Development', *The Journal of Law, Economics & Organization*, Vol. 11, No. 1, 1–31.

Weiler, J. H. H. (1981) 'The Community System: the Dual Character of Supranationalism', now in F. Snyder (editor) *European Community Law*, Vol. 1, Aldershot: Dartmouth Publishing, 161–200.

(1999) *The Constitution of Europe*, Cambridge University Press.

Wilks, S. (2005) 'Competition Policy', in H. Wallace, W. Wallace and M. A. Pollack (editors) *Policy-Making in the European Union* (5th edition) Oxford University Press, 113–39.

Williamson, O. E. (1985) *The Economic Institutions of Capitalism*, New York, NY: The Free Press.

Wilson, J. Q. (1989) *Bureaucracy*, New York, NY: Basic Books.

Wincott, D (1995) 'Institutional Interaction and European Integration', *Journal of Common Market Studies*, Vol. 33, No. 4, 597–609.

Winter, M. (2010) 'Zukunft der EU' ('The Future of the EU'), *Sueddeutsche Zeitung*, 25 February 2010.

Wittman, D. (1995) *The Myth Of Democratic Failure*, Chicago, IL: The University of Chicago Press.

Wolf, M. (2011) 'Managing the Eurozone Fragility', *Financial Times*, 3 May 2011, 5.

Wolfe, C. (1987) *The Rise of Modern Judicial Review*, New York, NY: Basic Books.

Wyplosz, C. (2000) 'Der Euro braucht klare Kompetenzen' ('The euro needs clear competences'), *Financial Times Deutschland*, 16 June 2000, 35.

INDEX

accession partnerships
  Central and Eastern Europe
    negotiations and, 44–5
  deepening integration in EU and,
    91–2
  feasibility analysis of, 63–4
accountability
  deficit of, 192–6
  performance evaluations of EU and,
    78–83
  in post-monetary union era, 313–16
  statutory regulation and, 166–7
acquis communautaire, 39–41
  closer cooperation paradigm and, 227
  de facto opt-outs from, 41–2
  functional vs. territorial integration
    and, 112–13
  implications of, 42–7
  integration through judiciary and,
    97–101
  as irreversible investment, 123
  monetary union and, 289–94
  'Pact for Competitiveness' and, 232
adverse selection
  acquis communautaire negotiations
    and risk of, 44–5
  collective responsibility and, 204–7
  euro zone debt crisis, 139–41
  monetary union rules and, 129–34
  transaction costs and, 119–21
African, Caribbean, and Pacific (ACP)
    conventions, WTO jurisprudence
    and, 107–10
African countries
  impact of precautionary standards
    in, 158

regional integration schemes in,
  280–1
age discrimination, negative
  integration and, 95–7
agency costs, delegation of powers and,
  129–34
Alesina, A., 129–34
Alter, Karen, 104
American Confederation of 1781,
  278–9
Amsterdam Treaty, 95–7, 104–5
  absence of trust and, 243–5
  closer cooperation paradigm and,
    226–32
  Schengen Agreement and,
    125–6
Andean Pact, 280–1
anti-competitive behaviour
  policy harmonization and control of,
    36–7
  unintended consequences of
    'more Europe' policy and, 232–5
anti-majoritarian institutions,
  accountability deficit in,
  194–6
Articles of Confederation (United
  States), 185–7
Asia
  European historical hegemony over,
    177–8
  regional integration schemes in,
    280–1
asset specificity, transaction costs
  of, 122
Attali, Jacques, 139–41
Attlee, Clement, 161–2

337